A Vietnamese Reference Grammar

Chapter 3 both

A Vietnamese Reference Grammar

Laurence C. Thompson

Previously published as
Mon-Khmer Studies XIII-XIV

University of Hawai'i Press
Honolulu

Originally published as *A Vietnamese Grammar*
Copyright © 1965 by the University of Washington Press
Copyright © 1987 by the University of Hawaii Press

All rights reserved
Manufactured in the United States of America

00   7 6 5 4

ISBN 0–8248–1117–8
ISSN 0147–5207

To my mother

and

the memory of my father

Table of Contents

Editor's Note

When Laurence Thompson's original *Vietnamese Grammar* first appeared in 1965, it went almost instantly to the top of the list of required reading for serious students of the Vietnamese language. It has stayed there ever since but, in recent years, the title has become almost impossible to find, either in bookstores or in libraries, where original copies have often grown woefully ragged and marked up or are now simply missing. In the meanwhile, the author has become aware of a number of minor infelicities and typographical errors requiring correction. Thus, both demand and scholarship have dictated this re-edition.

We would be remiss if we did not note two other reasonns for deciding to make this work available once more: the first is that it has proven an indispensible teaching tool. If, as seems likely, general interest in Viet-Nam increases as that nation begins to open itself up to the outside world, the number of people learning Vietnamese abroad will surely rise from the currently sparse enrollments. While several other descriptions of the language have appeared more recently, in both Vietnamese and French, Thompson's grammar remains far and away the best thing available in English and, thus, the most useful work for the greatest number of potential users. After more than two decades of answering student's questions on various points in the Vietnamese language, this editor still finds himself frequently turning to its pages for clarification and rarely without satisfaction.

Beyond these considerations, however, is our desire to pay tribute to the work of Laurence Thompson, Professor Emeritus in the Department of Linguistics at the University of Hawaii. Members of the profession are already aware of the breadth of his other academic endeavors, his pioneering work on North American Indian languages, and his teaching texts for Russian, to name but a few. The present volume best illustrates the unfailingly high quality and precision, the attention to detail which mark the true scholar. It represents craftsmanship as well as intellect, and while we may assume that the latter is necesary for any scientific undertaking, it is the former which is often lacking these days and which is so greatly to be appreciated here.

It remains for *Mon-Khmer Studies* to extend its thanks to the University of Washington Press for coöperation in making this re-edition possible.

Foreword to the Revised Edition

Following *Studies in Vietnamese (Annamese) Grammar* [1951], Professor Murray B. Emeneau's seminal work—a product of the wartime Army Specialized Training Course, 1943–1944—American linguists showed increasing interest in the language of Vietnam through academic courses offered for the first time in the 1950's at such universities as Cornell, Columbia, Yale and Georgetown, and also at the Foreign Service Institute of the U.S. Department of State. When the Army Language School at Monterey, California (later renamed the Defense Language Institute on the West Coast) began adding Vietnamese to its curriculum in 1954, a young Ph.D. was asked to join its teaching staff and organize the new department. Professor Laurence C. Thompson thus found himself in the enviable twofold position of an official promoter of Vietnamese language studies and a research scholar in both synchronic and diachronic linguistics.

His industriousness and ingenuity have resulted in *A Vietnamese Reader* (University of Washington Press, 1961), which he co-authored with Mr. Nguyễn Đức Hiệp, and *A Vietnamese Grammar* (University of Washington Press, 1965), which I know immensely pleased him as a descriptivist-structuralist. The discipline also owes him several articles and essays, all of which evidenced his rigorous methodology, his deep concern with backing up theoretical considerations with the real pragmatics of communcation as well as his many insights into "language-in-culture" contexts. We are now grateful to the University of Hawaii at Manoa for an overdue reprint edition of this excellent reference grammar.

This book has indeed served untold numbers of students of the language for two decades, during which numerous studies by both native linguists and non-Vietnamese linguists (American, Australian, British, Chinese, French,

Japanese, Russian, etc.) have also appeared. As a basic work of reference it meets all the criteria of linguistic analysis, namely, thoroughness, comprehensiveness, conciseness, and elegance. Among other features Profesor Thompson deserves the credit for calling attention to the endocentricity of Vietnamese constructions, to the existence of sub-syllabic morphemes, to a number of "relator-nouns" which previous authors had called "verbs" or "prepositions" (*trong, ngoài, trên, dưới,* etc.), to the notion of "focus" discovered in proper nouns, pronouns, and also circumstantial complements (of manner, place and time), and to a novel treatment of particles.

Although Professor Thompson has lately turned his attention to the Amerindian languages of the Pacific Northwest, his work in Việt-Mường historical linguistics in recent years continues to amaze specialists and laymen alike. I deem it therefore a signal honor for me to add these few inadequate lines to introduce again what I have once called "a classic"—indeed a superb tool forged and tempered by a superb polyglot-linguist in the U.S.A.

Dinh-Hoa Nguyen
Center for Vietnamese Studies
Southern Illinois University

Foreword

The production of a reference grammar of Vietnamese of the scope of the present work is a signal event not only for Vietnamese studies in particular but for Southeast Asian studies in general. And to the growing list of names of linguists who have made substantial contributions to Vietnamese scholarship—among them, Henri Maspero, Léopold Cadière, Lê văn Lý, Murray B. Emeneau, Nguyễn-Đình-Hòa, Robert B. Jones—must be added the name of Laurence C. Thompson.

Prior to World War II the languages of Southeast Asia were virtually unknown in the United States. At that time Thailand was the only independent country in the area. Burma and Malaya were under British control, Indonesia was in the hands of the Dutch, while Cambodia, Laos, and Vietnam were still dominated by the French. Moreover, to the great detriment of the proper development and expansion of knowledge, scholarly activities were quite parochial and tended strongly to conform to political spheres of influence. As a consequence, Burmese and Malayan studies were largely conducted by British scholars, Indonesian by Dutch scholars, and Cambodian, Laotian, and Vietnamese by French scholars. Thai studies, as might be expected, tended to be relatively neglected except for the work of a few missionaries, mostly (though not exclusively) American.

Great changes have taken place in the past twenty-five years not only in the realm of politics but in the world of scholarship as well. Colonialism has vanished from the area and scholarship, freed of its stifling parochialism, has been greatly enriched by ever-increasing internationalization. Southeast Asia, from being one of the least known, is rapidly becoming one of the best known areas.

For untold millennia Southeast Asia has been a crossroads between India and China and between these and the islands of the Pacific. The problems of genetic interrelationship are intricate and by no means fully resolved. According to the most widely accepted theory, most of the languages belong to the Sino-Tibetan family composed of Tibeto-Burman, Sinitic, and Tai (or Daic). Malay, of course, belongs to the well-established Austronesian (or Malayo-Polynesian) family, while Mon and Cambodian (Khmer) and a few less well-known languages have been grouped together in the Mon-Khmer family. Vietnamese, however, has never been definitively proved to be related to any of these. The most plausible assumption, that of a (possibly remote) affiliation with the Tai family, as promulgated by H. Maspero, remains unverifiable while scholars await the availability of fully reconstructed Proto-Tai forms to implement comparison of appropriate rigor.

But problems of genetic relationship are by no means the only challenging problems regarding these languages. For centuries the great civilizations of India and China exerted a strong influence in matters of religion, literature and the arts, and in manners. This is reflected in the various languages which often show a heavy overlay of borrowed words from Pali and Sanskrit and from Chinese. The Indic influence was particularly strong in Burma, Thailand, and Cambodia, while the Chinese influence was dominant in Vietnam. More recently the influence of European languages has not been negligible. Of these, Portuguese was perhaps the earliest, but Dutch, English, and French have also contributed their share. Moreover, at a deeper level we see that long contact among members of the various indigenous linguistic families has given rise to certain broad similarities characteristic of a linguistic area. Prominent cross-genetic features include the widespread use of status and kin-term pronominals, of numeral classifiers, and of complex verbal strings. As a consequence, any two languages of the area, whether related or unrelated, offer far greater ease of inter-translatability than either does with a European language.

Highly characteristic of both Vietnamese and Thai are rhyming and/or alliterative and/or ablauting derivatives (in the present work called "emphatics," section 7.5). In both languages many of these give the superficial impression of being nonce formations, but deeper study reveals that most of them are probably quite old, particularly since many of the types are nonproductive. Formations of this sort make genetic comparison extremely difficult since the normally expectable constituency of a morph as a sequence of phonemes with a definite meaning is blurred. Both languages are also characterized by a variety of "synonym" compounds (here called "reinforcing" compounds, 6.24) and they frequently combine elements of similar meanings with similar semantic results, e.g. Vietnamese *chọn lựa* 'select' (*chọn* 'choose', *lựa* 'choose'), Thai *khádlŷag* 'select, pick out' (*khád* 'choose', *lŷag* 'choose'). Moreover, the extended meanings of many morphs have an almost identical range in the two languages, as can readily be seen when Vietnamese *đến* 'go to, arrive at; all the way to, up to; concerning' (9.66) is placed beside Thai *thў̆ŋ* 'to reach, get to; to, up to (esp. with verbs of motion); of, about, concerning (esp. with verbs of talking, thinking, etc)'. Nor are such resemblances limited to these two languages. As often as not, Cambodian or Karen, if looked into, will reveal the same coincidence.

Dozens of other equally interesting points could be extracted from the book and used to reveal comparisons and contrasts with other languages. For we have here a valuable addition to our growing literature on the languages of Southeast Asia. There is a wealth of material to delight not only the student concentrating on Vietnamese but also the specialist in other languages of Southeast Asia, the comparitivist, and the diffusionist. The appearance of this book is consequently an important event both in the world of practical affairs (which now demands proficiency in many languages formerly considered too "exotic" to be learned) and in the world of scholarship which is obligated (1) to reexamine the problem of genetic affiliations for Vietnamese and to provide us with better information on the whole problem and (2) to bring together the features which delineate Southeast Asia as a linguistic area and to compare and contrast these with other nearby areas, such as those of India[1] and China.

Mary R. Haas

May, 1965
Berkeley, California

---

[1] M.B. Emeneau, "India as a linguistic Area," Language 32.3-16 (1956).

Preface

The project of creating a descriptive grammar of Vietnamese began a number of years ago when I had the opportunity to spend an extended period in southern Viet Nam collecting linguistic data (1951-53). The primary goal at that time was a study of the southern dialect, and I presented a structural analysis of Saigon speech as my doctoral dissertation at Yale University in 1954. For support during that period of residence I am grateful to Yale University, the American Council of Learned Societies, the Human Relations Area Files, and the Ford Foundation. I am also eternally indebted to the many kind people in Viet Nam, both those who served as patient and painstaking informants and those (sometimes the same individuals) who helped me with the many complications of living in another culture.

In 1954 I joined the staff of the U.S. Army Language School in Monterey, California, and was assigned, among other things, the responsibility for establishment of a course in Vietnamese and subsequent supervision of the training conducted in the language. Upon moving to the University of Washington in 1957 I continued my private study, working in particular in collaboration with Mr. Nguyễn đức Hiệp of Monterey on a collection of texts which could be graded and assembled to provide a cultural introduction to the written language, at the same time bridging to the extent possible the gap between a basic knowledge of the spoken tongue and the capacity to handle the considerable difficulties of modern printed works. This project, too, was supported by the American Council of Learned Societies. In 1960 the need for Vietnamese materials was recognized in connection with the efforts of the U.S. Office of Education to encourage study of neglected languages, and a contract was arranged which made possible the finalizing of the collection of texts just mentioned (published by the University of Washington Press as *A Vietnamese Reader*, 1961) and provided for further research into structural problems and the creation of this companion reference grammar for students of the language.

The present grammar thus represents the results of some twelve years of thinking about the language, based on the consideration of materials of quite varied nature, collected during my residence in the country and expanded during the subsequent period of research. As is inevitable with a work of this sort, the depth and coverage are uneven. I have thus often had occasion to point out where further research is needed. Given the nature of language and the characteristics of human nature, it is also inevitable that the present work contains samples of speech and writing which seem unnatural or in some other fashion questionable to some native speakers. However, all the forms cited were recorded as the natural creation of some speaker or writer, and were checked with various informants.

For the ideal of a rigorous linguistic description which seeks to capture the elusive general aspect and underlying nature of a language without dependence on the systems of other languages, I am of course indebted to my teachers, especially Bernard Bloch and Franklin Edgerton. In this approach to language structure I have also profited greatly from numerous discussions with Mary R. Haas over the last several years. In a way more directly related to the material at hand I am grateful to M.B. Emeneau, not only for his encouragement and generosity in making his extensive materials on Vietnamese available to me, but in particular for the enormous stimulation I have derived from his own deep penetration of the structure, reflected in the painstaking close analysis of a very large number of typical sentences. For much help at various times with the background in Chinese language and culture and for valuable discussions of similarities in structure I owe thanks to Kun Chang and F.-K. Li. The work has ultimately benefited, too, from discussions of various problems with Samuel E. Martin and Richard B. Noss.

It has seemed important to include in the book some theoretical background for readers who may not be familiar with the practice of linguists. This should afford a basis for understanding the definitions and testing frames for word classes and construction types that form the backbone of the syntactic system presented here so that this system may be extended to account for forms beyond those actually exemplified. Such forms can usually be placed in the general scheme of things (if the context in which they appear does not provide the necessary information) by checking with an informant their privileges and limitations of occurrence in accordance with the definitions provided.

The illustrative material presented is taken from a wide variety of sources and I have not attempted to identify the origin of each example. Literary quotations, however, are attributed to the authors or works involved, and folk sayings are so marked. Many examples are drawn from my own field notes. Many others are taken from the text of *A Vietnamese Reader*, thus increasing the utility of the two books as companion volumes. Other printed sources from which a good many examples are drawn are Trần trọng Kim et al 1950, R. Bulteau 1950, M.B. Emeneau 1951, and Nguyễn đình Hòa 1957a (see Bibliography).

It is of course impossible to name here all the persons who have furnished material and helped me in my continuing effort to understand Vietnamese structure. But I should like to give credit to at least some principal consultants from each dialect area. During my residence in Viet Nam the following southern speakers were especially helpful in providing linguistic material and advice: Messrs. Phan văn Cư, Lâm quang Hồng, Nguyễn văn Nha, Trần văn Dõng, Nguyễn văn Đẩu, Dr. and Mrs. Trương thoại Đẩu, Dr. and Mrs. Nguyễn văn Hiền, Mr. and Mrs. Nguyễn Khác Oanh, and Misses Nguyễn thị Cút and Trương thị Danh. For representation of central dialects I drew on the speech of (among others) Messrs. Thomas Khôi and Nguyễn văn Cẩn and Mrs. Lê thị Trinh. Among the informants who furnished material on northern dialects during this period were Mr. Lưu văn Kính and Miss Vũ Liên.

Back in the United States I have had frequent occasion to consult with Miss Lê thị Bài on southern dialect forms. In addition to Mr. Hiệp, several other northern speakers located at Monterey have provided linguistic material. Among them Messrs. Nguyễn Hữu Thụ, Nguyễn văn Thuần and Lê Cảnh Xuyên should be mentioned as particularly helpful. Finally, I collected samples of central pronunciation from Messrs. Nguyễn Bình and Phạm Đăng Tải, and Miss Trần thị Quỳnh-Châu.

In the consideration of traditional views on Vietnamese structure I am particularly indebted to Mr. Hiệp for explanations and assistance in interpreting statements of native grammarians. He also was enormously helpful in supplying examples at various points of the analysis, and in checking numerous items. As principal consultant in the recent stage of research he deserves much credit for helping to make available a fair variety of illustrative material. I must thank also his son, Nguyễn Phi Hùng, and his daughter, Nguyễn thị Nam-Hải, for assistance in checking the occurrence of various forms during the writing of the final draft.

Although the text was completed in the spring of 1963, the typing of the final draft was exceedingly slow, the arrangements for financing publication were fraught with administrative delays, and the preparation of the photomaster for printing has involved some extraordinary difficulties. For a reference work of this sort it seems essential to have available contrasting type faces in order to preserve clarity of statement and provide appropriate emphasis. Because of the orthographic complexities of Vietnamese and the obligation to remain with a "cold-type" process, the production of the photomaster has been an exceedingly time-consuming and troublesome matter. The VariTyper machine provided the only means of solving the apparent impasse, but it brought with it a number of technical problems of its own. Miss Leila Charbonneau assumed responsibility for editing the manuscript and directing the typist; she established the page format and general form, provided lettering for the map, and did some of the detail work in several tables. However, she found it necessary to withdraw before much progress could be made on the photomaster, and I am grateful to my wife Maranell for taking over at the eleventh hour and accomplishing the bulk of the editorial work, as well as preparing the index and assisting with the bibliography. The first typist, Mrs. Linda Hale, began with Chapter 3, but was obliged to stop work on the project before being able to complete more than a few pages beyond. I am especially grateful to Mrs. Avis Brewster, who then took up the work at a time when it was very seriously behind schedule and brought to completion this extraordinarily difficult job of typing. Stephen Q. Howell prepared the map and special figures and also supplied much helpful advice on the preparation of the tables. Finally, I am grateful to the University of Washington Press for advice throughout the project, help with the technical arrangements, and patience during the long succession of delays.

L.C.T.

Seattle, April 1965

Typography and Symbols

Forms cited as linguistic examples appear in italics. Special emphasis is provided by boldface type. In the explanatory text technical terms appear in boldface where they are introduced, so that their definitions may be easily located.

Glosses are enclosed in single quotation marks ('...') only where it has been necessary to mark their beginning or end. Where a more literal kind of translation seems called for it is enclosed in double quotation marks ("..."). In such literal translations each Vietnamese word is glossed by a single English word or by a phrase joined by hyphens so that the correspondence to items in the example is easily discerned. Literary sources are identified at the end of examples, set off from the translation immediately preceding by a dash (–).

Ordinary parentheses (...) are used to signal that material enclosed therein may be omitted from the example or statement. Within glosses this material translates elements in the Vietnamese citation which are superfluous or unnecessary in English. Before or after glosses such material clarifies references, extensions of meaning, and the like.

Square brackets [...] enclose phonetic transcriptions in the early chapters. They are also used to identify glosses which describe grammatical function or usage rather than lexical meaning. Within glosses they are used to identify elements which must be added in order to make intelligible or grammatical English, although they do not translate any Vietnamese form. Literal translations are also usually enclosed in brackets.

The diagonal .../... is used to show the end of a line of poetry where the citation continues directly in the same line of print.

In a few cases phonemic transcriptions are provided, and they are enclosed between diagonals.

A Vietnamese
Reference
Grammar

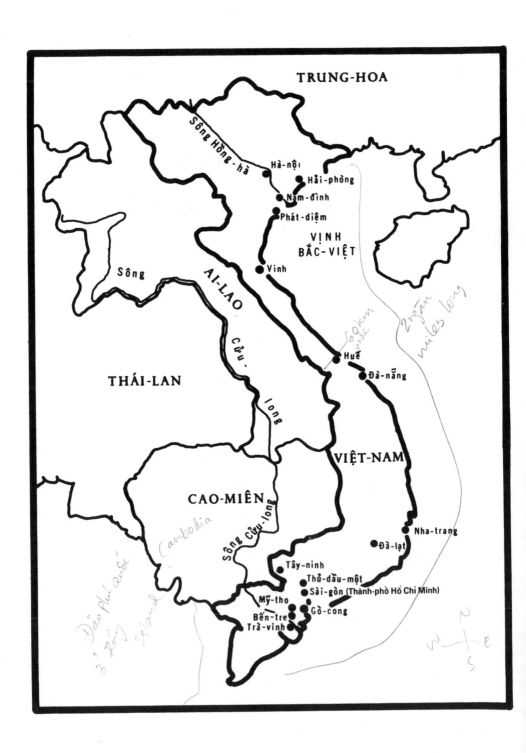

CHAPTER 1

Introduction to
Vietnamese Pronunciation

1.1. Standard Pronunciation. Although there is considerable fluidity
and a good deal of conflicting opinion, in general the pronunciation of
educated speakers from the Hanoi area of Viet Nam is the most widely
accepted as a sort of standard. School pronunciation involves a few
distinctions beyond those normally made in the dialect area: they reflect
differences in spelling which correspond to real differences in pronunciation in some dialects.[1] It seems most useful to present here this somewhat idealized pronunciation. For those interested in the details of pronunciation in Hanoi and Saigon, in phonological structure, in the general
picture of dialectal shifts, and in the background of the modern writing
system, a technical discussion of these matters is provided in Chapters
2-4.

Since the traditional orthography furnishes a good basis for discussing
standard pronunciation this presentation will treat sounds as renditions
of written symbols. Such an approach will also be most useful for students
already familiar with the orthography, as well as for those who wish to
progress rapidly to a reading acquaintance with the language. The tabular
form of the presentation will provide a rapid introduction to the sounds
for readers who wish to progress to the chapters on grammatical structure
as soon as possible, at the same time furnishing a means of checking
quickly the pronunciation of particular spellings.

---

[1] But no modern dialect yet studied shows all the distinctions implied in the traditional
orthography.

3

1.2. Consonants are listed in the following table with symbols of the International Phonetic Alphabet (IPA), rough English equivalents, and a minimum of pertinent remarks about their differences from the English sounds and other peculiarities, especially limitations on distribution. Pronunciations labeled "careful" generally disappear in natural conversation in favor of alternatives labeled "ordinary." (These "careful" pronunciations reflect spelling differences.) The English equivalents are at best only approximations of the Vietnamese sounds; those that are especially undependable or only suggestive are enclosed in parentheses. The terms "initial" and "final" mean syllable initial and syllable final.

Syllables which are written with no initial consonant—that is, the first symbol is a vowel letter (1.3)—actually begin with a glottal stop. Letter cues refer to notes at end of table.

SYMBOL	POSITION	IPA	ROUGH ENGLISH EQUIVALENT	REMARKS	EXAMPLES
b	initial only	[ɓ]	bad	fortis preglottalized imploded (cf. 2.22)	*ba* three
					biết know
c	initial, exc. before *i*, *e*, *ê*, *y*	[k]	scald	fortis, unaspirated	*cá* fish
					cũng likewise
	final after *u, o, ô*	[k͡p˺]	—	unreleased double closure (cf. 2.26)	*độc* poisonous
					học study
	final after other vowels	[k˺]	tic	unreleased	*khác* different
					mực ink
ch [b]	initial	[c]	(chop)	unaspirated palatal, less friction than in English	*chè* tea
					chọn choose
	final	[c˺]	—	unreleased, often backed	*cách* manner
					ích useful

Phiên ân Quốc tế

Letter	Position	IPA	English	Phonetic description	Vietnamese examples
d^c	initial only	[z]	zone	ordinary: lenis lamino-dental	*dùng* to use; *da* skin
		[ʒ]	azure	careful (distinguished from *gi*, *r*; cf. 3.21)	
đ	initial only	[dˀ]	done	fortis preglottalized, imploded (cf. 2.24)	*đá* stone; *đi* go
gh	initial before *i, e, ê*	[g]	gone	following immediately after syllable ending in *-ng*	*đáng ghi nhớ* noteworthy
		[ɣ]	–	elsewhere: voiced dorsovelar spirant	*ghi* to record
g	initial exc. before *i, e, ê, o, u, ơ, ô*		(s a m e)	as *gh*	*bằng gỗ* made of wood; *gỗ* wood
gi^c	initial followed by consonant, *ê* or nothing	[zi]	zebra	voiced lenis lamino-dental spirant plus high front vowel	*gin* keep; *giêng* January; *gì* what(ever)
	initial followed by any vowel other than *ê*	[z]	zebra	spirant only	*gia* establishment; *giàu* rich; *giờ* hour
h	initial only	[h]	hat		*hồ* lake; *hát* sing
k	initial before *i, e, ê, y*	[k]	sketch	fortis unaspirated (same as *c-*)	*kia* over there; *kén* choose; *kêu* call; *kỳ* to sign

(handwritten marginal notes)

bob
b + p = vô ə có voiced, ch ... có voiceless
= produced in the same way

on /ɔn/
house /haws/
→ cm |c|

SYMBOL	POSITION	IPA	ROUGH ENGLISH EQUIVALENT (Bach)	REMARKS	EXAMPLES
kh	initial only	[x]		lenis voiceless dorsovelar spirant	không not khỉ monkey khát be thirsty khu region
l	initial only	[l]	lot		lá leaf lúa rice growing lim ironwood
m	initial	[m]	mat		mạnh strong mua buy
	final	[m˺]	him	unreleased; shorter than in English postdental	tìm to search cam orange
n	initial	[n]	not		này this nữa in addition
	final	[n˺]	in	unreleased; shorter than in English	in print nên therefore bán sell
ngh	initial before i, e, ê	[ŋ]	singer		nghi suspect nghe listen nghề profession
ng	initial before other vowels	[ŋ]	(s a m e a s ngh-)		ngựa horse ngon tasty

	occurrence	phonetic	English	description	Vietnamese examples
	final after *u, o, ô* [a]	[ŋ͡m⁻]	—	short unreleased double closure (cf. 2.44)	*đúng* correct *ong* bee *ông* grandfather
	final after other vowels	[ŋ⁻]	sing	unreleased; shorter than in English	*vàng* gold *nhưng* but *nặng* heavy
nh	initial	[ɲ]	onion	palatal	*nhà* house
	final	[ɲ⁻]	—	unreleased, short, often backed	*lính* soldier *mạnh* strong
p	final only	[p⁻]	top	unreleased	*kịp* on time *tập* practice
ph	initial only	[f]	photo	lenis	*phá* destroy *phúc* happiness
qu	initial only	[kw]	square	fortis unaspirated	*quê* rural area *qua* cross over
r [c]	initial only	[z]	zebra	ordinary: lenis laminodental	*ra* go out *rẽ* turn off *rồi* already done
		[r]	—	careful: flap or trill (distinguished from *d, gi;* cf. 3.21)	

SYMBOL	POSITION	IPA	ROUGH ENGLISH EQUIVALENT	REMARKS	EXAMPLES
s[d]	initial only	[s]	ʃun	ordinary: lenis laminodental	sữa milk, sao star, sinh be born
		[ʂ]	(ʃhot)	careful: retroflex (distinguished from x; cf. 3.21)	
t	initial	[t]	stop	fortis, unaspirated dental	tôi I, tư fourth, tây west
	final	[t˺]	hat	unreleased	mát cool, mệt tired
th	initial only	[t']	Thomas	lenis aspirated dental	thôi stop, tháng month, thì then
tr[b]	initial only	[c]	(chop)	ordinary: fortis unaspirated palatal, less friction than in English	trẻ late, trang page
		[tʂ]	(strap)	careful: retroflex affricate (distinguished from ch; cf. 3.21)	

v	initial only	[v]	ʋan	lenis	và and về return vua king
x [d]	initial only	[s]	ʃun	lenis laminodental	xa far xe vehicle xưa in former times

NOTES

[a] Note also that **o** and **ô** have special pronunciations before *c*, *ng* (1.3).

[b] In ordinary Hanoi speech **ch-** and **tr-** are pronounced alike.

[c] In ordinary Hanoi speech **d-**, **gi-** and **r-** are pronounced alike.

[d] In ordinary Hanoi speech **s-** and **x-** are pronounced alike.

1.3. Vocalics are more complicated to discuss because some symbols play different roles in only slightly different positions. There are semi-vowels similar to those in English *yes, boy, wall, how, idea,* but they are represented by symbols which also serve to denote vowels in other cases.

The table below shows the pronunciation of the various symbols. In the case of each letter its most general use is covered first, then special cases are taken up; these combinations are indented beyond the general entry. Unless otherwise indicated, each symbol sequence occurs either initially in the syllable or directly after one of the initial consonants listed in 1.2. It then constitutes the rest of the syllable, unless it is followed by a hyphen, which indicates that it is followed by some other symbol. Similarly, a symbol preceded by a hyphen indicates that it is always preceded by some other symbol. Lettered cues refer to notes at the end of table.

SYMBOL	IPA	ROUGH ENGLISH EQUIV.	REMARKS	EXAMPLES	
a, a-	[a]	*f*ather		*Á* Asia	*ba* three
				đáp reply	*nam* south
				hát sing	*bàn* table
				gác upstairs	*vàng* gold
ach[a]	[ɐc][b]	–	= ă + *ch*	*sách* book	
anh[a]	[ɐɲ][b]	–	= ă + *nh*	*anh* elder brother	
ai[a]	[aɪ]	a*isle*		*mai* tomorrow	
ay[a]	[ɐɪ][b]	(b*i*te)	=ă + [ɪ]	*máy* machine	
ao[a]	[au]	cac*ao*		*sao* star	
au[a]	[ɐu][b]	(b*ou*t)	= ă + [u]	*sau* afterward	
See also *ia, ua, uya, ưa*					
ă-	[ɐ][b]	(h*a*t)	more central than in English	*cắp* pilfer	*năm* five
				đắt expensive	*ăn* eat
				bắc north	*nặng* heavy
â-	[ʌ][b]	b*u*t		*ngập* flooded	*đâm* stab
				rất very	*dân* citizen
				xấc ill-mannered	*vâng* obey
âu	[ʌu]	–		*đâu* where(ver)	

10

SYMBOL	IPA	ROUGH ENGLISH EQUIV.	REMARKS	EXAMPLES	
ây	[ʌɪ]	–	occasionally centralized (cf. 2.65)	*đây* here	
e, e-[c]	[ɛ]	(b*e*t)	slightly lower than in English	*nghe* listen *đem* carry *đen* black	*đẹp* beautiful *ghét* detest
eo[a]	[ɛʊ]	–		*mèo* cat	
ê	[eɪ]	th*ey*		*quê* rural area	
ê-[c]	[eˑ]	(b*e*t)	slightly higher than in English; except before -*ch, -nh*	*bếp* kitchen *hết* used up *đêm* night *nên* therefore	
êch	[eˑc⁻]	– ⎫	upper mid central un-	*ếch* frog	
ênh	[eˈʃ⁻]	– ⎭	rounded vowel	*bênh* defend	
êu	[eˈʊ]	–		*nếu* if	

See also -*iê-, uê-, uyê-, yê-*

i	[ɪi]	s*ee*	also spelled y on occasion (see y below)	*đi* go	*chị* elder sister
i-	[i]	b*ee*t		*kịp* in time *ít* be a small amount	*tìm* to search *in* print
ich	[ɪˈc⁻]	(*itch*) ⎫	lower high front un-	*ích* useful	
inh	[ɪˈʃ]	– ⎭	rounded vowel centralized	*lính* soldier	
ia[d]	[iə]	id*ea*		*chia* divide	
-iê-[d]	[ieˈ]	(d*ea*l)	vowel cluster (cf. 2.52); except before -*c, -ng*	*tiếp* continue *biết* know *miền* region	*nghiệm* to experiment
-iêc	[iək⁻]	–	diphthong	*việc* affair	
-iêng	[iəŋ⁻]	–	diphthong	*tiếng* noise	

SYMBOL	IPA	ROUGH ENGLISH EQUIV.	REMARKS	EXAMPLES
-iêu	[ieʰ ʊ] –		vowel cluster	*hiểu* understand
-iu	[iʊ]	–	diphthong	*chịu* suffer, endure

See also *ai, oi, ôi, ơi, ui, uôi, ưi, ươi*

o, o-	[ɔ]	*law*	slightly higher than in English	*nhỏ* small	*to* large
				chóp summit	*xóm* neighbor-
				ngọt sweet	hood
				ngon tasty	
oi	[ɔɪ]	(b*oy*)	lower than English diphthong	*dói* be hungry	
oo-	[ɔ]	–	used only in a few loan words	*soong* pot	
				boong deck [of ship]	
oc	[ɐukp̑⁻]	–		*dọc* read	
ong	[ɐ̃ũŋ̑m⁻]	–		*ong* bee	
oa, oa- ᵉ	[wa]	–	except before -*ch, -nh, -y*	*òa* burst into tears	
				góa be widowed	
				khoai potato	*toán* calculate

oach	[wɐc]	–	} cf. *ach, anh,* *ay*	{ *oách* well dressed
oanh	[wɐɲ]	–		*oanh* oriole
oay	[wɐɪ]	–		*xoay* turn [on axis]
oă- ᵉ	[wɐ]	–		*hoặc* or
				ngoắt turn around quickly
oe, oe- ᵉ	[wɛ]	*west*		*khỏe* healthy
				lòe-loẹt gaudy

See also *ao, eo*

ô	[ou]	sn*ow*		*cô* father's sister	
				bộ a set	
ô-	[o]	–		*hộp* box	*hôm* day
				tốt good	*bốn* four
ôi	[oɪ]	(b*oy*)	higher than in English	*tôi* I	*ngồi* sit
ôc	[ʌukp̑⁻]	–		*độc* poisonous	
ông	[ʌ̃ũŋ̑m⁻]	–		*ông* grandfather	

See also *uô-*

12

SYMBOL	IPA	ROUGH ENGLISH EQUIV.	REMARKS	EXAMPLES	
ơ	[ɤ ɯ]	–	upper mid back un-rounded diphthong	*mơ* dream	*sợ* be afraid
ơ-	[ɤ]	–	upper mid back un-rounded vowel	*hơn* more than *ớt* pepper *lớp* class	*cơm* cooked rice
ơi	[ɤɪ]	–		*với* with	

See also *uơ, uơ-*

SYMBOL	IPA	ROUGH ENGLISH EQUIV.	REMARKS	EXAMPLES	
u	[ʊu]	s*ue*		*ngủ* sleep	*thu* autumn
u-	[u]	(b*oo*t)	slightly lower than in English, not diphthongized	*chụp* snap [a picture] *bút* writing instrument	
ua	[u ə]	–	(except in *qua* [kwa])	*cua* crab	*mùa* season
ui	[uɪ]	b*uoy*	(except in *qui* [kwɪi])	*mũi* nose	*vui* pleasant
uô- [d]	[ue]	–	vowel cluster (cf. 2.58); except before -*c*, -*ng*	*buồm* [ship's] sail *chuột* rat *luôn* continually[f]	
uôc	[uək-]	–	diphthong	*luộc* cook by boiling	
uông	[uəŋ⁻]	–	diphthong	*chuông* bell	
uôi	[ueɪ]	–	vowel cluster	*đuôi* tail	
uê [e]	[weɪ]	s*ue*de		*thuê* to rent	
uêch [e]	[weɪ̞c]	–	cf. *êch*, *ênh*	*khuêch* amplify	
uênh [e]	[weɪ̞ɲ]	–		*huênh-hoang* showy	
uâ-	[wʌ]	*wo*n		*xuân* spring [season]	
uy [a,e]	[wɪi]	*wee*		*khuy* button	
uy- [e]	[wi]	*wee*p		*huýt* to whistle	

13

SYMBOL	IPA	ROUGH ENGLISH EQUIV.	REMARKS	EXAMPLES	
u y a[e]	[wiə]	–		*khuya* late at night	
u y ê-[e]	[wie⊦]	–	cf. *-iê-*	*tuyết* snow	*Nguyễn* [family name]
u y u[e]	[wiʊ]	–		*khuỷu* elbow	
u ơ	[wɤɯ]	–		*thuở* epoch	

See also *au, âu, êu, iu, iêu, ưu, ươu*

ư	[ɯ⊦ɯ] (good)[g]		high back unrounded rising diphthong	*tư* fourth	
ư-	[ɯ]	(good)[g]	high back unrounded vowel	*dứt* break [string]	*sức* strength *đừng* don't
ưa	[ɯə]	–	diphthong	*mưa* rain	
ưi	[ɯɪ]	–	diphthong	*ngửi* sniff	
ươ-	[ɯɤ]	–	vowel cluster	*ướp* to perfume *ướt* wet	*gươm* sword *vườn* garden
ươi	[ɯɤɪ]	–		*người* person	
ươu	[ɯɤʊ]	–		*rượu* alcoholic drink	
ưu	[ɯʊ]	–		*mưu* ruse	
y	[ɪi] *see*	replaces *i* in certain cases[h]		*Mỹ* America *kỳ* strange	
y-	[i] *beet*			*hýt-rô* hydrogen	
y ê-	[ie⊦]	–	replaces *-iê-* when initial	*yên* calm	
y êng	[iəŋ⁻]	–		*yểng* blackbird	
y êu	[ie⊦w]	–		*yêu* cherish	

See also *ay, ây, uy*

NOTES

ᵃ In general the final semivowels [ɪ, ʊ] are represented by **i** and **u**, respectively. However, there are some special cases: after *a* the spellings **-y, -u** represent the semivowels and also signal that the vowel is [ɐ], elsewhere written ă. In the same positions, the vowel [a] is signalled by writing -i and -o for the semivowels. In addition it is conventional to write -o for the [ʊ] semivowel after *e*. Note that the final consonants -ch, -nh also signal that the preceding a represents [ɐ].

ᵇ [ɐ] and [ʌ] are consistently shorter than other vowels.

ᶜ The vowels written e, ê are very similar (and difficult to distinguish) before final stops and nasals; e is slightly lower than the vowel in English *bet*, ê slightly higher.

ᵈ There are vowel clusters written -iê-, -uô-. In these clusters, which in Hanoi speech are heard only preceding final [p, m, t, n] and the semivowels [ɪ, ʊ], the second vowel is centralized, but clearly another vowel, not a semivowel (cf. 2.5). In other cases the second element is usually a lower mid back unrounded semivowel, sometimes centralized. Occasionally it is heard as a low back unrounded vowel. Note that when initial the writing iê is replaced by yê.

ᵉ The semivowel [w] is common preceding many vowels. This is usually written u, but before *a, ă* and *e* is written o. (The combination [kw], however, is always written qu-.) The combination uê- occurs only before -*ch*, -*nh* in a few rare forms, except where the u belongs to the initial sequence qu-. Uy- is rare before consonants. Uyê- appears only before -*t*, -*n*.

ᶠ We would expect the same pronunciation before -*p*, but no examples have appeared.

ᵍ The high back unrounded vowel represented by ɯ is heard in some dialects of American English in a few words replacing [ʊ]; actually it is somewhat lower than the Vietnamese vowel.

ʰ In some words y is an alternate for i; in others only one or the other is found. For a detailed discussion, see 3.34.

1.4. Tones are elements consisting of pitch contours combined with certain other features. Six distinctions are made by the standard orthography: one tone is unmarked, four others are represented by diacritics written over a vowel of the syllable, the last by a dot under a vowel of the syllable. Since other diacritics are used to distinguish vowel qualities (e.g., ă, â, ơ) there are often two diacritics accompanying the same vowel letter. The following table presents the tones of Hanoi speech. For clarity the tone symbols are written with the vowel a. (For more details see 2.71.)

15

1.4

SYMBOL	NAME	DESCRIPTION	EXAMPLES
a (unmarked)	(ngang)[2]	Mid or high-mid trailing pitch, nearly level when syllable is not final in pause group; in final syllables pitch falls to low range (citation forms often show level pitch)	ba three không not ăn eat tư fourth mơ dream
à	huyền	Low trailing pitch, often accompanied by breathy voice quality	và and gần near bằng made of cờ chess
á	sắc	High rising pitch, often heard as nearly high level in rapid speech	cá fish sách book số number bắn shoot cứ persist lớp class
ạ	nặng	Low dropping pitch, abruptly falling to bottom of normal voice range; syllable ends in stop or is cut off abruptly by glottal stop	mạ rice seedling nặng heavy chợ market ngựa horse lại come cập briefcase vật thing sạch clean được get
ả	hỏi	Mid-low dropping pitch, less abrupt than the tone just described accompanied in citation forms by rise at end	cả elder hỏi ask ổ nest thử try out
ã	ngã	High rising pitch, accompanied by glottal stop or "strangulated" vowel quality	đã [anterior tense marker] mỗi each chữ written word cũng likewise

[2] This tone is marked by the absence of any other tone symbol; its name is a technical term used by grammarians. The names of the other tones are in common use to designate the diacritics. Note that each name is an example of the tone it designates. (See also 3.38.)

16

1.5. Intonational elements are not represented in the traditional writing system except in a vaguely suggestive way (cf. 2.73, 3.54). It seems important, however, to mention them in this brief sketch of pronunciation.

For the immediate purpose it will suffice to say that three degrees of **stress** (relative loudness or force in the production of a syllable) are distinctive: most syllables are produced with **medium** loudness, but at least one in each pause group has **heavy stress** (louder than medium) and occasional syllables have **weak** stress (less loud than medium). Heavy stress isolates a syllable of the form which conveys the maximum new information or has the greatest importance in the phrase; weak stress accompanies syllables belonging to forms which add little or no new information—they are nearly predictable in the context. For further discussion of these matters, see 2.72, 5.22 and 12.5.

While it is likely that the real basis of other intonational distinctions lies in contours of loudness (see 2.73), it is most easily observable to the non-native ear—and most simply described and imitated—as deviations from the basic patterns of the tones (1.4). Most syllables are accompanied by the tonal contours as described, but before pause and occasionally in the middle of pause groups exceptional contours are heard.

Final syllables accompanied by tones beginning and ending lower than usual (**lowered tone**) signal the end of sentences which are produced with certainty—they convey the notion that the speaker expects his word to be taken, he expresses no doubt. This terminal intonation is most often represented on paper by a period, although the correspondence is not consistent. If, on the other hand, the final syllable has its tone beginning and ending higher than usual (**raised tone**), the sentence expresses some kind of uncertainty or indefiniteness—it often signals a question, but also accompanies a variety of emotionally colored statements and commands. The questions are typically written with a question mark at the end. Finally, there are syllables, both final and medial, which are accompanied by a tone contour that covers far more of the voice range than usual (**spread tone**). This intonation (sometimes symbolized in print by the exclamation point) signals a variety of exclamatory colorings, but also often signifies the lack of concern on the part of the speaker for the outcome of his utterance. For examples and more detailed description of intonational patterns, see 2.73 and 5.3.

CHAPTER 2

Hanoi Phonology

2.1. The Phonological System of Hanoi speech contains three major systems of sounds—consonants, vowels, and tones—and two minor systems of accompanying elements—stresses and intonations. The balance of the phonological structure has to do with the interrelationships of these elements and systems with one another—the ways in which they are combined to form syllables and pause groups. A brief characterization of each system is provided first. The remainder of the chapter is devoted to a description of the elements themselves. In the detailed discussion, examples are cited in the standard orthography. However, where it is desirable to call attention to special phonological features, broad phonetic transcriptions (using primarily the symbols of the traditional spelling) are sometimes added, enclosed, as is customary, between brackets: [...].

2.11. The Consonant System makes use of the distinctions fortis vs. lenis, voiced vs. voiceless and oral vs. nasal, and shows consonants primarily in four positions: labial, apical, laminal and dorsal. The elements are shown in Table 1, represented by the symbols with which they are written on at least some occasions in the standard orthography (Chapter 3), except that the voiced lenis consonant in laminal position is here represented by z (while in the traditional system it is written variously *d, gi* and *r*). Consonants are discussed in detail in 2.2-4.

18

TABLE 1. THE CONSONANT SYSTEM

		LABIAL	APICAL	LAMINAL	DORSAL	GLOTTAL
FORTIS ORAL CONSONANTS	Stops, voiceless	p	t	ch	k	
	Stops, voiced (preglottalized)	b	ḍ			
LENIS ORAL CONSONANTS	Voiceless	ph	th	x	kh	h
	Voiced	v	l	z	g	
N A S A L S		m	n	nh	ng	

Some of the symbols used in this table are digraphs (that is, they consist of more than one letter). However, they represent single elements. No difference in status is implied between the symbols consisting of a single letter and those consisting of two. The h's in **ph, th, ch, nh, kh** have nothing consistently in common with the single **h** in the glottal column, or with each other. The **t** and **th** are as distinct in Vietnamese as a comparable pair (*t* and *th*) in English are—although the distinctions involved in the the two languages are quite different. The letter **x** was chosen to represent an element similar to English *s* because the distinction between Vietnamese **s** and **x** is an important feature in certain other dialects, and the Hanoi sounds are most similar to those regularly written **x** (cf. 2.35, 3.21, 4.21).

2.12. The Vocalic System includes two subsystems of vowels and related semivowels: **upper vocalics**, six vowels and three semivowels formed relatively high in the mouth and characterized by a three-way position distinction (front, back unrounded, back rounded); and **lower vocalics**, five vowels and one semivowel formed relatively low in the mouth and characterized by a two-way position distinction (front, back). Sounds of the two systems are distributed somewhat differently in syllable structure (see 2.5, 2.6 and 2.82). The occurring sounds are shown in Table 2. Note that in the lower vocalic subsystem there are three distinctions of height in front, but only two in back: â includes both higher and lower low vowels. Vocalics are discussed in detail in 2.5-6.

TABLE 2. THE VOCALIC SYSTEM

		FRONT UNROUNDED	BACK UNROUNDED	BACK ROUNDED
	Semivowels	j	ư̭	w
UPPER	High Vowels	i	ư	u
	Upper Mid Vowels	ê	ơ	ô
	Lower Mid Vowels	e		o
LOWER	Higher Low Vowels	ă	â	
	Lower Low Vowels	a		
	Semivowel		â̭	

2.13. The Tone System consists of six elements composed of contours of musical pitch combined with certain other features of voice production. Table 3 shows the system in a comparative chart. Tones are discussed in detail in 2.71.

TABLE 3. THE TONE SYSTEM

TONE NAME	SYMBOL	PITCH LEVEL	CONTOUR	OTHER FEATURES
sắc	´	High	Rising	Tenseness
ngã	~	High	Rising	Glottalization
ngang	(unmarked)	High-Mid	Trailing-Falling	Laxness
huyền	`	Low	Trailing	Laxness, breathiness
hỏi	?	Mid-Low	Dropping	Tenseness
nặng	.	Low	Dropping	Glottalization or tenseness

2.14. Minor Systems are two: **stresses** (relative degrees of force or loudness with which each syllable is produced) and **intonations** (contours of diminishing force through each syllable with concomitant variations in tone contours). These systems are shown in Table 4. Stresses are discussed in detail in 2.72, intonations in 2.73.

TABLE 4. MINOR SYSTEMS

STRESSES	INTONATIONS
Heavy	Decreasing (normal tones)
Medium	Fading (lowered tones)
Weak	Sustaining (raised tones)
	Increasing (spread tones)

2.15. Hanoi Phonemics (Notes for Linguists). Considered from the point of view of phonemic analysis, the phonological structure of Hanoi speech emerges as still more systematized. (Since this systematization appears capable of producing some confusion for non-linguist readers it has not been used as the basis for general description. However, it seems useful to provide these notes for the benefit of those who are interested).

A more rigorous systematization of consonantal elements would recognize glottal stop as a phoneme. The voicing of [b] and [đ] would then be predictable allophones of /p/ and /t/ respectively, following initial /ʔ/. (**B,** initial only, and **p,** final only, must in any case belong to the same phoneme.) The fact that so-called initial [w] is always preceded by glottal stop suggests putting it with lenis [v], initial only. The semivowels [j, u̯], final only, combine respectively with [z, g], initial only. An /h/ phoneme can be defined to include modified anticipations and prolongations of vowel phonemes, thus accounting for [h-] and [-ạ]. The vowel system remains as presented in 2.12, but all the semivowels have been reassigned to the consonantal system.

Recognition of glottal stop as a phoneme forces a reconsideration of the tone system. The most economical phonemicization would recognize two tones, high and low; two degrees of tension, tense and lax. Other tone differences would be accounted for by final /-ʔ/, and the tonal contours would be predictable. Stresses and intonations would remain as presented in 2.14.

Table 5 shows this reanalysis, arranged so as to be comparable with earlier charts. It has not seemed particularly valuable to provide an accounting of the effect of the reanalysis on syllable structure. The charts provided in 2.8 can be converted mechanically. The most significant difference is the addition of a new type of syllable ending in /-ʔ/.

Nguyễn Bạt-Tụy 1959 reports experimental phonetic studies on the basis of which the author proposes some interesting treatments for certain aspects of the phonological system. He mentions in particular the difference between final consonantal elements following long vocalics (which he calls *lỏng* 'loose', presumably meaning 'lax, lenis') and those following short vocalics (termed *chặt* 'tight', i.e., presumably, 'tense, fortis'). He then considers differences in tension among initial consonants and identifies homorganic lax and tense elements in the two positions. He finds initial *b-* and *d-* (as well as *g-*) lax, while *t-* and *k-* (*c-*) are tense. So, for example, the distinctions /-ap : -ăp, -at : -ăt, -ak : -ăk/ he treats as /-ab : -ap, -ad : -at, -ag : -ak/, respectively. He also identifies final laminals /-ch, -nh/ with the final tense velars /-k, -ng/; for example, /-ich, -êch, -ăch/ are treated as /-ik, -êk, -ek/ (the contrast /-ăch : -ăk/ has been shifted to the

TABLE 5. PHONEMIC REINTERPRETATION

CONSONANTS

p	t	ch	k	ʔ
ʔp	ʔt			
ph	th	x	kh	h
w	l	j	g	
m	n	nh	ng	

VOCALICS

j	g	w
i	ư	u
ê	ơ	ô
e		o
ă		
a	â	
	h	

TONES

sắc	high tone, tense
ngã	high tone, tense, final /-ʔ/
ngang	high tone, lax
huyền	low tone, lax
hỏi	low tone, tense
nặng	low tone, tense, final /-ʔ/ or other stop

EXPLANATION OF CERTAIN COMBINATIONS

PREVOCALIC

/w-/ = [v-]
/ʔw-/ = [ʔw-]
/j-/ = [z-]
/g-/ = [g-]
/h-/ = [h-]

POSTVOCALIC

/-w/ = [-w]

/-j/ = [-j]
/-g/ = [-ṳ]
/-h/ = [-â̯]

vowel: /-ek : -ak/). It is interesting to note, in this connection, that he considers the laminopalatal closure of /-ch, -nh/ as subsidiary to the simultaneous velar closure he ascribes to these sounds in the same way that labial closure is a non-distinctive coarticulation in the case of /-k, -ng/ after /u, w/. In this way he establishes a reduced vowel inventory, having dispensed with our /ă, â/.

There are a number of problems with this treatment. For example, at the phonemic level there is considerable loss in economy elsewhere in the system: he is forced to set up five additional phonemes—tense varieties of nasals and semivowels (written here for convenience with capital letters): /M, N, NG, Y, W/—which occur only finally, and of which /Y, W/ have very limited distributions. On the phonetic level, I find the typification of b-, d- as lax quite contrary to reality, and the experimental basis for the characterization seems dubious. For this purpose elements were pronounced into one end of a V-shaped tube partially filled with a liquid, and relative readings of the rising of the liquid at the other end of the tube were recorded. This presumably records primarily the amount of air released rather than relative tension of production. The fact that *b-* and *d-* displaced the liquid a relatively small amount seems quite predictable, since they are regularly preglottalized and imploded, making for reduced exhalant air pressure. On the other hand, the identification of these differences in the tension of finals is interesting and may well lead to a deeper understanding of the phonological system.

An opposite treatment based on some of the same phenomena (in fact, inspired by the earlier work of Nguyễn Bạt-Tụy) appears in Haudricourt 1952. Here the number of short vowels is increased to six: /ă, â/ are the short vowels corresponding to /a, ơ/; in addition there are short varieties of /ê, e, ô, o/. Although again probably not preferable, as a phonemic system, this treatment does call attention to interesting features in the distributional table.

2.2. Fortis Stops are characterized by relatively strong articulation: at the beginning of syllables they are exceedingly fortis, except for **ch,** which is somewhat weaker. At the end of syllables they are about midway between the extremes of fortis and lenis. (It would be somewhat more accurate to call them non-lenis stops.) Those after short vocalics are generally more fortis than those after long vocalics.

They subdivide naturally into voiceless **p, t, ch, k;** and voiced **b, đ,** which are also preglottalized and often imploded. The voiced stops occur only initially, while the voiceless stops also occur finally, in which position they are unreleased; **p** occurs only finally (see 2.15).

2.21. p: bilabial stop (without any other closure in the mouth: in certain positions [k] involves a double closure, a labial closure accompanying the defining dorsovelar stop; cf. 2.26)—voiceless, unreleased: final only.

> *kịp* on time, *nếp* glutinous [rice], *tiếp* receive, welcome,
> *lớp* class, *ướp* to scent, *chụp* seize suddenly, *hộp* box,
> *đẹp* be beautiful, *thấp* be short, low, *tháp* tower

2.22. b: bilabial stop, voiced, preglottalized and often imploded (see below): initial only.

> *biết* know, *bên* side, *bữa* meal, *bờ* shore, *buồm* [ship's] sail,
> *bốn* four, *bè* raft, *bỏ* to suit, *bắn* to shoot, *bận* be busy,
> *ba* three

23

This sound is similar to English *b* but is much more strongly articulated. In addition, it is always preceded by glottal stop, which is seldom released before the beginning of the **b**, with the result that a partial vacuum is created between the throat and the lips; when the lip closure is released this vacuum is often still strong enough so that a little air is sucked in at the lips, giving the sound its characteristic strangeness to non-native ears.

2.23. **t:** apical stop, postdental–
Voiceless, unreleased: final only.

> *ít* small amount, *hết* be used up, *biết* know, *dứt* to break
> [string], *ớt* pimento, pepper, *ướt* be wet, *bút* writing
> instrument, *một* one, *chuột* rat, *ghét* detest, *ngọt* be sweet,
> *đắt* be expensive, *mất* to lose

Voiceless, sharply released: initial only.

> *tiền* money, *tết* [New Year's] holiday, *tư* fourth, *tờ* thin sheet
> [classifier], *tủ* cupboard, shelves, *tôm* shrimp, lobster,
> *té* to fall down [living being], *to* be large, *tay* hand, arm,
> *tây* west, *ta* you and I, *tòa* bureau, office

This sound differs sharply from English *t*, of which it is reminiscent. English initial *t* is fortis and voiceless, but it is also aspirated—that is, a puff of breath accompanies its release—and it is produced by the contact of the tongue tip to the ridge behind the upper teeth. Vietnamese initial **t** is fortis and voiceless, but in producing it the tongue tip touches the roots of the upper teeth, and the release is unaspirated. Final **t**, however, is more similar to English final unreleased *t* (except for position). When it comes at the end of a syllable which is followed immediately by a syllable beginning with *ch* or *nh*, the contact of the tongue tip is against the backs of the upper teeth: the transition to the following laminal articulation of the *ch* or *nh* (see 2.25, 2.43) thus involves less movement.

2.24. **đ:** apicoalveolar stop, voiced, preglottalized and often imploded (see below): initial only.

> *đi* go, *để* put, place, *đưa* hand over, *đơn* application, *đủ* be
> enough, *đôi* pair, couple, *đẹp* be beautiful, *đỏ* be red, *đọc*
> to read, *đông* winter, *đá* stone, *đoán* to guess

Đ is very similar to **b**: it is voiced and preglottalized, and this preglottalization often occasions an implosion with the release (cf. 2.22). It resembles English *d* in that it is alveolar.

2.25. **ch:** laminoalveolar stop–
Unreleased: final only.

> *ích* be useful, *ếch* frog, *sạch* be clean

Usually with slightly affricated release: initial only.

> *chia* divide, *chết* to die, *chưa* not yet, *chợ* market, *chủ* master, lord, boss, *chỗ* place, *chén* cup, *cho* give, *chẳng* definitely not, *chậm* be slow, *chạp* final month of year, *chuyện* conversation

Although reminiscent of the English *ch* in *child*, this Vietnamese sound differs in position: the English sound is generally produced by the tongue tip against the alveolar ridge with the blade touching just behind it, while in the Vietnamese sound the tongue tip is down near the backs of the lower teeth and the contact is made by the blade against the back of the alveolar ridge. The English sound is aspirated and affricated while the Vietnamese sound is unaspirated and only slightly affricated (sometimes not at all). Note that ch occurs finally only after *i, ê,* [ă].

After vowels the closure is often made somewhat further back—sometimes it involves an area of the tongue considerably behind the tip touching the roof of the mouth in back of the ridge (laminopalatal). This makes it difficult to distinguish from English consonants like those in *sick, seek.*

Jones and Thông (1957, 1960) analyze the sequences *ich, inh, êch, ênh, ach, anh* as /ik, ing, êk, êng, ăyk, ăyng/ respectively (reported here with the equivalent symbols of the present treatment). Nguyễn đình Hòa (1957b, 1959b) makes a similar analysis, with the difference that he interprets *êch, ênh* as /âyk, âyng/. These interpretations seem to me pedagogically less fortunate in that they tend to reinforce an English speaker's difficulty in hearing the sounds. There may be some question about the phonetic reality of these sequences. But I find it difficult to believe that the clear pronunciations of final palatal ch and nh which I have heard in my Hanoi informants' connected speech represent deviations in the direction of the official spelling. This is a feature which should be carefully investigated on the spot in Hanoi, since speakers who have migrated from their birthplaces do change their speech habits. (See also 2.15, discussion of Nguyễn Bạt-Tụy 1959).

2.26. k: voiceless dorsovelar stop—

Unreleased with simultaneous strong rounding (and often closure or near closure) of the lips: final only after *u* and [w].

> *lúc* time, instance, *học* [hặwk] to study, *cốc* [kắwk] [drinking] glass

Unreleased, plain: final only after vowels other than *i, ê, u, ô, o.*

> *mực* ink, *nước* water, *eng éc* [onomatopoetic: squealing of pig], *sắc* be sharp, *xấc* be ill-mannered, *các* [plural marker]

Sharply released: initial only.

> *kia* (over) there, *kêu* shout, call, *cửa* door, opening, *cờ* flag,
> *cũng* also, *cô* father's sister, *kém* be less, *con* animal
> [classifier], *cắt* put away, store, *cá* fish, *qua* cross over

Vietnamese **k** differs from the similar sound in English (as in *cake, quick, cookie*) primarily in lacking aspiration in initial position and in having the strong lip rounding (or sometimes double closure) after *u* and [w]. This strongly rounded **k** occasions considerable difficulty for learners of the language, since they will frequently think they are hearing **p** instead of **k** and must take care to distinguish the following contrasting syllable types:

> [-up: -uk] *dụp* three times, *dục* perforate
> [-ăp: -ăwk] *cắp* pilfer, *cóc* toad
> [-âp: -âwk] *chấp* bear a grudge, *chốc* moment, instant

This element is written with three symbols, distributed as follows:

> **k** before *i, y, ê,* or *e* of the official spelling (in the same syllable)
> **q** in the combination [kw]: **qu-**
> **c** elsewhere (before all other vowels and in final position)

2.3. Lenis Oral Consonants

are less strongly articulated than the fortis stops: occurring only in initial position (where fortis stops are very strongly articulated), they are about midway on the scale or somewhat toward the lenis extreme. They are mainly continuants, although **th** is a stop and **g** has a stop variant. The continuants are spirants, except for the lateral **l**. They occur in pairs, voiced and voiceless in each position, except for **h** (see 2.39 below).

2.31. ph: voiceless labiodental spirant.

> *phía* direction, *phê* criticize, comment on, *phương* method, way,
> *phở* noodle soup, *phu* coolie, *phố* street, *phép* rule, custom,
> *phó* entrust, *phòng* room, *Phật* Buddha, *phá* destroy

2.32. v: voiced labiodental spirant.

> *việc* affair, matter, work, *về* return, *vừa* to fit, suit, *vợ* wife, *vua*
> king, *vốn* capital, principal (sum), *vẽ* to draw, sketch, *vỏ*
> shell, skin, *văn* literature, letters, *vâng* obey, *và* and

2.33. th: voiceless apicodental stop with aspirated release.

> *thi* take an examination, *thế* manner, way, *thử* to try out, *thờ* to
> worship, *thua* to lose [e.g., a game], *thôi* to stop, *theo*

26

follow, *thọ* to live long, *thành* become, *thật* be real, true,
thang staircase, *thuế* taxes

The distinction between t and th in Vietnamese is difficult for speakers
of English because it entails some elements which are contrary to the
habits of English. Vietnamese t is fortis and unaspirated, th is lenis and
aspirated (opposed to the English *t* in *take, toad,* which is fortis and aspi-
ated, and the *d* in *dish, dawn,* which is lenis and unaspirated). There is
also, of course, the matter of position: Vietnamese th, like t, is formed
against the roots of the upper teeth.

2.34. l: voiced lateral (apicodental contact; accompanied by approximately
the coloring of the vowel *ơ*).

> *lính* soldier, *lên* go up, *lửa* fire, *lợn* pig, *lúc* time, instance, *lối*
> path, *leo* to climb, *lo* to worry, *lạnh* be cold, *lâu* to last a long
> time, *lá* leaf, *loài* species

Hanoi l is rather like the *l* in English *lay, let.*

2.35. x: voiceless laminodental spirant.

> *xin* to ask for, *xếp* to fold, *sữa* [xữậ] milk, *sợ* [xợư] to fear, *xuống*
> go down, *số* [xốw] number, *xe* vehicle, *xóm* neighborhood,
> *sách* [xǎch] book, *sống* [xǎwng] to live, *xa* be far away,
> *xuân* spring [season]

X is similar to English *s* in *see,* but is somewhat more palatalized, and a
little less shrill. In the official orthography it is represented sometimes by
x, sometimes by s; the spelling must be learned for each word.

2.36. z: voiced laminodental spirant (voiced counterpart of x).

> *gì* [zìj] anything, what(ever), *dễ* [zễj] be easy, *dưa* [zưậ] melon,
> *giời* [zờj] sky, heaven, *dùng* [zùng] to use, *rồi* [zồj] be
> already accomplished, *dẻo* [zẻw] be soft and pliable, *rõ* [zõ]
> be clear, *danh* [zǎnh] name, *giấc* [zấk] take a nap, *ra* [za]
> go out, *duyên* [zwiên] predestined affinity

Z is similar to English *z* in *zebra,* but is somewhat more palatalized. In the
official orthography it is represented by d (without a bar), r or gi (simply
g- before [i]) (for details, see 3.2-3).

2.37. kh: voiceless dorsovelar spirant (occasionally beginning with a
stop—see below).

> *khi* time when, *khế* carambola (kind of fruit-bearing tree), *khứ-hồi*
> round-trip, *khờ* be gullible, *khu* region, *khổ* be unfortunate,
> *khen* commend, *khó* be difficult, *khách* guest, *không* not,
> *khát* be thirsty, *khoai* potato.

Kh is created by narrowing the passage between the back of the tongue and the roof of the mouth, sometimes making a complete closure. Some speakers occasionally begin **kh** with a very short stop; this is especially common immediately after a preceding syllable ending in [k]—the [k] is simply held over and released with the new syllable.

2.38. g: voiced dorsovelar oral consonant—
    Stop: initial immediately following syllable ending in *ng*.
       thang gác stairs [leading up]
    Spirant: elsewhere (i.e., unless immediately preceded by syllable ending in *ng*).
       ghi to record, *ghế* chair, *gương* mirror, *gợi* to arouse [feelings],
       guốc clog, wooden shoe, *gỗ* wood, *ghen* be jealous, *gọi* to
       call, *gặp* to meet, *gần* be near, *gác* upstairs, *góa* be widowed
G is written **gh** before *i, ê, e.*

2.39. h: voiceless anticipation of immediately following vowel or semivowel. Although it might be referred to as a voiceless spirant in the glottis, **h** actually is simply the voicelessness which accompanies voiceless sounds in the same way that voicing accompanies voiced sounds. Each occurrence of **h**, then, is really a voiceless vowel having the same formation as the following vowel or semivowel (only [w] occurs).
       hiểu to understand, *hết* be used up, *hứa* to pledge, promise, *hơn*
       be more (than), *hút* inhale, *hộp* box, can, jar, *hè* summer, *hỏi*
       to ask (a question), *hay* be interesting, good, *hồng* rose, *hát*
       to sing, *hoàng* [hwàng] emperor

2.4. **Nasals** are fully voiced and about midway in relation to the extremes of lenis and fortis (those in final position after short vocalics are more fortis than others). They all occur both initially and finally; in the latter position they are unreleased. They differ sharply from similar nasals in English in final position in that they are very short—English nasals are prolonged, especially after short vowels. With *ngã* and *nặng* tones (see 2.71) in rapid speech they are chopped off almost before they are formed. However, enough of each nasal is heard in such cases so that it is possible to tell them apart. Vowels are frequently nasalized before or after nasals. They are always nasalized before [wng] and in all nasal-final syllables accompanied by *ngã* and *nặng* tones (see 2.63, 2.64).

2.41. m: labial nasal (without any other closure in the mouth—in certain circumstances **ng** involves a double closure, a labial closure accompanying the defining one in the dorsovelar area; cf. 2.44).

Mỹ America, *tìm kiếm* to go looking (for something), *mê* be unconscious, *đêm* night, *mứt* preserves. jam, *mở* to open, *sớm* be early, *lườm* give a threatening look, *mua* to buy, *chum* earthenware jar, *một* one, *hôm* day, *buồm* [ship's] sail, *mèo* cat, *đem* to carry, *mỏ* beak, bill, *xóm* neighborhood, *may* to sew, *năm* year, *mây* cloud, *đâm* to stab, *ma* spirit, ghost, *tám* eight

2.42. **n:** postdental apical nasal (in final position followed immediately by *ch* or *nh* the contact is against the backs of the upper teeth; cf. 2.25).

nín to hold back, keep from, *nên* be fitting, proper, *tiền* money, *nữa* still more, *nở* to bloom, *hơn* be more (than), *mượn* to borrow, *núi* mountain, *phùn* drizzle, *nổi* to rise to the surface, *bốn* four, *ném* to throw, *đèn* lantern, *non* be tender, young, *nặn* to model [clay], *nấu* to cook (esp. by boiling), *xuân* spring [season], *nạn* accident, calamity

2.43. **nh:** laminoalveolar nasal.

nhiều be abundant, much, *lính* soldier, *nhể* to extract with a sharp instrument, *bênh* to defend, *như* like, as, *nhớ* to remember, *nhục* to disgrace, *nhổ* to pull out, uproot, *nhẹ* be light [weight], *nhỏ* be small, *nhanh* be fast, *nhất* first, *nhà* house, *năm nhuận* leap year

Note that **nh** occurs finally only after *i, ê,* [ă].

This nasal has the same position as **ch** (2.25). Finally, especially after [i], the sound is frequently made a little further back in the mouth, with the contact somewhat back of the ridge behind the upper teeth. For this reason it sounds very much like the end of the English word *thing*, but the closure is not so far back (the English sound is velar).

2.44. **ng:** dorsovelar nasal—

With simultaneous strong rounding (and often closure or near closure) of the lips: final only after *u,* [w].

đúng be correct, *ong* [ăwng] bee, *ông* [âwng] grandfather

Plain: elsewhere (i.e., initial, and final after other vowels)

nghỉ to rest, take time off, *nghề* occupation, profession, *ngựa* horse, *đừng* don't, *ngờ* to expect, think, *người* person, *đường* sugar, *ngủ* to sleep, *ngồi* to sit [down], *xẻng* shovel, *nghe* to listen [to], *ngon* be good tasting, *xoong* saucepan, *ngắn* be short, brief, *nặng* be heavy, *ngân* silver, *vâng* to obey, *ngà* ivory, *làng* village, *ngoài* outside

Note that **ng** does not occur finally after [i, ơ], and is rare after [ê, e, ô, o] (cf. 2.82). The spellings *ong, ông* represent special combinations with the diphthongs [ăw, âw] (cf. 2.58, 2.62).

The strongly rounded **ng** occurring after *u* and [w] occasions the same kind of difficulty for foreigners as [k] in the same position. Care must be taken to distinguish the following syllable types:

[-um : -ung]   *chum* earthenware jar, *chung* assemble
[-ăm : -ăwng]   *đăm* to sink, *đóng* to shut
[-âm : -âwng]   *âm* sound, *ông* grandfather

This sound is written **ngh** before *i, ê, e*.

2.5. Upper Vocalics

2.5. Upper Vocalics have three distinctive positions: front (which includes variant vowels in central position), back unrounded, and back rounded. In each position there is a high vowel and semivowel, and an upper mid vowel. None of these vowels occur finally. Those which are written as single final vowels are actually diphthongs consisting of the vowel followed by its homorganic semivowel. Thus the writings **i, ê, ư, ơ, u, ô**, actually represent in final position the diphthongs [ij, êj, ưɤ̣, oɤ̣, uw, ôw].

It is also important to distinguish a variety of diphthongs from some vocalic sequences of rather different quality—vowel clusters, which contain two dissimilar vowels in sequence, neither of which is regularly enough less prominent than the other to qualify as a semivowel. These are the sequences written **-iê-** (or **yê-**) before [w, p, m, t, n], **uô-** before [j, m, t, n], and **ươ-** before all occurring finals. It is regularly observable that on occasion the first element is slightly more prominent, on occasion the second; sometimes it seems impossible to distinguish either vowel as more ·prominent. They are thus quite different from diphthongs like those written **ao, au, âu, ua**, etc., where the first element is regularly more prominent than the second. It is interesting that these vowel clusters involve only the upper vowels in sequence from higher to lower.

2.51.

2.51. i: high front or central (unrounded) vowel—

Lower high central: before final *ch, nh.*

  ích be useful, *lính* soldier

Upper high front: before [ê, ậ, p, m] in the same syllable.

  biết know, *chia* [chiậ] to divide, *miệng* [miậng] mouth, *kíp* be urgent, *tìm kiếm* search (for)

Lower high front: elsewhere (i.e., before [j, w, t, n] in the same syllable).

  di [dij] go, *gì* [zìj] what(ever), *chịu* [chịw] endure, suffer, *mưu* [miw] scheme (see below), *ít* be a small amount, *xin* to ask for

30

The diphthong [ij] is quite similar to that in English *see*. The variant of
i before *ch, nh* is similar to many pronunciations of the vowel in English
it. However, in other positions i is very high and front, like the element at
the very end of English *see*. English speakers will have difficulties especially before *p, m,* because the Vietnamese combinations *ip, im,* are unlike
the English sounds in *keep* and *seem* (which are usually diphthongs like
that in *see*).

In the official spelling the most common symbol is i: *ích* be useful, *ít*
be a small amount, *tìm kiếm* search for, *chia* to divide. However, after [w]
y is written: *quyển* [kwiên] volume, *ủy* [wǐj] to delegate, entrust, *Huỳnh*
[hwình] [a family name]. Y is written consistently as the first vowel of
the cluster [iê-] and the diphthong [iậ-] (followed by some final) when
otherwise the i would appear as the first letter of a syllable (the initial is
glottal stop, which is not represented in the orthography)—that is, whenever
otherwise the sequence of symbols *iê-* would stand first in a word: *yêu*
[iêw] to cherish, *yểng* [iậng] red-winged blackbird. The diphthong [ij] is
written simply i in most cases: *đi* [dij] go, *gì* [zìj] what(ever), *chị* [chij]
elder sister, *mì* [mìj] wheat flour. In some cases, however, y is written instead, and in a few forms y and i are interchangeable: *Mỹ* [mĩj] America,
hy, hi [hij] to hope.

In some dialects there are forms involving the sequences [ɯw, ɯow],
and they are written ưu, ươu. However, these sequences are not native to
Hanoi, where they are replaced in ordinary speech by [iw, iêw]. As a result there are some forms in Hanoi speech with [iw, iêw] which are written
ưu, ươu, respectively, while others are written iu, iêu: *chịu* [chịw] endure, suffer, *mưu* [miw] scheme, *hiểu* [hiểw] understand, *rượu* [ziệw] alcoholic beverage. (Even in Hanoi, of course, one hears spelling pronunciations
with [ɯw, ɯow].)

2.52. ê: upper mid front or central (unrounded) vowel—

Upper mid central: before final *ch, nh*; and after [i] before [w, p, m, t,
n] in the same syllable (slightly lower before [w]).

     ếch frog, *bênh* defend; *hiểu* [hiểw] understand, *tiếp* receive,
        welcome, *kiêm* be in charge of, *biết* know, *miền* region

Upper mid front: elsewhere (i.e., before [j, w, p, m, t, n] in the same
syllable) (slightly higher before [j]).

     để [dểj] put, place, *nếu* [nếw] if, *bếp* kitchen, *đêm* night, *hết* be
        used up, *đến* arrive

The diphthong [êj] is similar to that in English *they*, but the vowel is
higher. The vowel which occurs before *ch, nh,* and after [i] before [w, p,
m, t, n] is a little higher than the vowel often heard at the end of English

sofa, similar to the first vowel in a rapid pronunciation of *confusion* or *sustain.* In other positions ê is slightly higher than the vowel in English *bet.* However, this is the most serious difficulty, because Vietnamese e (2.6) is only slightly lower than this English vowel. Thus each vowel, when heard in isolation, will sound much like the vowel in *bet* to an English speaker. He must practice hearing and making this distinction, using such pairs as the following:

ê	e
kêu [kêw] to shout, call	*keo* [kew] be miserly
nếp glutinous [rice]	*nép* to hide [oneself]
đêm night	*đem* carry
hết be used up	*hét* to shriek
đền [Taoist] temple	*đèn* lantern

Not all cases where ê is written are pronounced [ê]: in the combinations *iêc, iêng,* ê has the value of the semivowel [ą] (see 2.66.) Note that [êj] is written simply ê.

2.53. [j]: high front unrounded semivowel—
Upper high: after *i.*
đi [dij] go, *gì* [zìj] what(ever)
Lower high: elsewhere ((i.e., after [ê, ư, ơ, u, ô, o, ă, a, â] (tenser after short vowels).
đế [đểj] put, place, *dễ* [zẽj] be easy, *ngửi* [ngửj] to sniff, *mời* [mòj] invite, *người* [ngờj] person, *núi* [núj] mountain, *tôi* [tôj] I, *tuổi* [tuổj] years old, *hỏi* [hỏj] ask a question, *tay* [tăj] arm, hand, *tây* [tâj] west, *tai* [taj] ear
This semivowel is very short and in rapid speech often becomes voiceless or nearly so before silence or a voiceless sound beginning the next syllable. English speakers tend to make this [j] too long (as in the comparable semivowel in English *boy*).
The representation of [j] in the official spelling (see also 3.34) is usually i: *tôi* I, *hỏi* ask a question, *củi* firewood. But after [i, ê] it is not written at all: *đi* go, *dễ* easy. After â it is always written y: *mây* cloud. The distinction between [a] and [ă] before [j] is symbolized by writing [j] as i in the first case, as y in the second: *mai* [maj] tomorrow, *may* [măj] be lucky.

2.54. ư: lower high back unrounded vowel.
ngửi to sniff, *tư* [tưɤ] fourth, *người* person, *lươn* eel, *ưa* to like, *đứt* to break [string], *sức* strength, *đừng* don't
In many dialects of American English, vowels of this sort do not occur or

32

are rare. It may be helpful in learning the sounds to practice saying the English word *too*, prolonging the vowel while gradually spreading the lips and keeping the tongue in the same position. This should give an upper high back unrounded vowel. The lower vowel can be obtained by opening the mouth a little wider. Some speakers of English use lower high back unrounded vowels commonly in words like *good, should*, especially in unstressed positions. Such vowels generally are variants of [u] in English, and this may mean that there will be real difficulty in learning to distinguish Vietnamese u and u (see 2.57). For persons with this difficulty, practicing exaggerated rounding for u and exaggerated lip spreading for u should be helpful. The following pairs of words are examples of the contrast.

u		u	
thứ [thứɯ]	kind, sort	*thú* [thúw]	(four-footed) animal
cưa [kuɐ̰]	to saw	*cua* [kuɐ̰]	crab
đứt	to break [string]	*đút*	to insert
đứng	to stand	*đúng*	be correct

The diphthong [uɯ] occurs only finally. It is similar to [ij] in that it involves movement from a vowel to a higher homorganic semivowel, and in that it is represented in the orthography by the symbol u alone. U is the regular writing for the vowel. Note, however, that the spellings uu and uou are actually [iw] and [iêw] in Hanoi pronunciation.

2.55. ơ: upper mid back unrounded vowel.

mời invite, *chợ* [chơɯ] market(place), *khớp* joint [of bones], *sớm* be early, *ớt* pepper, pimento, *sơn* to paint, *ướp* to scent, *lườm* give a threatening look, *ướt* be wet, *lươn* eel, *được* receive, *đường* sugar

No vowels of this sort occur in most dialects of English. It will probably be easiest for an English speaker to learn this sound after having learned u, then practicing ơ by opening his mouth wider. If he produces a sound like that in English *but* he has opened his mouth too wide. It is also possible to approximate this vowel by pronouncing the English word *go*, prolonging the vowel and spreading the lips without moving the tongue.

2.56. The ɰ semivowel is roughly the same as u or somewhat higher. It occurs only after *u* and *ơ* when no other consonants follow, and is not represented in the orthography. The diphthongs involved thus parallel [ij, uw].

Upper high back unrounded semivowel: after *u*.

tư [tɯɰ] fourth, *chữ* [chữɯ] written word

Lower high back unrounded semivowel: after *ơ*.

sợ [xơɰ̰] be afraid, *ở* [ởɰ] be located

2.57. **u**: high back rounded vowel—
   Upper high: before *p*, *m*.
      chup seize suddenly, *chum* earthenware jar
   Lower high: elsewhere (i.e., before [j, w, ô, ậ, t, n, k, ng] in the same
syllable).
      núi [núj] mountain, *mũ* [mũw] hat, *tuổi* years old, *chùa* [chùậ]
         (Buddhist) temple, *bút* writing instrument, *phùn* drizzle, *lúc*
         time, instance, *cũng* also
The diphthong [uw] is quite similar to that in English *too* (except for
speakers who have an unrounded vowel in this combination). The vowels
before *p*, *m* are as high as the end of this English combination. The other
variant is only slightly lower. It resembles the vowel in most pronunciations of English *wood*. The difficulty for English speakers having unrounded high back vowels in their speech is discussed in 2.54.

2.58. **ô**: upper mid back rounded vowel—
   Higher mean mid: before [j, w].
      tôi [tôj] I, *rồi* [zồj] be already accomplished, *cô* [kôw] father's
         sister, *lỗ* [lỗw] hole
   Mean mid strongly centralized: after *u*.
      buồn be sad, *quốc* [kwốk] country, *tuổi* [tuổj] years old, *chuột*
         rat
   Upper mid: elsewhere (i.e., before *p*, *m*, *t*, *n*)..
      tốp band, group, *hôm* day, *tốt* be good, *đồn* fort, military post
The cluster [ôw] is quite similar to the diphthong heard in some pronunciations of English *snow*, *boat*. However, many English speakers have unrounded back vowels (usually also lower) in such words, combinations
which are very similar to the Vietnamese diphthong [âw] (see 2.64-65).
They will need to practice carefully hearing and making the distinction
between [ôw] with a rounded vowel, and [âw] with an unrounded (and
much lower) vowel. Certain other English speakers have still different
vowels in *snow* or *boat*—central vowels. They may have difficulty distinguishing Vietnamese [ăw] (see 2.64) rather than [âw] from [ôw], or they
may confuse all three combinations. Examples of the three contrasting
diphthongs in Vietnamese follow:
   cô [kôw] father's sister   *câu* [kâw] sentence   *cau* [kăw] areca
   số [xôw] number   *xấu* [xâw] be ugly   *sáu* [xăw] six

   The cluster [ôj] is reminiscent of the diphthong in English *toy*, *boy*,
but the vowel is higher. Many English speakers will have difficulty learning to distinguish Vietnamese [ôj] from [oj] (see 2.62). They will need

to practice pairs like the following:

nối [nŏj] to join, add to   *nói* [nój] to speak

đối [đŏj] to reply to   *đói* [đój] be hungry

Before *p, m, t, n* Vietnamese ô is not a diphthong like the one usually heard in English *hope, home, boat, bone.* It is totally unlike the vowels in English words like *hop, Tom, cot, Don.* (Most speakers of English have low central unrounded vowels in these positions, although some have low or lower mid back rounded vowels.) Those who have difficulties with these combinations will need to practice starting with the vowel they have learned in the combinations [ôw, ôj], and remember that the ô in *ôp, ôm, ôt, ôn* is produced with the tongue raised just slightly higher. (With low tones the combination [ôp] sometimes has a slightly lower vowel: e.g., *hộp* box, can.)

Not all cases where ô is written correspond to [ô] in the pronunciation: in the combinations *uôc, uông,* ô has the value of [ậ] (cf. 2.66); the combinations *oc, ông* represent [âwk, âwng] respectively. Note also that [ôw] is written simply ô.

2.59. [w]: high back rounded semivowel—

Upper high: after [u].

đủ [đủw] be enough, *mũ* [mũw] hat

Lower high: elsewhere (i.e., preceding the vocalic nucleus of the syllable, and after [i, ê, e, ô, a, ă, â]) (tenser preceding vocalic nucleus than following it, and preglottalized when initial in syllable; tenser after short vowels).

> *òa* [wà] burst into tears, *tuần* [twần] week, *thuế* [thwế] taxes, *loài* [lwàj] species, *chuyện* [chwiện] talk, conversation, *xuân* [xwân] spring [season], *duyên* [zwiên] predestined affinity, *năm nhuận* [năm nhwận] leap year, *qua* [kwa] cross over, *khỏe* [khwẻ] be strong, healthy, *góa* [gwá] be widowed, *ngoài* [ngwàj] outside, *hoa* [hwa] flower

> *chịu* [chịw] endure, suffer, *nếu* [nếw] if, *đeo* [dew] wear (on body), *cô* [kôw] father's sister, *cao* [kaw] be high, *sau* [xăw] afterward, *xấu* [xâw] be ugly

Before vowels [w] is very similar to English *w* in *winter,* although it is tenser and perhaps a little higher. However, after vowels it is laxer; like [j] it is very short and in rapid speech often becomes voiceless or nearly so before silence or a voiceless sound in the next syllable. The [w] in the combinations [ăwk, ăwng, âwk, âwng] (cf. 2.64, 2.65) is especially short. English speakers tend to make postvocalic [w] too long (like the comparable semivowel in English *cow, crowd*).

35

The representation of [w] in the official spelling (see also 3.33) is usually **u**: *tuần* week, *thuế* taxes, *chuyện* talk, conversation, *thuở* epoch, *chịu* endure, suffer, *nếu* if, *xấu* be ugly. However, it is not written at all after [u, ô]: *ngủ* [ngủw] to sleep, *cô* [kôw] father's sister. After *e* and before *e, a, ă* it is written **o** (except that [kw-] is always written **qu-**): *mèo* [mèw] cat, *khỏe* [khwẻ] be strong, healthy, *góa* [gwá] be widowed, *hoặc* [hwặk] or, *qua* [kwa] cross over. The distinction between [a] and [ă] before [w] is symbolized by writing [w] as **o** in the first case, **u** in the second: *sao* [xaw] star, *sau* [xăw] afterward.

2.6. Lower Vocalics have only two distinctive positions: there are three vowels produced toward the front of the mouth, two toward the back. Three of the vowels are relatively long and appear in final position: **e, o, a**. The others (**ă** and **â**) are very short and do not occur finally.

2.61. **e**: lower mid front unrounded vowel.

> *nghe* listen, *bè* raft, *lẽ* cause, reason, *mèo* [mèw] cat, *thép* steel, *đem* carry, *ghét* detest, *đen* be black, *eng-éc* [onomatopoetic: squealing of pig], *sẻng* shovel

This sound is not much lower than the vowel in English *bet*, and for this reason there are many positions in which it is difficult for the English speaker to learn the distinction between **e** and **ê**. For some examples of this distinction, see 2.52.

In final position **e** itself occupies about the same amount of time as a diphthong such as [ew]. That is, *mè* 'tench' (a kind of fish) is about as long as *mèo* [mèw] 'cat'. In heavily stressed syllables, especially citation forms, one often hears [eậ] as an alternate for [e] in final position or before *-ng* (most commonly with low tones): *bè* [bè(ậ)] raft, *sẻng* [xẻ(ậ)ng] shovel. Before *ng* this [ậ] is extremely short.

2.62. **o**: lower mid back rounded vowel.

> *khó* be difficult, *cỏ* grass, *hỏi* ask a question, *chóp* summit, *xóm* neighborhood, *ngọt* be sweet, *ngon* be good tasting, *boong* [bong] deck (of ship), *họ* (extended) family, clan

This sound is very similar to that heard in most pronunciations of English *law*, although generally a little higher. Many English speakers have considerable difficulty with **o** before final consonants, because in their native speech a lower unrounded vowel occurs in words like *chop, Tom, cot, Don*. They will need to listen carefully to the Vietnamese words and compare them with similar English words in order to hear the differences before they will be able to practice the Vietnamese sounds.

Like *e*, o itself when final occupies about the same amount of time as a diphthong like [oj]. So *khó* 'be difficult' is about the same length as *khói* [khój] 'smoke'. In heavily stressed syllables, especially citation forms, one often hears [oậ] as an alternate for [o] both in final position and before [j] (most commonly with low tones): *cỏ* [kỏ(ậ)] grass, *hỏi* [hỏ(ậ)j] ask (a question).

The distinction between oi and ôi occasions difficulty for some. This is discussed in detail in 2.58.

Note that before *ng* [o] is written oo. (The spelling *ong* represents [ăwng], which is extremely common in Vietnamese, while [ong] is limited to a few borrowed words: see also 3.37.)

2.63. a: lower low front unrounded vowel.

> *nhà* building, *bài* lesson, *cao* be high, *đáp* to answer, *làm* to act, *hát* to sing, *bàn* table, *khác* be different, *làng* village, *mạ* rice seedling, *bạn* friend

For English speakers whose *a* in words like *father* is produced very far front in the mouth, Hanoi a presents few problems. But many have in *father* a vowel much like the ones in *hot, rob, hop,* which is farther back in the mouth (often described as "broader"). For them Hanoi a may most usefully be viewed as intermediate between the English vowels just mentioned and those in words like *cat, map, jam.* Specifically, it is lower than the latter, and farther front than the former.

In final position a itself occupies about the same amount of time as a diphthong such as [aj]. That is, *ma* 'ghost' is about as long as *mai* 'tomorrow'.

There may be considerable difficulty in learning to distinguish a from ă (2.64), which is not only shorter, but is also quite different in quality. Following are some examples of this contrast:

a	ă
mai [maj] tomorrow	*may* [măj] be lucky
sao [xaw] star	*sau* [xăw] afterward
sáp wax	*sắp* be on the point of
tham be greedy	*thăm* to visit
cát sand	*cắt* to cut
bán to sell	*bắn* to shoot
xác corpse	*sắc* be sharp
mang carry (on one's person)	*măng* bamboo shoots

Note that in the orthography the symbol a does not always represent [a]. Before *ch, nh* (where [a] does not occur) a represents [ă] and [ăj, ăw] are written ay, au, as distinct from ai [aj] and ao [aw].

2.64. ă: upper low central unrounded vowel.

> *máy* [măj] machine, *sáu* [xăw] six, *sắp* be on the point of, *thăm*
> to visit, *đắt* be expensive, *ăn* to eat, *sạch* [xăch] be clean,
> *mạnh* [mănh] be strong, *sắc* be sharp, *đằng* direction, area,
> *đọc* [đăwk] to read, *ong* [ăwng] bee

This sound resembles nothing in most English dialects. It can be learned
by producing the vowel in *cat, mat,* with the tongue slightly retracted. It is
essential to learn the distinction between ă and â. The latter is similar to
the sounds usually heard in English words like *but, fuss, sun* in stressed
positions. Without contrasting forms to compare it with ă often sounds like
â to an English speaker. Following are some examples of the contrast:

ă	â
máy [măj] machine	*mấy* [mâj] how(ever) many
sáu [xăw] six	*xấu* [xâw] be ugly
cắp pilfer	*cấp* level, degree
thăm to visit	*thâm* be black
đắt be expensive	*đất* ground, land
chăn to tend	*chân* foot, leg
sắc be sharp	*xấc* be ill-mannered
văng to throw out	*vâng* to obey
óc [ăwk] brain	*ốc* [âwk] snail
ong [ăwng] bee	*ông* [âwng] grandfather

In the standard orthography [ă] is usually written ă, but before *ch, nh*
(where [a, â] do not occur) it is written simply a: *cắp* pilfer, *ăn* to eat,
sạch be clean, *mạnh* be strong, The combination [ăj] is written **ay**. The
combination [ăw] is written **au** when final, but **o** before [k, ng]: *sáu* six,
óc brain, *ong* bee.

2.65. â: relatively low back unrounded vowel.

> Lower mid back, strongly centralized: after [w, b, ph, v, m] before [j].
>> *quấy* to stir, *bẩy* to display, *phẩy* comma, *vậy* as just described,
>> *mấy* how(ever) many
> Lower mid back: elsewhere.
>> *tây* west, *đâu* where(ver), *ngập* be flooded, *đâm* to stab, *rất* very,
>> *dân* citizen, *xấc* be ill-mannered, *vâng* obey, *ốc* [âwk] snail,
>> *không* [khâwng] not

The most common sound of â is very similar to the vowel in English *but,
fuss, sun* in stressed positions. The sound before [j] after labials, however, is nearly a central vowel, and the English speaker may have some
difficulties in distinguishing [âj] from [êj] in these positions. Some contrasting examples follow:

[âj]	[êj]
bày to display	*bè* border, edge
phẩy comma	*phê* comment on, criticize
vầy in the following manner	*về* to return
mây cloud	*mê* be unconscious
quẩy to stir	*quê* rural area

The distinction between [âw] and [ôw] is treated in 2.58. The distinction between [â] and [ă] is treated in 2.64.

/â/ is written â in the standard orthography except in the combinations [âwk, âwng], which are written ôc, ông, respectively.

2.66. The ặ semivowel is roughly the same as the vowel â–a lower mid back semivowel. It appears as a final after the upper high vowels [i, ɯ, u]; and as a prefinal before [k, ng] after the same vowels. Occasionally a still lower vowel is heard following [u], especially with low tones; this is also the vowel heard in the diphthongs [eặ, oặ] which appear as alternates of [e, o] in certain positions (cf. 2.61-62). After [i] before [k, ng] it is strongly centralized.

> *chia* [chiặ] to divide, *mưa* [mưặ] to rain, *mua* [muặ] to buy;
> *thuốc* [thúặk] medicine, *buồng* [bùặng] chamber, room,
> *việc* [viặk] matter, affair, *tiếng* [tíặng] noise, sound;
> *mùa* [mùặ] season (of year), *bè* [bè(ặ)] raft, *hỏi* [ho(ặ)j] ask
> (a question)

In the standard writing system this semivowel is represented by a in final position; and by ê after *i*, ô after *u* before [k, ng]. It is not written in the variants of forms in *-e, -o*.

2.7. Tones and Accompanying Elements. As the speaker of any language talks he gradually releases air from his lungs. This release is effected in brief uneven pulses, which are characterized by a beginning that is relatively forceful, and gradually decreasing force until the next pulse or a pause. In Vietnamese the sequence of consonants and vowels which goes with each chest pulse is a **syllable.** The makeup of syllables is described in 2.8.

Each syllable has certain additional distinctive features which are produced simultaneously with some or all of its consonants and vowels. First of all, the chest pulses which define syllables are unequal, varying from very forceful to very weak: three gradations of this forcefulness (**stresses**) are distinctive. At the same time, the force of each chest pulse dissipates gradually—that is, it begins strong and becomes gradually weaker. There are four different ways in which this is accomplished (**intonations**).

Finally, there are six **tones**–combinations of musical pitch and certain other aspects of voice production. Every syllable in connected speech is accompanied by one element from each of these sets.

2.71. Tones in Hanoi speech combine relative heights and contours of pitch with differences in glottal stricture. It remains unclear precisely how these tonal differences are perceived, but it is at least evident that loss of voicing impairs perceptibility considerably (cf. Lê văn Lý 1948 and Miller 1961). There are a number of theoretical difficulties involved in the interpretation of these phenomena (cf. 2.15), but the most generally useful description handles the material in the same way as the traditional orthography.

Sắc tone is high and rising (perhaps nearly level at the high point in rapid speech) and tense. In sequences of several syllables with this tone, one accompanied by heavy stress (2.72) is highest and those preceding it are successively higher as the heavy stress is approached. After the heavy stress subsequent syllables with *sắc* tone begin lower and build up their own series of increasing height. It is symbolized by the acute accent:

cá fish, *khó* be difficult, *tốt* be good, *thuốc* medicine

Ngã tone is also high and rising (in other words, the contour is roughly the same as that of *sắc*), but it is accompanied by the rasping voice quality occasioned by tense glottal stricture. In careful speech such syllables are sometimes interrupted completely by a glottal stop (or a rapid series of glottal stops). It is symbolized by the tilde: ~.

dã [anterior marker], *sữa* milk, *muỗi* mosquito, *cũng* likewise

Ngang tone is lax; in contour it is nearly level in non-final syllables not accompanied by heavy stress, although even in these cases it probably trails downward slightly. It starts just slightly higher than the mid point of the normal speaking voice range. In syllables accompanied by heavy stress (2.72) it starts somewhat higher and falls more noticeably. Final syllables in the pause group have this latter contour unless one of the special intonations is involved (see 2.73), in which case quite different contours are heard. In isolated citation forms one frequently hears the level contour typical of non-final syllables. This tone is symbolized in the writing system by the absence of any tone mark.

ba three, *tay* hand, *xe* vehicle, *răng* tooth

Huyền tone, also lax, starts quite low and trails downward toward the bottom of the voice range. It is often accompanied by a kind of breathy voicing, reminiscent of a sigh. It is symbolized by the grave accent:

cờ chess, *làng* village, *giày* shoe, *về* to return home

Hỏi tone is tense; it starts somewhat higher than *huyền* and drops rather abruptly. In final syllables, and especially in citation forms, this is followed by a sweeping rise at the end, and for this reason it is often called the "dipping" tone. However, non-final syllables seem only to have a brief level portion at the end, and this is exceedingly elusive in rapid speech. It is symbolized by an accent made of the top part of a question mark: ˀ.

ᴄᴏ́ *cỏ* grass, *khỏe* be strong, healthy, *ngủ* to sleep, *ảnh* photograph

Nặng tone is also tense; it starts somewhat lower than *hỏi*. With syllables ending in a stop [p, t, ch, k] it drops only a little more sharply than *huyền* tone, but it is never accompanied by the breathy quality of that tone. Other syllables have the same rasping voice quality as *ngã*, drop very sharply and are almost immediately cut off by a strong glottal stop. This tone is symbolized by a subscript dot: ₌ . (For a recent study of this tone in Hanoi speech, see Donaldson 1963.)

mạ rice seedling, *mạnh* be strong, *dẹp* be beautiful, *chợ* market-(place)

Note that the name for each tone is itself an example of that tone. These names are known to literate Vietnamese as the designations of the diacritics which symbolize them. For this reason the name *ngang* is not generally known; for the most part it is to be found only in technical works, while the other words are common property.

With the various intonations tone contours are somewhat different. These differences are discussed in connection with the intonations themselves (2.73).

2.72. Stresses are not symbolized in any way in the traditional orthography. Where it has seemed important to indicate them in this work, a single superior vertical stroke (') is used before the first letter of the syllable to symbolize **heavy stress**, a small superior circle (°) for **weak stress**, while **medium stress** is left unmarked.

In ordinary speech the majority of syllables are accompanied by medium stress. In sequences of several such syllables alternate ones are slightly louder, but this is not a distinctive matter. Each pause group has at least one heavy stress. Weak stresses are fairly frequent in rapid passages, rarer in careful speech.

Tôi °không 'biết. I don't know

'Nói phải 'có người nói 'đi nói 'lại, chớ 'bắt °người °ta 'nói °một mình 'hoài! For a conversation you ought to have people talk-

41

ing together, not make somebody talk alone all the time!
["speak ought exist person speak go speak come and-not
constrain someone speak alone continually"]

2.73. **Intonations** are probably perceived as shifting contours of fading
syllabic stress—that is, the way the force of each syllable dies away; however, there are also differences in the contours of the tones. Some extensive
and careful research on natural speech is needed to provide a better basis
for understanding these phenomena.

For the moment it may be simply stated that there seem to be four ways
in which the force of a syllable is dissipated. The most common fashion is
here accepted as normal intonation: **decreasing** stress contour involves a
gradual diminishing of force from the beginning of the syllable; it accompanies the vast majority of syllables. Final syllables in pause groups are
frequently accompanied by **fading** intonation, characterized by a more
rapid decline in force. The tones of such syllables are **lowered**—that is,
they begin and end lower than syllables with the same tones and decreasing stress. Also quite frequent with final syllables is **sustaining** intonation, in which the initial force of the syllables is maintained for a short
while before decreasing. The tones of these syllables are **raised**—starting
and ending higher than with regular decreasing stress. Occasional syllables (both medial and final) are accompanied by **increasing** intonation,
in the production of which the initial force increases before it starts to
fade away. The tones of these syllables are **spread**—they cover a greater
proportion of the voice range than the same tones accompanied by decreasing stress.

The pitch contours described in 2.71 are those which occur with decreasing intonation. The effect of the other intonations on the tones is
described in detail in the following paragraphs.

With **fading intonation** tones are somewhat lower. *Sắc* and *ngã* syllables like *má* 'cheek' and *sữa* 'milk' begin a little lower and do not rise
as high. *Ngang* syllables like *ma* 'ghost' start lower and fall slightly. *Hỏi*
syllables like *mả* 'tomb' start lower and usually have only a slight rise at
the end or none at all. *Nặng* syllables like *mạ* 'rice seedling' and *đẹp* 'be
beautiful' start lower and fall abruptly. *Huyền* syllables such as *mà* 'but'
start lower and fall to the bottom of the speaker's normal speaking voice
range. This intonation is common at the end of simple statements.

> *Tôi đi xuống.* I'm going down.
> *Tôi đi lên.* I'm going up.
> *Tôi đi ngủ.* I'm going to bed.
> *Tôi không mệt.* I'm not tired.
> *Tôi đi chùa.* I'm going to the (Buddhist) temple.

42

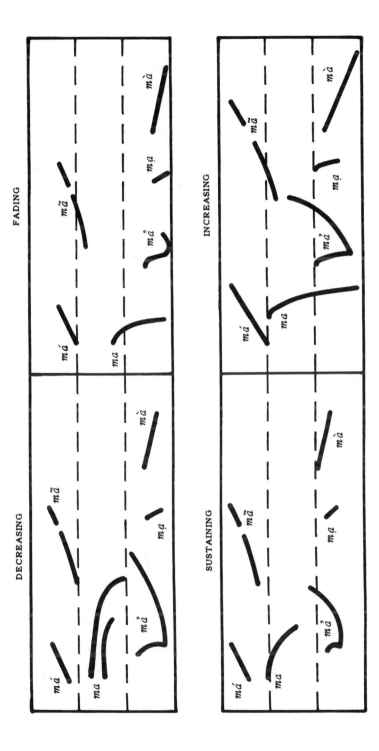

Fig. 1. Tonal Contours with Different Intonations

With **sustaining intonation** tones are somewhat higher. *Sắc* and *ngã* syllables start higher and rise somewhat more abruptly. *Ngang* syllables start higher and fall back to about the middle of the voice range. *Hỏi* syllables start at about the same level as with decreasing intonation, but do not fall as far and rise noticeably at the end. *Nặng* syllables again start at about the same level as with decreasing intonation and drop abruptly to a level only slightly lower; they often sound simply level, but higher than with decreasing intonation. *Huyền* syllables start higher and do not fall so low as with decreasing intonation. A complicating factor with *ngang* tone involves relative stress: in sequences of several *ngang* tones the one accompanied by the heaviest stress is the highest (the last of the following examples). This intonation is frequent in questions.

> *Khi nào ông đi xuống?* When are you going down?
> *Ông thích không?* Do you like [it]?
> *Khi nào ông đi ngủ?* When are you going to bed?
> *Tại sao ông mệt?* Why are you tired?
> *Ông nói gì?* What did you say?
> *Ông 'đi không?* Are you going?

With **increasing intonation** tones cover more of the voice range. *Sắc* and *ngã* syllables start lower and rise higher. *Ngang* syllables start higher and fall all the way to the bottom of the normal speaking voice range. *Hỏi* syllables start a little higher, dip rapidly and rise to a point around the middle of the voice range. *Nặng* syllables start higher and fall abruptly. *Huyền* syllables start higher and fall to the bottom of the normal speaking voice range. This intonation is generally heard in exclamative sentences like the following.

> *Sao ông không đi xuống!* Why aren't you going down?
> *Sao ông không đi!* Why don't you go!
> *Sao ông không đi ngủ!* Why don't you go to bed!
> *Sao ông không mệt!* How come you're not tired!
> *Ông ấy không nói gì!* He didn't say anything!

Figure 1 provides an impressionistic comparative drawing of the tonal contours with the different intonations.

Intonations are not directly represented in the official writing system, although they are often suggested by conventional punctuation symbols (see 3.54). They involve some special problems of meaning which are best treated as morphemic entities (5.3).

2.8. Syllable Structure.

The sequence of sounds accompanying each chest pulse constitutes a syllable. Every syllable has at least a vowel and a tone, accompanied by a relative stress and an intonation. In some syllables the vowel is followed by a semivowel, a consonant, a semivowel and a consonant, or a second vowel and a consonant. The vowel and whatever follows it is the **nucleus** of the syllable. All syllables also have a consonant at the beginning—if not one of the ones treated in 2.2-4, then a glottal stop (which is not represented in the regular orthography, so the vowel appears as first letter). Most of these consonants appear in some syllables followed by the semivowel [w], making a cluster. Glottal stop is followed by [w], and in this case the symbol (o- or u-) representing the [w] is the first letter written. These consonants and clusters are **initials**. The composition of the syllable may now be restated simply: each syllable contains an initial, a nucleus and a tone.

There are no limitations on the kinds of syllables which occur with the various stresses and intonations. But there are a number of special features about the internal structure of syllables and they are described in the following sections.

Syllables vary in length with the degree of relative stress which accompanies them: the heavier the stress the longer the syllable. Syllables accompanied by [⁰] are extremely rapid.

Syllables with the same relative stress are approximately equal in length. That is, those containing a vowel cluster, diphthong or triphthong take approximately the same time as those containing a single vowel, and so on. However, there are some special differences which are worth noting. Syllables ending in stops preceded by a single vowel are shorter than other types. On the other hand, the vowel [a] is often somewhat longer than other vowels in comparable positions.

Very short:
> *ích* be useful, *hết* be used up, *dút* to break [string], *lớp* class, *hút* to inhale, *một* one, *đẹp* be beautiful, *ngọt* be sweet, *cắp* pilfer, *thấp* be short, low

Slightly longer:
> *tháp* tower, *in* to print, *đến* arrive, *muốn* to want, *đường* sugar, *đi* go, *người* person, *biết* know, *được* receive, *sau* afterward, *nghe* listen

Still longer:
> *cam* orange, *hai* two, *sao* star, *xa* be far

2.81. Initials

2.81. Initials include all of the consonants described in 2.2-4 except [p]. Where the traditional writing shows a vowel symbol as initial, it is, in fact, preceded by a glottal stop. All initial clusters have [w] as second member. This includes the case in which the symbol representing [w] appears first—in pronunciation it is preceded by glottal stop. Table 6 shows the occurring combinations. Possible clusters are shown by including [w] in parentheses after the consonants with which it occurs. The entry (w) in the glottal column symbolizes the glottal stop initial, which sometimes clusters with [w].

TABLE 6. INITIALS

	LABIAL	APICAL	LAMINAL	DORSAL	GLOTTAL
FORTIS	—	t(w)	ch(w)	k(w)	(w)
	b	d(w)			
LENIS	ph	th(w)	x(w)	kh(w)	h(w)
	v	l(w)	z(w)	g(w)	
NASAL	m	n	nh(w)	ng(w)	

tôi I, *tòa* [twà] bureau, office, *chợ* market, *chuyện* [chwiện] conversation topic, *cá* fish, *qua* [kwa] cross over, *in* to print, *oà* [wà] burst into tears, *bên* side, *đến* arrive, *đoán* [dwán] to guess, *phá* destroy, *thờ* to worship, *thuế* [thwếj] taxes, *sách* [xǎch] book, *xuân* [xwân] spring [season], *khen* commend, *khoai* [khwaj] potato, *hỏi* ask (a question), *hoàng* [hwàng] emperor, *vừa* to fit, suit, *lá* leaf, *loài* [lwàj] species, *gì* [ʐìj] what(ever), *duyên* [zwiên] predestined affinity, *gần* be near, *góa* [gwá] be widowed, *Mỹ* America, *núi* mountain, *nhớ* remember, *năm nhuận* [năm nhwận] leap year, *nghe* listen, *ngoài* [ngwàj] outside

Clusters with [w] occur with nearly all non-labial consonants. The important exception is [n]. There are a few forms in dictionaries which would suggest a cluster [nw]: e.g., *noãn* [nwãn] womb (listed in dictionaries with the meanings: egg; testicle), *noạ* [nwạ] lazy, *nuy nhân* [nwịj nhân] dwarf. However, these are learnèd forms, all Chinese borrowings, of extremely limited occurrence in the everyday language. It thus seems more realistic to consider the cluster [nw] as marginal. A very few French loan forms have [w] clusters with labials—e.g., *(ô-tô-)buýt* [ôw tôw bwít] bus (Fr. *autobus*)—but they are also marginal. The cluster [gw] seems to be represented by only the single form *góa* [gwá] be widowed. However, unlike the items suggesting [nw], this form is extremely common in everyday speech and is a native word of long standing.

The cluster [lw] is absent from the speech of many Hanoi people. In these cases the [w] is replaced by the vowel [u] before [i, â], and by the vowel [o] before [a, ă] thus establishing additional vowel clusters:

lũy [lwĩj, lũi]fence, hedge, *luật* [lwật, luật] law, *loài* [lwàj, loàj] species, *loăng-quăng* [lwăng kwăng, loăng kwăng] to run about.

2.82. Nuclei are **simple,** containing only a single vowel (and no final consonant or semivowel); **two-element,** containing a vowel followed by a consonant or semivowel; and **three-element,** containing a cluster of two vowels or a diphthong followed by a final consonant or semivowel.

Simple nuclei consist of one of the vowels **e, o, a.** Syllables in **e** and **o** have occasional variants in [eậ, oậ], which are, of course, two-element nuclei (cf. 2.61, 2.62).

nghe listen, *nhỏ* be small, *cá* fish, *lẽ* cause, reason, *họ* clan, *mạ* rice seedling

Two-element nuclei contain any of the eleven vowels as first element, and (with certain limitations) one of the following as final element: [j, ɰ, w, ậ, p, m, t, n, ch, nh, k, ng]. Table 7 shows the possible combinations. Examples follow.

TABLE 7. TWO-ELEMENT NUCLEI

VOWELS	j	ɰ	w	ậ	p	m	t	n	ch	nh	k	ng
i	ij		iw	iậ	ip	im	it	in	ich	inh		
ê	êj		êw		êp	êm	êt	ên	êch	ênh		(êng)
ư	ưj	ưɰ		ưậ			ưt				ưk	ưng
ơ	ơj	ơɰ			ơp	ơm	ơt	ơn				
u	uj		uw	uậ	up	um	ut	un			uk	ung
ô	ôj		ôw		ôp	ôm	ôt	ôn				(ông)
e			ew	(eậ)	ep	em	et	en			ek	eng
o	oj			(oậ)	op	om	ot	on				ong
ă	ăj		ăw		ăp	ăm	ăt	ăn	ăch	ănh	ăk	ăng
â	âj		âw		âp	âm	ât	ân			âk	âng
a	aj		aw		ap	am	at	an			ak	ang

đi [đij] go, *mưu* [miw] scheme, *chia* [chiậ] to divide, *kíp* be urgent, *lim* ironwood, *ít* be a small amount, *in* to print, *ích* be useful, *lính* soldier

để [đẻj] put, place, *nếu* [nẽw] if, *bếp* kitchen, *đêm* night, *hết* be used up, *đến* arrive, *ếch* frog, *bênh* defend, *côông-kêng* carry [a person] astride over one's shoulders

ngửi [ngửj] to sniff, *tư* [tưɰ] fourth, *mưa* [mưậ] to rain, *đứt* to break [string], *súc* strength, *đừng* don't

mời [mòj] invite, *mơ* [mơ̰] to dream, *lớp* class, *sớm* be early, *ớt* pepper, pimento, *sơn* to paint,

núi [núj] mountain, *đủ* [đủw] be enough, *mua* [muə̰] to buy, *chụp* seize suddenly, *chum* earthenware jar, *phút* minute, moment, *bùn* mud, *lúc* time, instance, *đúng* be correct

tôi [tôj] I, *cô* [kôw] father's sister, *tốp* band, group, *hôm* day, *một* one, *đồn* fort, military post, *côông-kêng* [kông kêng] carry [a person] astride over one's shoulders

mèo [mèw] cat, *bè* [bèə̰] raft (see 2.61), *đẹp* be beautiful, *đem* to carry, *ghét* detest, *đen* be black, *eng éc* [eng ék] [onomatopoetic: squealing of pig]

hỏi [hỏj] ask a question, *nhỏ* [nhỏə̰] be small (see 2.62), *chóp* summit, *xóm* neighborhood, *ngọt* be sweet, *ngon* be tasty, *boong* [bong] deck [of ship]

tay [tăj] hand, arm, *sáu* [xǎw] six, *cắp* pilfer, *thăm* to visit, *tắt* [tăt] to extinguish, *ăn* to eat, *sách* [xăch] book, *hành* [hănh] onion, *sắc* be sharp, *vắng* be absent

tây [tâj] west, *xấu* [xâw] be ugly, *cấp* level, degree, *đâm* to stab, *rất* very, *dân* citizen, *xấc* be ill-mannered, *vâng* to obey

hai [haj] two, *sao* [xaw] star, *tháp* tower, *làm* act, *mát* be cool, *bàn* table, *khác* be different, *làng* village

Sometimes the final semivowels [w, ə̰] are as prominent as the preceding vowel in the combinations [iw, iə̰, ɯə̰, uə̰] (occasionally even more prominent); the diphthongs are then really vowel clusters: [iu, iâ, ɯâ, uâ]. Speakers who have no initial cluster [lw] have one special two-element nucleus which otherwise does not occur: [oa] as in *loa* 'megaphone', where other speakers have [lwa] (cf. 2.81).

Some of these combinations are rare. [ɯt] is not common, and the lack of examples in [ɯn] is perhaps connected. Forms in [ek, eng] are very few, and seem for the most part to be onomatopoetic. Forms in [ong] are extremely limited, and all the examples observed are borrowings from French. Words in [êch, ênh] are also relatively infrequent and some of them have variants in [ich, inh]. The combinations [êng, ông] are attested only in the single form *côông-kêng* cited above (cf. Nguyễn đình Hòa 1955: p. 26).

Three-element nuclei contain the vowel clusters and diphthongs oâ]; cf. 2.61, 2.62), followed by certain of the following finals: [j, w, p, m, t, n, k, ng]. The occurring combinations are shown in Table 8.

TABLE 8. THREE-ELEMENT NUCLEI

VOCALIC SEQUENCES	*j*	*w*	*p*	*m*	*t*	*n*	*k*	*ng*
iê		iêw	iêp	iêm	iêt	iên		
iậ							iậk	iậng
ươ	ươj		ươp	ươm	ươt	ươn	ươk	ương
uô	uôj			uôm	uôt	uôn		
uậ							uậk	uậng
(eậ)								(eậng)
(oậ)	(oậj)							
ăw							ăwk	ăwng
âw							âwk	âwng

hiểu [hiểw] understand, *tiếp* to welcome, *nghiệm* to experiment, *biết* know, *miền* region

việc [viậk] matter, affair, *tiếng* [tiậng] sound, noise

người [ngườj] person, *ướp* to scent, *lườm* give a threatening look, *ướt* be wet, *vườn* garden, *nước* water, *đường* sugar

tuổi [tuổj] years old, *buồm* [ship's] sail, *chuột* rat, *buồn* be sad

guốc [gúậk] clog, wooden shoe, *ruộng* [zuậng] rice field

xẻng [xẻậng] shovel, *hỏi* [hỏậj] ask a question

học [hăwk] to study, *cõng* [kãwng] carry on one's back, *ốc* [ấwk] snail, *ông* [âwng] grandfather

The nuclei [eậng, oậj] are alternates of [eng, oj] (see 2.61, 2.62). The nucleus [uôm] is very rare, and the non-occurrence of [uôp] is perhaps connected. Note that [iậ-, uậ-] before [k, ng] correspond to [iê-, uô-] before other finals.

In the clusters [iê, ươ, uô] the second vowel is frequently more prominent than the first. This occasionally also happens with the diphthongs [iậ, uậ], in which a vowel cluster then results: [iâ, uâ].

Speakers having no initial [lw] cluster have the following three-element clusters after *l* which otherwise do not occur: [uât, uân, oăj, oăt, oănh, oăng, oaj, oat, oan, oak, oang]. E.g., *luật* [luật] law, *loanh-quanh* [loănh kwănh] go around and around, *loài* [loàj] species.

2.83. Combinations of Nuclei with Tones.
In general, most of the nuclei described in 2.82 occur with all tones. Non-occurrences are for the most part accidental and not structurally significant. There is one important

exception: nuclei ending in stops occur only with *sắc* and *nặng* tones.

> *kíp* be urgent, *ít* be a small amount, *sách* [xǎch] book, *khác*
> be different, *đẹp* be beautiful, *vịt* duck, *sạch* [xặch] be
> clean, *học* [hǎwk] to study, *tiếp* to welcome, *biết* know,
> *việc* [viậk] matter, affair, *được* receive

2.84. Combinations of Nuclei with Initials.

A large number of the syllabic nuclei occur with each initial described in 2.81. For the most part non-occurrences are the result of accident—that is, no words with these particular shapes happen to occur, although there is no pattern which would suggest that they are not possible sequences. However, one limitation is structurally significant: with a single exception (*quốc* [kwốk] country), no initial clusters with [w] occur before back rounded vowels [u, ô, o] or before [ɯ], and they are very rare before [ơ]. Three examples of the latter have been recorded:

> *quơ* [kwơɰ] to gather, seize, *quờ* [kwờɰ] to grope for, *quở*
> [kwởɰ] to scold

Initial clusters with [w] are also very rare before nuclei ending in [w]. Only [kw, khw, ngw] have been observed; the nuclei involved are [iw, êw, ew, aw] and the number of forms is small:

> *khuỷu* [khwǐw] elbow, *khuỵu* [khwịw] to collapse, *khoèo*
> [khwèw] be bent, curved, *ngoẹo* [ngwẹw] to turn, branch
> off, *ngoẻo* [ngwẻw] to die (slang), *ngoao* [ngwaw] meow
> [onom. of cat's mewing] (also *ngoeo* [ngwew]), *ngoáo*
> [ngwáw] hobgoblin, *ngoéo* [ngwéw] to hook onto, into,
> *quào* [kwàw] to claw, *quạu* [kwặw] to scold severely, *quấu*
> [kwẩw] to pinch, *queo* [kwew] be curved, *quèo* [kwèw]
> hook, *quẹo* [kwẹw] to turn, branch off, *quểu-quào* [kwểw
> kwàw] be sloppily, illegibly written

2.9. Pause Groups

are sequences of syllables occurring between two pauses without any intervening pauses. They vary in length from a single syllable to a dozen or more, but the average length is around five to eight syllables. In extremely rapid speech speakers generally make few pauses, and the groups are longer, while slow, deliberate speech has a great many short groups.

There are two items of distributional interest about pause groups. First, every pause group has at least one heavy stress ([']) (2.72); second, the three special intonations (fading, sustaining and increasing, cf. 2.73) are typically heard at the ends of pause groups. While increasing intonation is common enough medially, fading and sustaining intonations are almost limited to final position. (In extremely rapid speech they do occasionally occur without an immediately following pause, but analysis of the material always shows that the speaker is actually running sentences together, and it is almost certain that if asked to repeat what he has just said he will make pauses at specifically these points.)

These matters are discussed further in 5.3, and it will be apparent that these pause groups are the larger building blocks of sentences (5.4).

CHAPTER 3

The Writing System

3.1. History. For over a thousand years (207 B.C. to 939 A.D.) the territory of the Vietnamese was a province of China. During this long period
the semicivilized people whom the Chinese had come to dominate gradually became more and more influenced by the already extremely advanced
culture of their conquerors. When the Vietnamese gained their independence in the tenth century it was mainly a political change, for they had
been profoundly and lastingly affected by Chinese culture. Thus it is not
surprising that Chinese long after remained the cultured language of the
court, and the writing system which had been adopted along with other
cultural elements was used for official documents of all sorts as well as
for the considerable body of artistic literature produced during that period.

There are vague references to an earlier writing system, presumably of
Indic origin, like that of Cambodian and Thai, but no real evidence seems
to have survived. (Cf. Cordier 1932: 10; Nguyễn văn Liễn 1934: 63. Both
refer, the latter with a quotation, to Trương vĩnh Ký 1883, which has not
been available to consult.) In any case, it is most likely that Chinese
characters came into extensive use in the country long before Vietnamese
independence.

The pronunciation of the wealth of Sino-Vietnamese forms (that is, Vietnamese words of Chinese origin) indicates that around the ninth or tenth
century these forms left the stream of development of Chinese dialects and
joined that of Vietnamese phonetic evolution. From this it is clear that
these words—and presumably their written forms—must have been in current use at that time.

It is impossible to say just when the Vietnamese began to write their
own adaptations of Chinese characters to express native words. It is reasonable that the need may have arisen early to record some native place
name or personal name which had no Chinese designation. And there may

well have been literary artists who were very early inspired to create in
their native language as well as in the official tongue and who sought to
write down their efforts in some way. On the other hand, it is clear that
only Chinese enjoyed real prestige during that long period, even for several centuries after independence: Vietnamese was not considered a wor-
thy vehicle for either literary efforts or official communications.

Nevertheless, a native Vietnamese adaptation of Chinese characters
did develop. Whatever the impetus for its creation, it is clear that it had
already evolved well before the mid-point of the fourteenth century: in
Ninh-bình province of modern northern Viet Nam there has been discovered
a stone inscription dating from 1343 listing in adapted characters the
names of some twenty villages and hamlets. This stele at Hộ-thành-sơn is
the earliest irrefutable piece of evidence of this writing system, which is
called in Vietnamese **chữ nôm** (*chữ* 'written word', *nôm* 'popular language',
probably ultimately related to *nam* 'south'—note that the Vietnamese often
call themselves simply *người Nam* 'people of the south' and their land
nước Nam 'southern country'). One estimate, on the basis of indirect evidence, places the beginnings of this system as early as the eighth century.
In any case, the concrete evidence from 1343 suggests a system already
well developed. By the early part of the next century there were manu-
scripts of literary compositions written in this fashion, some of which
have survived to the present day.

The system of *chữ nôm* makes use of Chinese characters, either simply
or in various combinations not occurring in Chinese writing. Sometimes the
Chinese writing is used unchanged to suggest either the meaning or the
pronunciation of a Vietnamese syllable. (Typically each Chinese character represents a syllable.) However, a large proportion of the characters
combine two or more of the original Chinese elements together, one part
suggesting the meaning, another the pronunciation. The principle is not
new to the system, but this extension of it results in symbols which are
quite unrecognizable to a Chinese reader. For a more detailed description
of *chữ nôm* see Maspero 1912 (pp. 5-9), Dương quảng Hàm 1951 (pp. 100-
104), and Nguyễn đình Hòa 1959a.

Chữ nôm apparently existed for several centuries alongside the standard written Chinese of the royal court (called **chữ nho** 'scholar's characters' or **chữ hán** 'Han [i.e., Chinese] characters'). With increasing na-
tionalism the native adaptation might well have replaced the Chinese
writing, had it not been for a rival—although unrelated—development.

When Catholic missionaries from Europe began their efforts to Chris-
tianize the country in the sixteenth and seventeenth centuries, they were
very early concerned with establishing some sort of writing system which

could be easily taught to large numbers of people in order to extend their influence beyond the momentary reach of their voices. Again it is not very clear exactly how this work began, but by the 1620's there were certainly adaptations of the Roman alphabet in use to represent Vietnamese words. In 1624 Alexandre de Rhodes came to the Cochinchinese Mission, where earlier work had concentrated. He is reported to have learned the language with amazing rapidity and skill, speaking it fluently and idiomatically in a short six months. Later he went north to establish a new mission and continued his enthusiastic work on the language. It was he who assembled the efforts of earlier workers to develop an efficient writing system. He codified it and used it to produce extensive materials in support of his missionary activities. Most interesting from the point of view of the language is his monumental compilation, *Dictionarium annamiticum, lusitanum et latinum* (Annamese-Portuguese-Latin Dictionary), published in Rome in 1651. Such is the origin of the romanized writing system called **quốc-ngữ** (literally 'national language').

From that time on the romanized script was in increasing use among the missionaries and their followers, and gradually it spread beyond their ranks. It had obvious advantages over the official *chữ nho* and the semi-official *chữ nôm*—both of these systems were difficult to learn, involving long and careful study and extensive practice, while *quốc-ngữ*, because it made use of the alphabetic principle (each symbol representing for the most part a structurally significant phonetic entity—i.e., phoneme), was simple and direct, and it could be learned in relatively few hours without especially arduous practice. This is not to suggest that it swept the country like wildfire, taking over and replacing the other systems in a short time. Traditions are changed or eliminated only extremely slowly. So it seems not to have been until the first years of the present century that officials recognized and sanctioned what must have been by then a *fait accompli*: the earliest reference to official use of the system is a circular of 1910 in which the Résident supérieur of Tonkin (northern Viet Nam) required that all public documents be transcribed into *quốc-ngữ*. Nevertheless, the revolution, once accomplished, was complete. Aside from a small class of scholars, there are scarcely any Vietnamese today who read *chữ nôm;* and the few people who read Chinese characters generally have this proficiency because of some important connection with China rather than out of a primary concern for Vietnamese classical literature. There have been some changes in the system since de Rhodes' time, and it is unclear exactly how they came about. In a few cases they show historical changes in the language, but for the most part they have to do with the representation of vocalic elements which seem to have been very similar to those of the modern language.

The origin of the name for this script is also unclear, although it most
certainly has some connection with the fact that the lingua franca of educated Chinese (fundamentally Mandarin, learned as a second language by
educated speakers of various other Chinese dialects) is called *kuo yu*,
for which the Sino-Vietnamese pronunciation is *quốc-ngữ*. Part of the regular education of Chinese children in the various provinces and in overseas
Chinese settlements (including those in Viet Nam) is learning to speak
kuo yu. It goes hand in hand with their study of Chinese characters, and
their texts regularly reflect this communal dialect rather than local divergent uses of the writing system. The Vietnamese feel that throughout the
colonial period (which coincides roughly with the period of the spread of
the romanized script) the French were eager to keep them aware of their
local differences and disagreements, presumably on the basis of the theory
of "divide and conquer." Apparently dialect differences (which actually
are only a little more pronounced than those of American English) were
often cited in this connection. The writing system, then, may have become
a symbol of Vietnamese unity, even as *kuo yu*—although in a different way,
and for different reasons—is for the Chinese, whose mother tongues are
often not at all mutually intelligible.

The nature and details of the system are discussed thoroughly in the
following sections, but it remains to mention here something about the origin of its idiosyncrasies. The early missionaries who devised the script
were extremely heterogeneous in background. It appears that the majority
came from a variety of localities in Italy, Portugal, and southern France,
although Spaniards and perhaps other nationalities were also represented.
Spelling habits which have nothing to do with Vietnamese presumably relate to these diverse backgrounds. What is perhaps most puzzling is that
Alexandre de Rhodes, who was responsible for the basic codification,
was a native of Avignon in southern France, yet the writing system probably shows more oddities relating to Portuguese than to any other one
language. In this connection, it is significant that de Rhodes' dictionary
included specifically Portuguese—besides the expected Latin—rather
than French. Throughout this early period it was the Portuguese trading
and shipping interests that represented the most considerable European
commitments in the area, and as a result Portuguese was likely enough
the most widely used European language of the time.

3.2. The Phonological System Implied by Quốc-ngữ.

For the most
part, the form of modern written Vietnamese represents the phonological
system of a northern dialect at some period between the seventeenth
century and the present. Its changes from the orthography of Alexandre de

Rhodes' dictionary (3.1) imply some alterations in the structure; yet the system does not fit exactly any modern dialect yet observed. The writing very likely demonstrates the "jelling" of a tradition more than a real dialectal stage, but it is nonetheless useful to guess at the kind of phonological reality which it seems to have represented. It is of course impossible to establish with certainty the phonetic facts of speech which can no longer be heard. So it is necessary to attempt to reconstruct a system on the basis of all the information available.[1]

A careful philological investigation of writings at various periods may eventually make it possible to date this hypothetical dialect a little more precisely. It is fortunate that the seventeenth-century missionaries were as interested in the language and as careful observers as they were. Although by modern standards their phonetic training was limited, they were nevertheless enormously perceptive about the phonetic details they observed. A great deal of information about the language can be gleaned from the description of sounds (de Rhodes 1651b), as well as from the letters of the Roman alphabet which were used to represent the distinctive elements (phonemes). The writing system seems to have been very close to phonemic, which is little short of amazing for that period. To these sources can be added several kinds of indirect evidence: the presumed pronunciation of words borrowed from Chinese, the forms of words borrowed from Vietnamese into other languages of the area, the comparison of Vietnamese words with presumably related words in other languages, the dialectal variations evidenced in Vietnamese itself, and the phonetic reality of modern Vietnamese dialects. This task was undertaken by Maspero in his monograph on the historical phonetics of the language (1912), and that work remains the most penetrating analysis of the subject to date.

More recently there have been some discussions of the background of the symbols chosen to represent Vietnamese sounds by the early missionaries (Haudricourt 1949, Emeneau 1951: 1, Nguyễn Khắc Xuyên và Phạm dình Khiêm 1961, Nguyễn Khắc Xuyên 1963), but none of them appear to be definitive. Presumably a careful consideration of the earliest documents in romanized spelling and scrutiny of the accounts of pertinent dialects of the European languages concerned should reveal some interesting things—

[1] That is, unless there are recordings which can be listened to and studied by modern linguists, a language of the past is known only by written records, which represent only certain aspects of the total phonetic reality. The aspects represented often reflect the particular background or bias of the speakers who devised the writing system, or cultural influences under which they fell. Other aspects of the phonological reality either go unnoticed or are considered unimportant. Occasionally some of these factors are mentioned in descriptions of the sound pattern; again some of them may be deduced from various pieces of evidence—the symbols used to write certain sounds, comments which hint at a phonetic aspect which is not understood, features of distribution, relationship to forms in other languages, and so on.

not only about the written symbols themselves but hopefully about the pronunciation of this earlier period of Vietnamese.[2]

3.21. The Consonant System implies five main positions, as opposed

to the four of Hanoi speech, and more distinctions of manner than in the Hanoi system. It apparently had two different positions in which the tongue tip formed consonants: one against or near the backs of the upper teeth, the other farther back in the mouth—around the alveolar ridge or even in back of it. It is more difficult to say exactly what the manners were, because some of the phonetic detail is lacking. In particular, it is not clear which sounds were fortis or lenis, although this may well have been as significant a distinction as it is today. The written symbols suggest an opposition between voiceless and voiced stops, accounting for two manners; voiceless aspirated stops and spirants seem to form a third manner; the fourth category was obviously nasals; the remaining consonants are voiced oral continuants. Table 1 shows the presumed system.

Many of the consonants were apparently very similar to those heard in Hanoi speech today: **t, ch, k, th, h, g, l, m, n, nh, ng.** In some other cases, however, it is clear that quite different entities were involved.

Of the labials, **ph** was probably bilabial, rather than labiodental as it is today (Maspero 1912: 46); the time of the change is difficult to estimate. It would appear that the distinction between orthographic **p** and **b** was no more a distinction even in the seventeenth century than it is today: **p** occurred only finally, **b** only initially. That both **b** and **d** were preglottalized and usually imploded at that time is not as certain, although this is also to be suspected from descriptions of the sounds. (These factors would, of course, lead to a reinterpretation of the system similar to that outlined in 2.15, but such considerations go beyond the purpose of this discussion. The intention of this treatment is to suggest what phonetic features underlay the choice of symbols of the writing system, since this will make the symbolization more understandable.)

The added position with the tongue tip approaching the roof of the mouth well in back of the upper teeth involves one sound which does occur in Hanoi speech—the one written **d**, in which the tongue tip forms its closure against the alveolar ridge. The other stop in this position, written **tr**, probably had a position still further back—the tongue tip presumably touched the back of the ridge, or perhaps the hard surface just behind it. In its production the tongue tip was most likely curled up and back toward

---

[2] Since this writing, Kenneth Gregerson has conducted a study of the de Rhodes dictionary and description of sounds (1651a and b) and has reconstructed a phonological system for the seventeenth-century language (Gregerson 1963).

the rear of the mouth (retroflexed). The stop was apparently released with a spirant (secondary articulation). A spirant in much the same position was written s; it may be assumed that it resembled the *sh* in English *shirt* except that again the tongue tip was curled back, not true of most pronunciations of the English sound. The r was apparently a tongue-tip flap or trill against the alveolar ridge; it has become [z] in the speech of Hanoi today.

In the other set of consonants produced by the action of the tongue tip, t, th, and l were probably much like their modern counterparts in Hanoi pronunciation. However, the sound represented by d (without a bar) was a sound outside the modern system—the descriptions indicate a stop formed by the tongue tip against the backs of the upper teeth with perhaps also the blade of the tongue against the ridge behind the teeth (secondary articulation, palatalization). At the time the writing system was created this sound was apparently more reminiscent of the *d* sounds in the Romance languages that the missionaries spoke than was the sound written đ. This palatalized dental stop apparently extended over the northern dialect area (Tonkin) and the northern part of central Viet Nam. In the latter area Maspero observed some dialects retaining this pronunciation in his day, but elsewhere it had disappeared; today in Hanoi and the surrounding area it has evolved to [z]. In careful speech it is often pronounced as a voiced spirant similar to the z in English *azure* in order to distinguish it from gi. The sound represented by n presumably had some variants formed by contact with the teeth (finally before *t, th* in an immediately following syllable), but elsewhere it was. like đ, alveolar.

TABLE 1. THE CONSONANT SYSTEM OF WRITTEN VIETNAMESE

	Labial	Apical Dental	Apical Alveolar	Laminal	Dorsal	Glottal
Voiceless Stops	p	t	tr	ch	k	
Voiceless Aspirated Stops and Spirants	ph	th	s	x	kh	h
Voiced Stops	b	d	đ	gi		
Voiced Oral Continuants	v	l	r	}	g	
Nasals	m		n	nh	ng	

58

Among the laminal sounds, **ch** and **nh** were probably much like modern Hanoi [ch, nh]. The sound represented by **x** was presumably similar to Hanoi [x] as described in 2.35. However, the choice of representing this sound by the letter **x**, in contradistinction to **s** for the spirant formed by the tongue tip near the alveolar ridge, suggests that the early Vietnamese distinctions were similar to differences heard between Portuguese *x* and *s* of that period. The symbol **gi** was borrowed from the orthography of Italian, and represented a sound heard as similar to that in Italian words like *Giovanni, giorno*, not unlike the consonant sounds in English *judge*. This, like **d**, came to be pronounced [z] in Hanoi and much of the surrounding area. It is noteworthy that the space provided for a voiced oral continuant formed by the tongue blade is vacant: apparently no consonant of this category existed in the seventeenth-century language. It is, of course, specifically this articulation which characterizes modern Hanoi [z], the sound to which older **d** and **gi** both evolved.

In the dorsal column, **g** occupies both the space for voiced stops and that for voiced oral continuants: presumably it was earlier, as today in Hanoi, a stop in some situations, a spirant in others (cf. 2.38). The sound represented by **kh** is generally described as a stop released with aspiration—that is, relating to [k] as Hanoi [th] does to [t]. If this is true, then it has since evolved to the spirant described in 2.37 in all dialects.

It is difficult to say whether glottal stop had a role in the earlier language similar to the one it plays in modern dialects. If it did, this fact was not understood by the creators of the writing system, which includes no suggestion of such an element as structurally significant.

3.22. Distribution of Consonants.

In the earlier language, consonants were apparently distributed in syllables in much the same way as they are in modern Hanoi speech. Initials are assumed to have included clusters with an element like Hanoi [w] after initial consonants. The representation of this element by vowel symbols **u**, **o**, is undoubtedly derived from the usages in several Romance languages—cf. Italian *buono*, Spanish *muy*, Portuguese *João*, and so forth. Table 2 shows the initials implied by the orthography. Finals are treated as part of nuclei (3.24).

In de Rhodes' time there were three additional initial clusters which have since disappeared from all the modern dialects recorded (although they appear in the Mường dialects, which constitute the only language clearly related to Vietnamese). These were written **bl**, **tl**, **ml** (dialectal variants in **mnh**). They have been replaced by other initials in all the modern dialects; for details, see Maspero 1912. For recent comparative work with Mường see Barker 1963.

59

TABLE 2. INITIALS

t(w)	tr(w)	ch(w)	k(w)	[(w)][1]
ph	th(w)	s(w)	x(w)	kh(w)	h(w)
b	d(w)	d(w)	gi	g(w)
v	l(w)	r		
m	n(w)[2]		nh(w)	ng(w)

3.23. The Vocalic System was apparently not too different from that of modern Hanoi. However, the writing suggests that the sound written ă was simply a short variety of that written a. Later descriptions seem to bear this out: they further say that â was the short variety of ơ. This notion is supported in both cases by the fact that the Vietnamese names for the "short" vowel letters are derived from the other letters involved: ă is read (in spelling aloud) [á], â is read [ớɤ], while a is read simply [a], and ơ [ơɤ] –in other words, high rising tone identifies the derived signs. This suggests a simpler system of vowels:

$$i \quad ư \quad u$$
$$ê \quad ơ \quad ô$$
$$e \quad a \quad o$$

In general, they may have been phonetically very much like those observed in modern Hanoi speech. The main identifiable differences from the modern system have to do with the distribution of vowels in clusters, which is treated in 3.24.

It seems likely that semivowels similar to those of modern dialects were present in the earlier language. That these should have been written with vowel letters is quite in keeping with the heritage on which the designers drew (cf. 3.22).

3.24. Nuclei. The official writing system suggests that there was a complex system of vowel clusters similar to that of modern Hanoi speech, but of still more regular and balanced pattern. The two- and three-element nuclei implied by *quốc-ngữ* are shown in Tables 3 and 4 respectively.

---

[1] The notation [(w)] suggests that orthographic initial vowel symbols may actually have represented syllables beginning with glottal stop before a vowel or [w] as in modern Hanoi speech. (If this was the case, a modern phonemic interpretation would recognize glottal stop as a phoneme, and the [w] would be part of the phoneme containing [v]: cf. 2.15.)

[2] Initial [nw] was rare; cf. 2.81.

These may be compared with Tables 7 and 8 (Chapter 2) and the examples in 2.82. It is uncertain whether the simple final vowels i, ê, ư, ơ, u, ô represented (as assumed here) diphthongs like those in Hanoi [ij, êj, ưɣ, ơɣ, uw, ôw] or simply long vowels in final position. The quality of the final -a following other vowels is also uncertain: the writing suggests that it is to be identified with [a], although it seems more likely that it was (as in modern Hanoi speech) a semivowel resembling [â].

The older system apparently had the sequences [ưw, ươw], which are replaced in Hanoi speech by [iw, iêw] respectively (see 2.51).

Note that Hanoi [iậk, iậng, uậk, uậng] have apparently replaced older [iêk, iêng, uôk, uông], which formed parallels to other three-element nu-

TABLE 3. TWO-ELEMENT NUCLEI

FINALS

VOWELS	j	ɣ	w	ậ	p	m	t	n	ch	nh	k	ng
i	ij		iw	iậ	ip	im	it	in	ich	inh		
ê	êj		êw		êp	êm	êt	ên	êch	ênh		
ư	ưj	ưɣ	ưw	ưậ			ưt				ưk	ưng
ơ	ơj	ơɣ			ơp	ơm	ơt	ơn				
u	uj		uw	uậ	up	um	ut	un			uk	ung
ô	ôj		ôw		ôp	ôm	ôt	ôn			(âwk)	(âwng)
e			ew		ep	em	et	en			ek	eng
o	oj				op	om	ot	on			(ăwk)	(ăwng)
ă	ăj		ăw		ăp	ăm	ăt	ăn	ăch	ănh	ăk	ăng
â	âj		âw		âp	âm	ât	ân			âk	âng
a	aj		aw		ap	am	at	an			ak	ang

TABLE 4. THREE-ELEMENT NUCLEI

FINALS

VOCALIC SEQUENCES	j	w	p	m	t	n	k	ng
iê		iêw	iêp	iêm	iêt	iên	iêk	iêng
ươ	ươj	ươw	ươp	ươm	ươt	ươn	ươk	ương
uô	uôj			uôm	uôt	uôn	uôk	uông

clei beginning in [i, ɯ, u]. The nuclei [âwk, âwng, ăwk, ăwng] were at some point interpreted as filling the positions of missing nuclei [ôk, ông, ok, ong], and thus are written ôc, ông, oc, ong. However, it is fairly clear from the earlier orthography that even in de Rhodes' day they were diphthongs. For example, the early notation for the word 'bee' (modern ong, Hanoi [ăwng]) was aố. (This is reminiscent of the Portuguese writing ão, which represents a nasalized diphthong.)

3.25. Tones in seventeenth-century Vietnamese apparently involved six distinctions. It is unclear whether these were primarily pitch height and contour distinctions or whether, as in modern Hanoi speech, they combined pitch with other factors. In any case, their status as elements functioning similarly to vowels and consonants was recognized—as opposed to the function of intonational pitch distinctions in typical European languages. The relationship of the written tones to their Hanoi pronunciations is presented in 2.71 and need not be repeated here.

3.3. Spelling Conventions. The spelling of various forms has been discussed in several connections earlier in this chapter and in Chapter 2. In general, sounds are written with the symbols used to represent them in 3.2 above. However, there are a few special cases, which are discussed in the following sections (see also 3.42). All pronunciations cited are those of modern Hanoi speech.

3.31. Gi is the basic symbol for what was apparently a voiced laminal (affricated) stop in de Rhodes' time. It has become [z] in modern Hanoi speech. It has an alternant spelling **g-**, which appears only before *i* and *iê*. *G-* before *a*, *o*, *u* represents [g] (see 3.32).

This is presumably borrowed from Italian spelling. By the time Italian had developed, what had earlier been a voiced dorsal stop had developed into a palatal affricate not unlike the *j* in English *joke* or the *g* in *generous* when it preceded a high front vowel—written *i* or *e*. Before other vowels, however, the dorsal stop survived. The result was that the spellings *gi*, *ge* really referred to a different initial consonant from that of the spellings *gu*, *go*, *ga*. At the same time this j-like consonant also occurred before the vowels *a*, *o*, and *u*: these combinations were written *gia*, *gio*, *giu*. In the Vietnamese borrowed spelling convention, **gi-** is now written before all vowels except *i*, where the writing of two *i*'s together was avoided. Thus *gi-* appears before *e*, while the Italian system would suggest simply **ge** (which does, in fact, appear in older Vietnamese texts). The spellings for [k, g, ng] relate to this and other similar developments in orthographies of Romance languages.

Spelling g: *gì* [zìj] what(ever), *giết* [ziết] to kill

Spelling gi: *giữ* [zữ] to hold, protect, *giời* [zờj] heaven, sky, *giúp* [zúp] to help, *giỗi* [zỗj] get angry, *gieo* [zew] to sow, cast, *giỏi* [zỏj] be good, capable, *giặt* [zặt] to launder, *giàu* [zầw] be rich, *già* [zà] be old, aged

Theoretically, we might expect the writing *gia* to be ambiguous, representing either [za] or [ziậ]. In fact, the latter sound sequence occurs in modern Hanoi speech, but is always written *dia* or *ria*; apparently this nucleus did not occur with the old initial represented by *gi-*.

3.32. Dorsal Consonants

are for the most part represented by letters which vary in value in West European languages depending on what vowel they precede. The only exception is [kh], which is always written **kh.**
[k] is written **c** except when followed by *i, ê, e*, in which cases **k** is written; or [w], in which case the combination is written **qu-**:

Spelling c: *cưa* [kuậ] to saw, *cờ* [kờ] chess, *cũng* [kũng] also, *có* [kó] exist, *cắp* [kắp] pilfer, *cần* [kần] be needed, need, *cá* [ká] fish, *việc* [viậk] affair, matter, *học* [hặwk] to study, *sắc* [sắk] be sharp (Note that this **c** has no connection with the writing **ch**, which always represents the sound [ch].)

Spelling k: *ki-lô* [kij lôw] kilogram, *kia* [kiậ] over there, *kỳ* [kìj] fixed unit of time or space, *kêu* [kêw] to shout, call, *kéo* [kéw] to pull, drag

Spelling q: *quả* [kwả] fruit, *quyển* [kwiển] volume (classifier for books), *quét* [kwét] to sweep

The representation for [g] is **g** before *ư, ơ, u, ô, o, ă, â, a*, but **gh** before *i, ê, e*. The combination **gi** represents another sound (see 3.31).

Spelling g: *gởi* [gởj] to send, *gỡ* [gỡ] disentangle, *guốc* [gúậk] clog, wooden shoe, *gối* [gốj] pillow, *gõ* to knock, rap, *gắp* to pick up with chopsticks, *gần* be near, *gà* chicken, hen, *góa* [gwá] be widowed

Spelling gh: *ghi* [gij] to record, *ghế* [gếj] chair, *ghét* [gét] to detest

The representation of [ng] is analogous to that of [g]: that is, **ngh** is written before *i, ê, e*, even though there is no different sound represented by *ngi*; everywhere else **ng** is written.

Spelling ngh: *nghĩa* [ngĩậ] idea, *nghề* [ngềj] profession, *nghe* [nge] to listen

Spelling ng: *ngữ* [ngữ] language, *ngờ* [ngờ] to suspect, *ngủ* [ngủw] to sleep, *ngồi* [ngồj] to sit down, *ngon* be good tasting, *ngắn* be short, *ngập* be flooded, submerged, *ngà* ivory, *xẻng* shovel, *đúng* be correct, *làng* village

3.33. [w] is not written at all after [u, ô] (*ngủ* [ngủw] to sleep, *cô* [kôw] father's sister). Otherwise it is represented by either **u** or **o** in a complicated fashion. The initial cluster [kw] is always written **qu**: *quý* or *quỉ* [kwỉj] demon, *quét* [kwét] to sweep, *quân* [kwân] army, *quả* [kwả] fruit.

Except after [k] it is regularly written **o** before *e*, *ă*, *a*, and after *e*: *khỏe* [khwẻ] be healthy, *hoặc* [hwăk] or, *toán* [twán] band, group, *òa* [wà] to burst into tears, *ngoảnh* [ngwảnh] to turn [head] away, *mèo* [mèw] cat.

After **a**, [w] is written **u** to show that the **a** represents [ă], **o** to show that the **a** represents [a]: *sau* [xăw] afterward, *sao* [xaw] star. However, when the diphthongs [ăw, âw] precede final dorsals [k, ng], they are written **o**, **ô**, respectively: *đọc* [đăwk] read, *ong* [ăwng] bee, *ốc* [áwk] snail, *hồng* [hằwng] rose.

Elsewhere [w] is written **u**–before [i, ê, ɔ, â]; and after [i, ê, ɯ, ươ, â]. After **u** representing prevocalic [w], [i] is regularly written **y** (see 3.34): *tuy* [twij] although, *thuế* [thwếj] taxes, *thuở* [thwỏ̵] epoch, *tuần* [twần] week; *chịu* [chịw] endure, suffer, *khuỷu* [khwỉw] elbow, *nếu* [nếw] if, *hiểu* [hiểw] understand, *mưu* HN [miw] scheme, *rượu* HN [ziệw] alcoholic beverage, *dầu* [zầw] oil.

3.34. **i** is the usual representation for [i] and [j]. However, **y** is also used—optionally in some cases, obligatorily in others. The use of **y** has spread since de Rhodes' time, and it is uncertain what the exact timing of its extension or the reasons for it were.

Only **y** appears in the following situations: (a) as the first letter of a syllable followed by *ê*; (b) after [w] except in the combination *qu* (see 3.33); (c) after *qu* and followed by *ê* or *nh* in the same syllable; (d) after [ă] (combination written **ay**) and [â] (**ây**):

(a) *yến* [iến] swallow [bird], *yêu* [iêw] to love, cherish

(b) *úy* [wíj] officer [of lower ranks], *tuy* [twij] although, *khuya* [khwiậ] be late at night, *chuyện* [chwiện] conversation, *huýt* [hwít] to whistle

(c) *quyển* [kwiển] volume [book], *quyết* [kwiết] to decide, *quýnh* [kwính] be nervous, upset

(d) *máy* [mǎj] machine, *đầy* [đằj] be full

Only **i** is written in the combinations **ui, ơi, ươi, ui, ôi, uôi, oi, ai**: *ngửi* [ngửj] to sniff, *mời* [mờj] to invite, *người* [ngườj] person, *củi* [kủj] firewood, *tôi* [tôj] I, *cuối* [kuốj] end, *hỏi* [hỏj] ask a question, *bài* [bàj] lesson

Note that in two cases the written distinction between **i** and **y** actually serves to specify the value of the preceding vowel letter: **u** before *i* has the value [u] (except after q), before *y* the value [w] (*sui* [xuj] be related through marriage, *suy* [xwij] to consider); a before *i* has the value [a] but before *y* the value [ă] (*mai* [maj] tomorrow, *may* [măj] to sew).

Note also that [j] is not written at all following [i, ê]: *di* [dij] go, *Mỹ* [mĩj] America, *về* [vèj] to return.

In other cases there is no regular pattern for the writing of [i]. The spelling of each form must be learned. However, some generalizations about frequency may be helpful. **Y** is more common than **i** as the only letter in a syllable: *y* [ij] he, *ý* [íj] thought, idea, but *ì* [ìj] be motionless. Beyond this, with a few rare exceptions, **y** is limited to positions where it represents [ij] after the following initials: *m, t, l, k, qu, h*; and often after *qu* and *h* the words have an alternant spelling with **i**:

> *Mỹ* [mĩj] America, *ty* [tij] bureau, office, *lý* [líj] reason, common sense, *ký* [kíj] to sign, *quỷ* or *quỉ* [kwỉj] demon, *hy* or *hi* [hij] to hope

3.35.
[ă] is written **ă** except before [j, w, ch, nh]. Before [ch, nh] it is always written simply **a**; there is no possible ambiguity because [a] does not occur in that position. Before [j] it is always written **a**, and the value [ă] is shown by using the letter **y** to represent [j] (while **i** is written to show the value [a]; cf. 3.34). Before [w] it is written **a** unless the [w] is followed in turn by [k, ng], in which case the cluster [ăw] is written **o**. (The value [a] before [w] is indicated by using **o** to represent [w], while **au** means [ăw]; cf. 3.33.)

> Spelling **a**: *sách* [xắch] book, *anh* [ănh] elder brother, *may* [măj] to sew (cf. *mai* [maj] tomorrow), *sau* [xăw] afterward (cf. *sao* [xaw] star)
> Spelling **o** for [ăw]: *học* [hăwk] to study, *ong* [ăwng] bee
> Spelling **ă**: *săp* be on the point of, *lăm* to a great extent, *căt* [kăt] to cut, *ăn* to eat, *bắc* [băk] north, *văng* be absent

3.36.
[â] is usually written **â**, but the combination [âw] before [k, ng] is written **ô** (parallel to the writing **o** for [ăw] in the same positions; cf. 3.35).

> Spelling **ô** for [âw]: *óc* [áwk] snail, *hồng* [hàwng] rose
> Spelling **â**: *lấy* [lấj] to take, *dầu* [zàw] oil, *ngập* be flooded, *đâm* to stab, *rất* [zất] very, *dân* [zân] citizen, *xấc* [xấk] be ill-mannered, *vâng* to obey

The related semivowel [ậ] is written **a** after *i, ư, u*.

> Spelling **a**: *nghĩa* [ngĩậ] idea, meaning, *mưa* [mưậ] to rain, *mua* [muậ] to buy

In Hanoi speech [ậ] occurs in the combinations [iậk, iậng, uậk, uậng], which are written (respectively) **iêc, iêng, uôc, uông**:

 việc [viậk] affair, matter, *tiếng* [tiậng] noise, sound, language, *quốc* [gúậk] clog, wooden shoe, *uống* [úậng] to drink

3.37. Other Special Conventions Concerning the Writing of Vocalics.

Just as [j] is not written after [i, ê] (3.34) and [w] is not written after [u, ô] (3.33), so [ɰ] is not written after [ɯ, ơ]: *tư* [tɯɰ] fourth, *sợ* [sơɰ] be afraid.

The sound [o] is regularly written **o**. However, because of the special use of **o** before *c, ng* to represent [ăw] (3.35) the combination [ong] (rare, occurring only in a few borrowed words) is written **oong** : *boong* [bong] deck [of ship].

An analogous spelling **ôông** is reported for [ông], appearing only in the form *côông-kêng* 'to carry [a person] astride over one's shoulders' (Nguyễn dình Hòa 1955: 26; note that this unusual form contains also the only occurrence of the combination [êng]). The letter **o** is also used to represent [w] in certain cases (3.33).

The sound [a] is regularly written **a**. However, the letter **a** also has other values in certain positions—before *ch, nh, y, u* it symbolizes [ă] (3.35); after *i, ư, u* it represents [ậ] (3.36).

The word *quốc* [kwốk] 'country' represents the only case of an initial [w] before a back rounded vowel (cf. 2.84). In the speech of many persons it is [kwắk]. It is interesting to note in this connection that it appears spelled *cuốc* in de Rhodes' dictionary, while somewhat later the spelling *quấc* is quite common. What this fluctuation in spelling means is not clear, but it may be suspected that the rendition [kwốk] was originally a spelling pronunciation.

The word *cái* (general classifier) is pronounced [káj] when accompanied by heavy or medium stress but with weak stress it has the variant [kấj].

A very few forms spelled **giê-** represent [zê-], rather than the regular [ziê-] or [ziâ-]: *giền* [zền] amaranth (quoted from Emeneau 1951: 30).

Here and there throughout the country are place names which reflect by their spelling the fact that they are borrowed from other languages. This is especially the case with Cambodian and Cham names in southern Viet Nam.

3.38. Tone Marks are written with the vocalic portion of the syllable.

Where there is only a single vowel letter they appear over (or, in the case of *dấu nặng*, under) that letter.

 mả tomb, *nặng* heavy, *lần* instance, *rẻ* inexpensive, *đến* arrive, *vì*

because, *ngọt* sweet, *hồ* lake, *phở* noodle soup, *đúng* correct, *những*
[plural marker], *Mỹ* America

Where there are two or more vowel letters the tone mark accompanies one
of them according to the following principles:

(1) If they include a letter with one of the other diacritics (denoting
vowel quality differences), the tone mark accompanies that letter.

tuần week, *xấu* bad, ugly, *hoặc* or, *thuế* taxes, duties, *nguyệt* moon,
chuối banana, *hiểu* understand, *thuở* epoch, *cừu* sheep

(2) In the case of ươ (where there are two letters with diacritics), the
tone mark accompanies ơ.

đường sugar, *mười* ten, *rượu* alcoholic beverage

(3) Otherwise, the tone mark accompanies the letter which denotes the
prominent vowel of the syllable, unless this is word final [see (4)].

nghĩa meaning, *nửa* half, *mùa* season, *bài* lesson, *máy* machine, *mèo*
cat, *áo* tunic, *máu* blood, *đoán* to guess, *khoèo* be bent, curved,
khuỷu elbow

(4) Where the prominent vowel is represented by a word final vowel letter without diacritic, there is a strong tendency to place the tone symbol
with the preceding vowel letter. Thus *u* and *o* are often found with tone
marks, even though they may actually represent the [w] of an initial cluster. There is a good deal of variation in this matter, even in the writing of
the same author or printing of a single work. However, tone marks are not
shifted back to the *u* of the combination *qu-* or the *i* of *gi-* .

tùy according to, *thủy* water, *khỏe* be healthy, *hóa* peace; *quỉ* demon, *quả* fruit, *già* old, *gió* wind   *hoà*

There is a strong tendency to omit tone marks with proper names.
Names of well-known places often appear in print in the form they typically
assume in ordinary French publications: e.g., *Hanoï*, *Saïgon*. Place names
of foreign origin are also apt to forego tone marks: e.g., *Soc-trang*, *Sa-đec*
(towns in the south with names of Cambodian origin); *Đalat* (a well-known
resort town of the south-central interior plateau—the name comes from the
local mountain tribal language). In handwriting all diacritics are commonly
omitted from individual personal names; this practice, however, does not
extend to printed material.

3.4. Dictionaries

3.4. Dictionaries list in alphabetical order meaningful units which for
the most part are one syllable long. Longer items are usually listed as
subentries to their first syllable. The kinds of units involved and their
interrelationships are discussed in more detail in 5.5.

Lexicography in Viet Nam is much less developed than in Western
Europe and America or in China and Japan. The student simply cannot ex-

pect to find a single reference work which will list all or even a large proportion of the forms he will meet in reading texts in the language. In fact, the wholesale coinage of new terms during the last decade makes recent texts quite difficult for foreign readers until they have acquired a deep sense of the wordbuilding habits of the language and the intimate knowledge of a large number of basic meaningful forms.

The most helpful work for American students is certainly *Hòa's Vietnamese-English Dictionary* (Nguyễn đình Hòa 1959b). Although it does not have a very extensive coverage, it provides a good deal of valuable information about the forms it does include. The most scholarly lexicographic work today remains Đào duy Anh, *Pháp-Việt Từ-điển* (French-Vietnamese Dictionary), 1936 (reprinted in 1950), but because of its nature it is really helpful only for the more advanced students. For other dictionaries see the Bibliography.

3.41. Alphabetical Order is in general based on the usual order of the Roman alphabet as in English and the various other European languages which make use of it. Because of the special extensive complications with diacritics, however, certain further conventions are needed. Letters without diacritics precede characters which have been modified: thus d precedes đ; e precedes ê; o is followed by ô, then ơ, and so forth. The diacritics distinguishing vowel qualities have their own fixed order: the breve or short mark (as in ă) precedes the circumflex (as in â, ê, ô), which, in turn, precedes the hook identifying unrounded vowels (as in ơ, ư). These principles establish the following basic order for alphabetization:

a ă â b c d đ e ê g h i k l m n o ô ơ p q r s t u ư v x y

All this ordering is completed prior to the introduction of tonal distinctions. Then for each syllable type (without tone symbol) the various occurring combinations with tone marks are ordered according to any of several systems. These all agree in one respect: they list syllables with the unmarked tone first. The two most common orders for tone marks are ´ ` ? ~ . (e.g., in Nguyễn đình Hòa 1959b) and ` ´ . ? ~ (e.g., in Lê văn Hùng 1955). The following sample of alphabetical order uses Hòa's ordering:

ma má mà mả mã mạ mác mạc mách mạch mai mái mài mải mãi mại

In some works (e.g., Hòa's) two- and three-letter combinations representing unitary sounds are treated as if they were unit symbols when they appear first in an entry; these symbols are placed in order following the letter with which they begin. An entirely separate section is set up for words beginning with **ch**-, which follows the section containing all others

beginning with c-. Similarly, there are special sections for **gi-, kh-, ng-**
(and **ngh-**), **nh-, ph-** (separate from a few rare entries with simple initial
p-), **th-**, and **tr-**. For further alphabetization within sections, however, each
letter is considered a separate entity. Other dictionaries (e.g., Hùng's)
follow the latter principle throughout, so that, for example, items beginning
with **ch-** follow those beginning **câ-** and are in turn succeeded by those
beginning **co-**, and so forth.

3.42. Spelling Variations in Dictionaries presumably represent forms

of the same word from different dialects which over the years have under-
gone different phonetic development. In the written language many of these
alternants have come to be used for stylistic variety, and some of them
have passed along into the conversational usage of educated speakers.
Until a great deal more careful research on Vietnamese dialects has been
accomplished, it will be impossible to untangle many of the complexities
which this situation presents.

Dictionaries frequently list alternants of this sort, sometimes relating
them to one another, sometimes not. More often only one alternant appears
in a given compilation. For this reason it is helpful for the foreign student
of the language to have some knowledge of the possible alternations. The
following lists are suggestive rather than in any sense complete. A great
deal of further research must be done to identify and make more sense of
the patterns of alternation and to understand their historical significance.
(For a discussion of some of these matters, see Maspero 1912.)

The items treated here are considered acceptable in print. It is important to mention that there are many other variations occurring in printed
materials, especially in newspaper copy, which are considered spelling
errors. Beside genuine inaccuracies in setting type there are those er-
roneous spellings which a speaker of a particular dialect will produce because a distinction implied in the official writing system is absent from
his own speech. Thus Hanoi speakers will sometimes confuse **d-** and **gi-**
and **r-**, **ch-** and **tr-**; southern and central speakers will confuse the tones
hỏi and *ngã*; and so on. The student will do well to familiarize himself
with the dialect variations described in Chapter 4 as a basis for dealing
with these problems. He should bear in mind that this sort of confusion
operates in two directions: first, a speaker may write a form in the way
that he hears it in his dialect area; second, he may write a form in a different way from what his hearing suggests, thinking that he is correcting
himself, and arriving sometimes at a hypercorrection. For example, a Hanoi
speaker might write the word *trạng* 'master, expert' with initial **ch-** because
he pronounces it with the same beginning sound as in *cha* 'father', *chưa*

'not yet', *cho* 'give', and a host of other common words. Operating in the other direction, however, he might write **tr**- instead of the correct **ch**- in the word *chiến* 'to fight, struggle, make war', thinking that he was correcting himself on the analogy of *trạng*, written with **tr**-. Such errors are especially frequent with words which fall outside everyday colloquial usage.

In the following list each alternation is exemplified only once under the letter which appears earlier in alphabetical order.

INITIAL ALTERNATIONS

c- : **tr-**   *cừu, trừu* sheep

ch- : **x-**   *chung-quanh , xung-quanh*
       all around

d- : **đ-**   *dĩa, đĩa* plate

d- : **gi-**   *dây, giây* string, wire

d- : **n-**   *dĩa, nĩa* fork

d- : **nh-**   *dơ, nhơ* be dirty, *dện,*
       nhện spider

gi- : **tr-**   *giời, trời* sky, heaven,
       giai, trai male human

l- : **nh-**   *lăm, nhăm* five (cf. 8.41),
       lời, nhời words, speech

ng- : **ngo-**   *ngảnh, ngoảnh*
       turn [head] away

nh- : **r-**   *nhức đầu, rức đầu*
       headache, *nhắm, rắm*
       to close one's eyes

s- : **th-**   *sũng, thũng* dropsy

s- : **tr-**   *sống, trống* male

s- : **x-**   *sẻng, xẻng* shovel

th- : **x-**   *thanh, xanh* be blue,
       green

Forms exemplifying these alternations are not necessarily interchangeable. They should be used for help in recognition, not for learning new forms.

VOWEL ALTERNATIONS

[a : iê]   *an, yên* be peaceful;
       doan, duyên fate, exist-
       ence; *trào, triều* court

[a : ô]   *bản, bổn* origin

[a : ơ]   *mai, mơi* morning; *thế-*
       giái, thế-giới world; *đan,*
       đơn be simple

[a : ươ]   *đang, đương* in the act of

[a : i]   *ngàn, nghìn* thousand

[ă : â]   *bàu, bầu* be master; *tàu,*
       tầu China; *cày, cầy* to
       plow

[ă : i]   *chánh, chính* to adminis-
       ster, govern; *sanh, sinh*
       be born

[â : iê]   *nhậm, nhiệm* function,
       charge; *tấn, tiến* advance;
       thật, thiệt be true

[â : ơ]   *chân, chơn* foot, leg;
       nhân, nhơn person

[â : i]   *tâm, tim* heart

[â : ư]   *bâng, bưng* carry in front
       with arms outstretched;
       nhất, nhứt first

[âw : uw]   *dầu, dù* although; *thâu,*
       thu autumn

[ê : i]   *bệnh, bịnh* illness;
       lệnh, lịnh order, command

[ê : iê]   *đều, điều* matter, thing

[i : ơ]   *thi, thơ* poetry

Alexandre
de Rhodes

VOWEL ALTERNATIONS (continued)

[iê : ơ]	*hiệp, hợp* unite	[ơ : ươ]	*cỡi, cưỡi* to mount
[o : u]	*phó, phú* give, bestow	[u : uô]	*cục, cuộc* disposition
[ô : u]	*hội, hụi* group, society	[u : ươ]	*phúc, phước* happiness;
[ơ : ư]	*thơ, thư* letter; *gởi, gửi* send		*phụng, phượng* phoenix

OTHER NUCLEAR ALTERNATIONS

[ang : ănh : ênh]	*mang, mạnh, mệnh* human life
[ăng : inh]	*bằng, bình* be equal
[ât : ưk]	*thật, thực* be true, real

3.5. The Writing of Larger Elements. Intonations are only imperfectly suggested by conventional symbols of punctuation (cf. 2.73), and stresses are not written at all. However, there are a number of conventions involved in writing elements larger than the syllable, which are summarized in the following sections.

3.51. Capital Letters (called **chữ hoa** 'flower character' or **chữ cái** 'principal, largest character') are used in much the same way they are in English, although there are certain special conventions and enormous variety in individual usage. The first word in a sentence begins with a capital letter. In titles of books, paintings, and so forth, the principal forms usually begin with an upper-case letter, although there is a good deal of variation. In the citation of a work in the body of a text, usually only the initial letter of the title is a capital unless there are other reasons to capitalize forms within. Some editors follow this principle even for titles appearing as headings. On the other hand, titles and authors' names on the title page of books are most often in block capitals, and this principle often extends to headings of chapters and sections as well. The variety is so great that there seems little point in citing examples.

For names of places there is more of a basic pattern: only the first letter of the name is properly upper-case unless one of the succeeding syllables is itself a proper name in its own right:

> *Việt-nam, Trung-quốc* China, *Mỹ-quốc* America, *Pháp* France, *Tây-ban-nha* Spain, *La-mã* Rome, *Hà-nội, Sài-gòn*; but *Bắc-Việt* North Viet Nam, *Trung-Việt* Central Viet Nam, *Nam-Việt* South Viet Nam, *Đông-nam-Á* Southeast Asia (in which *Việt*, the word designating the Vietnamese people, and *Á* 'Asia' are proper names).

Personal names involve capital letters, but the usage is complex and is treated with other details about the names themselves in 3.52.

In the names of places, words specifying the kind of place are most often not themselves capitalized, even when they stand first:

> *đường Lê Lợi* Lê Lợi Street, *đại-lộ Duy-tân* Duy-tân Boulevard, *sông Hồng-hà* the Red River (note the redundant use of *sông*, the native Vietnamese word for 'river' before the name, which contains the Sino-Vietnamese borrowed element *hà* 'river'), *nước Tầu* China, *hồ Hoàn-kiếm* Lake of the Returned Sword (in Hanoi)

This principle extends to the names of artificial entities such as shops, restaurants, temples: *hiệu Hải-Anh* (a restaurant), *đền Ngọc-sơn* Jade Mountain Temple. In a few cases such elements are capitalized—they are apparently felt to be part of the name, e.g., *Hồ-tây* West Lake (in Hanoi), *Sông Ngân* Silver River (the Milky Way), *Chợ-lớn* (suburb of Saigon, lit. "big market").

The names of dynasties (actually kings' family names) and historical periods begin with a capital letter: *Lê, Lý, Trần, Nguyễn; Trung-cổ* Medieval Period, Middle Ages.

The names of supernatural and personified entities start with an upper-case character: *Giời* Heaven, *Tơ-hồng* [Mr.] Pink-Thread (mythical being who unites the life strands of married couples), *Cóc* Toad (as a character in a fable).

The names of holidays (*Nguyên-đán* New Year's, *Chúa Giáng-sinh* Christmas), religions (*Công-giáo* Catholicism), and various official entities (*Quốc-gia* the Nation) use capital letters.

However, the names of months are not capitalized, as they are in English: *tháng giêng* January (or the first month of the lunar year), *tháng chạp* December (or the last month of the lunar year), *tháng sáu* June (or sixth month of the lunar year).

In printing or writing, various terms of address or reference are often capitalized to suggest courtesy, respect: *Chào Ông!* Good day, Sir! *Cái này có phải của Bà không?* Does this belong to you? (addressing a lady).

As a result, the designations for kings and high-ranking officials are very frequently capitalized—nearly always when they refer to specific persons.

3.52. Personal Names

nearly always contain at least two parts: the family name (**tên họ**), which comes first when the full name is stated; and the given name (**tên đẻ** 'birth name'), which comes last. Either element may be polysyllabic, although compound given names are by far the more common. Many names have also a middle syllable (called **tiếng lót** 'lining word' in Nguyễn Bạt-Tụy 1954 and typified as really not a name but rather an indicator of sex or [dubiously] a euphonious device). Which syllables are connected by hyphens and which are written with an initial capital letter depends on their value as part of the name. In general, any syllable which itself is a name (rather than a noninitial part of a title) properly begins with an upper-case character; similarly, the initial letter of a title is a capital. Other elements, including the *tiếng lót*, usually begin with a lower-case letter. For the use of hyphens in personal names see 3.53(f).

Examples of names containing *tiếng lót* are *Nguyễn* **văn** *Tố*, a famous twentieth-century scholar, president of the permanent committee of the first Viet Minh government parliament, 1946-47; *Trần* **quốc** *Tuấn*, the thirteenth-century general whose troops turned back the Mongols.

For very special reasons individuals sometimes acquire compound family names, and they are then, of course, passed along to their descendants. An adopted child, for example, typically adds the family name of his new family to his own surname (the new name preceding): **Đặng-Trần** *Côn*, a famous eighteenth-century author, was the adopted son of a family named *Đặng*; his original name was *Trần Côn*. On occasion a king gave a new family name to a man and allowed him to retain his old surname as the second element in a compound. Such, for example, is the case of *Huỳnh Đức*, who was given the name *Nguyễn* by the celebrated king Gia Long, becoming **Nguyễn-Huỳnh** *Đức*. Other reasons for double surnames include adoption of a second element following a very common name as a distinguishing element and the prefixing of a new name in order to disguise the original. (Examples are from Nguyễn Bạt-Tụy 1954, which may be consulted for further details on Vietnamese names.)

If compound given names are more common, their origin, on the other hand, is often more difficult to trace. Two main categories may be distinguished: those which are actually titles (in these, noninitial elements begin with a lower-case letter), and true given names (in which subsequent elements begin with a capital letter). Examples of titular given names are *Lê* **Thái-tổ**, royal name of the famous fifteenth-century king Lê Lợi, founder of the Later Lê Dynasty(1428-1793) (*thái-tổ* 'dynasty founder'); and *Trần* **Hưng-đạo**, titular name (bestowed by the king) of *Trần quốc Tuấn* (see above) (*hưng-đạo* from *Hưng-đạo Vương* 'Prince [who] makes the way prosperous', the full epithet).

Ordinary compound given names are chosen for a variety of personal reasons. Examples are *Nguyễn* **Công-Trứ**, man of letters of the turn of the nineteenth century; *Hồ* **Xuân-Hương**, a brilliant poetess of the early nineteenth century; and *Chu* **Mạnh-Trinh**, late nineteenth-century poet.

3.53. Hyphens (called **gạch nối** 'joining dash', **gạch giữa** 'dash between; or, more formally, **ngang nối** 'joining horizontal') have been used widely in writing *quốc-ngữ* forms. In general they signal combinations of syllables which form units from the point of view of their use in sentences. To some extent their use relates to the problem of just what a word is in Vietnamese (see 5.53 and 5.57). The recent trend is away from the extensive writing of hyphens, and it is possible to specify the cases where they are considered most appropriate in fairly rigorous terms. The general usage is (and is likely to remain) quite lacking in uniformity even within the body of single published works. At one extreme there are publications which do not use them at all.

Only rarely are more than two syllables linked by hyphens in most modern texts. The notable exceptions to this are place names (*Thủ-dầu-một*, a town some 30 km north of Saigon; *Phi-luật-tân* 'the Philippines') and borrowed words (*ca-lô-ri* 'calorie').

The following kinds of two-syllable sequences are commonly written with connecting hyphen:

(a) Forms borrowed from foreign languages: *ô-tô* 'automobile', *cà-phê* 'coffee', *va-li* 'suitcase' (from French *auto, café, valise*). This includes an enormous number of forms borrowed from Chinese: *quốc-ngữ* 'national language; the romanized spelling system', *phi-cơ* 'airplane', *sinh-viên* 'student.' However, many of the syllabic elements borrowed from Chinese have become independent in Vietnamese and are used in sequences with native words. Some are used with other forms which were originally borrowed elements, but the new combinations are Vietnamese. Such forms are not generally written with hyphens: for example, *tầu thủy* 'steamship' contains the native element *tầu* 'conveyance of relatively large proportions' and the Chinese borrowed form *thủy* 'water'; *bạn thân* 'close friend' contains two Chinese loans, *bạn* 'friend' and *thân* 'be intimate', but the sequence is apparently a Vietnamese creation (a Chinese loan form would have the two elements in the reverse order; see 6.33-34).

(b) Forms in which at least one syllable has by itself no identifiable meaning related to the over-all meaning: *vui-vẻ* 'be cheerful' (cf. *vui* 'be cheerful', but *-vẻ* does not recur by itself with any meaning relatable to this form); *rõ-ràng* 'be clear' (*rõ* 'be clear' and dependent element *-ràng*) (see 7.56); *thình-lình* 'be sudden, unexpected' (neither element occurs by itself with a related meaning).

(c) Sequences which denote a general category of things suggested by the meanings of the constituent forms (called generalizing compounds; 6.22): *bàn-ghế* 'furniture' ('tables, chairs, etc.'), *quần-áo* 'clothes' ('trousers, tunics, etc.'), *nhà-cửa* 'household' ('buildings, doors, etc.'), *cầy-cấy* 'to engage in farming' ('to plow, plant, etc.').

(d) Forms involving an exact repetition of the basic constituent where this basic constituent is not a noun (8.63) or verb (9.55): *luôn-luôn* 'always', *thường-thường* 'usually.'

(e) Place names (both native and foreign): *Việt-nam, Hà-nội, Sài-gòn, Ba-lê* 'Paris', *La-mã* 'Rome'. (Note, however, that very common place names are often written in the form they would have in French: *Paris, Hanoï, Saïgon.*)

(f) Elements in personal names which are themselves units. This includes compound family and given names (for details about personal names and further identification of the following examples, see 3.52):

> *Đặng-Trần Côn*, eighteenth-century author; *Nguyễn-Huỳnh Đức*, mandarin at the court of Gia Long; *Lê Thái-tổ*, royal name of Lê Lợi; *Trần Hưng-đạo*, thirteenth-century general; *Nguyễn Công-Trứ*, man of letters; *Hồ Xuân-Hương*, poetess; *Chu Mạnh-Trinh*, poet.

In older usage (which still survives in many contemporary publications) all the elements of a personal name were connected by hyphens. The recent tendency away from profusity of hyphenation has perhaps operated with less consistency here.

3.54. Clause and Sentence Punctuation

makes use of the period (**chấm**), comma (**phẩy** or **phết**), colon (**hai chấm**), semicolon (**chấm phẩy** or **chấm phết**), parentheses (**dấu ngoặc đơn** 'simple hook marks'), question mark (**chấm hỏi**), and exclamation point (**chấm nhểu**), much as does English or French. Only departures from this general similarity are mentioned here.

A comma is used to set off a phrase or clause which is parallel to the preceding element; however, there is generally no second comma to mark the end of such an element which is interposed in the middle of the sentence.

> *Tục chơi hoa thủy-tiên cũng phổ-thông như cành đào, nhưng vì hoa này đắt quá, hằng năm phải nhập-cảng từ bên Tàu sang nên chỉ những gia-đình giầu mới dám chơi.* 'The custom of enjoying the narcissus [at New Year's] is as common as the peach branch, but because this flower is very expensive, having each year to be imported from China, so only the wealthy families can permit themselves the luxury.' (From the English point of view, a comma would be expected between *sang* and *nên*.)

The question mark is often used to mark indirect questions, which in English would simply end with a period. (This usage is characterized as incorrect by some native grammarians, cf. Bùi đức Tịnh 1952: 298.)

> *Tôi sẽ hỏi ông ấy có biết chăng?* 'I'm going to ask him whether he knows [about it] or not.'

3.55. Quotations are symbolized in several ways which are rather different from English usage. The most common device is a horizontal bar (called **gạch dài** 'long dash') (usually called a dash in English) to mark the beginning of a speech which is reported in print. The end of the quotation is not marked but left up to the reader to deduce from the context. (This device is characteristic of French usage in similar instances.)

> —*Thưa thầy, cột to bằng này, cậu Thanh vừa nói vừa cho đũa và quấy trong cái liễn đựng cơm.* '"Sir, the pillars [of the house] are this big," said Thanh, making a stirring motion with his chopsticks in the dish containing the rice as he spoke.'

Quotation marks, called **dấu ngoặc kép** 'double hook marks' (« ») are also borrowed from French: they symbolize elements borrowed from the speech or writing of others or singled out for special attention. They are sometimes used for a quotation within a quotation (the framing quotation symbolized by a *gạch dài*), and around the titles of books, songs, and the like. Some type fonts have instead quotation marks like those used in American printing.

In newspapers occasionally a third device is used to signal a quotation (perhaps because the font of type in use lacks or has only a limited supply of the items described above): three periods (**ba chấm** or **chấm chấm**) on the line before an item single out the following phrase as a quotation. Again the reader must recognize for himself the end of the quoted element.

> *Chúng tôi nhận thấy một người đứng bên sửa- soạn cho tài- tử cái* ... *búi tó.* 'We noticed an actor sitting before a mirror, with one person winding a turban for him, and another standing to one side preparing to give him the "traditional bun [of hair]".'

Both the dash and the three successive periods are also used in a way analogous to English usage. Dashes at the beginning and end of an element within a sentence signal a kind of parenthetical expression or aside. The three periods often have the value of suspensive points—signaling something omitted or expressly left to the reader's imagination.

3.6. Reading Pronunciation, which gives a very different impression from ordinary speech, may be characterized as follows. In general, the stress pattern of ordinary reading pronunciation is a more or less regularly alternating succession of medium and heavy syllables, with a heavy syllable regularly terminating each pause group. Occasional syllables have weak stress, which seems to carry its normal value, but the alternation of medium- and heavy-stressed syllables certainly does not indicate any kind of emphatic distinction between the two types. In reading pronunciation each syllable is very distinctly pronounced, and tones tend to be

76

exaggerated. Each syllable with medium or heavy stress occupies approximately the same amount of time; weakly stressed syllables are considerably shorter. This gives reading its characteristic measured, rhythmic quality and makes it notably different from normal speech, where there is far more elasticity in the length of syllables and the stress distinctions are fully exploited.

A special kind of "reading pronunciation" with dramatic overtones is used in some theatrical productions in classical style: many lines are simply spoken, more or less as in ordinary conversation, but highly significant or dramatic lines are accompanied by instrumental music (one or more stringed instruments and sometimes a flute) and are spoken in this stylized fashion. The net effect is reminiscent of *recitative* in Western opera, but note that the utilization of this style corresponds rather to the *aria*, or to the song in Western musical comedy. The practice probably stems from the Chinese-inherited opera, where such passages are interspersed with lines which are sung—a tradition corresponding more nearly to Western opera but with less clear definition of arias.

CHAPTER 4

Dialectal Variations

4.1. Vietnamese Dialects were divided by Henri Maspero (1912) into two main groups: on the one hand, the Haut-Annam group, comprising numerous local dialects of the small villages stretching from the north of Nghệ-an province to the south of Thừa-thiên province; on the other, Tonkinese-Cochinchinese, encompassing all the remainder.

Haut-Annam dialects had been little studied at Maspero's writing, and so far as I can determine this is still the case today. (In addition to his own observations Maspero mentions Cadière 1902, which he characterizes as treating only the southern part of the area, and as having an unfortunately small number of examples, most of which are not related to specific places. Cadière 1958 gives extensive examples and emphasizes material collected in the region of Huế. While numerous individual dialectal forms are in evidence throughout, the general impression reasserts the basic unity of the language as a whole. Valuable as the work is for its penetrating view of the syntax, it furnishes no real basis for serious dialectal study. In private correspondence with me in 1961 Nguyễn Bạt-Tụy indicated that he had been conducting instrumental phonetic studies on several dialects, including some of these, but to my knowledge he has not yet printed a description of this work.)

Certain things about Maspero's division are not too clear. The southern extremity of the Haut-Annam territory would include the city of Huế, and he mentions employing informants from that area. But the speech of present-day Huế seems quite inseparable from the complex of integrating dialects spoken from there on south to the southern tip of the country and in the Red River valley and delta in the north. And the Vinh language which M.B. Emeneau describes (1944, 1951) seems intermediate in many respects between Tonkinese and the speech of modern Huế. The most striking differences in both Vinh and Huế are in the tones, and it may be that these

78

factors influenced Maspero to place both localities in his Haut-Annam category. In both Huế and Vinh the influence of the literary standard language is to be reckoned with, and it may well be that those informants whose speech has been observed have actually altered their habits extensively in that direction.

On the other hand, the few details Maspero gives of the speech of the northern part of the Haut-Annam area, which he himself observed while traveling there, suggest a form of the language quite distinct from that spoken at Hanoi, Vinh, Huế or Saigon. Judging from the comments of contemporary informants these divergent ways of speaking have not yet disappeared under the influence of the metropolitan standards, but only a thorough modern investigation of them will reveal their deeper natures and their relationships to one another and to the language as a whole. Such an investigation is especially important in connection with the effort to understand more about the history of the language.

For the rest of the speech area, if it is fairly clear that the whole represents a series of intergrading dialects—that is, ways of speaking in each village which vary in only a few slight details from the neighboring villages, but forming a gradually shifting picture such that remote points are very noticeably different from one another—it is none the less apparent that many interesting investigations of local speech remain to be made across the Vietnamese countryside in these regions as well.

There are several modern studies which provide the basis for perceiving the overall picture of gradually changing patterns from north to south. Hanoi speech has most often been the basis of descriptions of the language, although many of these—especially the earlier ones—seem to represent an idealization departing from the actual pronunciation of Hanoi natives in the direction of assuring all the distinctions implied in the official spelling system (3.2). Accounts of other dialects are less affected by normalizing tendencies. It seems useful to offer here a kind of general impressionistic description of several dialect areas and their interrelationships so far as it is possible. In this account innovations which are mentioned for each successive locality should be construed as a part of the basic shifting pattern, except where they are specifically affected by subsequently mentioned differences; for example, the retroflexed consonants which are missing in Hanoi speech but clearly present in Vinh, remain characteristic of the speech of Huế, Đà-nẵng and Saigon. Such a survey is necessarily conjectural because there is insufficient information on most intermediate areas. The sources I have most relied on are Lê văn Lý 1948 (northern metropolitan speech, probably somewhat idealized), Emeneau 1944, 1951 (for Vinh and Tonkin), Smalley and Nguyễn văn Vạn 1954 (for Đà-nẵng speech), H. Maspero

1912 (for information on various dialects), Cadière 1911 (for Bas-Annam dialects), and my own observations (of speakers from Hanoi, Phát-diệm, Huế, Đà-nẵng, Dalat, Saigon, Gò-công, Mỹ-tho, Bến-tre, Trà-vinh).

Following this survey of the overall speech area Saigon dialect is described in greater detail (4.2) and a tentative chart of dialect correspondences is provided for some typical localities where descriptions are generally adequate for the purpose (4.3).

4.11. Tonkin. As the observer moves from Hanoi southward in the Tonkinese delta land he notices gradual changes in pronunciation and phonological structure. The clustered vowels of the Hanoi area shift almost imperceptibly in quality from village to village in the delta region itself: the second vowels in the Hanoi clusters [iê, ươ, uô] tend toward [â]. Note that the beginnings of this tendency are already apparent in Hanoi—[iêw, iêp, iêm, iêt, iên, uôj, uôm, uôt, uôn] but [iậk, iậng, uậk, uậng], while the official spelling suggests [iêk, iêng, uôk, uông].[1] Also, the vowels [ê, ô] as the second member of the clusters which do occur are centralized, noticeably different from their variants as simple vowels. The clusters beginning with [i] and [u] have [â] as second member in the speech of Phát-diệm on the southern margin of the delta. (And in this dialect this [â] is frequently more prominent than the preceding vowel.) In some localities of the delta the clusters [ưw, ươw] (written *ưꞷ, ươꞷ*) are to be found, while Hanoi replaces them by [iw, iêw].

4.12. Vinh. By the time Vinh is reached the retroflex position of tongue-tip consonants (tongue curled back) has become distinctive: here speakers distinguish orthographic tr from ch, s from x, and r from d and gi. These distinctions almost certainly obtain in some areas in Tonkin, but there is so little detailed information on dialectal variations there that it is difficult to determine just which ones. Maspero 1912: p. 27, characterizes the area as pronouncing **ch** for **tr** everywhere except in a few small, clearly defined pockets. However, some of my informants have asserted that universal [ch] is a characteristic rather of the urban centers, while tr is distinguished in rural areas—here educated speakers often have a retroflexed stop, while uneducated people have [t]; e.g., *trâu* water buffalo: HN [châw], rural educated [trâw], rural popular [tâw]. Certainly the influence of the official spelling is a complicating factor. (Cf. also Lê văn Lý 1948: p. 14.)

For further details on Vinh pronunciation see Emeneau 1951. The presentation here involves a few reinterpretations from his phonemic system. There are a number of respects in which this dialect area seems to be quite

---

[1] Whether such clusters are or were actually pronounced in some dialects or whether those writings represent a normalizing tendency on the part of the inventors of the writing system is of course not certain.

special, and it is interesting to note that Vietnamese from other regions frequently mention Vinh speech as "peculiar" or the subject of ridicule. The characteristics of the tones are particularly interesting and certainly merit further study. Those with glottal stricture might perhaps be analyzed as containing a glottal stop phoneme, like similar Hanoi sequences. However, from Emeneau's description it appears that they do not fit very well with any other contours, and the glottal stricture affects most or all of the syllable, while there is apparently not usually a full glottal stop at any consistent point. These peculiarities tend to support the relationships of Vinh speech to Maspero's Haut-Annam group, but many other characteristics place Vinh as simply intermediate between Hanoi and Huế.

Tr, s and **r** all have the tongue tip curled back; the first is a stop usually released with a spirant, the second a voiceless spirant, the third its voiced counterpart, although usually with less friction—**r** resembles English r in *run* to some extent, but lacks the English lip rounding and has somewhat more friction. In the distance from Phát-diệm to Vinh, too, the vowel clusters have lost their distinctive quality of vacillating prominence and become regular diphthongs—that is, the first vowel of the (orthographic) sequences iêu, iêp, iêm, iêt, iên, iêc, iêng, ươi, ươu, ươp, ươm, uôi, uôm, uôt, uôn, uôc, uông, is regularly prominent. The second element is then a semivowel of the type of Hanoi postvocalic [j, w]. Of the simple vowels [ǎ] is replaced by [e] before [ch, nh]. Vinh tones are different from those of the Hanoi area, but there remain the six distinctions implied by the orthography (2.71, 3.25). Table 1 shows the consonant and tone systems of Vinh speech; the vocalic system is the same as that of Hanoi, although there are differences in distribution, as suggested above.

TABLE 1. VINH CONSONANTS AND TONAL DISTINCTIONS

CONSONANTS

p	t	tr	ch	k	
b		đ			
ph	th	s	x	kh	h
v	l	r	z	g	
m	n		nh	ng	

TONES

Sắc	High rising
Ngang	High level
Ngã	Mid level with glottal stricture
Hỏi	Mid dropping with glottal stricture
Nặng	Low level
Huyền	Low falling

ORTHOGRAPHY	HANOI	VINH	
chưa	[chưậ]	[chưậ]	not yet
trâu	[châw]	[trâw]	water buffalo

ORTHOGRAPHY	HANOI	VINH	
xa	[xa]	[xa]	be far
sách	[xǎch]	[sǎch]	book
da	[za]	[za]	skin
gì	[zìj]	[zìj]	what(ever)
ra	[za]	[ra]	go out
hiểu	[hiểw]	[hỉậw]	understand
biết	[biét]	[bíật]	know
người	[ngưòj]	[ngừậj]	person
muốn	[muốn]	[múận]	to want

4.13. Huế. Passing the Haut-Annam area and arriving at Huế, the observer
is confronted by a number of further differences. While the tones implied
by the standard orthography are apparently all distinguished in some way
or other throughout Tonkin and as far south as Vinh, Huế has only five
distinctions—words written with *hỏi* and *ngã* tones are pronounced alike
with a long rising contour, beginning in lower mid range and accompanied
by glottal stricture, which frequently interrupts the voicing about midway
through the syllable. (In examples this tone is represented by the symbol
for *ngã* tone.) Words with *sắc* tone have the same pitch contour without
glottal stricture. *Nặng* tone starts low, falls abruptly, and ends with glottal
stop or one of the other stops. *Huyền* tone begins considerably higher than
in Hanoi and Vinh and trails downward. It is often difficult for the foreigner
to distinguish from the unmarked tone (*ngang*), which is higher mid level.
As in other dialects, the latter tone has a higher variant with sustaining
intonation and a high falling contour with increasing intonation. With fading intonation it starts at higher mid and falls to the bottom of the voice
range.

Hanoi and Vinh initial [z] are replaced in Huế by a semivowel [j],
much like the *y* in English *yes* (and like the final [j] in this and other
dialects of Vietnamese).

More outstanding are differences in final consonants. Final [ch, nh] of
Tonkin and Vinh are replaced by [t, n]. Final **t, n** of the orthography correspond to Huế [t, n] only after [i, ê] (not after *iê-*, which is pronounced
[iậ-]); elsewhere they are replaced by [k, ng].

ORTHOGRAPHY	HANOI	HUE	
sách	[xǎch]	[sǎt]	book
anh	[ǎnh]	[ǎn]	elder brother
ít	[ít]	[ít]	be a small amount
đến	[dến]	[dến]	arrive

ORTHOGRAPHY	HANOI	HUE	
biết	[biết]	[bíậk]	know
dứt	[dứt]	[dứk]	to break [string]
ớt	[ớt]	[ók]	pimento, pepper
hơn	[hơn]	[hơng]	be more (than)
một	[một]	[mộk]	one
khen	[khen]	[kheậng]	commend (for [ậ] see below)
ngon	[ngon]	[ngong]	be tasty

Certain shifts in vocalic elements appear in Huế. The orthographic sequences **iêp, iêm, ươp, ươm** are usually pronounced with the first element most prominent; the second element, however, is not as clearly semivocalic as in **iêt, iên, iêc, iêng, ươt, ươn, ươc, ương**, where it is clearly the semivowel [ậ] that is involved. Before -*p, -m* these second elements are vowels somewhat lower and more central than the first vowel (the prominent element).[2] But the cluster **uôm** belongs in the second category [uậm].

ORTHOGRAPHY	HANOI	VINH	HUE	
tiếp	[tiếp]	[tíập]	[tíip]	continue
tìm kiếm	[tìm kiếm]	[tìm kíậm]	[tìm kíim]	to search
ướp	[ướp]	[ứập]	[ứưp]	to perfume
lượm	[lượm]	[lựậm]	[lựưm]	pick up
biết	[biết]	[bíật]	[bíậk]	know
tiếng	[tíậng]	[tíậng]	[tíậng]	noise, sound, language
nước	[nưóc]	[nứậk]	[nứậk]	water
vườn	[vườn]	[vừận]	[vừậng]	garden
buồm	[buồm]	[bùậm]	[bùậm]	[ship's] sail

Before the final semivowels [j, w], the clusters **iê, ươ, uô** have lost their second element, so that the sequences **iêu, ươi, ươu, uôi** (triphthongs in Vinh) are pronounced as diphthongs indistinguishable from **iu, ưi, ưu, ui**.

---

[2] While this is reminiscent of Hanoi pronunciation, it also presages the treatment of these sequences farther south where the second element has disappeared entirely (cf. 4.16). I am indebted to Herbert Izzo for information on Hue speech from his unpublished field notes representing work he conducted in that city. (Mr. Izzo read a paper at the annual meeting of the Linguistic Society of America in December 1961 in which he characterized Hue speech as intermediate between Hanoi and Saigon.) This supplements and corroborates my own observations of the speech of several persons from Hue.

ORTHOGRAPHY	HANOI	VINH	HUE	
hiểu	[hiểw]	[hịə̯w]	[hīw]	understand
người	[ngừ̛ờj]	[ngừ̛ə̣j]	[ngừj]	person
rượu	[ziễw]	[rə̣w]	[r̥w]	alcoholic beverage
tuổi	[tuổj]	[tửə̣j]	[tūj]	years old

In citation forms, the prominent vowels representing the last clusters are often longer than the corresponding vowels in words with orthographic two-element nuclei. (This appears to be a kind of spelling pronunciation.)

Some other aspects of vocalic elements are elusive and need further study. Incomplete data make it impossible to state the entire pattern with certainty, but certain characteristics may be mentioned here. The diphthongization of **e** before [ng] which is already an alternate in Hanoi seems to have become a constant phenomenon in Huế: *xẻng* [xẽə̣ng] shovel, *sen* [seə̣ng] HN [xen] lotus. Sequences involving prevocalic [w] in more northerly speech have special treatments in Huế, which seem not to be duplicated in any other dialects, except for the special pronunciations of some Hanoi speakers in replacing [lw] clusters by [l] and a following vowel cluster. The orthographic sequence -**uâ**- seems regularly to be pronounced as a very rapid vowel cluster [uâ] preceded by strongly labialized initial consonants. Before front vowels [i, ê, e, ă], [w] appears much as in other dialects. But orthographic sequences with -**oa**- are pronounced in some cases as a vowel cluster [ôa], in which the second vowel is prominent (finally and before [ng]); in others as a diphthong [oạ](before [j]).

ORTHOGRAPHY	HANOI	HUE	
luật	[lwật]	[luậk]	law
xuân	[xwân]	[xuâng]	spring [season]
tuần	[twần]	[tuầng]	week
lũy	[lwĩj]	[lwĩj]	rampart
thuế	[thwếj]	[thwếj]	taxes
ngu-ngoe	[nguw ngwe]	[nguw ngwe]	[animal] wags its tail
loăng-quăng	[lwăng kwăng]	[lwăng kwăng]	to run about
góa	[gwá]	[gôá]	be widowed
toán	[twán]	[tôán]	calculate
loài	[lwàj]	[lòạj]	species
ngoài	[ngwàj]	[ngòạj]	outside

4.14. Đà-nẵng (formerly widely known by the name **Tourane**). Just south of Huế the tone system is different again: in Đà-nẵng *sắc* tone is again high rising (much like that of Hanoi and Vinh), and syllables written with *hỏi* and *ngã*, although still pronounced alike with a long mid rising contour, lack the glottal stricture they have in Huế. (In all the dialects where *hỏi* and *ngã* tones are pronounced alike the tilde is here adopted to represent the fusion of the two tones in the transcription.) *Nặng* tone has glottal stricture, but it is less forceful and consistent than in Huế speech, and the pitch contour is different: low level with final stops, otherwise low dipping. *Huyền* tone is somewhat lower than in Huế, but not as low as in Hanoi.

The initial cluster [hw] has disappeared in Đà-nẵng speech, replaced by simple [w]. (These comments on Đà-nẵng speech are based primarily on Smalley and Nguyễn văn Vạn 1954, supplemented by my own observations of Đà-nẵng speakers in Dalat and Saigon. Whether this initial [w] is regularly preceded by glottal stop, as in Hanoi, is not certain from either source.) After [w] the vowel [â] is replaced by [ɯ] before [k, ng]. Before final [j, w] the vowel [ă] is replaced by [a'], so that forms in -ay and -au sound (respectively) exactly like those in -ai and -ao.

ORTHOGRAPHY	HANOI	HUE	DA-NANG	
hoài	[hwàj]	[hwàj]	[wàj]	continuously
xuất	[xwất]	[xuấk]	[xwúk]	to exit
xuân	[xwân]	[xuâng]	[xwɯng]	spring [season]
mai	[maj]	[maj]	[maj]	tomorrow
may	[măj]	[măj]	[maj]	to sew
sao	[xaw]	[saw]	[saw]	star
sau	[xăw]	[săw]	[saw]	afterward

In this dialect there are some problems which cannot be resolved without further field work. Involved is the pronunciation of forms written with -*ich*, -*inh*; -*ut*, -*un*; -*uc*, -*ung*. Resolution of these apparent anomalies may shed interesting light on dialectal correspondences. (See Smalley and Vạn 1954, book 2, p. 28, for phonetic details.)

4.15. Bas-Annam.

The general characteristics of Đà-nẵng speech apply for the most part to the balance of the territory of south central Viet Nam. There are some interesting developments in local speech communities of the region, but their scope is limited, and the details are complex and not very thoroughly documented. The most significant of these developments is the simplification of various initial clusters with [w], a characteristic we shall observe again in the speech to the south of Saigon. Somewhere not far north of the Saigon region [v] disappears; it is replaced by [j], which everywhere from Huế south resembles English y in *you*, *yes*. An early picture of this area is presented in Cadière 1911. The correspondence of Cochinchinese [j] to [v] of other dialects is discussed historically in

Maspero 1912 (pp. 41-42, 70-74). A detailed treatment of [w] and related sounds is Cadière 1908-09.

4.16. Saigon. The difference between south central Viet Nam and the Saigon area has mainly to do with variants of the vowels. Saigon [i, ê] have some variants which are central, others which are strongly centralized front vowels. All vowels except [a] have lower variants with non-high tones tones (*nặng*, *huyền*, and the fused *hỏi-ngã* tone); in the same positions [a] has variants which are further back in the mouth. The replacement of [â] by [ɯ] before [k, ng] (occurring after [w] in Đà-nẵng speech) is extended in Saigon to syllables beginning with [ch, nh]. The tones themselves are very similar to those of Đà-nẵng, except that *huyền* is clearly lower than *nặng*, and *nặng* syllables end in glottal stop (if there is no other stop) but are not generally accompanied by glottal stricture. One difference has less to do with the characteristics of individual sounds than with the system they present: Saigon consonants involve a different kind of manner distinction from that of the dialects farther north (4.21).

The reduction of three-element nuclei to two elements (which begins at Huế) is carried still farther in Saigon: **iêp, iêm, ươp, ươm, uôm** are pronounced the same as **ip, im, up, ưm, um.** This leaves in the system only three-element nuclei ending in dorsals, except for the alternate pronunciation [oậj] of the diphthong **oi** (cf. 4.26).

ORTHOGRAPHY	HANOI	HUE	SAIGON	
tiếp	[tiếp]	[tíip]	[típ]	continue
tìm kiếm	[tìm kiếm]	[tìm kíim]	[tìm kím]	to search
ướp	[ướp]	[ứɯp]	[úp]	to scent
lượm	[lượm]	[lɯ̣ɯm]	[lụm]	pick up
buồm	[buồm]	[bùậm]	[bùm]	[ship's] sail

It is interesting to note that educated speakers, wishing to distinguish, for example, a syllable in **iêm** from one in **im**, produce a longer vowel in the first. This is intermediate between the usual Saigon pronunciation and that of Huế, where the second element is lower and centralized, but phonetically quite close to the first. Saigonese pronunciation is treated in greater detail in 4.2.

4.17. Southern Cochinchina. South of Saigon there are still further differences. Materials are lacking for a systematic description but some general observations can be made. In some rural speech initial **ph** is a lax aspirated [p]. All initial clusters with [w] are lacking (cf. 4.15): [kw, ngw] are replaced by [w]; [gw] does not occur; in all other cases [w] has disappeared, leaving the single initial consonant. (The one word *góa* 'be widowed' which represents the cluster [gw] elsewhere, is lacking; it is replaced by [já], which seems not to be written. It is insufficient evidence for saying that SG [gw] is replaced by rural [j].) In some areas [x] is formed by the tongue blade, as in Hanoi, and it corresponds to both [x] and [s] in Saigon. There are fewer vowel distinctions in general and phonetically there are very few front vowels: [ă] is replaced by [â] except before [k, ng]; [i, ê] are replaced by [ɯ, ơ] before [t, n]; [ơ, o] are replaced by [ô] before [p, m]. On the other hand, diphthongs are more frequent and by and large they involve greater changes in position: for example, the words *đi* 'go', *tư* 'fourth' and *ngủ* 'to sleep' have diphthongs which start much lower than in Đà-nẵng or even in Saigon, and the [i] and [u] are strongly centralized. These remarks are based on limited observation of speakers from Gò-công, Mỹ-tho, Bến Tre, and Trà-vinh. Thorough study should be made of these and other Cochinchinese dialects. See also Grammont 1909-10.

ORTHOGRAPHY	SAIGON	SOUTHERN COCHINCHINA	
qua	[kwa]	[wa]	cross over
ngoài	[ngwàj]	[wàj]	outside
tuần	[twừng]	[từng]	week
xoài	[xwàj]	[xàj]	mango
truyện	[trwị âng]	[trị âng]	story
duyên	[jwiâng]	[jiâng]	predestined affinity
cắp	[kắp]	[kắp]	pilfer
lắm	[lắm]	[lắm]	to a great extent
sách	[sắt]	[xắt]	book
lạnh	[lăn]	[lận]	be cold
ít	[ít]	[ứt]	be a small amount
định	[dịn]	[dựn]	decide, determine
hết	[hết]	[hớt]	be used up
đến	[dến]	[dớn]	arrive
lớp	[lớp]	[lốp]	class
cơm	[kom]	[kôm]	cooked rice
cọp	[kọp]	[kộp]	tiger
xóm	[xóm]	[xốm]	neighborhood

4.18. Summary. As can be seen from this survey the majority of Vietnamese dialects form a chain extending from north to south, each involving a few differences from the patterns of its neighbors to either side. The large urban centers (especially Hanoi, Huế and Saigon) stand out as supporting rather special dialects, showing the influence of large classes of educated speakers and more extensive contact with other areas.

There are other differences among dialects—a few morphological and syntactic variations and numerous words and expressions with strongly local flavor. The most important special grammatical features typical of Saigon are dealt with in connection with related items in Hanoi speech. In addition there are examples cited from my Saigonese materials, and these are marked (S) wherever they seem alien to northern speakers. A few lexical items characteristic of Huế are also mentioned. It is not, however, the purpose of this work to treat systematically the differences of local usage.

4.2. Saigon Phonology involves rather different systems and arrangements of consonants, vowels and tones from those implied by the official spelling and especially from those of Hanoi speech. In one important respect the Saigonese consonants are closer to those of the writing system than their Hanoi equivalents: they show the distinction between plain and retroflexed sounds formed by the tip of the tongue.

Examples in the following sections are cited in the standard orthography. This is followed by a phonetic notation representing Saigon pronunciation where this is not clear from the *quốc-ngữ* form, and by a second phonetic notation marked HN when the Hanoi pronunciation differs.

4.21. The Consonant System makes use of the distinctions fortis vs. lenis, stop vs. continuant, and oral vs. nasal, and shows consonants primarily in five positions: labial, apical plain, apical retroflex, laminal and dorsal. Table 2 shows the elements, making use of the symbols of the standard orthography as far as it is possible. Comparison with 2.11 (Table 1) will make clear some of the differences in status of elements similar to those of Hanoi speech. Other details are discussed below.

TABLE 2. SAIGON CONSONANTS

		Labial	Apical Plain	Apical Retroflex	Laminal	Dorsal	Glottal
FORTIS ORAL CONSONANTS	Stops, voiceless	p	t	tr	ch	k	
	Stops, voiced	b	đ				
	Continuants	ph	x	s		kh	
LENIS ORAL CONSONANTS		v	th	r	l	g	h
NASALS		m	n		nh	ng	

The sounds [p, t,ch, k, b, đ, th, m, n, nh, ng] are virtually identical with their Hanoi counterparts except for their distributions (cf. 4.25-26).

> cấp [kắp] pilfer, tôi [tôj] I, ít be a small amount, cho give,
> các [plural marker], bài [bàj] lesson, đá stone, theo [thew]
> follow, mèo [mèw] cat, làm act, nên therefore, nhà house,
> nghe [nge] listen, đúng be correct

Fortis continuants [ph, x, s, kh] contrast with similar lenis sounds in Hanoi. Some of these sounds also involve differences in position. Saigon [x] resembles Hanoi [x], but is produced by the tongue tip rather than the blade. Saigon [s] is produced by the tongue tip curled back toward the roof of the mouth; it is reminiscent of the s in English sugar, or the sh in short.

> phá destroy, xe vehicle, số [sốw] HN [xốw] number, khoai
> [khwaj] potato

The lenis oral consonants in Saigon [v, th, r, l, g, h] are very noticeably more relaxed than their Hanoi counterparts. In addition there are a few other differences. Saigon [v] appears only before the semivowel [j] (4.22) and is itself palatalized in anticipation. Saigon [l] differs from its Hanoi counterpart in that it has approximately the vocalic coloring of [e]— that is, the front of the tongue is raised toward the roof of the mouth during its production—and the contact generally involves the blade against the alveolar ridge, rather than the tip. [r] is discussed in connection with [tr] below.

> vợ [vjọɤ] HN [vọɤ] wife, thu [thuw] autumn, làm act, gà hen,
> chicken, hôm day

The initial cluster [vj] corresponds to Hanoi initial [v]. Actually, this is a spelling pronunciation on the part of educated speakers in Saigon: the majority of the Saigonese (including many educated people) pronounce simply [j] in these forms. Some, then, add a [v] before the [j], knowing that the form is spelled with v. There are a few who pronounce a [b] sound before [j] in the same forms; this sound is also lenis (quite unlike the sound heard in bài lesson).

The retroflex stop [tr] is formed by touching the under side of the tip of the tongue against the alveolar ridge; it is usually slightly affricated— that is, released with a very short spirant. [r] has the same general position, but varies rather widely in manner—one hears interchangeably (sometimes in the speech of a single person) a flap or short trill, a voiced spirant (similar to the sound written z in English azure), or a combination of this spirant with a flap or trill. (Note that the position is similar to that of r in English run, but the concurrent lip rounding characteristic of

the English sound is lacking). Final [t, n] in a syllable immediately preceding [tr] have variants with the tongue tip touching the ridge, but only
[n] is retroflexed in such cases.

> *trắng* HN [chẳng] be white, *ít trà* a small amount of tea (cf.
> HN *ít chè*), *anh trả* [ăn trã] you pay (cf. HN *anh giả* [ănh
> zả]), *ra* HN [za] go out

4.22. The Vocalic System is similar in structure to that of Hanoi speech,
but there are a number of differences in distribution (4.26), and the actual
qualities of many vowels are noticeably different. Nearly all the vowels
have more widely scattered variants—this fact accounts for a good share of
the distinctive acoustic effect of Saigonese speech. Further, the two elements [ă, â] are paired together by two features—they are both relatively
shorter than other vowels in comparable positions, and they are distinguished to a great extent by the presence (in [ă]) or absence (in [â]) of
lip spreading. (This contrasts with the rest of the system where it is rather
the presence or absence of lip rounding which is involved.)

With non-high tones (see 4.23) the vowel [a] has variants which are
farther back than those occurring with high tones; with non-high tones other
vowels have variants which are lower than those occurring with high tones.

> *ba* three, *bà* grandmother, *thi* [thij] take an examination, *thì*
> [thìj] then, *cô* [kôw] father's sister, *cổ* [kổw] be ancient,
> *thứ* [thứɤ] kind, sort, *thử* [thửɤ] try out

After initial [ch, j, nh] the vowels [i, ư] have variants which are farther
front than after other initials.

> *chi* [chij] what(ever) [polite], *đi* [đij] go, *díp* [jíp] HN [zíp]
> [vehicle] spring, *kíp* be urgent, *như* [nhưɤ] similar to, *tư*
> [tưɤ] fourth

The vowels [i, ê] have central variants before [t, n]. (However, [i] is
farther front after initial [ch, j, nh]; see above.)

> *ít* be a small amount, *in* to print, *chết* to die, *đến* arrive

Initially[3] and after [th, ch, j, nh, h] before [p, k] the vowel [a] has variants which are very far front in the mouth and somewhat higher than in
other positions.

> *áp* oppress, *thác* [thák] waterfall, *chạp* last month of year,
> *giáp* [jáp] armor, *nhạc* [nhạk] music, *hát* [hák] HN [hát]
> sing

Some occurrences of the vowel [â] are very difficult for English
speakers to recognize: before final [j] there are variants which are central

---

[3] Actually initial vowels are usually preceded by glottal stop, although smooth onset
also occurs (see 4.25 end).

and somewhat higher than those which resemble the vowels in English *but,*
some. The variation has two conditioning factors—the relative stress which
accompanies the syllable and the initial which precedes the vowel. After
labials [b, ph, v, m, w], laminals [ch, j, l, nh] and dorsals [kh, g, ng]
(but not [k]) these central vowels occur, regardless of the relative stress;
with medium and weak stress they occur after all initials.

    bầy [bằj] to display, *mấy* [mấj] how(ever) many, *giấy* [jấj]
    paper, *gậy* [gâj] cane, *thấy* [thấj] perceive, *cây số* [⁰kây
    số w] kilometer

Compare the following forms with heavy stress or other finals:

    tây ['tâj] west, *dây* ['dâj] here, *thấy* ['thấj] perceive, *nấm*
    mushroom, *dầu* [jầw] oil, *tập* to practice

The vowel [ă] has front variants before [k, ng], central vowels elsewhere; all are accompanied by strong lip spreading.

    mắt [măk] be expensive (sometimes written *mắc*) (replaced in
    Hanoi by *dắt*), *ăn* [ăng] to eat; *gặp* to meet, *ong* [ăwng]
    bee, *sách* [săt] HN [xăch] book, *manh* [măn] HN [măṇh]
    be strong

There are some other minute variations of Saigonese vowels, but their
distributions are complex: it does not seem pertinent to cover them here.[4]
    Final [w, j, ɰ, ậ] are as in Hanoi, except that there are some differences
in distribution (cf. 4.26).

    mèo [mèw] cat, *tôi* [tôj] I, *tư* [tɰ] fourth, *chia* [chiậ] to
    divide, *mưa* [mưậ] to rain, *mùa* [mùậ] season, *đường*
    [dừậng] HN [dường] sugar, *biết* [bíậk] HN [biết] to know

Prevocalic [w] is different in that it is not preceded by glottal stop in
syllable initial; there are also some differences in its distribution in initial
clusters (cf. 4.26). And in Saigon [j] occurs before vowels, replacing
Hanoi [z] (written **d- gi-**): it is much like the *y* in English *yes, yacht,*
although tenser than most pronunciations of this sound. It also occurs in
the initial cluster [vj] (see above).

    òa [wà] burst into tears, *xuân* [xwɰng] HN [xwân] spring
    [season], *da* [ja] HN [za] skin, *giỏi* [jöj] HN [zỏj] be
    skillful, *vợ* [vjɵɰ] HN [vɵɰ] wife

4.23. The Tone System
involves three levels of pitch (high, mid, low)
and rising and falling contours (with a few level contours as variants).
There are five tones: as everywhere else in central and southern Viet Nam,
the *hỏi* and *ngã* tones of the official orthography are pronounced alike.

[4] For further details on these and other features of Saigon phonology see Thompson 1959.

Very similar to their Hanoi counterparts are high rising (*sắc*) and low trailing (*huyền*) tones.

má cheek, *mà* but, *ốc* [ắwk] snail, *làng* village

The fused *hỏi-ngã* tone has a long rising contour beginning in low mid range and rising sometimes as high as *sắc* tone, sometimes somewhat lower (depending on relative stress and intonation). With weak stress it is quicker and has a much sharper rise. (It is represented in transcriptions of pronunciation by the tilde ~.)

mả [mã] tomb, *cũ* [kũw] be old, *củ hành* [kũw hẳn] HN [kủw hẳnh] onion

The *nặng* tone is quite low (although not so low as *huyền* most of the time) and is level with syllables ending in [p, t, k]; with other syllables (which all end in glottal stop) it dips slightly, then rises. However, with weak stress all syllables are level. The level contour gives a kind of "monotonous" acoustic impression.

đẹp be beautiful, *sạch* [sặt] HN [xặch] be clean, *được* [dựậk] HN [dược̣k] receive, *mạ* rice seedling, *mạnh* [mặn] HN [mặnh] be strong

The *ngang* tone (unmarked) has several variants depending on relative stress and intonation and the position of the syllable in the pause group. Within a pause group (that is, not accompanying the final syllable) it is level with medium or weak stress and about one fifth of the way down from the top of the speaker's normal talking voice range. With heavy stress it starts a little higher and falls back to this level. With the final syllable of a pause group it has the same variants with decreasing intonation, but with fading intonation it begins lower, and with heavy stress falls to the bottom of the voice range; with medium or weak stress it falls somewhat below mid range. (In the latter case it is difficult to tell precisely what happens because the voicing fades so rapidly.) With sustaining intonation it starts a little higher, falls a short way and is maintained a short time at that level. With increasing contour it starts quite high and falls abruptly to the bottom of the voice range.

Khi nào ông đi, ... [khij nàw âwng 'đij...] Whenever you go, ...
Khi nào tôi đi, ... [khij nàw 'tôj đij ...] Whenever *I* go, ...
Tôi không đi. [tôj khâwng 'đij.] I'm not going.
Ông có biết không? [âwng °kắ 'bíhk! khâwng.] Do you know (or just surmise)?
Đi không? [đij 'khâwng?] Are [you] going [or not]?
Tôi không đi! [tôj khâwng 'đij!] I'm not going!

4.24. Stresses and Intonations are very similar to their Hanoi counterparts (cf. 2.72-3).[5] However, the variants of tonal contours which go with the various intonations are somewhat different for the unmarked tone (cf. 4.23 end). A noticeable difference in stressing habits in Saigon speech may be described impressionistically: there seems to be generally a much more pronounced difference in intensity or loudness between heavy and medium stresses; and weak stress is accompanied by very short syllables. This gives the typical conversational language a much more syncopated rhythmic impression than Hanoi speech.

It is convenient to mention one distributional feature here: syllables ending in [o] with medium or heavy stress are replaced by syllables ending in [â] under weak stress. (Aside from a few marginal exclamatory forms this is the only occurrence of final [â].)

Để tôi làm cho. [dễj tôj làm 'cho.] Let me do it (for someone else).
Để tôi làm cho ông. [dễj tôj 'làm ᵒchâ âwng.] Let me do it for you.

4.25. Initials are shown in Table 3, which may be compared with the Hanoi initials shown in 2.81 (Table 6). The clusters [vj, kw] seem obviously secondary introductions into the system based on knowledge of the spelling of the words involved; less educated speakers have simply [j, w] in these forms, and educated speakers, too, often use them in less careful speech. The [hw] of Hanoi is replaced by [w] in Saigon. None of the learnèd forms suggesting [nw-] (2.81) were recorded for this dialect. As in Hanoi, [gw-] is represented by the single form *góa* be widowed.

TABLE 3. SAIGON INITIALS

	Labial	Apical Plain	Apical Retroflex	Laminal	Dorsal	Glottal
		t(w)	tr(w)	ch(w)	k(w)	
Fortis	b	đ(w)				
	ph	x(w)	s(w)		kh(w)	
Lenis	vj	th(w)	r	l(w)	g(w)	h
Nasal	m	n		nh(w)	ng(w)	
Semivocalic	w		j(w)			

tôi [tôj] I, *tòa* [twà] bureau, office, *trễ* [trễj] be late, *truyện* [trwị ậng] HN [chwiện] story, *chợ* [chợɤ] market(place), *chuyện* [chwị ậng] HN [chwiện] conversation topic, *cá* [ká] fish, *qua* [kwa] cross over
ba three, *đến* arrive, *đoán* [dwáng] HN [dwán] to guess
phá destroy, *xa* be far, *xuân* [xwɤng] HN [xwân] spring [season], *sách* [sắt] HN [xắch] book, *soạn* [swạng] HN

---

[5] Thompson 1959 posits four degrees of relative stress. I now think that for Saigonese speech, as for Hanoi, there are only three distinctions. What I earlier called extra-loud stress is an extra-loud variant of heavy stress accompanying increasing intonation.

[xwạn] arrange, *khen* [kheăng] commend, *khoai* [khwaj] potato

vừa [(v)jừậ] HN [vừậ] to fit, suit, *thờ* [thờɤ] to worship, *thuế* [thwếj] taxes, *ra* HN [za] go out, *lá* leaf, *loài* [lwàj] species, *gà* hen, chicken, *góa* [gwá] be widowed, *hỏi* [hõj] HN [hõj] ask a question

Mỹ [mĩj] America, *núi* [núj] mountain, *nhớ* [nhớɤ] remember, *năm nhuận* [năm nhwɤng] HN [năm nhwận] leap year, *nghe* [nge] listen, *ngoài* [ngwàj] outside

òa [wà] burst into tears, *hoa* [wa] HN [hwa] flower, *gì* [jìj] HN [zìj] what(ever), *duyên* [jwiậng] HN [zwiên] predestined affinity

Syllables which begin with none of these initials have either a direct vowel onset or a glottal stop, in free variation; this is different from the Hanoi habit, where glottal stop seems always to be present.

ai [aj] who(ever), *ướt* [ứậk] be wet, *em* younger sibling

4.26. Nuclei follow patterns similar to those of Hanoi (2.82). **Simple nuclei** consist of one of the vowels [e, o, a].

nhẹ be light [weight], *họ* (extended) family, clan, *mạ* rice seedling

Two-element nuclei are shown in Table 4, which may be compared with Table 7 in 2.82.

TABLE 4. TWO-ELEMENT NUCLEI

VOWELS	j	w	ʉ	ậ	p	m	t	n	k	ng
i	ij	iw		iậ	ip	im	it	in		
ê	êj	êw			êp	êm	êt	ên		
ɯ	ɯj	ɯw	ɯʉ	ɯậ					ɯk	ɯng
ơ	ơj		ơʉ		ơp	ơm			ơk	ơng
u	uj	uw		uậ	up	um			uk	ung
ô	ôj	ôw			ôp	ôm			ôk	ông
e		ew			ep	em			(ek)	
o	oj				op	om			ok	ong
a	aj	aw			ap	am			ak	ang
ă					ăp	ăm	ăt	ăn	ăk	ăng
â	âj	âw			âp	âm			âk	âng

i: *đi* [dij] go, *riu-rít* [riw rít] to chatter, chirp, *chia* [chiậ] to
divide, *kíp* be urgent, *lim* [lim] ironwood, *ít* be a small
amount, *in* to print, *ích* [ít] be useful, *lính* [lín] soldier

ê: *để* [dẽj] put, place, *nếu* [nḗw] if, *bếp* kitchen, *đêm* night, *hết*
be used up, *đến* arrive, *ếch* [ḗt] frog, *lênh-bênh* [lên-bên]
[life] is unstable

ư: *ngửi* [ngũj] to sniff, *mưu* [mɯw] HN [miw] scheme, *tư* [tɯɣ]
fourth, *mưa* [mɯậ] to rain, *đứt* [dứk] to break [string], *sức*
[súk] strength, *đừng* don't

ơ: *mời* [mòj] invite, *nớu* [nớw] alveolar ridge*, *mơ* [moɣ] to
dream, *lớp* class, *sớm* be early, *ớt* [ớk] pepper, pimento,
son [song] to paint

u: *núi* [núj] mountain, *đủ* [dũw] be enough, *mua* [muậ] to buy,
chụp seize suddenly, *chum* earthenware jar, *phút* [phúk]
minute, moment, *bùn* [bùng] mud, *lúc* [lúk] time, instance,
đúng be correct

ô: *tôi* [tôj] I, *cô* [kôw] father's sister, *hộp* box, *hôm* day, *một*
[môk] one, *bốn* [bống] four

e: *mèo* [mèw] cat, *đẹp* be beautiful, *đem* to carry, *eng éc* [eậng
ék] [onomatopoeic: squealing of pig]

o: *hỏi* [hõj] ask a question, *chóp* summit, *xóm* neighborhood, *ngọt*
[ngọk] be sweet, *ngon* [ngong] be tasty, *boong* [bong]
deck [of ship]

a: *hai* [haj] two, *tay* [taj] hand, arm, *sao* [saw] star, *sáu* [sáw]
six, *tháp* tower, *làm* do, make, *mát* [mák] be cool, *bàn*
[bàng] table, *khác* [khák] be different, *làng* village

ă: *cắp* [kắp] pilfer, *thăm* to visit, *sách* [sắt] HN [xắch] book,
hành [hằn] HN [hằnh] onion, *tắt* [tắk] extinguish, *ăn* [ăng]
eat, *sắc* [sắk] HN [xắk] be sharp, *vắng* [(v)jắng] be
absent

â: *tây* [tâj] west, *xấu* [xấw] be ugly, *cấp* [kấp] level, degree,
đâm to stab, *rất* [rấk] HN [zất] very, *dân* [jâng] HN [zân]
citizen, *xấc* [xấk] be ill-mannered, *vâng* [(v)jâng] obey

Three-element nuclei end in [k, ng] preceded by one of the sequences
[iậ, ɯậ, uậ, eậ, ăw, âw]. They are shown in Table 5, which may be compared with Table 8, in 2.82. Of these diphthongs, note that [eậ, ăw] occur
only in these combinations.

---

* Not found in Hanoi colloquial usage.

TABLE 5. SAIGON THREE-ELEMENT NUCLEI

	FINALS	
DIPHTHONG	k	ng
iậ̆	iậ̆k	iậ̆ng
ư̆ậ̆	ư̆ậ̆k	ư̆ậ̆ng
uậ̆	uậ̆k	uậ̆ng
eậ̆	eậ̆k	eậ̆ng
ăw	ăwk	ăwng
âw	âwk	âwng

iậ̆: biết [bíậ̆k] know, việc [(v)jiậ̆k] affair, matter, tiền [tìậ̆ng] money, tiếng [tíậ̆ng] noise, sound

ư̆ậ̆: ướt [ứậ̆k] be wet, vườn [(v)jừậ̆ng] garden, dược [dự̆ậ̆k] receive, đường [dừậ̆ng] sugar

uậ̆: chuột [chuậ̆k] rat, buồn [bùậ̆ng] be sad, guốc [gúậ̆k] clog, wooden shoe, chuông [chuậ̆ng] bell

eậ̆: ghét [géậ̆k] detest, đen [deậ̆ng] be black, eng éc [eậ̆ng ék] [onomatopoetic: squealing of pig]

ăw: học [hặwk] to study, ong [ăwng] bee

âw: ốc [ấwk] snail, ông [âwng] grandfather

A number of the three-element nuclei implied in the orthography (and heard in Hanoi speech) appear simplified to two-element nuclei in Saigon.

ORTHOGRAPHY	HANOI	SAIGON	
hiểu	[hiểw]	[hĭw]	understand
tiếp	[tiếp]	[típ]	continue
tìm kiếm	[tìm kiếm]	[tìm kím]	to search
người	[ngườj]	[ngừj]	person
rượu	[ziệw]	[rựw]	alcoholic beverage
ướp	[ướp]	[úp]	to scent
lượm	[lượm]	[lụm]	pick up
tuổi	[tuổj]	[tũj]	years old
buồm	[buồm]	[bùm]	[ship's] sail

The two-element nucleus [oj] is replaced in some individuals' speech by the three-element nucleus [oậ̆j].

hỏi [hõj, hõậ̆j] ask a question, nói [nój, nóậ̆j] speak

4.27. Saigon Phonemics (Notes for Linguists). We may review here
salient features of the structural analysis of Saigonese phonology presented in detail in Thompson 1959. As in Chapter 2 (cf. 2.15), this more
systematic description was not chosen for the purpose at hand because
its relationship to the standard writing system involves some confusing
complexities for the non-linguist.

As in the Hanoi system, glottal stop appears as a phonemic entity, and
preglottalized [b, d] are recognized as allophones of /p, t/, respectively,
following initial [ʔ]. Although initial [w] is not distinguished from [v]
by being preglottalized, the fact that [v] occurs only before [j], where
[w] does not appear, places them together in a /w/ phoneme, as in Hanoi
speech. (For those speakers who have a lenis stop before [j] this [b]
clearly belongs to the /w/ phoneme, in place of the [v] just discussed).
The semivowel [j] is seen to fill the empty position in the laminal column,
and [ɯ, ậ] may be interpreted as allophones of /g, h/ respectively, as in
the northern dialect.

The tone system allows for little reinterpretation: glottal stop is connected only with *nặng* tone, and the contour is not sufficiently similar to
any other tone to suggest any phonemic identity.

Table 6 shows the results of this reanalysis, arranged so as to be comparable with earlier charts (cf. 2.15, 4,21).

TABLE 6. PHONEMIC REINTERPRETATION OF SAIGONESE

CONSONANTS							VOCALICS		
p	t	tr	ch	k		ʔ	j	g	w
ʔp	ʔt						i	ɯ	u
ph	x	s	j	kh			ê	ɤ	ô
w(j)	th	r	l	g	h		e		o
m	n		nh	ng			ă	ậ	
							a		
							h		

EXPLANATION OF CERTAIN COMBINATIONS

PREVOCALIC	POSTVOCALIC
/wj-/ = [vj-]	/-w/ = [-w]
/w-/ = [w-]	
/g-/ = [g-]	/-g/ = [-ɯ̯]
/h-/ = [h-]	/-h/ = [-ậ̯]

4.3. Dialectal Correspondences are summarized in the charts on the
following pages. The charts are arranged in alphabetical order for the key
elements cited in the standard orthography with pronunciations for the

major dialects discussed in 4.1. Letter cues refer to notes at end of each table.

INITIALS

ORTHOGRAPHY	HANOI	VINH	HUE	DA-NANG	SAIGON	TRA-VINH
b	b	b	b	b	b	b
c	k	k	k	k	k	k
ch	ch	ch	ch	ch	ch	ch
d	z	z	j	j	j	j
đ	đ	đ	đ	đ	đ	đ
g[a]	g	g	g	g	g	g, -(w)[b]
gh	g	g	g	g	g	g
gi	z	z, tr[c]	j, tr[c]	j, tr[c]	j, tr[c]	j, tr[c]
h	h	h	h	h, -(w)[b]	h, -(w)[b]	h, -(w)[b]
k	k	k	k	k	k	k
kh	kh	kh	kh	kh	kh	kh
l	l	l	l	l	l	l
m	m	m	m	m	m	m
n	n	n	n	n	n	n
ng(h)	ng	ng	ng	ng	ng	ng, -(w)[b]
nh	nh	nh	nh	nh	nh	nh
ph	ph	ph	ph	ph	ph	ph
qu	kw	kw	kw	kw	(k)w	w
r	z	r	r	r	r	r
s	x	s	s	s	s	s
t	t	t	t	t	t	t
th	th	th	th	th	th	th
tr	ch, z[c]	tr	tr	tr	tr	tr
v	v	v	v	v	(v)j	j
x	x	x	x	x	x	x

NOTES

[a] Before -*i*, *g* = *gi*-.

[b] Does not occur before [w].

[c] The correspondence of HN [z-] (written *gi*-) to [tr-] (written *tr*-)elsewhere characterizes only certain words: for a further discussion of this, see Maspero 1912. Some less extensive special correspondences e. g., [l-: nh-] are not included in these charts because their local distributions are not documented.

98

NUCLEI

ORTHOGRAPHY	HANOI	VINH	HUE	DA-NANG	SAIGON	TRA-VINH
a	a	a	a .	a	a	a
ac	ak	ak	ak	ak	ak	ak
ach	ăch	ech	ăt	ăt	ăt	ât
ai	aj	aj	aj	aj	aj	aj
am	am	am	am	am	am	am
an	an	an	ang	ang	ang	ang
ang	ang	ang	ang	ang	ang	ang
anh	ănh	enh	ăn	ăn	ăn	ân
ao	aw	aw	aw	aw	aw	aw
ap	ap	ap	ap	ap	ap	ap
at	at	at	ak	ak	ak	ak
au	ăw	ăw	ăw	aw	aw	aw
ay	ăj	ăj	ăj	aj	aj	aj
ăc	ăk	ăk	ăk	ăk	ăk	ăk
ăm	ăm	ăm	ăm	ăm	ăm	âm
ăn	ăn	ăn	ăng	ăng	ăng	ăng
ăng	ăng	ăng	ăng	ăng	ăng	ăng
ăp	ăp	ăp	ăp	ăp	ăp	âp
ăt	ăt	ăt	ăk	ăk	ăk	ăk
âc	âk	âk	âk	âk, ɯk[a]	âk, ɯk[b]	âk, ɯk[b]
âm	âm	âm	âm	âm	âm	âm
ân	ân	ân	âng	âng, ɯng[a]	âng, ɯng[b]	âng, ɯng[b]
âng	âng	âng	âng	âng, ɯng[a]	âng, ɯng[b]	âng, ɯng[b]
âp	âp	âp	âp	âp	âp	âp
ât	ât	ât	âk	âk, ɯk[a]	âk, ɯk[b]	âk, ɯk[b]
âw	âw	âw	âw	âw	âw	âw
ây	âj	âj	âj	âj	âj	âj
e	e	e	e	e	e	e
ec	ek	ek	ek	ek	ek	eậk
em	em	em	em	em	em	em
en	en	en	eậng	eng	eậng	eậng
eng	eng	eng	eậng	eng	eậng	eậng
eo	ew	ew	ew	ew	ew	ew
ep	ep	ep	ep	ep	ep	ep
et	et	et	ek	ek	eậk	eậk
ê	êj	êj	êj	êj	êj	êj
êch	êch	êch	êt	êt	êt	ɤt

99

ORTHOGRAPHY	HANOI	VINH	HUE	DA-NANG	SAIGON	TRA-VINH
êm	êm	êm	êm	êm	êm	êm
ên	ên	ên	ên	ên	ên	ơn
ênh	ênh	ênh	ên	ên	ên	ơn
êp	êp	êp	êp	êp	êp	êp
êt	êt	êt	êt	êt	êt	ơt
êw	êw	êw	êw	êw	êw	êw
i	ij	ij	ij	ij	ij	ij
ia	iậ	iậ	iậ	iậ	iậ	iậ
ich	ich	ich	it	ưt[c]	it	ưt
iêc	iậk	iậk	iậk	iậk	iậk	iậk
iêm	iêm	iậm	iim	iim	im	im
iên	iên	iận	iậng	iậng	iậng	iậng
iêng	iậng	iậng	iậng	iậng	iậng	iậng
iêp	iêp	iập	iip	iip	ip	ip
iêt	iêt	iật	iậk	iậk	iậk	iậk
iêu	iêw	iậw	iậw	iw	iw	iw
im	im	im	im	im	im	im
in	in	in	in	in	in	ưn
inh	inh	inh	in	ưn[c]	in	ưn
ip	ip	ip	ip	ip	ip	ip
it	it	it	it	it	it	ưt
iu	iw	iw	iw	iw	iw	iw
o	o	o	o	o	o	o
oa	wa	wa	ôa[d]	wa	wa	(w)a[e]
oac	wak	wak	ôak?[d]	wak	wak	(w)ak[e]
oach	wăch	wech	wăt	wăt	wăt	(w)ât[e]
oai	waj	waj	oạj[d]	waj	waj	(w)aj[e]
oam	wam	wam	wam?[d]	wam	wam	(w)am[e]
oan	wan	wan	ôang[d]	wang	wang	(w)ang[e]
oang	wang	wang	ôang[d]	wang	wang	(w)ang[e]
oanh	wănh	wenh	wăn	wăn	wăn	(w)ân[e]
oao	waw	waw	waw?[d]	waw	waw	(w)aw[e]
oat	wat	wat	ôak?[d]	wak	wak	(w)ak[e]
oay	wăj	wăj	wăj	waj	waj	(w)aj[e]
oăc	wăk	wăk	wăk	wăk	wăk	(w)ăk[e]
oăm	wăm	wăm	wăm	wăm	wăm	(w)âm[e]
oăn	wăn	wăn	wăng	wăng	wăng	(w)ăng[e]
oăng	wăng	wăng	wăng	wăng	wăng	(w)ăng[e]
oăt	wăt	wăt	wăk	wăk	wăk	(w)ăk[e]

ORTHOGRAPHY	HANOI	VINH	HUE	DA-NANG	SAIGON	TRA-VINH
oc	ăwk	ăwk	ăwk	ăwk	ăwk	âwk
oe	we	we	we	we	we	(w)e[e]
oen	wen	wen	weậng	weng	weậng	(w)eậng[e]
oeo	wew	wew	wew	wew	wew	(w)ew[e]
oet	wet	wet	wek	wek	weậk	(w)eậk[e]
oi	oj	oj	oj	oj	o(ậ)j	oậj
om	om	om	om	om	om	ôm
on	on	on	ong	ong	ong	ong
ong	ăwng	ăwng	ăwng	ăwng	ăwng	âwng
oong	ong	ong	ong	ong	ong	ong
op	op	op	op	op	op	ôp
ot	ot	ot	ok	ok	ok	ok
ô	ôw	ôw	ôw	ôw	ôw	ôw
ôc	âwk	âwk	âwk	âwk	âwk	âwk
ôj	ôj	ôj	ôj	ôj	ôj	ôj
ôm	ôm	ôm	ôm	ôm	ôm	ôm
ôn	ôn	ôn	ông	ông	ông	ông
ông	âwng	âwng	âwng	âwng	âwng	âwng
ôông	ông	ông	ông	ông	ông	ông
ôp	ôp	ôp	ôp	ôp	ôp	ôp
ôt	ôt	ôt	ôk	ôk	ôk	ôk
ơ	ɤ̆	ɤ̆	ɤ̆	ɤ̆	ɤ̆	ɤ̆
ơi	ɤj	ɤj	ɤj	ɤj	ɤj	ɤj
ơm	ɤm	ɤm	ɤm	ɤm	ɤm	ôm
ơn	ɤn	ɤn	ɤng	ɤng	ɤng	ɤng
ơp	ɤp	ɤp	ɤp	ɤp	ɤp	ôp
ơt	ɤt	ɤt	ɤk	ɤk	ɤk	ɤk
u	uw	uw	uw	uw	uw	uw
ua	uậ	uậ	uậ	uậ	uậ	uậ
uân	wân	wân	uâng	wɯng	wɯng	(w)ɯng[e]
uâng	wâng	wâng	uâng	wɯng	wɯng	(w)ɯng[e]
uât	wât	wât	uâk	wɯk	wɯk	(w)ɯk[e]
uây	wâj	wâj	uâj? [d]	wâj	wâj	(w)âj[e]
uc	uk	uk	uk	uwk[e]	uk	uk
uê	wêj	wêj	wêj	wêj	wêj	(w)êj[e]
uêch	wêch	wêch	wêt	wêt	wêt	(w)ɤt[e]
uên	wên	wên	wên	wên	wên	(w)ɤn[e]
uênh	wênh	wênh	wên	wên	wên	(w)ɤn[e]

101

ORTHOGRAPHY	HANOI	VINH	HUE	DA-NANG	SAIGON	TRA-VINH
uêt	wêt	wêt	wêt	wêt	wêt	(w)ɔt[e]
ui	uj	uj	uj	uj	uj	uj
um	um	um	um	um	um	um
un	un	un	ung	ung[c]	ung	ung
ung	ung	ung	ung	uwng[c]	ung	ung
uôc	uậk	uậk	uậk	uậk	uậk	uậk
uôi	uôj	uậj	uj	uj	uj	uj
uôm	uôm	uậm	uậm	uậm	um	um
uôn	uôn	uận	uậng	uậng	uậng	uậng
uông	uậng	uậng	uậng	uậng	uậng	uậng
uôt	uôt	uật	uậk	uậk	uậk	uậk
uơ	wɤ̯	wɤ̯	wɤ̯ʔ[d]	wɤ̯	wɤ̯	(w)ɔɤ̯[e]
uơn	won	won	uơng?[d]	wong	wong	(w)ong[e]
uơt	wɔt	wɔt	uɔk?[d]	wɔk	wɔk	(w)ɔk[e]
up	up	up	up	up	up	up
ut	ut	ut	uk	uk[c]	uk	uk
uy	wij	wij	wij	wij	wij	(w)ij[e]
uya	wiậ	wiậ	wiậ	wiậ	wiậ	(w)iậ[e]
uych	wich	wich	wit	wɤt[c]	wit	(w)ɤt[e]
uyên	wiên	wiận	wiậng	wiậng	wiậng	(w)iậng[e]
uyêt	wiêt	wiật	wiậk	wiậk	wiậk	(w)iậk[e]
uynh	winh	winh	win	wɤn[c]	win	(w)ɤn[e]
uyt	wit	wit	wit	wit	wit	(w)ɤt[e]
uyu	wiw	wiw	wiw	wiw	wiw	(w)iw[e]
ư	ɯɤ̯	ɯɤ̯	ɯɤ̯	ɯɤ̯	ɯɤ̯	ɯɤ̯
ưa	ɯậ	ɯậ	ɯậ	ɯậ	ɯậ	ɯậ
ưc	ɯk	ɯk	ɯk	ɯk	ɯk	ɯk
ưi	ɯj	ɯj	ɯj	ɯj	ɯj	ɯj
ưn	ɯn	ɯn	ɯng	ɯng	ɯng	ɯng
ưng	ɯng	ɯng	ɯng	ɯnɜ	ɯng	ɯng
ươc	ɯɔk	ɯậk	ɯậk	ɯậk	ɯậk	ɯậk
ươi	ɯɔj	ɯậj	ɯj	ɯj	ɯj	ɯj
ươm	ɯɔm	ɯậm	ɯɯm	ɯɯm	ɯm	ɯm
ươn	ɯɔn	ɯận	ɯậng	ɯậng	ɯậng	ɯậng
ương	ɯɔng	ɯậng	ɯậng	ɯậng	ɯậng	ɯậng
ươp	ɯɔp	ɯập	ɯɯp	ɯɯp	ɯp	ɯp
ươt	ɯɔt	ɯật	ɯậk	ɯậk	ɯậk	ɯậk
ươu	iêw	ɯậw	ɯw	ɯw	ɯw	ɯw
ưt	ɯt	ɯt	ɯk	ɯk	ɯk	ɯk
ưu	iw	ɯw	ɯw	ɯw	ɯw	ɯw

ORTHOGRAPHY	HANOI	VINH	HUE	DA-NANG	SAIGON	TRA-VINH
y	ij	ij	ij	ij	ij	ij
yêm	iêm	iậm	iim	iim	im	im
yên	iên	iận	iậng	iậng	iậng	iậng
yêng	iậng	iậng	iậng	iậng	iậng	iậng
yêt	iêt	iật	iậk	iậk	iậk	iậk
yêu	iêw	iậw	iw	iw	iw	iw

NOTES

ᵃ After [w].

ᵇ After [ch, nh, w].

ᶜ Problematic in Đà-nẵng phonology; cf. 4.14 end. The notations [wk, wng] mean double closure (labial and dorsal), as opposed to simple dorsal closure [k, ng], for this dialect.

ᵈ Problematic in Huế phonology; cf. 4.13 end. Question marks indicate guesses based on the material available.

ᵉ No [w] after the initials [t, đ, x, th, tr, s, ch, j, l, nh, kh].

TONES*

	HANOI	VINH	HUE	DA-NANG	SAIGON AND TRA-VINH
Sắc	High rising	High rising	Mid rising	High rising	High rising
Ngang (unmarked)	High trailing	High level	Mid-high trailing	Mid-high trailing	High trailing or falling **
Ngã	High rising (glottal stricture)	Mid level (glottal stricture)	Mid rising (glottal stricture)	Mid rising	Mid rising
Hỏi	Low dropping (and rising)	Mid dropping (glottal stricture)	Mid rising (glottal stricture)	Mid rising	Mid rising
Huyền	Low trailing	Low falling	Mid-low trailing	Mid-low trailing	Low trailing
Nặng	Low dropping (glottal stricture or stop final)	Low level	Low level or dipping (glottal stricture)	Low level or dipping (glottal stricture)	Low level or dipping (stop final)

* Tones are characterized here on the basis of their variants occurring in isolated (citation) forms.

** Citation forms usually have high falling contour; occasional trailing (or even level) contour is probably an idealization of the tone, which is traditionally described as level.

CHAPTER 5

Grammatical Structure

5.1. Morphemes. Any utterance in a language may be divided into component parts, each of which carries an identifiable meaning recognizable as contributing to the meaning of the whole. Each of these parts, provided that it contains no smaller meaningful bits which contribute to the over-all meaning, is a **morph.** Every morph belongs to a **morpheme**–the class of all morphs having precisely the same meaning. Some morphs belonging to a particular morpheme sound alike, others sound different. Those which sound alike constitute a subclass called an **allomorph.** Different allomorphs of the same morpheme never contrast with one another: where one is found, others will never occur and vice versa.

For example, consider these English sentences:
> *The child played.*
> *The child slept.*

These sentences contain the morphs (minimum meaningful units) *the, child, play, -ed, the, child, slep-,* and *-t.* None of these can be divided any further into meaningful units. Of these there are some which sound alike and have the same meaning: *the* and *the, child* and *child. Play* and *slep-* have different meanings and belong to different morphemes. But *-ed* and *-t,* although they sound different, are recognized as belonging to the same morpheme, which means something like 'past action.' Each belongs to a different allomorph of that morpheme: *-ed* recurs in *prayed, -t* recurs in *crept,* but *-ed* is never found with *slep-* or *crep-,* and *-t* is never found after *play* or *pray. Slep-* represents one allomorph of a morpheme which shows a different sounding member *sleep* in *The child sleeps.* Here again *sleep* appears before *-s* but not before *-t,* while *slep-* precedes *-t* but not *-s.* This is called **complementary (noncontrastive) distribution.**

Vietnamese has a variety of morphs of the sort we have identified in English *sleep, slep-, -ed, -t, the,* and so forth. They consist of consonants,

105

vocalics, and tones. In addition there are other meaningful elements which accompany them in sentences—the intonational elements, or features of phrase rhythm and melody. Technically, in the opinion of many linguists, these elements should also be analyzed as morphs belonging to special morphemes, but the technicalities need not concern us here. It is simpler to treat them as occurrences of stresses (2.72) and intonations (2.73) accompanying syllables which make up the vast majority of morphs. They single out certain elements for special attention and convey notions about the speaker's attitude toward what he is saying. Their functions in these connections are discussed in 5.2-3.

Usually in speaking about the composition of larger linguistic forms it is convenient to say that morphemes **occur**. Strictly speaking, on any one occasion only a morph occurs; this morph represents some morpheme. In the following discussion, however, the convention is adopted that morphs and allomorphs will be mentioned only where specifically pertinent to the matter at hand, otherwise the term *morpheme* will be used.

The overwhelming majority of Vietnamese morphemes are composed of allomorphs precisely one syllable long. It is for this reason that Vietnamese has often been described as a "monosyllabic" language. However, there are in addition some morphemes with allomorphs comprising less than a syllable, and others with allomorphs of two or three syllables.[1]

Less than a syllable: đ- (with first register tones) 'relative location' in đ-ây 'here'
-ây (with even tones) 'near speaker' in đ-ây 'here'
'just mentioned' in bẩ (S) 'lady just mentioned, she' (cf. bà lady)

One syllable: sớm early, đi go, có exist, ghế chair, tôi I
Two syllables: thình-lình sudden, Sài-gòn Saigon, va-li suitcase
Three syllables: Thủ-dầu-một (town approximately 30 km north of Saigon), com-mi-nít (S) communist

5.2. Stresses (2.72) denote three degrees of emphasis, varying from very great to very little. Each syllable is accompanied by one stress. In cases where stress is pertinent to the discussion in this book it is marked by the symbols described in 2.72.

5.21. Degrees of Emphasis. Heavy stress singles out the syllable or syllables of each pause group which carry the heaviest burden of convey-

[1] For a more detailed discussion of this matter see Thompson 1963. Unfamiliar terms in the following examples are explained in 7.12.

ing information. **Weak stress** accompanies syllables which bear the low-est information conveying load in the pause group. They often refer to things which have been brought up earlier or which are expectable in the general context. Other syllables are accompanied by **medium stress**.

> °*Tôi* °*không* '*biết.* I don't know. ["I not know"]
> °*Không* '*biết!* Don't *know!* (i.e., 'stop asking me.') ["not know"]
> '*Nói phải* '*có người nói* '*đi nói* '*lại chớ* '*bắt* °*người* °*ta* '*nói* °*một mình* '*hoài!* For a conversation [you] ought to have people talking back and forth, not make somebody talk alone all the time! ["speak ought exist person speak go speak come prohibit constrain some-one (*người ta*) speak alone (*một mình*) continually"]

5.22. Emphatic Patterning. In noncontrastive situations, heavy stress typically accompanies a particular kind of element in each pause group. Certain other elements regularly have weak stress, the remainder, medium stress. This distribution of stresses constitutes the emphatic patterning of the pause group. Since emphatic patterning can only be described in terms of the elements which stresses accompany—elements which have not yet themselves been described—a detailed description must be delayed. Certain individual features of the system are discussed in connection with other items of the grammatical structure (Chapters 6-11); the over-all sys-tem itself is treated in 12.5.

5.3. Intonations (2.73) convey certain general attitudes of speakers to-ward what they are saying. The majority of syllables are accompanied by **decreasing intonation**, which signals primarily that the speaker intends to continue. It is basically distinctive only in contrast with other intona-tions, which for the most part accompany only final syllables in pause groups. The latter are **terminal intonations**.

5.31. Decreasing Intonation accompanies syllables which are not sin-gled out for attention in intonational terms. A pause group ending with this intonation conveys the notion that the speaker has not completed his speech. At the end of an utterance it may mean that he has been interrupted by some thought or external stimulus, or simply that he is leaving some-thing unsaid. Internally in an utterance it signals that the sentence con-tinues in the following pause group. Pause groups ending with decreasing intonation are sometimes symbolized in print by a comma (,) at the end, and occasionally by a sequence of three periods (...).[2]

[2] This symbol also has other meanings; cf. 3.54.

Tôi 'đến nhà, má tôi mở cửa 'ra, tôi 'vô. (S) I arrived at the house, my mother opened the door, and I went in. ["I arrive house, mother I open door exit, I enter"]

Nếu tôi không 'đi được ... If I can't go ... ["If I not go successfully"]

5.32. Increasing Intonation (spread tone) occurs occasionally with medial syllables, although it is more common with final syllables. Within a pause group it singles out a form which the speaker wishes to emphasize particularly, often in a contrastive way. It is sometimes suggested in printed texts by italicization or in writing by underlining or some other such device, but it is mainly a feature of conversation or expressive reading which goes unmarked in the written language.

Ông °có 'biết không? Do you *know* (or just surmise)? ["gentleman exist know! not"]

Accompanying final syllables it signals a lack of concern for or a certain detachment from the result of the speech. It includes exclamative statements and commands, and questions to which the answer is of relatively small interest to the speaker. It is occasionally symbolized in the written language by an exclamation point (!); however, many sentences followed by a period or question mark might well be spoken with this intonation.

Tôi không 'đi! I'm not going! ["I not go!"]

Chừng nào °cưới 'vợ làm cho °người ta 'hay! (S) When you get married, let people know! (slightly annoyed) ["point-in-time whichever give-marriage-gifts-for wife act give someone (*người ta*) find-out!"]

Ông đi 'không! Are you going or not! ["gentleman go not!"]

Muốn hỏi °về chuyện 'gì! What did you want to ask about? (I'm so tired of asking that I don't really care.) ["wish ask concerning conversation-topic whatever!"]

5.33. Fading Intonation (lowered tone) accompanies the final syllable (occasionally two or more syllables) of a pause group. It signals that the speaker assumes a certain result from his speech—that the hearer will react in a certain way. It includes commands, statements of fact which the speaker assumes the hearer will accept as true, and questions to which the speaker assumes the answer. In print the large majority of occurrences of the period (.) suggest this intonation. However, many questions (written or printed with question marks at the end) are spoken with this intonation.

Ông cho tôi 'coi. (S) Let me see. ["gentleman give I inspect."]

Tôi đi °*Sài-*'*gòn.* I'm going to Saigon. ["I go Saigon."]

Ông °có '*biết* không? Do you *know?* (assumes negative reply: i.e., 'I realize you suspect, but can you be certain?') ["gentleman exist know! not."]

5.34. Sustaining Intonation (raised tone) accompanies the final syllable (occasionally two or more syllables) of a pause group. It signals that the speaker is unable or for some other reason fails to predict the result of his speech. It includes doubtful statements, emotionally colored and indecisive imperatives and exhortations, and informational questions. Questions are generally symbolized by the question mark (?); indecisive or doubtful statements are also occasionally so indicated. Other sentences of this sort are generally printed with a period at the end.

Chừng nào ông '*đi* °*Sài-gòn?* When are you going to Saigon? ["point-in-time whichever gentleman go Saigon?"]

°*Tôi muốn* '*hỏi ông.* I'd like to ask you a question. (doubtful as to whether the hearer is agreeable) ["I wish ask gentleman ?"]

'*Nói* °*chuyện đi.* Go ahead and talk! (impatient) ["speak conversation-topic go?"]

5.35. Other Intonational Features. Vietnamese speakers also make use of more exaggerated devices—as do speakers of most linguistic communities—for conveying a variety of emotional attitudes. Most common is the use of a generally higher level of pitch for an utterance—the entire range is raised. Several such successive levels may be observed in many speakers; it appears that the higher the pitch range of an utterance, the more emotional intensity is conveyed. None of these features is represented in any way in the written language. A detailed study of these phenomena remains to be accomplished.

A colorful device which is frequently heard in colloquial usage consists of the repetition of a key form in a very high register (and prolonged a good deal) immediately after its first occurrence, followed in turn by a second repetition in normal register.

°*Con* '*chó ấy,* '*to,* '*to!* [very high pitch] '*to.* That dog's *big*—oh, so big! ["animal dog just-mentioned large large! large."]

5.4. Constituent Analysis. Every utterance in any language may be analyzed into component parts. One type of analysis is extremely helpful in understanding the structure of utterances: it is the analysis into two or more parts which balance one another in the makeup of the whole. Each of these parts may then be subjected to similar analysis, and so on until the

level of single morphemes is reached and no further divisions can be made
The parts of a given section of an utterance in such an analysis are the
immediate constituents of that section. For example, in the English sentence *John's brother is playing tennis* the immediate constituents are
John's brother and *is playing tennis.* In turn, the immediate constituents
of *John's brother* are *John's* and *brother,* and those of *is playing tennis*
are *is playing* and *tennis. John's* has the immediate constituents *John*
and *'s; is playing* has *is* and *playing,* and *playing* in turn is composed of
play and *-ing.* Thus the sentence has been divided into immediate constituents in successive steps until only indivisible morphemes remain; these
are the **ultimate constituents.** (For a native speaker of a language or for
a linguist who knows the language well, division into immediate constituents seems relatively simple and straightforward in a majority of cases.
They recognize intuitively that the analysis *John's* plus *brother is playing
tennis* and *John's brother is* plus *playing tennis* are not as valid as the
analysis *John's brother* plus *is playing tennis.* This intuition really represents a deep sense of the structure of the language. There are, of course,
cases where it is difficult to choose between two or more apparently
equally acceptable divisions. For a more detailed discussion of the subject and rigorous techniques for the application of the theory, see Hockett
1958, Chapter 17; and Wells 1947.)

All items isolated in this type of analysis are **constituents** of the
passage in question. Constituents consisting of more than one word (5.53)
are **phrases.**

In any passage of more than two forms there are sequences which, although they involve items in the order in which they occur in the passage
at hand, are not constituents of that passage. For example, in the English
sentence just analyzed such sequences as *is play-, 's brother, -ing tennis*
are obviously not constituents; in the same way *John's brother is* is not a
constituent of this sentence. *Playing tennis* is not a constituent of this
sentence, although the identical sequence in the sentence *Playing tennis
is fun* would be a constituent. In other words, a constituent of a given
passage is one of the immediate constituents of the next larger constituent of that passage.

From the point of view of a particular constituent, the larger phrase of
which it is one immediate constituent is its **constitute,** and each of the
other immediate constituents is a **partner.** In the example cited in the
preceding paragraph *John's brother* is one of the immediate constituents
of the constitute *John's brother is playing tennis,* and *is playing tennis*
is its partner. Similarly, *is playing* and *tennis* are the partner immediate
constituents of the constitute *is playing tennis.*

110

5.41. Sentences. In spoken Vietnamese sentences are set off from one another by terminal intonations. The first sentence begins after silence on the part of a particular speaker and ends with the first terminal intonation. The next sentence begins immediately after this terminal intonation and ends with the next terminal intonation, and so on. In printed material, of course, sentences are marked with a capital letter at the beginning, and a period, question mark, or exclamation point at the end (3.54).

In immediate constituent analysis, intonations and stresses are isolated first, leaving the balance of the sentence. Since this part of the analysis does not add anything to the discussion of individual sentence analyses, it is presumed to have been already accomplished in the detailed discussions below.[3]

Responsive utterances are those in which a speaker responds to something in a directly preceding utterance by another speaker; speeches which are not thus characterized are **independent utterances**. Sentences which occur in at least some environments as opening sentences in independent utterances are **independent**; other sentences (that is, those occurring only as second or later sentences in utterances or as opening sentences in responsive utterances) are **dependent**. It is useful to make these distinctions in order to provide a firm basis for defining various sentence types. Certain constructions form independent sentences; others do not.

5.42. Models. The syntactic structure of any language is observable as a relatively small number of patterns in each of which the elements (although consisting of infinitely varied morpheme sequences) bear the same basic relationship to one another. Longer sequences are seen to have the same function as far shorter sequences—that is, a longer sequence bears the same relationship to its immediate constituent partner as a shorter sequence in the same position. This is conveniently described by saying that the shorter sequence is the **model**[4] of the longer one, and that the longer one is an **expansion** of the shorter one. For example, in the English sentence analyzed in 5.4 (*John's brother is playing tennis*) a model for *John's brother* is *Jim*, as in *Jim is playing tennis*. Similarly, a model for *is playing tennis* is *works*, as *John's brother works*. Conversely, *John's brother* and *is playing tennis* are expansions respectively of *Jim* and *works*.

Often in Vietnamese one of the immediate constituents of a particular constitute is a model of that constitute. Such a constitute is a **nuclear**

---

[3] A similar preliminary analysis was likewise omitted from the English examples above.

[4] This is a different use of the term 'model' from that in Wells 1947, although it is derived from the concept involved there.

model, provided that the referential relationship remains the same when
the model is substituted for its constitute in the context. To state it somewhat differently, a nuclear model is an immediate constituent which can
replace its constitute in the larger context, maintaining the same basic
grammatical and referential relationship to that context. Sometimes a constitute has more than one nuclear model. The method of analysis into constituents is illustrated in the following example.

> *Ngày xưa có người hiếu-lợi, một hôm ra chợ, gặp ngày chợ phiên vừa
> đông người đến buôn bán vừa lắm đồ hàng.* Once upon a time there
> was a greedy person, [who] one day went out [into] the market
> place on the day of a fair [when there were] both a great many
> people who had come to do business and a great deal of mer-
> chandise.

This sentence consists of the two immediate constituents *Ngày xưa
có người hiếu-lợi* plus *một hôm ra chợ, gặp ngày chợ phiên vừa đông người
đến buôn bán vừa lắm đồ hàng.* The first is a (nuclear) model of the sentence as a whole, since it could replace the entire sentence in this context—the beginning of a story.

Ngày xưa có người hiếu-lợi is itself a constitute containing the immediate constituents *ngày xưa* 'days of old' and *có người hiếu-lợi* 'there was
a greedy person.' The second is a model, but its partner is not. The sentence containing only this second element in this position occurs elsewhere[5] with the same relationship of parts: *Có người hiếu-lợi, một hôm ra
chợ ...* (etc.) 'There was a greedy person, [who] one day went out [into]
the market place ...' The other constituent, *ngày xưa*, also occurs in this
position with the partner, but the relationship of the two parts is different:
ngày xưa một hôm ra chợ... 'once upon a time [someone] one day went
out [into] the market place ...' *Ngày xưa* is analyzed into *ngày* plus *xưa*,
with the model *xưa*: this analysis is based on the existence of the constitute *xưa có người hiếu-lợi* 'In former times there was a greedy person' with
the same interrelationship of parts. *Ngày* 'day', however, does not occur
in this position.

The immediate constituents of *có người hiếu-lợi* are *có* 'exist' and
người hiếu-lợi 'greedy person'; *có* is a model of the constitute: in the
phrase *ngày xưa có* 'once upon a time there was' the same basic relationship of parts is preserved. (Such a constitute is possible as a whole sentence, for example, in answer to another speaker's question 'Do you suppose there ever was such a greedy person?') *Người hiếu-lợi*, however, is

---

[5] In practical terms the analyst need not go through a large amount of material to find
such constitutes. He may simply ask an informant—a native speaker of the language—
whether a given constitute is possible.

not a model of this constitute; it does not occur with this same relationship to *ngày xưa*. *Người hiếu-lợi* itself contains the model *người* 'person' and *hiếu-lợi* 'greedy' (not a model). *Hiếu-lợi* is composed of *hiếu* 'be fond of' and *lợi* 'profit'; neither is a model, since neither combines with *người* in this sort of constitute.

In the remainder of the sentence, which is itself not a nuclear model of the whole sentence, the first division is into *một hôm ra chợ* 'one day went out [into] the market place' and *gặp ngày chợ phiên vừa đông người đến buôn bán vừa lắm đồ hàng* 'met with the day of a fair [when there were] both a great many people who had come to do business and a great deal of merchandise',[6] each of which is a model of the over-all constitute.

Một hôm ra chợ consists of *một hôm* 'one day' and *ra chợ* 'went out [into] the market place', and the latter is a model. *Ra chợ* has the model *ra* 'go out'. *Một hôm* has the immediate constituents *một* 'one' and *hôm* 'day', neither of which is a model.

The balance of the sentence consists of *gặp ngày chợ phiên* 'ran into a fair day' (a model) and the rest of the phrase, which is not a model. The first phrase has the model *gặp* 'meet up with' and the non-model *ngày chợ phiên* 'day of a fair'. *Ngày* 'day' is a model of its constitute; its partner, also a model, is further analyzable into *chợ* 'market(place)' and *phiên* 'a turn in orderly succession' (both models). (*Chợ phiên* refers to the fair which takes place at regular intervals at a particular market.)

Vừa đông người đến buôn bán vừa lắm đồ hàng 'both crowds of people arriving to do business and lots of merchandise' has three immediate constituents: the correlative *vừa ... vừa* 'both ... and' (not a model), *đông người đến buôn bán* 'teeming [crowds of] people arriving to do business', and *lắm đồ hàng* 'many things and merchandise' (both models). *Đông người* 'teeming [crowds of] people' is a model, while its partner *đến buôn bán* 'arriving to do business' is not. The former contains *đông* 'be in crowds' (not a model) and the model *người* 'person'. *Đến buôn bán* 'arrive to do business' contains the models *đến* 'arrive' and *buôn bán* 'do business' (in which *buôn* 'buy [for reselling]' and *bán* 'sell' are both models). Finally, *lắm đồ hàng* contains *lắm* 'much, many' (not a model) and *đồ hàng* (a model), the latter containing *đồ* 'thing' and *hàng* 'goods, merchandise' (both models).

Some constituents are **discontinuous**; that is, they are in two or more parts which are separated by part or all of other constituents. In the example above the correlative *vừa ... vừa* 'both ... and' is such a discontinuous constituent.

[6] The translation of parts of the sentence under study are intended to point up the relationships of the parts. There are therefore some minor differences from the somewhat freer translation given earlier of the sentence as a whole.

Some constituents are models of their constitutes, others are not. It is typical that constitutes which are themselves models nearly always are analyzable into immediate constituents at least one of which is a nuclear model. Non-models are frequently not so analyzable.

5.43. Heads and Complements.

Nuclear models of those constitutes which are themselves either nuclear models or complete sentences are called **heads.** Non-model partners of heads are called **complements.** The analysis of the sentence of 5.42 is repeated below in schematic form with (nuclear) models, heads, and complements labeled.

Ngày xưa có người hiếu-lợi (model, head)
   ngày xưa (complement)
      ngày 'day'
      xưa 'in former times' (model)
   có người hiếu-lợi (model, head)
      có 'exist' (model, head)
      người hiếu-lợi (complement)
         người 'person' (model)
         hiếu-lợi 'be greedy'
            hiếu 'be fond of'
            lợi 'profit'
một hôm ra chợ, gặp ngày chợ phiên vừa đông người đến buôn bán vừa lắm đồ hàng (complement)
   một hôm ra chợ (model)
      một hôm (complement)
         một 'one'
         hôm 'day'
      ra chợ (model, head)
         ra 'go out' (model, head)
         chợ 'market (place)' (complement)
   gặp ngày chợ phiên vừa đông người đến buôn bán vừa lắm đồ hàng (model)
      gặp ngày chợ phiên (model, head)
         gặp 'meet [with]' (model, head)
         ngày chợ phiên (complement)
            ngày 'day' (model)
            chợ phiên (model)
               chợ 'market (place)' (model, head)
               phiên 'a turn in orderly succession' (model, head)
      vừa đông người đến buôn bán vừa lắm đồ hàng (complement)

vừa ... vừa 'both ... and'
đông người đến buôn bán (model)
  đông người (model, head)
    đông 'be in crowds' (complement)
    người 'person' (model, head)
  đến buôn bán (complement)
    đến 'arrive' (model)
    buôn bán (model)
      buôn 'buy [for reselling]' (model, head)
      bán 'sell' (model, head)
lắm đồ hàng (model)
  lắm 'many, profuse' (complement)
  đồ hàng (model, head)
    đồ 'thing, item' (model, head)
    hàng 'merchandise' (model, head)

5.44. Analysis of Complement Constitutes.

Complements often have no nuclear models among their immediate constituents (e.g., *một hôm* 'one day' in the phrase *một hôm ra chợ* 'went out into the market one day' analyzed in 5.42). It is similarly true that the nuclear model of a phrase serving as a complement is sometimes different from the nuclear model of the same phrase with the same meaning when it is itself a model. Consideration of a large number of sentences shows that the kinds of elements which occur as complements are extremely varied. Thus nuclear models of complement constitutes reveal considerably less about the structure than nuclear models of larger nuclear models. For this reason complement constitutes are more meaningfully analyzed the same way as identical phrases occurring themselves as nuclear models.

In the sentence analyzed in 5.42-43 the following constitutes (among others) were identified as complements: *ngày xưa* once upon a time, *người hiếu-lợi* greedy person, *một hôm* one day, *ngày chợ phiên* fair day. Each of these occurs elsewhere as a head, as demonstrated in the following sample analyses.

Ngày xưa ấy có người hiếu-lợi. In those days of old of which we have been speaking there was a greedy person.
  ngày xưa ấy 'days of old just mentioned' (complement)
    ngày xưa (model)
      ngày 'day' (model, head)
      xưa 'in former times' (complement)
    ấy 'just mentioned'
In this example the difference in analysis is important as exemplary of the

general principle: *ngày xưa* as a complement has the nuclear model *xưa*, which occurs by itself in this complement position; but the expanded constitute *ngày xưa ấy* reveals a different analysis of its nuclear *ngày xưa*: here *ngày* is model, since *ngày ấy* 'the days just mentioned' occurs, while **xưa ấy* does not.[7]

Có người hiếu-lợi ấy. [There] existed the greedy person referred to.
   có 'exist' (model, head)
   người hiếu-lợi ấy 'greedy person just mentioned' (complement)
      người hiếu-lợi 'greedy person' (model)
         người 'person' (model, head)
         hiếu-lợi 'greedy' (complement)
      ấy 'just mentioned'

The analysis of the constitute *người hiếu-lợi* as a complement in the original sentence happens not to be different from its analysis as a nuclear model, demonstrated here.

Một hôm lạnh ra chợ. One cold day [he] went out [into] the market place.
   một hôm lạnh 'one cold day' (complement)
      một hôm 'one day' (model)
         một 'one' (complement)
         hôm 'day' (model, head)
      lạnh 'be cold'
   ra chợ 'went out [into] the market place' (model, head)

This example clarifies the analysis of *một hôm*, unanalyzable in the original sentence.

By this extension of the nuclear model principle all parts of all sentences can be analyzed down to the word level; the analysis of complex words (such as *hiếu-lợi* 'greedy') is discussed in 5.55.

5.5. Morphology.

While morphemes are the smallest isolable units which convey meaning (5.1) and are the ultimate constituents (5.4) of any sentence in the language, it is difficult or impossible to understand the structure of sentences as simple sequences of morphemes. It is necessary to identify larger units, themselves composed of morphemes, which appear in varying relationships to one another as constituents of sentences. These larger units are **words**: they are the minimum freely distributed units of which sentences are composed.

Traditionally each Vietnamese syllable has been regarded as a word. As a matter of fact, a great proportion of Vietnamese words—especially

---

[7] Here and elsewhere the asterisk (*) is used at the beginning of a form which does not occur.

those most current in the spoken language—are just one syllable long. The generalization is presumably to some extent based on this fact. Probably equally strong in the traditional attitude is another factor: Vietnamese was first written with symbols borrowed from the Chinese, and Chinese characters typically represent one syllable each and are traditionally considered to represent as well one word each.

However, it is not really accurate to say that each Vietnamese syllable is a word or each word a syllable. In the first place, there are quite obviously indivisible forms—morphemes—consisting of more than one syllable: *thình-lình* 'sudden', *Sài-gòn* 'Saigon', *va-li* 'suitcase', *Thủ-dầu-một* (name of a town about 30 km north of Saigon), *com-mi-nít* (S) 'communist', and so forth. Secondly, a far greater number of morphemes (which themselves do consist of one syllable each) behave in quite a different way from most of the minimum forms which were isolated as ultimate constituents of the sentences analyzed in 5.4. And finally there are a great number of polysyllabic forms containing elements which are described by native speakers as having no meaning by themselves (that is, outside the combination at hand). It is then obviously necessary to define words in reference to something other than syllables. It is also important to recognize different types of morphemes in terms of their relative freedom of occurrence.

The study of the makeup of various kinds of words is **morphology.** Syntax (5.6) is the study of arrangements of words in phrases and sentences. The word thus furnishes the line of separation between these two major divisions of grammar: morphology concerns the grammatical relationships of elements below the word level; syntax concerns the grammatical relationships of elements at the word level and above.

5.51. Basic Free Forms. Minimum pause groups are the smallest bits

of a normal conversational speech which occur by themselves, isolated by preceding and following pauses (although not necessarily constituting whole sentences).[8] Each minimum pause group includes one stress (5.2) for each of its syllables and one or more intonations (5.3). Beside these intonational elements there is at least one (ordinary) morpheme (5.1). Any pause group containing more than one morpheme is minimum if none or only one of those morphemes occurs in other speeches as a (different) minimum pause group. Any constituent which occurs on some occasion as a minimum pause group is a **basic free form.**

'*Đi*. Go [ahead]. (e.g., said to a child who has asked permission to
to go somewhere)

---

[8] Any syllable, of course, can be pronounced by itself, but this citation of individual forms is not part of ordinary conversation. For the purposes of this definition such speech events are excluded.

º*Cũng* '*di.* [He] went, too. (e.g., in answer to a question such as
'What happened to him?')

º*Liên-*'*hiệp quốc.* The United Nations. (e.g., in answer to the question 'What agency sponsored the conference?')

Quốc-'*gia.* The [federal] government. (e.g., in answer to the question 'Do you work for the government or a private company?')

Each of these examples is a minimum pause group and each morpheme sequence is a basic free form. In the first example, *di* 'go' is a single morpheme. The second contains two morphemes, *cũng* 'likewise' and *di* 'go', but only *di* occurs elsewhere (e.g., in the first example) as a minimum pause group (i.e., as a basic free form); *cũng* is not found in this position. The third contains three morphemes, *liên* 'unite', *hiệp* 'join', and *quốc* 'nation', of which only *hiệp* occurs also as a basic free form. The immediate constituents (5.4) of the third example are *liên-hiệp* 'unite' and *quốc* 'nation.' *Liên-hiệp* occurs elsewhere as a basic free form. In *quốc-gia* neither *quốc* 'nation' nor *gia* 'household; establishment' occurs anywhere as a basic free form.

5.52. Morpheme Types. A morpheme which occurs either as a basic free form or (on at least some occasions) as the partner of an immediate constituent which is greater than a basic free form is a **free morpheme.** Other morphemes (those which do not occur either as basic free forms or as partners of immediate constituents greater than a basic free form) are **bound morphemes** (called *restricted words* in Emeneau 1951).

In the examples of 5.51, *di* 'go' and *hiệp* 'join' (which occur as basic free forms) and *cũng* 'likewise' (which occurs as partner of immediate constituents greater than a basic free form) are free morphemes. *Cũng*, for example, occurs in the constitute *cũng như cha tôi* 'like my father'; here the immediate constituents are *cũng* plus *như cha tôi*, and *như cha tôi* 'like my father' is larger than a basic free form, since it contains two morphemes (*cha* 'father' and *tôi* 'I') which occur themselves in other situations as basic free forms. *Liên* 'unite' and *quốc* 'nation' (which do not occur either as basic free forms or as partners of constituents larger than a basic free form) are bound morphemes.

5.53. Words. Single free morphemes (5.52) and basic free forms (5.51) containing no more than one free morpheme (or none at all) are **words.** That is, words are either (1) single free morphemes such as *di* 'go' or *cũng* 'likewise' in the examples of 5.51; or (2) basic free forms consisting entirely of bound morphemes, such as *quốc-gia* 'nation, country' (containing the bound morphemes *quốc* 'nation' and *gia* 'household; establishment'); or (3) basic free forms containing one free element and one or more bound morphemes, such as *liên-hiệp* 'unite' (bound morpheme *liên* 'unite' and free morpheme *hiệp* 'join'), *Liên-hiệp quốc* 'United Nations', or *rõ-rệt* 'be very clear, obvious' (containing the free morpheme *rõ* 'be clear' and a bound morpheme denoting intensification in the allomorph - *rệt*). Words of type (1) are **simple,** containing only one morpheme; those of types (2) and (3) are **complex,** containing more than one morpheme.

Words are **independent,** occurring as basic free forms (e.g., *đi* go, *quốc-gia* nation, country, *liên-hiệp* unite); and **dependent,** not occurring as basic free forms (e.g., *cũng* likewise). Dependent words in general are relatively few, and only a handful of complex dependent words have been identified. Independent words, on the other hand, are extremely numerous, both simple and complex. The large majority of words in the everyday spoken language are simple, whereas complex words more frequently belong rather to written or formal style.

5.54. Simple Words are largely monosyllabic, consisting of morphemes with monosyllabic allomorphs (5.1), but there are also many polysyllabic simple words.

Some dissyllabic simple words are **reduplicative**—their two syllables are similar in sound. There are **perfect reduplicative words,** consisting of two identical syllables, and **partial reduplicative words,** containing similar (but not identical) syllables. Those in which the similarity of syllables consists of identical initial consonants or clusters are called **alliterative.** Those in which the similarity lies in the nucleus (vocalic, with final consonant, if any) are called **riming.** Reduplicative simple words appear exactly like reduplicative complex words (7.11).

Many reduplicative simple words have onomatopoetic meaning. Many nonreduplicative polysyllabic simple words are place names. Trisyllabic simple words include a few place names and some common words (mostly borrowings from foreign languages).

> Monosyllabic simple words: *đi* go, *cũng* likewise, *sớm* early, *có*
> exist, *ghế* chair, *tôi* I
> Dissyllabic simple words, nonreduplicative: *Sài-gòn* Saigon, *va-li*
> suitcase
> Dissyllabic simple words, reduplicative: *cạc- cạc* cry of a duck
> (perfect); *thỉnh- thoảng* now and then, *oái- oăm* be complicated in a
> strange way (initial [w-]) (partial, alliterative); *thình-lình* sudden,
> *đồi-mồi* marine tortoise (partial, riming)
> Trisyllabic simple words: *Thủ-dầu-một* (a town approximately 30 km
> north of Saigon), *com-mi-nít* (S) communist

5.55. Complex Words contain one or more bound morphemes and one free morpheme (or none at all). Bound morphemes having only a single mono-syllabic allomorph each (5.1) are **pseudo-bases.** Other bound morphemes (having multiple allomorphs or allomorphs shorter than one syllable) are **affixes.** Words containing pseudo-bases are **pseudo-compounds.** Words containing affixes are **derivatives.**

Pseudo-compounds resemble compounds and their pseudo-bases resemble the bases of compounds (5.56). They often contain only pseudo-bases, but there are also many forms containing one free morpheme. Pseudo-compounds are treated in detail in Chapter 6.

> Examples containing only pseudo-bases: *quốc-gia* nation, country (*quốc* 'nation' and *gia* 'household; establishment'), *bình-an* be well, safe (*bình* 'be calm, peaceful' and *an* 'be assured, peaceful, safe'), *tác-giả* author (*tác* 'create something artistic' and *giả* 'one who accomplishes something').
>
> Examples containing a free morpheme: *Mỹ-quốc* America (with free morpheme *Mỹ* 'America'), *bình-yên* be well, safe (with free morpheme *yên* 'be calm, quiet'), *học-giả* scholar (with free morpheme *học* 'study').

With a few important exceptions derivatives contain an affix as one immediate constituent and as the other an element which appears elsewhere as a basic free form (i.e., is a word by itself). The latter is the **base** of the derivative. Bases are of various sorts, as the examples below demonstrate. A very few derivatives have no base; they consist of two affixes each. Derivatives are treated in detail in Chapter 7.

> Baseless: *đây* 'here': *đ-* (with first register tones) 'relative location', *-ây* (with even tones) 'near speaker'
> Free morpheme as base: *rõ-rệt* 'be very clear, obvious': *rõ* 'be clear'
> Compound as base: *bàn-ghế bàn-ghiếc* (S) 'any old sort of furniture': *bàn-ghế* 'furniture'
> Derivative as base: *sạch-nhách sạch-nhẹ* 'be completely clean; all finished, exhausted': *sạch-nhách* id.

It is likely that there are derivatives having pseudo-compounds as bases, but no examples have been recorded.

5.56. Compound Words. In general a sequence of two or more free morphemes (5.52) constitutes a sequence of two or more words (5.53). However, there are borderline cases where such sequences appear to be more like complex words (5.55). Such sequences are called **compound words** or simply **compounds.** The formal characteristics of compounds are not entirely clear, and in many individual cases it is difficult to determine whether a morpheme sequence constitutes a compound or a phrase. How-ever, compounds are generally distinguished from phrases on the basis of the following factors: compounds have only two immediate constituents; they regularly have a heavier stress (5.2) accompanying their final constituent except in circumstances where both constituents have medium stress; they are always themselves constituents and do not correspond to expanded forms with either of their constituents complemented by another element. Phrases are not limited in any of these ways.

For example, the sequence *người ở* consists of two free morphemes *người* 'person' and *ở* 'be located, reside [at a certain place]'. The sequence occurs sometimes as a phrase meaning 'person located (or residing)', sometimes as a compound meaning 'servant'. The sequence is ambiguous in the following sentence: *Nhà này không có người 'ở* . It may mean either 'There is no one living in this house' or 'There is no servant in this house.' However, a comparable phrase occurs with *người* modified by the demonstrative *nào*: *Nhà này không °có người nào 'ở*. 'There is no one (at all) living in this house'. The analysis of the constituent *người nào ở* is clearly *người nào* plus *ở*, and *người* is the nuclear model of *người nào*: thus the relationship of *người* and *ở* is similar. No such possibility exists for the compound. A sentence meaning 'There is no servant (at all) in this house' occurs—*Nhà này không °có người 'ở nào* —with the element *người ở* still a constituent, modified by *nào*.

Người 'ở nhà này °là 'bạn tôi is similarly ambiguous: it means either 'The person living in this house is my friend' or 'The servant in this house is my friend.' However, with weaker emphasis on *ở* than on *người* it is clear that the phrase—not the compound—is involved: *Người °ở nhà này °là 'bạn tôi*. 'The person (living) in this house is my friend.'

Like compounds in English and other languages, Vietnamese compounds frequently have meanings which are recognizable as related to the meanings of their constituents but appear to involve specialized relationships of the underlying elements. Sometimes the meaning of the compound seems extremely remote from that of its constituents: *người ta* 'one, someone, people in general' contains the elements *người* 'person' and *ta* 'you and I'; it contrasts with a phrase meaning 'our people.'

Compounds are treated in detail in Chapter 6.

5.57. Vietnamese Designations for Meaningful Elements.
There are a number of native forms which are used to refer to wordlike units. Since the definition of "word" provided here is outside the tradition, there is naturally no Vietnamese expression which fits it exactly. The forms which do occur lack precision in other ways as well. It will be helpful to discuss the more common elements here.

The free morpheme **chữ** most often refers to a written or printed syllable—the unit appearing with a space preceding and following—although it sometimes refers to a longer sequence, the syllables of which are connected by hyphens. In some contexts it means a Chinese-type character, in others a letter of the romanized script or some other written symbol (the latter use presumably derived from the former). As a bound element in many literary forms and in a few common words there is the pseudo-base tự with a similar range of meanings. These forms refer fairly regularly to monosyllabic elements identified here as morphemes.

For reference to elements of the spoken language there are more forms in everyday use. The most common is the free morpheme **tiếng**, which in some contexts means simply 'sound, noise' and in others 'language, spoken language, dialect'. It is also widely used to refer to individual syllables as units in the spoken language, and sometimes to groups of syllables having much the same characteristics as the words defined in 5.53. The free morpheme **lời** 'word, words, expression, speech' generally refers to elements constituting the whole or a part of a particular speech act. (It thus contrasts with *tiếng*, which refers to the abstract entity that recurs in various speech acts.) Corresponding pseudo-bases are **ngôn** 'speech, (spoken) word' and **từ** 'word, expression, part of speech.'

In this connection it seems important to suggest that the student should attempt to define precisely for himself the sphere of reference of each Vietnamese morpheme—especially of each pseudo-base—he meets with. For example, compare *từ-điển* 'dictionary (containing citations of words and expressions)' and *tự-điển* 'dictionary of monosyllabic morphemes (with Chinese characters).'

The vague status of definable words is reflected in the written language by considerable vacillation about the writing of polysyllabic items. In general, the following kinds of polysyllabic words are hyphenated (3.53): (a) Sino-Vietnamese forms (pseudo-compounds) which have not become so common that their origin has been generally forgotten; (b) derivatives (5.55) containing syllables which are meaningless as isolated elements; (c) derivatives with the connotation of attenuation (7.43); and (d) compounds denoting collectives (6.22). Many other compound and complex words are written simply as successive (apparently independent) syllables. Of them the Vietnamese speaker will often say something like *Hai (ba ...) chữ (tiếng) này đi với nhau.* 'These two (three ...) words go together.'

5.6. Syntax is the study of the arrangements of words in phrases and sentences (cf. 5.5 and 5.53). Constituent analysis (5.4) makes it possible to identify interrelationships of words occurring in groups in the flow of speech. Certain words are so severely limited in distribution that they provide a guide to more intricate relationships of other words. By means of these guide words and the relationships revealed by constituent analysis, classes of words are established, each class containing all those words which have the same grammatical function. This type of analysis replaces the traditional Vietnamese system of "parts of speech," which clearly rests on the grammatical structure of other languages (primarily French). Since the grammatical classes thus established are necessarily somewhat different from the traditional ones, the formal grounds on which they are based will be clearly stated so that the student can learn to identify and classify forms for himself.

5.61. Phrases and Constructions. Phrases are constituents consisting of more than one word (5.4, 5.53). From the point of view of their own make-up, phrases are, of course, always constitutes. Phrases containing quite different words are, however, often comparable in a more general way: their constituents are identifiable as the same kind and they occur in the same order. That is, phrases are analyzed as shown in 5.43-44 into constituents which are either heads or complements. Phrases which have the same arrangement of heads and complements are formed by the same **construction type.**

In the sentence analyzed in 5.42-44 the elements *ngày xưa có người hiếu-lợi* 'once upon a time there was a greedy fellow' and *một hôm ra chợ* 'one day [he] went out [into] the market place' are each phrases. They have in common the fact that they are each analyzed into two immediate constituents, the first of which is a complement, the second a head. This similarity demonstrates that they are formed by the same construction type.

A construction which forms phrases with more than one head is **coordinating.** Other constructions (forming phrases containing only one head each) are **subordinating.** There are also **mixed** constructions, which are basically coordinating (they form phrases containing more than one head) but which also have a complement. Subordinating constructions are **restrictive,** forming phrases with the order complement-head, and **descriptive,** forming phrases with the order head-complement. All Vietnamese syntactic relationships may be understood in terms of these different kinds of construction: coordinating (including mixed), restrictive, and descriptive.

The over-all sentence analyzed in 5.43 is formed by a descriptive construction—the first immediate constituent is the head, the rest is the complement: *Ngày xưa có người hiếu lợi* plus *một hôm ra chợ, gặp ngày chợ phiên vừa đông người đến buôn bán vừa lắm đồ hàng.* 'Once upon a time there was a greedy person, [who] one day went out into the market place on the day of a fair [when there were] both a great many people who

123

had come to do business and a great deal of merchandise.' Application of the kind of analysis described in 5.44 reveals that the sequence *vừa đông người đến buôn bán vừa lắm đồ hàng* 'both teeming (crowds of) people arriving to do business and many items of merchandise' is a mixed coordinating phrase: it contains the two heads *đông người đến buôn bán* and *lắm đồ hàng*, and the complement *vừa … vừa* 'both … and'.

The same sentence furnishes several examples of restrictive phrases, for example:

> *ngày xưa* (complement) plus *có người hiếu-lợi* (head) 'once upon a time there was a greedy person'
> *một hôm* (complement) plus *ra chợ* (head) 'one day went out [into] the market place'
> *một* (complement) plus *hôm* (head) 'one day'

Similarly, it contains many descriptive phrases, for example:

> *có* (head) plus *người hiếu-lợi* (complement) '[there] existed a greedy person'
> *ra* (head) plus *chợ* (complement) 'went out [into] the market place'
> *ngày* (head) plus *chợ phiên* (complement) 'day of a fair'

5.62. Centers.

In the analysis of sentences into smaller and smaller constituents it is often the case that successive layers involve the same type of construction. The resulting appearance is that of nested elements, each head containing a head and complement in the same order as the next larger constitute. In such nested sequences, called **complexes**, the smallest head (containing no smaller constituents arranged according to the construction of the complex) is the **center**. In such a complex, complements are relatively **outer** or **inner** as they are isolated early or late in immediate constituent analysis. The first isolated is **outermost** complement, the last **innermost**.

> *con chó nhỏ này* 'this small dog' (descriptive complex)
>   *con chó nhỏ* (model)
>   *con chó* (model, head)
>   *con* 'animal' (model, head, center)
>   *chó* 'dog' (innermost complement)
>   *nhỏ* 'be small' (inner complement)
>   *này* 'this' (outermost complement)

> *sẽ không đi chợ* 'won't go to market' (restrictive complex)
>   *sẽ* 'subsequently' (outermost complement)
>   *không đi chợ* (model)
>   *không* 'not' (innermost complement)
>   *đi chợ* (model, head, center)
>   *đi* 'go' (model, head)
>   *chợ* 'market (place)' (complement)

5.63. Markers. There are words in Vietnamese which are always complements, never heads (5.43). Some of them are independent, others are dependent (5.53). A few of these are severely limited in distribution: they are called **markers.** As complements they are limited not only in relative position to their heads; they appear only with some of the forms which regularly occur as heads in the general construction type involved. In other words, with markers only certain types of words and phrases occur. With reference to markers, then, it is possible to subdivide the three basic construction types into subtypes.

5.64. Word Classes. It was observed in 5.44 that complements are extremely varied: they are in general more varied than heads. And of complements, descriptive (i.e., following) complements are considerably more varied than restrictive (i.e., preceding) complements. In fact, literally all kinds of phrases that can be identified by other criteria appear in some contexts as descriptive complements. (This, however, is not true of individual words—certain types of words do not appear as descriptive complements at all.) It is this extreme variety of descriptive complements that gives the language the appearance of permitting a great deal of freedom in the selection of items for syntactic combination. And it is probably this feature, coupled with the limited amount of morphology, which often leads native Vietnamese speakers to say that their language "has no grammar."

On the other hand, there are severe limitations on the types of elements which are found together in other syntactic relationships. These limitations (often signaled by markers, 5.63) form the basis for definition of **word classes.** In certain positions some words are found to occur, while others do not: all the words that occur there belong to the word class defined by that position. Those word classes which involve the severest limitations are the most helpful in making clear the syntactic structure of the language. Such classes are described in detail in Chapters 8-11.

5.65. Sentence Structure is describable in terms of the types of constructions by which the sentences and their constituents are formed. On this basis it is possible to discern several kinds of sentences and observe something about their typical parts (Chapter 12). Beyond this level certain statements can be made about the relationships of sentences to one another and to the general context. For the most part these considerations belong to the realm of style, some aspects of which are treated in Chapter 13. Some other aspects of the choice of words and expressions within sentences are discussed in Chapter 14.

125

CHAPTER 6

Compounds and
Pseudo-Compounds

6.1. General. In a language like Vietnamese, which is strongly syntactic or isolating (as opposed to synthetic languages like Latin or Russian or even English), it is not surprising that the distinction between the word and the phrase is not as clear as in languages where word boundaries are usually unambiguous. Every language seems to have some troublesome borderline cases (in English, for example, are *jack-in-the-pulpit* and *jack of all trades* words or phrases?). Perhaps there seem to be more problems of this sort in Vietnamese because investigation of them has been so limited to date. The pattern which emerges is not too clear, and precise definitions are difficult to make. However, it seems useful to present the salient facts here with the warning that this aspect of the language invites a great deal more study.

Although compounds and pseudo-compounds are different in underlying structure (5.55-56), they have many important similarities. And the dividing line between the two can be only vaguely defined, since pseudo-bases tend to become free forms—that is, many of them come to be used more and more widely, eventually appearing as dependent or independent words (5.53). (This is one of the apparent directions of evolution which the language shows.) It is for these reasons that they are treated together.

6.2. Compounds are morpheme sequences with two immediate constituents generally occurring with a heavier stress on the second constituent and never appearing in any environment in expanded form with one of their elements complemented by an additional element (cf. 5.56).

One kind of compound is further marked phonologically: **idiom compounds** have weak stress with their first syllable in ordinary (noncontrastive) contexts. All other compounds fall into two general categories: **syntactic compounds** typically are paralleled by syntactic phrases

126

which contain the same elements in the same order; **nonsyntactic compounds** have no such parallel phrases.

Syntactic compounds very frequently have weak stress with their first base, while the phrases they parallel more often have medium stress. They are conveniently divided into two types on the basis of the parallel phrases: **generalizing compounds,** paralleling coordinate phrases (8.33, 9.65); and **specializing compounds,** paralleling descriptive phrases (8.34, 9.62).

Nonsyntactic compounds are divided into two types on the basis of their apparent internal structure: **reinforcing compounds** appear to contain two heads; **attributive compounds** resemble sequences with the order complement-head.

Compounds are perhaps the least understood elements of Vietnamese grammar. Further analysis may well reveal further subtypes or a different basis for classification. It is expected that a deeper study of the stress system may clarify some of the points now in doubt. Details of the classes outlined here are presented in the following sections.

→ Bà-con

6.21. Idiom Compounds have weak stress with their first syllable in noncontrastive contexts. They often parallel syntactic phrases of quite distinct—often totally unrelated—meanings.[1] These compounds are also distinct from many other compounds in being extremely common in the everyday spoken language and less frequently found in more formal usage.

°*bà con* [be] related: *bà* grandmother, *con* child; cf. phrase *bà con* [a] child's grandmother

Ông ấy °**bà** '**con** °*với tôi.* (S) He's related to me.

Bà con °*đi* '*chợ rồi.* My grandmother's gone to market (said by a child to its parent).

°*một mình* alone: *một* one, *mình* oneself; cf. phrase *một mình* one body

Tôi '*ở đây* °**một mình.** I'm staying here by myself.

Côn-trùng mỗi thứ có **một mình** '*khác nhau.* Each kind of insect has a different body. ["insect each sort exist one body different reciprocally"]

°*người ta* one, someone, they, you, people (indefinite; similar to the French *on*, German *man*): *người* person, *ta* you and I; cf. phrase *người ta* our people

Chừng nào °*cưới* '*vợ làm cho* °**người ta** '*hay!* (S) When you get married, let people know about it!

---

[1] Because of this irregularity in correspondence of meanings, these forms are not classed with syntactic compounds in which there appears to be a more or less consistent relationship between the meanings of the compounds and the phrases they parallel.

Người ta *rất khỏe* '*mạnh* ⁰*và sung-*'*sướng.* Our people are very healthy and happy.

⁰*nhà nước* (federal) government: (*nhà* building, establishment, *nước* country); cf. phrase *nhà nước* building belonging to the nation *Ông ấy làm* ⁰*cho* ⁰**nhà** '**nước.** He works for the (federal) government.

Nhà chúng tôi '*ở* ⁰*là* **nhà** '**nước.** The house we live in is government property.

⁰*nhà quê* countryside, rural area: (*nhà* building, establishment, *quê* native village); cf. phrase *nhà quê* country house *Ông ấy* '*ở* ⁰**nhà quê** *mới* '*đến* ⁰*Hà-nội.* He's just come to Hanoi from the country.

Chúng tôi ở ⁰*Hà-nội cũng* '*có* **nhà quê** ⁰*ở gần Nam-định.* We live in Hanoi, and have a country house near Nam-định, too.

6.22. Generalizing Compounds are syntactic compounds paralleling

coordinate phrases (8.33, 9.65). They are composed of bases denoting different items of reality; the forms have the general meaning 'these two items and other similar ones, making up a general class'. Like idiom compounds, many generalizing compounds are common in conversational usage. However, there are members of this group which are quite bookish and others which hardly ever occur in conversation. These forms are very often written with a hyphen connecting their two parts. They frequently occur with weak stress on their first syllable, while the parallel additive phrases do not.

> *bàn-ghế* furniture: *bàn* table, *ghế* chair; cf. *bàn ghế* tables and chairs
>
> *quần-áo* clothes: *quần* trousers, *áo* tunic; cf. *quần áo* trousers and shirt
>
> *bát-đĩa* dishes, dinnerware: *bát* bowl, *đĩa* plate; cf. *bát đĩa* bowl and plate
>
> *mưa-gió* inclement weather; (fig.) vicissitudes, experience with the difficulties of life (somewhat bookish): *mưa* to rain, *gió* be windy; cf. *mưa gió* to rain and be windy
>
> *mua-bán* ~~~~~~~~~~~~ *mua* buy, *bán* sell; cf. *mua bán* buy and sell
>
> *giấy-bút* stationery goods: *giấy* paper, *bút* writing instrument; cf. *giấy bút* paper and pencil
>
> *con-cháu* youngsters, children: *con* child, offspring, *cháu* grandchild, nephew, niece; cf. *con cháu* children and grandchildren (of a particular person)

chải-chuốt take great pains with one's appearance, be meticulous (formal, unlikely to occur in conversation): *chải* to brush, comb, scrub, *chuốt* to polish; cf. *chải chuốt* to scrub and polish

học-tập to learn: *học* to study, *tập* to practice; cf. *học tập* to study and practice

This classification is troublesome in one respect: there are a number of morpheme sequences of this general aspect which seem not to be paralleled by phrases with coordinating construction. In any case, since the formal definition of compounds (5.56) involves an elusive distinction, it is often difficult to establish whether one is dealing with a compound or a phrase. The reality of the language as it is here viewed is that there are many sequences like those listed above in which there seems to be a clear and consistent distinction from nearly homonymous phrases; there are many other forms where no such distinction is clear, and others where obviously phrases with coordinating construction are involved. Some examples of borderline cases follow (those which are common with weak stress on their first syllables are so marked):

°*cây-cỏ* vegetation: *cây* tree, plant, *cỏ* grass

°*cày-cấy* engage in farming: *cày* to plow, *cấy* transplant

buôn-bán do business: *buôn* buy for resale, *bán* sell

°*ăn-ở* to live; behave: *ăn* eat, *ở* reside, be located

ai nấy everyone: *ai* anyone, who(ever) , *nấy* that very one (just referred to)

lễ-tục ceremonies and customs, rites and traditions:*lễ* ceremony, *tục* custom, tradition

sốt rét (pop.) malaria: *sốt* be hot, feverish, *rét* be cold, have chills

ảnh-hưởng influence: *ảnh* shadow, image, *hưởng* echo

giăng-hoa flirtation, ephemeral romance: *giăng* moon, *hoa* flower(s)

6.23. Specializing Compounds are syntactic compounds paralleling descriptive phrases (8.34, 9.62). Their meanings are fundamentally related to the meanings of the corresponding phrases, but are generally highly specialized in reference. In noncontrastive contexts their initial syllable nearly always has weak stress.

°*người ở* servant: *người* person, *ở* be located, reside; cf. phrase *người ở* person residing

°*dây thép* telegram: *dây* string, cord, wire, *thép* steel; cf. phrases *dây thép* electric wire, and *dây thép gai* barbed wire (with *gai* thorn)

làm việc to work: *làm* do, make, act; *việc* matter, affair; cf. phrase
   làm việc to accomplish a [particular] thing

The status of this category is the most doubtful of all. The language is
rich in descriptive phrases (cf. 8.34, 9.62-63). Many of them describe quite
directly the entities referred to, others are obviously suggestive, involving
extended meanings:

   làm ruộng engage in farming: *làm* do, make, *ruộng* rice field
   ăn cơm have a meal: *ăn* eat, *cơm* cooked rice
   nói chuyện converse, talk: *nói* speak, *chuyện* conversation topic
   nhà thương hospital: *nhà* establishment, *thương* be wounded
   đầu tầu locomotive: *đầu* head, *tầu* large conveyance

Still others designate a wide variety of phenomena by means of figurative
or suggestive extensions from the literal meanings of the individual words
involved. These are reminiscent of the kennings observed in many Western languages. Some items are obviously loan translations from Chinese,
others apparently are native inventions.

   nước đá ice: *nước* water, *đá* stone
   chiếu bóng show movies; movies: *chiếu* to project, *bóng* shadow
   xe lửa (railway) train: *xe* vehicle, *lửa* fire (cf. Chinese loan word
     hỏa-xa train: *hỏa* fire, *xa* vehicle)

It may well be that the specialized forms recognized here as specializing
compounds are simply cases of descriptive phrases with extended meanings. On the other hand, it must be recognized that even forms like *ăn cơm,*
nói chuyện, chiếu bóng, and *nước đá* (see above) are treated syntactically
as units and must at least be considered closely knit idioms.

6.24. Reinforcing Compounds are nonsyntactic compounds containing

two apparent heads; these two components usually denote identical or very
similar items of reality. The resulting forms often have a more figurative
or abstract reference than either of their bases. These compounds belong
almost wholly to the written or formal spoken language, although a few
occur now and then in conversation—even then they have a special formal-
istic flavor. Some also occur with their bases in reverse order.

   sợ-hoảng be terrified: *sợ* be afraid, *hoảng* be panic stricken
   buồn phiền be distressed: *buồn* be sad, *phiền* to bother, be bothered
   biến-mất to vanish: *biến* to disappear, *mất* to lose, be lost
   kén chọn choose carefully: *kén* ▓▓▓▓, *chọn* choose
   chọn lựa to select: *chọn* choose, *lựa* choose (also in reverse order:
     lựa chọn)

quen biết have an acquaintance with: *quen* be acquainted with, *biết* know

tìm kiếm to search: *tìm* to search, *kiếm* to search

biên-chép to write down, transcribe: *biên* jot down, make a note of, *chép* note down, copy

giàu có be wealthy: *giàu* be rich, *có* be existent

bền chặt be lasting, enduring: *bền* be durable, firm, solid, *chặt* be solid, secure, tight

tấn tới make progress: *tấn* to advance, *tới* to reach, attain

bởi vì because: *bởi* on account of, *vì* because

giúp đỡ to help: *giúp* to help, *đỡ* to help by taking on a burden

kỳ lạ be extraordinary, strange: *kỳ* be extraordinary, strange, *lạ* be different, strange, new

ca hát to sing: *ca* sing, *hát* sing

mưu-kế schemes and ruses, strategy: *mưu* scheme, plot, *kế* ruse, trick

dạ-thưa be polite, address with respect: *dạ* [polite responsive particle], *thưa* [polite vocative particle]

ngày giờ time (in general): *ngày* day(time), *giờ* clock time, hour

For obvious reasons these forms are often called synonym compounds. There are some interesting features about synonyms in Vietnamese. On the surface, at least, it would appear that there are a great many—the impression of the foreigner learning the language is that there are more forms referring to more or less the same bits of reality than in other languages with which he has dealt. [2] In any case, the reinforcing compounds add enormously to the number of synonyms. Often the native speaker finds it difficult or impossible to define differences of meaning among synonymous forms, but we may suspect that there are tiny nuances, suggestive overtones, which are different for each form. Such nuances seem especially likely in reinforcing compounds. For example, *kỳ lạ* and *kỳ-quái* both mean 'be strange'; *kỳ* 'be strange', combines with *lạ* 'be strange, unfamiliar' in the one instance, with *quái* 'be queer' in the other; *kỳ lạ* seems to have overtones of 'unusual, unexpected', while *kỳ-quái* suggests something a little abnormal.

One type of reinforcing compound contains dialectally distributed forms —that is, each of the components is used by itself with the same meaning, but is characteristic of a particular locality. For example, the compound *tìm kiếm* 'to search' contains the bases *tìm* 'to search', which is used

---

[2] A careful study of this matter should be undertaken, but it is obviously a long and exacting project; I know of no thoroughgoing attempt, either completed or under way, to get to the bottom of its possible structural significance.

singly in Tonkin, and *kiếm* 'to search', which is the common form in Cochinchina. (*Tìm* is understood in Saigon but is regarded as northern or literary.) Other examples of such compounds are *hư hỏng* 'spoil, break down', in which *hư* is southern, *hỏng* northern; *chọn lựa* 'select', in which *chọn* is northern, *lựa* southern.

Another type of reinforcing compound joins synonyms which have reference to two different kinds of thing belonging to the same general class, or two different attitudes toward the same thing. The resulting form often suggests a more general category including several similar things. In this respect these forms are very similar to generalizing compounds, but they seldom occur with weak stress on the first element.

> *sửa soạn* make preparations: *sửa* arrange, repair; *soạn* prepare

The figurative or abstract meaning of many reinforcing compounds is also an interesting matter. Many simple forms, of course, also have figurative or abstract meanings; at the same time, many compounds are mainly concrete or direct in their reference. But the pattern of abstraction is too common to ignore completely. Examples of figurative or abstract compounds based on (more) concrete bases are:

> *bền chặt* be lasting, enduring: *bền* be durable, firm, solid, *chặt* be solid, secure, tight
> *tấn tới* make progress: *tấn* to advance, *tới* to reach, attain
> *chài-lưới* [occupation of] fishing: *chài* fish net, *lưới* net, netting

6.25. Attributive Compounds

6.25. Attributive Compounds are nonsyntactic compounds characterized by the apparent order complement-head. These compounds differ from (syntactic) restrictive phrases (5.61)—the complement elements resemble greatly those elements generally found as descriptive complements, following their heads. This construction is the same as that of the vast majority of pseudo-compounds borrowed from Chinese, where the order complement-head is the regular one (cf. 6.33). A great many of these compounds are, in fact, composed of Chinese borrowed elements which have come to be used individually as free forms in Vietnamese. Presumably the rest are recent coinages, formed on the analogy of the Chinese borrowed forms. Some of these contain one form of Chinese origin and one native Vietnamese form; others contain no Chinese borrowed forms. In the following examples, Chinese borrowed elements are in boldface.

> **học** *trò* schoolchild, pupil: **học** to study, *trò* school-age child
> *chung cùng* together: *chung* be common, mutual, *cùng* to follow; and, with

Nam-Á South Asia: *nam* south, *Á* Asia
Bắc-Mỹ North America: *bắc* north, *Mỹ* America
Tây hồ West Lake (in Hanoi): *tây* west, *hồ* lake
thành-phần component, constituent: *thành* become, be the result,
　phần part

6.3. Pseudo-Compounds are morpheme sequences with two immediate

constituents at least one of which is bound (5.52). They are far more common than compounds, especially in more formal usage. They can be divided into subclasses partly on the analogy of the compounds which they resemble, but it must be borne in mind that this classification is based on semantic criteria rather than formal grounds. There are **generalizing pseudo-compounds,** which appear to contain two parts in coordinate relationship and have meanings very much like those of generalizing compounds; **reinforcing pseudo-compounds,** which appear to contain two parts in coordinate relationship and have meanings very much like those of reinforcing compounds; and **attributive pseudo-compounds,** which appear to have the relationship complement-head between their two parts, thus resembling attributive compounds. In addition there are **descriptive pseudo-compounds,** which resemble descriptive phrases (8.34, 9.62).

Historically the basis of this entire category lies in Chinese. It is the wealth of Chinese loan words which exhibit these relationships predominantly; and it seems likely that the similar compounds in Vietnamese constitute a spread of the principles from these borrowed elements. From the point of view of Vietnamese, however, pseudo-compounds are probably best understood in the way presented here—as collocations of bound forms which resemble true compounds.[3]

These bound elements borrowed from Chinese are reminiscent of similar elements in English borrowed from Greek. For example the English word *geography* is ultimately from a Greek word composed of two elements, one meaning 'earth', the other 'writing; description.' The element *geo-* is seen to recur in certain other words also borrowed from Greek, such as *geometry.* Further, it appears in words like *geology, geophysics, geocentric, geostatic, geothermic,* which, although they are composed of elements ultimately borrowed from Greek, are not traceable to words of this shape in the original language. The element *-graphy* appears in some other Greek borrowings, such as *biography, calligraphy,* and in many other words made up outside of Greek using Greek borrowed elements, such as *paleography,*

---

[3] Some of the forms apparently belong to similar compound classes in Chinese, while others are syntactic phrases. However, the over-all aspect of compounding in Chinese is quite different. For a brief account of compounds in Mandarin see Chao 1948: 41-44.

ethnography. More recently it has come to be used with elements of non-Greek origin, as in *roentgenography.* The recognizably related element *-graph-* appears in many recently coined words like *mimeograph* and *dictograph;* and as the word *graph,* now a free form in English, it enters into regular syntactic relationships and into native English compounds like *line-graph* and *bar-graph.* The situation with Chinese borrowed elements in Vietnamese is very similar, with two important exceptions: the number of borrowed elements in Vietnamese is vastly greater; the complications of form (so characteristic of the Greek borrowed elements) are very few. However, the difficulty of defining precise meanings for elements that will fit all occurrences; their unpredictable appearances now as bound elements, now as free forms; their use in scientific and literary coinage; their predominantly formal, educated, or technical flavor—all these characteristics are very similar in the two cases. So in dealing with the enormous complexity of this aspect of Vietnamese, it may be helpful to keep in mind the parallel of Greek elements in English.

The four types outlined above are discussed in more detail in the following sections. In the examples, free morphemes are in boldface type, other morphemes are bound (pseudo-bases).

The stress patterns of pseudo-compounds need more careful study. For the most part they have medium stress on each syllable. When they have heavy stress, it generally falls on the final syllable; however, there are some forms which appear with heavy stress on the first syllable—in the following examples such cases of initial heavy stress are marked. In forms consisting of three syllables the initial syllable sometimes has weak stress. Otherwise weak stress is rare in pseudo-compounds: it occurs with the initial syllable of a few dissyllabic forms which are current in conversational usage.

6.31. Generalizing Pseudo-Compounds contain elements which denote different items of reality and have the general meaning 'these two items and other similar ones, making up a general class'.

> *thi-***văn** literature (as a body): *thi* poetry, *văn* literature, especially prose
> **ca-***tụng* to praise, eulogize: *ca* sing, *tụng* to praise
> *xuất-nhập* go in and out: *xuất* put out, go out, *nhập* bring in, enter

6.32. Reinforcing Pseudo-Compounds contain elements which denote identical or similar items of reality. Like the corresponding compounds, they often have an abstract or figurative reference; and some occur as

well with their elements in reverse order. Such pseudo-compounds add to
the stock of synonyms discussed in 6.24, and again the differences in
meaning usually amount to subtle nuances.

kỳ-dị be odd, strange, abnormal: kỳ be strange, dị be odd,
  different (cf. synonyms kỳ lạ, kỳ-quái discussed in 6.24)
liên-hiệp to unite, ally: liên unite, associate, hiệp unite, join
  together
ái-tình romantic love: ái to love, tình sentiment, love (also in
  reverse order: tình-ái)
nhân-dân citizenry, people (of a country): nhân human being,
  person, dân person, citizen
gia-tộc family, household: gia family, household, tộc family, clan
thì giờ time (in general): thì time, giờ clock time, hour

6.33. Attributive Pseudo-Compounds contain elements in the apparent
order complement-head. Of all pseudo-compounds they constitute the majority and lend the most characteristic formal or literary flavor to the contexts in which they occur. However, some of them have come into current
conversational usage identifying concepts under current discussion.

quốc-gia state, nation: quốc nation, gia household; establishment
quốc-ngữ national language, romanized script: quốc nation, ngữ
  language
quốc-văn national literature: quốc nation, văn literature
náo-động to stir up, agitate: náo be noisy, động to move, disturb
'Mỹ-quốc America: Mỹ America, quốc nation
°Liên-'hiệp quốc United Nations: liên-hiệp unite (cf. 6.32), quốc
  nation
°sung-sướng be happy: sung be abundant, complete, sướng be
  happy
tác-giả author: tác to create, giả agent, actor, doer
cộng-tác to collaborate: cộng be in common, tác to create
cộng-sản communism: cộng be in common, sản property
'thi-nhân poet: thi poetry, nhân individual, human being
nhân-tạo be artificial, man-made: nhân human being, person, tạo
  to create

6.34. Descriptive Pseudo-Compounds contain elements in the appar-
ent order head-complement, and their meanings are very similar to those
of descriptive phrases (8.34, 9.62).

hạ-thủy to launch [a ship]: hạ to lower, thủy water

xuất- cảng to export: *xuất* put out, go out, *cảng* port
nhập- cảng to import: *nhập* bring in, enter, *cảng* port

There are comparatively few of these pseudo-compounds. They represent a different kind of relationship in the Chinese language from which they were borrowed. However, there are members of this class that make use of Chinese elements which remain bound in Vietnamese but are found in the regular Vietnamese order for descriptive phrases.[4]

long- thổ earthworm (lit. "earth-dragon"): *long* dragon, *thổ* earth
lính *thủy* sailor: *lính* soldier, *thủy* water
tầu *thủy* steamship: *tầu* large conveyance, *thủy* water

6.4. Interlocking Order of compounds and pseudo-compounds with other closely related forms is found in formal speech and writing. In conjunction with a monosyllabic form, this single form is repeated between the two immediate constituents of the compound or pseudo-compound. In conjunction with a dissyllabic form, the second syllable of one ‘form appears between the two syllables of the other.

Hai °vợ chồng lấy vàng đưa 'về **làm giầu làm 'có,** *ăn tiêu sung-* '*sướng.* The husband and wife took the gold home with them, it made them rich, and they spent it with pleasure. (*làm* ‘do, make, act’, *giầu có* ‘be wealthy [a reinforcing compound, 6.24])

Trước °thì còn 'riêng °các cụ bô-lão và quan-viên kỳ-cựu 'họp **bàn mưu tìm 'kế,** *sau phải hội toàn 'dân cũng không ai 'có °ý-kiến gì.* First separately the village notables and elder officials got together to discuss strategy, later they had to assemble the entire populace, and still no one had any [constructive] idea. (*bàn tìm* ‘discuss in quest of’ [coterminous phrase, cf. 9.65], *mưu- kế* ‘schemes and ruses, strategy’ [a reinforcing compound, 6.24])

°Dù ai **buôn đâu 'bán đâu,** *Mồng 10 tháng 8 chọi 'trâu °thì 'về.* Wherever anyone may be doing business, come the tenth of August buffalo fight he returns home. (*buôn bán* ‘do business’ [a generalizing compound, 6.22], *đâu* ‘anywhere, wherever’)

6.5. Polysyllabic Forms. Most of the compounds and pseudo-compounds cited thus far have been dissyllabic, each base or pseudo-base comprising a single syllable. However, there are a few longer forms belonging to these classes. Both compounds and pseudo-compounds of three syllables are found. The four-syllable forms observed are all compounds.

---

[4] Although a large proportion of the elements in such pseudo-compounds are of Chinese origin, they do not occur in these combinations in Chinese.

ᵖ*Liên-'hiệp quốc* United Nations (attributive pseudo-compound): *liên-hiệp* unite, *quốc* nation

ngôn-'ngữ học linguistics (attributive compound): *ngôn-ngữ* language (reinforcing pseudo-compound containing the pseudo-bases *ngôn* 'speech, word', *ngữ* 'language'), *học* to study

vô-tuyến điện-thoại radio telephone (attributive compound): *vô-tuyến* wireless (attributive pseudo-compound containing pseudo-bases *vô* 'without, lacking', *tuyến* 'wire, line'), *điện-thoại* telephone (attributive pseudo-compound containing the free morpheme *điện* 'electricity' and the pseudo-base *thoại* 'speech, conversation')

There seems to be a tendency away from such forms in favor of dissyllabic forms (see also 13.5). Many two-syllable forms appear to be shortenings of less common trisyllabic forms with virtually identical meanings:

vô-nghĩa be meaningless, nonsensical (beside *vô nghĩa-lý*) (pseudo-compounds): *vô* without, lacking, *nghĩa-lý* meaning, good sense (extended from basic meaning 'the right idea': reinforcing compound of *nghĩa* 'the right, justice' and *lý* 'common sense, justice') (an alluding form, cf. 6.6)

6.6. Alluding Forms

6.6. Alluding Forms are compounds, pseudo-compounds, or phrases consisting of elements at least one of which carries with it connotations of homonymous morphemes or other complex forms of which it is a part. Such forms are relatively common in artistic literature; even many very common words have such overtones. This is one of the many techniques which have been borrowed from Chinese literary tradition.

truyền-tụng 'to pass on reverently by oral tradition something which is valued': *truyền* 'transmit', *tụng* 'recite aloud' and *tụng* (pseudo-base) 'to praise'; glossed in Vietnamese: *ca-tụng, nhắc-nhở và truyền đi xa* 'to eulogize, remind about and spread far and wide'

nghĩa-lý 'meaning, good sense': *nghĩa* 'meaning, sense' and *nghĩa* 'the right, justice', *lý* 'common sense, justice'; glossed in Vietnamese: *chính-nghĩa và công-lý; nghĩa bóng: ý-nghĩa, nghĩa đúng, hợp theo với lẽ phải* 'righteous cause and justice; figurative sense: meaning, the correct idea, together with reason [i.e., common sense]'

hiền-hậu 'be mild, kind, benevolent': *hiền* 'be good, gentle', *hậu* 'generous, good'; glossed in Vietnamese: *hiền-lành trung-hậu* 'be good, gentle, and loyal' (*trung* 'faithful, loyal')

(Vietnamese glosses cited in the above examples are from Thanh Nghị 1952)

The classification of many such forms is difficult because the status of the homonymous parts in the modern language is sometimes different. For example, the first form cited above analyzed as containing *tung* 're-cite aloud' (a free morpheme) would be classed as a descriptive phrase (9.62). But *tung* 'to praise' is bound; if this is the element involved, then the form is presumably a descriptive pseudo-compound. This points up the shifting lines between compounds, pseudo-compounds, and phrases (6.1, 6.3).

Read

CHAPTER 7

Derivatives

7.1. General. The study of derivatives leads to classification according to the similarities of form which are involved. This classification has little consistent relationship to syntactic categories (Chapters 8-11). In fact, forms belonging to very different word classes often appear together in the same morphological class.

7.11. Formal Types. The great majority of derivatives are **reduplicative:** they are polysyllabic forms in which the affixal syllables have some kind of consistent phonetic resemblance to their bases. Such affixes, which appear in allomorphs directly dependent on the phonetic shape of bases, are **chameleon affixes.** They are of various subtypes, depending on the nature of the resemblance.

Perfect chameleon affixes have exactly the same phonetic shape as the bases with which they occur. (There are frequently differences in stress among the syllables, but these differences seem largely dependent on the position of the whole form in the pause group rather than on any internal structuring.) Because of this identity it is impossible to specify whether these affixes are prefixal or suffixal, and since other chameleon affixes are of both kinds, they offer no grounds for a decision.

> *nói nói* keep talking and talking (base *nói* 'talk')
> *sạch sạch* be rather clean (base *sạch* 'be clean')

Tonal chameleon affixes differ from their bases only in tone. Both prefixes and suffixes are found.

> *bự-bự* (S pop.) be very big (base *bự* 'be big' S pop.) (prefix)
> *den dẻn* be rather black (base *den* 'be black') (suffix)

Vocalic chameleon affixes differ from their bases only in vowel. Both prefixes and suffixes are found.

lẻu-láo [lɛ̆w láw] be ill-mannered (base *láo* 'be impertinent, insolent') (prefix)

mập-mạp be fat, chubby (base *mập* 'be fat') (suffix)

Riming chameleon affixes retain the nucleus of bases, which usually (but not always) includes the tone. Both prefixes and suffixes are found.

bối-rối be uneasy, troubled (base *rối* 'be tangled up') (prefix)

khóc-lóc cry, whimper (base *khóc* 'weep') (suffix)

sach-nhách be absolutely clean (base *sạch* 'be clean') (suffix, with different tone)

Alliterative chameleon affixes retain the initial of bases. Both prefixes and suffixes are found.

la-lết do with much pain or difficulty (base *lết* 'drag about painfully') (prefix)

rõ-rệt be very clear (base *rõ* 'be clear') (suffix)

Bases written in the standard orthography with no initial consonant have initial glottal stop (regularly in some dialects, sporadically in others: see 2.11, 4.1-2). This is the alliterative element in affixes of this kind.

óng-ả [ǎwng ả] shine [of fabric] (base *óng* id.)

These should not be confused with bases having initial [w] (preceded in some dialects by glottal stop), which are written with an initial *o-*. (Similar bases beginning with *u-* representing [w] would be expected, but no examples occur in the material.)

oằn-oại writhe [as with pain] (base *oằn* 'bend down, as with heavy burden')

Non-chameleon affixes are few, and without exception the derivatives in which they appear are limited to a few forms. However, some of the most common words in the language are involved. Two rather different formal types are observed: in the case of **demonstratives** (7.2) forms are made up of two elements, each consisting of less than a syllable, and only arbitrarily may one be designated as base; **anaphorics** (7.3), which seem limited to the southern speech area, involve a tonal affix.

7.12. Tone Alternations. Derivatives display special relationships of the various tones to one another. There are two registers and three types, as shown in Table 1. In the most common patterns the tone of the affix is in the same register as that of its base.

Traditionally the even tones (called **thanh bằng**) are distinguished from all the rest (called **thanh trắc** 'uneven, slanting tones'), and this distinction is important in rules for versification. The further patterning of distinctions between short and long tones is not recognized in this tradition, and becomes clear only in the examination of derivatives.

140

TABLE 1. TONE RELATIONSHIPS IN DERIVATIVES

	EVEN	SHORT	LONG
REGISTER			
FIRST	ngang	sắc	hỏi
SECOND	huyền	nặng	ngã

7.13 Consonant alternations. Limitations on the distribution of certain consonants in syllable final position (2.82) come into play in chameleon affixes. Final stops occur only with *sắc* and *nặng* tones. In chameleon affixes involving other tones, these stops of bases are replaced by their corresponding homorganic nasals, as shown in Table 2. Final [ch, nh] occur only after [i, ê , ă]. In chameleon affixes involving other vowels, these sounds of bases are replaced by [k, ng], as shown in Table 3. On the other hand, [k, ng] do not occur after [i, ê]. In chameleon affixes involving these vowels, [k, ng] of bases are replaced by [ch, nh] as shown in Table 4.

TABLE 2. REPLACEMENTS OF FINAL STOPS

Final of Base	Final of Chameleon Affix with Even or Long Tone
p	m
t	n
ch	nh
k	ng

đẹp be beautiful: *đèm-đẹp* be rather pretty
tốt be good, fine: *tôn-tốt* be rather good
sạch be clean: *sành-sạch* be rather clean
chắc be certain: *chăng-chắc* be more or less certain

TABLE 3. REPLACEMENTS OF FINAL [ch, nh]

Final of Base	Final of Chameleon Affix Vowel other than [i ê ă]
ch	k
nh	ng

lệch be tilted, slanted: *lệch-lạc* id.
quỳnh be emotionally upset: *quỳnh-quáng* be careless

TABLE 4. REPLACEMENTS OF FINAL [k, ng]

Final of Base	Final of Chameleon Affix with [i ê]
k	ch
ng	nh

cục be crude, course, boorish: *cục-kịch* id.
thùng barrel, large container: *thùng-thình* be too large, fit like a barrel [speaking of clothes]

One consonantal alternation appears to be only sporadic. Vocalic cha-meleon affixes accompanying bases in [ô] often have [w] before the charac-teristic vowel where this forms a possible cluster with the initial consonant. However, forms without [w] are also found.

sồm be shaggy [of beard]: sồm-soàm id. (also sồm-sàm)

This is very likely a matter of dialect variation ([w] clusters are far less frequent in some dialects; see 4.1).

7.2. Demonstratives constitute a closed class of forms with some appar-ently related marginal elements. Traditional grammar regards them as single, indivisible words, but a division into smaller elements with recurrent mean-ings brings out more about their interrelationships. The basic forms are shown in Table 5. In the sections that follow, these and related forms are discussed in detail.

TABLE 5. BASIC DEMONSTRATIVES

	Unspecified -ao/-âu (even)	Close to Speaker or Newly Introduced -ay/-ây (even)	Remote or Already Identified -ây/-o (short)
PLACE d̶- (first register)	dâu 'wherever'	dây 'here'	dấy 'there'
REFERENCE n- (second register)	nào 'whichever'	này 'this'	nọ '(an)other, that'
PROPORTION b- (first register)	bao 'to whatever extent'	bây 'to this extent'	bấy 'to that [such] extent'
MANNER s- (first register) / v- (second register)	sao 'however'	vầy 'this way, thus'	vậy 'that way, so'

7.21. Semantic Range. Note that the characteristic register of the tones of these forms is a property of the initial morpheme (the only inconsistent form in this respect is sao 'however, in whatever way, for whatever reason'). On the other hand, the tone type is a feature of the nuclear morpheme.

The meanings of the nuclear morphemes are broad and difficult to define; some further characterization is in order. The forms in the first column have

in common an indefinite meaning. They are often called interrogative words
(to be translated roughly *dâu* where? *nào* which? *bao* to what extent? *sao*
how, why?), because they occur frequently with sustaining intonation and
the resulting sentences are generally questions. However, they are also
extremely common in sentences with fading intonation and go together with
other forms to convey indefinite or negative notions. (These and other indefinites are discussed more fully in 14.2). The forms in the second column
share the notion of positional or conceptual proximity to the speaker. In
many circumstances a special connotation appears: the speaker uses one
of these forms to signal that something new is being introduced. Opposed
to these forms are those of the third column, which suggest a certain re-
moteness from the speaker and often presuppose a basis for comparison or
refer to an object or idea already identified.

The meanings of the initial morphemes are somewhat more specific. It
is convenient to use them as a basis for the detailed description of individual forms in the following sections.

7.22. Place Demonstratives (see 10.46) share the notion of relative
position. In addition to the forms in Table 5, there is a second form which
belongs in the third column:

> **đó** (S) 'there' (note formal similarity to *nọ*) replaces *đấy* (and also
> to a great extent *ấy*) in southern colloquial usage; it has a
> limited independent use in northern speech.

Some examples of the use of these forms follow.

> *Ai ở* **dâu,** *thì ở* **đấy.** Wherever someone is, he should stay there.
> *Ông ấy đi* **dâu?** Where did he go?
> *Ông ấy có đi* **dâu** *không?* Did he go somewhere?
> *Mời Ông ngồi* **đây.** Please sit here.
> **Đây** *là nhà của tôi.* This is [one of] my house [s].
> *Ông đi xuống* **đấy.** You go down there [that way]. (giving
> directions)
> *Lúc trước tôi ở Sài-gòn lâu năm. Ở* **đó** *thì vui lắm.* (S) Formerly
> I lived in Saigon for many years. [We] used to have a fine time
> there.
> *Cô ở* **đó** *rồi mà Ông thấy.* (S) She's over there already, as you
> [can] see.

A specialization of these forms appears in their use as descriptive
complements very similar to contained postpositive particles (11.82). Their
meanings in these cases are roughly as follows:

đâu [not] at all, at any cost, anyhow, whatever

đây right here, as I'm showing you (less frequent in this use)

đấy (S **đó**) there, near hearer, as just shown, noticed (nearly
  always with weak stress; southern form especially common)

Ông ấy không khỏi lại nhà tôi **đâu.** He mustn't fail to come to my
  house at any cost.

Ông đi đâu **đó?** (S) Where are you going [now]?

Ai **đó?**(S) Who is it? Who's there? (the stock phrase used as initial
  utterance in answering a telephone)

Ông làm gì **đấy?** What are you doing there? (emphasis on the
  relationship of the activity to the hearer rather than on the
  place)

Bà ấy không biết gì **đâu.** She doesn't know anything at all.

Sớm mơi tới giờ anh làm chi chi **đâu?** (S) What in the world have
  you been doing from morning till now?

Tôi có biết **đâu.** I have no idea. (How do you expect me to know?)

Tôi đi **đâu.** Why should I go? (I have no reason to go.)

7.23. Reference demonstratives are manner focuses (10.45) which are
very frequent as descriptive complements, marking substantival heads (8.1,
8.5). They indicate the relation of an object or idea to something in the
context or situation. They differ from place demonstratives in grammatical
function: as descriptive complements they appear only with substantival
heads, while place demonstratives are frequent in verbal phrases (9.62).

Of the basic forms in Table 5, **nọ** '(an)other, that' is relatively infrequent. It generally refers back to some entity already identified in the context. Sometimes it has a vague reference: 'somewhat remote from immediate
circumstances.' Occasionally it means specifically 'another than the one
mentioned.'

Năm ba mươi hai cô Lan đi Hà-nội thăm bạn. Hồi **nọ** *cậu Ngọc mới
  ra thủ-đô học.* In '32 Miss Lan went to Hanoi to visit a friend.
  Just a little earlier young Mr. Ngọc had come to the capital to
  study.

Hôm **nọ** *tôi gặp ông Lâm ở thư-viện. Lâu năm rồi chúng tôi không
  gặp nhau.* The other day I ran into Mr. Lâm at the library. It
  had been years since we'd seen one another.

Mùa hè các bạn ở ngoài bể nghỉ mát, làm cái **nọ** *cái kia thì vui
  lắm.* In the summer the friends were at the seashore for a vacation—they had a fine time doing this and that.

Nầy làm **nọ** *chịu.* (S) Some people suffer for others' misdeeds.
  ["this-one do, another suffer"]

144

The form **nây** is found in a limited number of expressions replacing *này*
or *nầy* (S) 'this'; it appears only as a descriptive complement.

Ở bên **nây** *sang bên kia.* [Someone] went over there from here.

Certain other forms are more common in situations where *nọ* might be
expected in relation to *này* and *nào*. In reference to some person or thing
already mentioned **ấy** 'just mentioned' is far more frequent in northern
speech. In the south the place demonstrative **đó** appears as an extremely
common complement meaning 'that, those; just mentioned' (see also 7.3).
In central colloquial usage the form **nớ** is current (see below).

Hai người **đó** *khó quá!* (S) Those two people are very difficult!

Ông Thanh có tiền nhiều. Ông **đó** *luôn-luôn đi chơi.* (S) Mr. Thanh
      has a lot of money. He's always going out to have a good time.

Northern **này** 'this' is **nầy** in the south.

Khi nào ông sang bên **này**? When did you come over here?

Chừng nào ông qua bên **nầy**? (S) When did you come over here?

There is a presumably closely related form **nay** 'present time', a temporal
focus (10.47) which appears as descriptive complement after certain substantives (8.1) denoting temporal categories. *Này* (S *nầy*) does not generally occur in these expressions.

    bữa **nay** today (with a vague non-northern flavor)

    ngày **nay** today (reference to future)

    hôm **nay** today (northern in flavor)

    năm **nay** this year

    sáng **nay** this morning (S *sớm mơi nầy*)

    đêm **nay** tonight

    chiều **nay** this afternoon

    tối **nay** this evening

However, unlike the principal reference demonstratives it is not limited as
a descriptive complement to substantival expressions.

    lâu **nay** for a long time now

    từ hôm ấy đến **nay** from that day to the present time

    Phong-tục thay đổi, trước kia nam nữ không được trò chuyện
      với nhau. **Nay** *thì các bậc phụ-huynh đã cho phép con*
      gái được tiếp bạn giai ở nhà. Customs change; in olden
      times boys and girls were not permitted to have social
      relations. Nowadays elders have given permission to
      girls to receive their male friends at home.

In Huế popular speech both *này* and *nay* are rendered by **ni**. *Nào* and *đâu*
are rendered by **mô**. **Nớ** serves for *nọ* and *ấy*.

    bên **ni** (H pop.) here, this place, this side

    bữa **ni** (H pop.) today

Bữa **ni** *mạ ở nhà hay đi* **mô** *rồi?* (H pop.) Is [your] mother home
today or has she gone somewhere already?

Ông nớ lấy cái **mô?** (H pop.) which one did he take?

Nãy (sometimes written **nẫy**) '[time] just past, a moment ago, a little
while ago' is presumably related to *nay* 'present time.' It has a limited distribution, appearing after a few substantives denoting temporal periods:

lúc **nãy,** ban **nãy,** hồi **nãy** just a little while ago

Lúc **nãy** *Ông hỏi tôi ăn cơm chưa?* A little while ago you asked
me whether I'd eaten or not.

The form **nấy** 'specifically that one' is a correlative word referring back to
an indefinite *ai* 'whoever' or *nào* 'whichever.'

Cha **nào,** *con* **nấy.** Like father, like son.

Mạnh **ai nấy** *được.* Whoever is strong[est] will get it.

Người **nào,** *giữ phận* **nấy.** Everyone should attend to his proper
duty. (i.e., 'People should mind their own business.' Also
'People should keep their proper place in society.')

There is a word **nao** 'whichever' which appears only in poetry. Presumably it is an indefinite similar to *nào*, but it seems to occur only or primarily in interrogative uses.

Đêm trăng nầy chàng nghỉ mát phương **nao?** This moonlit night
where is he taking his stroll, [I wonder]?—Đoàn thị Điểm

7.24. Proportion Demonstratives have a limited distribution and cover
a semantic range which is more difficult to delimit than that of place and
reference demonstratives. They suggest comparison in terms of quantity,
extent, or (occasionally) a point in time with well-known standards or
references in the context. Grammatically they are prepositive particles
(11.81). They combine with a few other words: some of these combinations
are extremely common, others are rare. Some occurring examples follow.

COMMON

bao giờ whenever, at some time	*bây giờ* now	*bấy giờ* then, at that time
bao nhiêu however much	*bây nhiêu* (L) this amount, demonstrable amount	*bấy nhiêu* that much
bao lâu however long		*bấy lâu* for that length of time

LESS COMMON

bao năm however many years	*bấy năm* for so many years
bao ngày however many days	*bấy ngày* that many days; that day
bao thuở at whatever time	*bấy thuở* (L) at that time
bao lớn however big	*bấy lớn* that big
bao xa however far	*bấy xa* that far
bao lần however many times	*bấy lần* that many times
	bấy chầy (L) for a long time

Có **bao nhiêu,** *xài* **bấy nhiêu.** Whatever [you] have [you] spend.
Bây giờ *mấy giờ?* What time is it now?
Chừng nào ông về Mỹ, **bấy giờ** *tôi sẽ về Sài-gòn.* (S) Whenever you go back to America, I'll go back to Saigon then.
Tôi thấy tình-cảnh đó, sanh lòng thương **bấy.** (S) When I saw that scene I was *so* moved by pity.
Bao nhiêu *cũng được.* Any amount will do.
Bao ngày *Ông đi khỏi, tôi vẫn ở nhà.* However many days you're away, I'll still be at home.
Việc đó không ích gì **bao.** (S) That thing isn't very useful.
Con anh năm nay **bao lớn?** (S) How old is your child this year?
Công việc đó tốt biết dường **bao.** (S) That business—it's really impossible to say how good it is. ["abstract-unit affair there good know manner however"]
Bao nhiêu *nhà ở trong làng cháy hết.* All the houses in the village were burned. ["However many houses there were in the village, they burned completely."]
Ông có **bao nhiêu** *mẫu ruộng?* How many [Vietnamese] acres of rice land do you have?
Cử-chỉ của anh đáng khen biết **bao nhiêu.** Your attitude deserves a good deal of praise.

7.25. Manner demonstratives (cf. 10.45) refer to the way something is accomplished. This portion of the paradigm seems to involve suppletion: the word **sao** 'however, in whatever way, for whatever reason' also has a broader semantic range than either **vầy** 'this way, thus, as I am demonstrat-

147

ing (or about to demonstrate)' (rare in Hanoi, but common in many other areas) or **vậy** 'that way, so, as was demonstrated (or mentioned).'

> *Có làm* **sao,** *nói làm* **vậy.** Whatever [you] do, [you] should make it known.
>
> *Có nói* **sao,** *phải làm* **vậy.** Practice what [you] preach.
>
> *Con chó đó dữ lắm, con chó nầy thật cũng dữ như* **vậy.** (S) That dog is very vicious, this dog is really just as bad.
>
> *Cái xe hỏng rồi. Ông phải làm* **sao?** The car has broken down. What are you going to do about it?
>
> **Sao** *Ông không đến nhà tôi chơi?* Why don't you come to see me?
>
> *Ông đi chợ* **sao?** Oh, so you're going to market! (surprised)
>
> **Sao** *cũng ráng gởi cho tôi.* (S) Whatever happens, try to send it to me anyhow.
>
> *Tại* **sao** *bữa nay anh đi lại trễ hơn hôm qua?* (S) Why did you come later today than yesterday?
>
> *Sự nầy xảy ra như* **vậy:** *anh Bính mệt lắm, thì lái xe không coi chừng. Còn có một cái xe khác đi mau lắm, hai cái đụng nhau.* (S) It happened this way: Bính was very tired and drove carelessly. There was another car going fast, the two [cars] collided.

In Hanoi **vầy** is generally replaced by **như thế (nầy),** and **thế** alone is extremely common in expressions which generally involve **vậy** in other dialect areas.

7.3. Anaphorics (S) are formed from a limited number of words; they belong to the spoken language and are to be heard very commonly in the southern and south central dialect areas. (The dividing line seems to be somewhere just north of Đà-nẵng, where they are recorded by Smalley and Vạn 1954; they are not used in Huế. They refer back to a person, time, or place which has just been mentioned or somehow otherwise called to attention (e.g., shown in a photograph, observed on the street, etc.) [1]

Bases of anaphorics are mostly general categoricals (8.62), but words of a few other classes are found as well. The most common forms are those based on categoricals that are basically kinship terms, many of which have

---

[1] Henderson 1961 discusses problems of interpretation of these forms. Although the forms cited cover a good deal of the same ground as those reported here, the interesting examples which are included emphasize some rather special limitations of usage with reference to formality and courtesy. The forms which I collected in Viet Nam, while certainly colloquial and not regarded as appropriate written style, did not have any unusual connotations of discourtesy or lack of respect. I suspect that possibly Miss Henderson's examples suggesting rudeness may be a product of the contexts in which they came to the informants' minds rather than a necessary concomitant of the forms themselves. Certainly the forms I recorded were in everyday use in quite polite situations. This phenomenon invites a good deal of study.

extended uses for reference to persons unrelated to the speaker (13.2). However, relator nouns (8.63) are also extremely common. In the following list, kinship terms have been separated and listed first.

KINSHIP TERMS

anh elder brother, male equal: **ảnh** he

bà grandmother; lady: **bả** she

cậu mother's brother: **cẩu** he

cha father: **chả** he

chị elder sister; female equal: **chỉ** she

cụ great-grandparent; elder venerated person: **củ** he or she

cô father's sister; young unmarried lady: **cổ** she

dì mother's sister: **dỉ** she

dượng aunt's husband: **dưởng** he

mẹ mother: **mẻ** she

mợ mother's brother's wife: **mở** she

ông grandfather; gentleman: **ổng** he

OTHER WORDS (categoricals except where otherwise indicated)

bên side, area: **bển** that side, there

chưa (negative) not yet: **chửa** likewise not yet

chừng certain amount, extent, limit measure: **chửng** to that extent, that much, then

đằng location: **đẳng** there

hôm day: **hổm** that day, then

không (negative) not: **khổng** also not, likewise not

ngoài (relator noun) outside, exterior, out: **ngoải** outside there, outside [of it]

thằng inferior person (male): **thẳng** he

trên (relator noun) top, upper surface: **trển** on top [of it]

trong (relator noun) inside, interior: **trỏng** inside [it]

No anaphorics have been observed based on forms ending in stops. None at all have been recorded with bases having *sắc* tone. These forms correspond for the most part to phrases consisting of the base followed by **ấy** in the northern dialect. In fact, a similar phrase type is found in the south alongside these derivatives; however, **đó** is generally used rather than *ấy*. It has been suggested that the southern derivatives with mid-rising tone represent an anticipation of the high-rising tone of *ấy* in words directly preceding it at an earlier stage of the dialect when *ấy* was used as it is in the north today; later the *ấy* was dropped, leaving the preceding word with modified tone. Presumably words having *sắc* tone (like *ấy*) were not affected in this position; thus there are no derivatives having bases with *sắc* tone, although there are examples of sentences having words with *sắc* tone in the same syntactic functions as these derivatives. (If this is indeed the origin of the formation, the principle has since been extended to forms without corresponding phrases; e.g., *khổng, chửa.*)

> *Hôm qua ông Lâm đến nhà tôi.* **Ổng** *sung-sướng lắm.* Yesterday Mr. Lâm came to my house. He was very happy.

> *Hôm qua tôi làm một cái chuồng cho con chim. Bữa nay nó ở* **trỏng.** Yesterday I made a cage for the bird. Today he's in it.

> *Ông không trả tiền, tôi* **khổng** *làm nữa.* If you don't pay [me], I won't work any more.

> *Ông tên chi?* What's your name? **Ổng** *tên chi?* What's his name? (Cf. [N] **Ông ấy** *tên gì?*)

> *Họ đương làm gì ở ngoài vườn?—Họ đương ăn cơm ở* **ngoải.**(or...*ở* **ngoài đó.**) What are they doing out in the garden?—They're eating out there.

> *Ở đằng nầy có tiệm ăn không?—Dạ không. Ở* **đẳng** *mới có.* Is there a restaurant over this way?—No, only over there (place already identified).

> *Ở dưới cái tách có gì?—Ở* **dưới** *có cái dĩa.* What's under the cup? —There's a saucer under it.

> *Ở đây không có nhà ở, chừng nào lên* **trển?** [Since] there's no house to live in here, when are you going up [to a place in the mountains]? (referring to a place already mentioned)

> *Ông chưa nói, tôi* **chửa** *làm.* You haven't said [anything about it] yet, [so] I haven't done [it] yet.

> *Tôi có chừng ấy, ông cũng có* **chửng.** I have so much, you have just as much.

> *Chừng hai mươi lăm người đi Sài-gòn, phải không?—* **Chửng.** [There were] about twenty-five people going to Saigon, weren't there? —About [that].

7.4. Specializing derivatives

7.4. Specializing derivatives are formed from a great variety of bases with perfect chameleon affixes. It is a productive formation—new derivatives are coined freely.

The meanings of these derivatives vary a good deal from form to form and from context to context. They have in common a specialization or limiting in applicability of the semantic range of the base. To some extent the varying meanings among forms may be distinguished along the lines of the syntactic classes to which the bases belong, but there are intermediate and conflicting cases.

Roughly four semantic centers are identifiable, and it is most useful to consider the majority of forms in relation to these. Problematic forms are treated in a separate section (7.45). **Distributives** (7.41) are formed nearly exclusively from substantives (8.1): they have in common the notion 'each unit or group in turn.' **Iteratives** (7.42) are based on verbs (9.55); they convey the notion '...continually or repetitively.' **Attenuatives** (7.43) are for the most part based on verbals (9.5), especially those denoting states; they weaken the force or scope of the base: 'more or less..., rather..., somewhat..., ...-ish' and the like. **Intensives** (7.44) are formed from a variety of miscellaneous bases; they strengthen the force or scope of the base: 'exceedingly..., definitely..., completely...,' and the like.

Noun and verb derivatives are usually written without hyphens; other derivatives are often hyphenated (3.53d).

7.41. Distributives are based on substantives (8.1). They establish plural reference and suggest further 'each unit or group individually, or in turn.'

> **Chi chi** *rồi cũng vậy.* (S) No matter what [you do—you try one thing after the other], it turns out the same.
>
> **Nhà nhà** *đều treo cờ, khi lễ độc-lập.* (S) All the houses hang out flags on independence day.
>
> *Tôi vô nhà ổng, thấy* **sách sách** *không biết bao nhiêu.* (S) I went into his house and saw book after book—I don't know how many.
>
> *Trong tủ tôi có nhiều sách;* **cuốn-cuốn** *đều (được) giữ kỹ-lưỡng.* (S) In my bookcase there are many books; each volume is kept in its place [carefully arranged].
>
> *Tết người ta đi chợ từng tốp* **hai-hai ba-ba** *vui lắm.* (S) On New Year's people go to market in groups of two or three [and] have a fine time.
>
> **Mỗi-mỗi** *người đều phải lo ăn tết.* (S) Each person individually is supposed to occupy himself with celebrating the New Year.
>
> *Ông hẹn với tôi* **mai mai mốt mốt** *hoài, không bao giờ làm xong.* (S) You keep promising me tomorrow or the next day and never finish [some work I've given you to do].
>
> *Chúng ta đi xem lễ.* **Họ họ** *đều vui,* **ta ta** *cũng thích.* We [you and I]'ll go watch the ceremony. They'll all enjoy it, [and] we'll all like it [too].
>
> *Khi vui thì gọi* **anh anh em em,** *khi giận thì nói* **tao tao nó nó.** When they're happy [people] use [polite terms] *anh* and *em,* when they're angry they say *tao* and *nó.*
>
> **Sao-sao** *cũng ráng gởi cho tôi.* (S) No matter what happens, try to send it to me.
>
> *Đếm cái gì* **năm-năm bảy-bảy** *hoài mà không rồi?* What are you counting by fives and sevens and never finish?

151

7.42. **Iteratives** are based on verbs (9.55). They establish unusual extension or repetition of some action or state, often with an added connotation of undesirability.

> *Tôi đi chợ* **coi coi** *đã, rồi sẽ mua.* (S) [Let] me go to market and look around, [if there are any of those things you want, I] will buy [some].
>
> *Bồi! Đứng đó* **coi coi** *hoài, không làm công việc!* (S) Hey, boy [speaking to servant]! What are you doing standing there gawking and not working?
>
> *Ông ở đó* **làm làm** *hoài.* (S) You're still working there [should be finished].
>
> *Tôi hay* **quên quên** *hoài.* (S) I'm always forgetting.
>
> *Ông đó* **đau đau** *hoài, không làm gì hết.* (S) He's always sick, never does anything.

7.43. **Attenuatives** are based mostly on verbals (9.5), especially those denoting states and conditions. Sometimes they clearly indicate reduced force or scope, but often they simply achieve a more cautious, less definite statement, a vaguer kind of assertion.

> *đẹp* be beautiful: ~~đẹp đẹp~~ be rather pretty
> *nhiều* be a large amount: **nhiều-nhiều** be a rather large amount
> *cười* laugh: **cười cười** laugh a little
> *đợi* wait: ~~đợi đợi~~ wait a little while
> *nhỏ* be small: ~~nhỏ nhỏ~~ be rather small
> *trắng* be white: ~~trắng trắng~~ be whitish
> *Hai bên đường có nhà cất* **đều đều.** (S) On the two sides of the street there were houses built [spaced] more or less equally [from one another].
> *Cái hộp đó hơi* **không không.** (S) That box is more or less empty.
> *Công việc đó* **vậy-vậy.** (S) That's more or less the way things are.
> *Ở đây người ta* **chơi chơi** *một chút.* Amusement is mediocre here.
> *Hôm qua tôi đau ít, bữa nay tôi đau* **hơn hơn** *một chút.* (S) Yesterday I was a bit sick, today I'm a little sicker.
> *Tôi* **quen quen** *cô ấy.* I know her slightly [we are casually acquainted].
> *Cái gì* **động động** *trong tủ áo.* Something's moving a little in the wardrobe.
> *Lá* **rung rung** *trên ngọn cây.* Leaves were gently rustling in the tree-tops.

Cánh hoa **rơi rơi** *xuống trước nhà.* Flower petals were falling, a few at a time, down in front of the house.

These forms are sometimes preceded by the prepositive particle *hơi* 'slightly' (11.81).

Tôi chữa mãi, máy xe **hơi chạy chạy** *rồi lại dừng hẳn.* I kept repairing [it]—the car's motor ran for a little while then stopped again entirely.

Cô ấy ốm nặng, hôm nay mới **hơi cười cười.** She's gravely ill—today only smiled a little bit.

Some forms seldom occur without this particle; for example,

hơi *đau đau* (S) be rather sick
  sai sai be rather incorrect
  rõ rõ be rather clear
  đúng đúng be fairly correct
  nực nực be rather warm [weather]

This use of *hơi* is one way of eliminating the inherent ambiguity of certain forms, since there are in some cases homonymous forms with iterative meaning (7.42). There are also attenuatives formed with a tonal chameleon affix which lack this ambiguity (7.61).

7.44. Intensives are formed from a wide variety of bases, although less commonly from substantives or verbals. They strengthen the force or scope of the base.

thường often: **thường-thường** usually, regularly
hoài continually: ~~hoài hoài~~ incessantly
mau (S) rapidly: **mau-mau** (S) very rapidly
vụn in small pieces: **vụn-vụn** in very small pieces
luôn still continuing [without break]: **luôn-luôn** always, forever
không not: **không-không** definitely not
đã previously (anterior marker): **đã-đã** ages ago
đời life, generation, period of existence: **đời-đời** eternity
rồi be finished, over with: **rồi-rồi** be completely finished
hết be used up: **hết hết** be completely used up

  Tôi thường đi chợ. (S) I often go to market
  Tôi **thường-thường** *đi chợ, không lỗi một ngày nào.* (S) I go to market regularly, never miss a day.
  Tôi đi chợ luôn. I'm continuing to go to market [anyway, although it was suggested that I not go any more].
  Tôi đi chợ **luôn-luôn.** I always go to market [every day, every week, etc.].

Tôi không ở Dà-lạt **luôn-luôn,** *phải đi về Sài-gòn mỗi tháng.* (S)
I'm not in Dalat all the time, I have to go back to Saigon each
month.

Mau-mau, *chúng ta phải đi.* (S) Hurry up, we should be leaving.

Bây giờ việc đó đã **rồi rồi.** This business is completely finished
now.

Nói **lớn lớn** *một chút đi!* (S) Speak a little louder.

Đường **hết hết** *rồi.* The sugar is absolutely all used up.

Công việc đó tôi **đã-đã** *nói rồi.* That matter I mentioned ages ago
already.

Tôi **không-không** *hề nói láo.* I never, never lie.

7.45. Miscellaneous Forms with intermediate, imprecise, and conflicting meanings are frequently found among specializing derivatives. In some
sentences, the emotional attitude of the speaker seems to be the main issue.

Anh nói **gì gì** *đó?* (S) What are you saying? (annoyed)

Sớm mơi tới giờ anh làm **chi chi** *đâu?* (S) What in the world have
you been doing from morning till now?

Sometimes it is difficult to tell which of two or more different implications
may be involved.

Việc đó dễ, làm như **chơi chơi.** (S) That work is easy, [you] work
as if you're amusing yourself. ('keep on enjoying' or 'play a
little'?)

Máy nầy chạy **đều đều** *không hư.* (S) This machine runs normally
without breaking down. (*đều* 'be even, regular, steady', *đều
đều* 'be more or less steady' or 'be absolutely regular'?)

Tôi đi chợ **mau-mau,** *sợ trễ giờ.* (S) I'm going to market soon,
[I'm] afraid it's late. ('very soon' or 'rather soon'?)

7.5. Emphatics are formed with extremely diverse affixes. Their meanings
range over a large semantic area from simply stylistic variants with a
slightly more picturesque flavor through directly attenuative and intensive
forms to derivatives with highly specialized, figurative, or extended connotations. There seems to be no clear limitation on the kinds of words
which serve as bases, but verbs are overwhelmingly predominant. Any
attempt to classify these forms according to common semantic elements
inevitably cuts across the formal lines. It is more useful to consider the
various forms involved. They have in common the feature that all the affixes involved are of the partial chameleon type. The derivatives are all
regularly written with hyphens.

The formations are for the most part nonproductive: there seem to be
no cases of new forms being coined by analogy with existent derivatives.

There are, however, two productive types, which are discussed in 7.6.

Often the meaning of a derivative is roughly the same in one or more respects as that of the base, but the special uses of the two forms differ. This is especially true of the extended or figurative uses of forms. How- ever, for the sake of simplicity in the following exemplary material, where there is a common core of meaning this is presented as the gloss of the base and the derivative follows it without a gloss.

The forms cited below are presented to demonstrate the types of affixes involved: no attempt has been made to treat the material exhaustively. The systematization offered here differs considerably from that of Emeneau 1951 (Chapter 5), which describes the patterns exemplified by reduplicative forms taken as a whole. whether or not the clear designation of a base and affixal element is possible. The reader is referred to this work for the difference in approach and for the wealth of examples, including many isolated forms which appear to suggest patterns outside the main scheme but which afford too meager a basis for setting up new categories.

This portion of the language invites a good deal more study. Three fac- tors make investigation especially difficult and time consuming. First, many of the forms belong rather to the written language than to ordinary speech and there is evidence of considerable dialectal variation as well. Second, the meanings and usage of the forms are very difficult to get at: dictionary glosses tend to be misleading, and informants are very often hard put to it to explain the subtle connotations. A thorough consideration would necessarily involve the scrutiny of a very large body of texts, and this should be an important part of the creation of a comprehensive diction- ary. Third, many forms which look very much like reduplicative derivatives turn out to be compounds, phrases, or single morpheme words (see also 7.58).

Some examples of the use of a few of these forms appear in 7.8.

7.51. Emphatics with tonal affixes are formed with tonal chameleon pre-
fixes (derivatives have in their initial syllable a tone different from that of the base) and suffixes (derivatives have in their final syllable a tone dif- ferent from that of the base). A productive prefix of this type is treated in 7.61. The remaining forms are suggestive of some minor types of tonal al- ternation in which the affix regularly has a tone of the opposing register. This is different from the pattern exhibited by the majority of reduplicative derivatives, the common tone relationships of which are described in 7.12. The patterns involved here may be regarded as basic for the treatment of some other reduplicative material omitted from this treatment as marginal (cf. Emeneau 1951: 5.5.4.3). Of this relatively limited material by far the predominant patterns are those which create forms having *sǎc* tone in the

155

first syllable, *nặng* tone in the second; thus bases with *nặng* tone have prefixes with *sắc* tone, while bases with *sắc* tone have suffixes with *nặng* tone.

Short tone of opposing register:

PREFIXES

bự (S pop.) be big: *bứ-bự* (S pop.) be very big

xẹp be flattened, become flat: *xép-xẹp* be completely flattened

mệt be tired: *mết-mệt* be somewhat tired, vague

kịch sound of something moving, striking against something hard: *kích-kịch*

SUFFIXES

cứng be hard: *cứng-cựng* (pop.) be very hard

khét have odor of something burning: *khét-khẹt* have odor of something badly burned

xốp be spongy: *xốp-xộp* be very spongy

nhớt be viscous: *nhớt-nhợt* be very viscous

rít be rough [because dirty]: *rít-rịt* be very rough

sít be close together: *sít-sịt* be very close together

A single form in the material suggests that this pattern may also have bases with other tones:

PREFIX

ngầm do something in secret: *ngẩm-ngầm*

Another single form suggests an opposing pattern:

Even tone of opposing register:

PREFIX

teo be extremely lonely, sad: *tèo-teo* [rejected by some informants]

A number of forms show *hỏi* tone in the affix:

PREFIXES

con be small: *cỏn-con* be very small

teo be shriveled: *tẻo-teo* be very shriveled

lặng be quiet: *lẳng-lặng* be very quiet

vẹn be finished, perfect, complete: *vẻn-vẹn* be completely finished; only, just

hoài constantly: *hoải-hoài* incessantly

SUFFIXES

thâm be deep: *thâm-thẩm* be very deep, far

đen be black: *đen-đẻn* be rather black (S)

A single form has a base with *hỏi* tone and a suffix with *ngang* tone:

mảy a tiny amount: *mảy-may*

The material also has two three-syllable derivatives:

hỏm be hollow, recessed: *hỏm-hòm-hom*

sạch be clean: *sạch-sành-sanh* be very clean (cf. 7.61 and 7.13)

The majority of these forms seem marginal to most informants and there is a good deal of disagreement on the validity of some.

7.52. Emphatics with vocalic affixes

7.52. Emphatics with vocalic affixes are formed with prefixes (derivatives have in their initial syllable a vowel different from that of the base) and suffixes (derivatives have in their final syllable a vowel different from that of the base). Prefixes are extremely rare, but the suffix type with *-a-* is quite common.

PREFIXES

-ê-

rao to announce, make known: *rêu-rao* spread scandal

oải be tired, worn out: *uể-oải* [wẻj wảj] be tired, lazy

-u-

nhát be cowardly: *nhút-nhát* be timid, shy

SUFFIXES

-a-

hốc hole, hollow: *hốc-hác* be emaciated, gaunt

sồm be shaggy [of beard]: *sồm-soàm* (or *sồm-sàm*)

mơn to caress: *mơn-man*

dễ be easy: *dễ-dãi* [zễj zãj] be easy-going, generous

rỗi be unoccupied: *rỗi-rãi* have leisure time

mếu screw up mouth to cry, weep: *mếu-máo* [mếw máw]

hếu be credulous: *hếu-hảo*

mập be fat: *mập-map*

ướt be wet: *ướt-át*

mất lose: *mất-mát*

vấp hit obstacles: *vấp-váp*

quýnh be emotionally upset: *quýnh-quáng* be careless

khuều be clumsy: *khuều-khoào*

đớt speak unclearly: *đớt-đát*

mút to suck: *mút-mát*

vênh stick one's nose up, be haughty: *vênh-vang*

-ă-

lệch be tilted, slanted: *lệch-lạch*

chín be ripe: *chín-chắn* be very ripe

hung be bad, wicked: *hung-hăng*

vùng shake: *vùng-vằng* be shaking with anger

-e-

móp be hollow, flattened: *móp-mép* be flattened, deformed

móm be toothless: *móm-mém* chew without teeth

-i-

múp be fat: *múp-míp* be fat, plump

cục be crude, coarse, boorish: *cục-kịch*

thùng barrel, large container: *thùng-thình* be too large, fit like a barrel [speaking of clothes]

Emeneau 1951 describes dissyllabic forms of this type as involving alternations of back and front vowels at the same level: *u:i, ô:ê, o:e* (5.5.6.34). A large proportion of the forms cited appear to be single morphemes, and this description fits them well. The suffixes with *-e-* and *-i-* exemplified above create forms which look very similar. However, the formations with *-a-* and *-ă-* seem unrelated. (See also 7.58.)

7.53. Emphatics with riming prefixes have initial syllables which rime with their bases but have different initial consonants. Most common are **b-** and **l-**, but there are also examples with **ch-** and **t-**.

b-

*ngùi** be moved [emotionally]: *bùi-ngùi* be very much moved

nhàu be wrinkled [çloth]: *bàu-nhàu* be very wrinkled

*hoải** (S) be nervously tired: *bải-hoải* (S) be very tired

rối be confused: *bối-rối* be troubled, perplexed, upset

thụng be roomy [of clothes]: *bụng-thụng* be too large, ill fitting

thùng barrel, etc. [large container]: *bùng-thùng* be ill fitting [like a barrel]

ch-

rộn be noisy, troublesome, disorderly: *chộn-rộn* be agitated, troubled, anxious

l-

nhẳng be trailing behind: *lẳng-nhẳng*

quỳnh be emotionally upset: *lính-quỳnh* be in awe

vụn be in small pieces: *lụn-vụn*

*choi** be unstable: *loi-choi* jump around, unable to be still

túng be reduced to poverty: *lúng-túng* not to know what to do to get out of a situation

mò grope for [in dark or water]: *lò-mò* grope feverishly

thưa be thin, sparse [vegetation, growth]: *lưa-thưa*

mờ be dim, vague, unclear: *lò-mờ*

thụng be roomy [of clothes]: *lụng-thụng* be too big [of clothes]

t-

mò grope for [in dark or water]: *tò-mò* be curious, want to know all

mờ be dim, vague, unclear: *tò-mờ*

mò-mẫn grope a long time: *tò-mò tẫn-mẫn* (cf. 7.72)

7.54. Emphatics with riming suffixes have final syllables which rime with their bases, but have different initial consonants. A few suffixes also have different tone from the base.

---

* Free morpheme of severely limited distribution.

b-

ten be torn: *ten-ben*

ch- (with different tone)

mét (S) be pale: *mét-chẹt* be
very pale

lùn be short [not tall]: *lùn-chủn*
be very short, dwarfed

l-

khóc weep: *khóc-lóc*

tham be greedy: *tham-lam* be
greedy, covetous

khéo be skillful, dexterous: *khéo-
léo*

l- (with different tone)

khét have odor of something
burned: *khét-lẹt* have odor of
something badly burned

xẹp be flattened, become flat:
xẹp-lép be completely flattened

m- (with different tone)

tịt be plugged up: *tịt-mít* remain
silent

ng- (with different tone)

khét have odor of something
burned: *khét-nghẹt* (S) have odor
of something very badly burned

cụt be short or lacking: *cụt-ngút*
be very short, *cụt-ngủn* id.

nh-

tạp be mixed, miscellaneous: *tạp-
nhạp* be mixed

cười to laugh: *cười-nhười* to tease,
joke

nh- (with different tone)

sạch be clean: *sạch-nhách* be completely clean; all finished, exhausted

qu- (with different tone)

sạch be clean: *sạch-quách* be completely clean; cleaned out, all
gone

7.55. Emphatics with alliterative prefixes have initial syllables which
begin with the same consonants as their bases but have different nuclei,
often also different tones. Tone relationships are regular as described in
7.12.

-a (with even tone)

(common with dissyllabic bases)

thiết have an interest in: *tha-
thiết* be earnest, insistent

lết drag about painfully: *la-lết* do
with much pain or difficulty

lụng-thụng be too big [of clothes]
lụng-thà lụng-thụng

đủng-đỉnh go slowly, leisurely:
đủng-đa đủng-đỉnh

õng-ẹo behave affectedly: *õng-à
õng-ẹo*

nhí-nhảnh be lively, sprightly:
nhí-nha nhí-nhảnh

đỏng-đảnh be difficult, exacting
(7.56): *đỏng-đa đỏng-đảnh*

-ai (with even tone)

láng abound: *lai-láng* overflow

-ao (with even tone)

khát be thirsty: *khao-khát*

-ăc

rối be mixed up, tangled: *rắc-rối*
be complicated, intricate

-ăn (with short tone)

đo to measure, gauge: *đắn-đo*
weigh both sides of a question

-âm (with short tone)

*ngùi** be moved [emotionally]:
ngậm-ngùi be grieved

* Free morpheme of severely limited distribution.

-âm

tắc to click [tongue]: tấm-tắc
click tongue in sign of
admiration

-âp

phồng swell up, inflate: phập-
phồng swell up and deflate
alternately; be worried

ngừng to stop, interrupt: ngập-
ngừng hesitate

-i (with even tone)

cóp* gather, collect: ky-cóp build
up bit by bit, economize

ngút* to rise [of smoke]: nghi-ngút
rise in curls [of smoke]

thùng sound of drum: thì-thùng

-ơn (with short tone)

đau be painful; sorrowful: đón-đau

-u (with even tone)

khờ be gullible, naive, dull: khù-
khờ be slow-witted

rờ feel one's way: rù-rờ be slow

7.56. Emphatics with alliterative suffixes are by far the most numer-
ous and diverse. They have final syllables which begin with the same consonants as their bases but have different nuclei, often also different tones.
Tone relationships are regular as described in 7.12.

-a (with even tone)

nôm demotic script: nôm-na
popular language

nguy be high, steep: nguy-nga be
grandiose, impressive

rầy annoy, pester: rầy-rà be
troublesome, complicated

mặn be salty; hearty, kindly: mặn-
mà be cordial

nết morals, [good] manners: nết-
na be well behaved

thiết have an interest in: thiết-tha
be earnest, insistent

xấu be bad, ugly: xấu-xa be
wicked

đẫy be stocky, fat: đẫy-đà be
very fat

-a (with short tone)

hèn be base, low, vile: hèn-hạ

quấy act recklessly: quấy-quá be
careless, sloppy

-a (with long tone)

hối be in a hurry: hối-hả

dối be false: dối-dả

bươn* hurry toward: bươn-bả

giục urge, stimulate: giục-giã

ròng* throughout: ròng-rã throughout, unceasingly

êm be tranquil: êm-ả

nong to force, squeeze into: nong-
nả

nhàn be idle; leisurely: nhàn-nhã

nhục be disgraced: nhục-nhã

oi be hot and muggy: oi-ả

óng shine [of fabric]: óng-ả

rộn be noisy, disorderly: rộn-rã be
vehement

rời come unstuck: rời-rã

vồn* to hurry: vồn-vã

buồn be sad: buồn-bã

-ac

đĩnh be extraordinary: đĩnh-đạc

*Free morpheme of severely limited distribution.

-ac (continued)

bàn discuss, deliberate: *bàn-bạc*

đồ thing, object: *đồ-đạc* thing, tool, utensil

ngơ ignore: *ngơ-ngác* be stupefied, unable to pay attention

nháo be in disorder: *nháo-nhác* be distraught, frightened

rải spread, sow, distribute: *rải-rác* be scattered around

rời come unstuck: *rời-rạc* be discontinuous, inharmonious

trọn* be wide-eyed: *trọn-trạc* give a menacing look

xao* be in motion: *xao-xác* make noise

-ach

phá destroy, demolish: *phá-phách* plunder, pillage

hiển be clear, obvious: *hiển-hách* be illustrious

-ai (with even tone)

đất land: *đất-đai* territory

rạc be exhausted: *rạc-rài*

-ai (with short tone)

hăng be ardent, eager: *hăng-hái* be enthusiastic

mềm be soft, flexible: *mềm-mại* be very soft; supple

quằn be bent under heavy burden: *quằn-quại* squirm, writhe

oằn bend downward [as with heavy burden]: *oằn-oại* writhe [as with pain]

-ai (with long tone)

rộng be wide, spacious: *rộng-rãi*

bừa be disorderly, untidy: *bừa-bãi*

mảnh be slender: *mảnh-mải*

-am (with short tone)

hôi to stink: *hôi-hám*

điềm be calm: *điềm-đạm*

-an (with even tone)

khô be dry: *khô-khan*

mê be unconscious: *mê-man*

nồng be intense [of feelings]: *nồng-nàn*

tồi be bad, mediocre: *tồi-tàn* be dilapidated

-ang (with even tone)

nở to blossom: *nở-nang* be full-blown

cũ be old: *cũ-càng*

gọn arrange with care: *gọn-gàng*

sẵn be ready: *sẵn-sàng*

sửa prepare: *sửa-sang*

trễ be late: *trễ-tràng*

bộn be numerous, encumbering: *bộn-bàng*

dễ be easy: *dễ-dàng*

nhẹ be light [weight]: *nhẹ-nhàng*

khoe to boast: *khoe-khoang* be boastful

rõ be clear: *rõ-ràng*

rộn be noisy, disorderly: *rộn-ràng* bother, disturb

giỏi be good, skillful: *giỏi-giang*

-ang (with short tone)

bỉ make fun of: *bỉ-báng*

-anh (with even tone)

sắm make preparations: *sắm-sanh*

tập to practice, exercise: *tập-tành*

dỗ to coax: *dỗ-dành*

-anh (with short tone)

nhặt pick up, glean: *nhặt-nhạnh*

vặt be miscellaneous: *vặt-vạnh*

so compare: *so-sánh*

-anh (with long tone)

vặt be miscellaneous: *vặt-vãnh*

đỏng* be difficult, exacting: *đỏng-đảnh*

*Free morpheme of severely limited distribution.

-ao (with even tone)

gắt be strong, harsh, violent: *gắt-gao* be keen, intense

lớn be big, great: *lớn-lao* be grandiose

khát be thirsty: *khát-khao*

nghẹn be choked: *nghẹn-ngào* be choked with tears

nôn vomit: *nôn-nao* be nauseous

xanh be blue, green; pale, sickly: *xanh-xao* be pale, sickly

hỗn be impolite, rude: *hỗn-hào*

bảnh be attractive, elegant: *bảnh-bao* be elegant, well adorned

-ao (with short tone)

khờ be gullible, naive, dull: *khờ-khạo*

tỉnh to wake up: *tỉnh-táo* be wide awake

trộn to mix: *trộn-trạo*

vênh stick one's nose up, be haughty: *vênh-váo*

-ao (with long tone)

đông be crowded [with people]: *đông-đảo*

sắc be sharp: *sắc-sảo* be keen, smart

-ap

ấm be warm: *ấm-áp*

cứng be hard: *cứng-cáp*

chậm be slow: *chậm-chạp*

nhắm to sample, taste, snack: *nhắm-nháp*

-at

cứng be hard: *cứng-cát*

to be large: *to-tát*

xô push, shove: *xô-xát* to scuffle, brawl

-ay (with short tone)

dơ be dirty: *dơ-dáy* be filthy

-ay (with long tone)

bóng be bright: *bóng-bảy* be shiny

nóng be hot: *nóng-nảy* be irritable, easily angered

-ac

lâu be a long time: *lâu-lắc* be a very long time

nồng be strong, intense: *nồng-nặc* be penetrating [of odor]

sâu be deep: *sâu-sắc* be very deep

-ăm (with even tone)

tối night; be dark: *tối-tăm* be dark

xa be far: *xa-xăm* be very far

-ăm (with short tone)

rối be mixed up, tangled: *rối-rắm* be complicated

-ăn (with even tone)

muộn be slow, late: *muộn-mằn* be late [in having a child]

cộc be easily angered, vicious: *cộc-cằn* be boorish

nhọc be tired: *nhọc-nhằn*

khó be difficult: *khó-khăn*

-ăn (with short tone)

chắc be solid, sure: *chắc-chắn*

đo to measure, gauge: *đo-đắn* weigh both sides of a question

đầy be full: *đầy-đặn*

đều be equal, regular: *đều-đặn*

già be old: *già-giặn* be experienced

giỏi be good: *giỏi-giắn* (S)

may be lucky: *may-mắn*

tươi be fresh: *tươi-tắn* be smiling

nhỏ be small: *nhỏ-nhắn*

khỏe be healthy: *khỏe-khoắn*

nhũn be courteous, polite, humble: *nhũn-nhặn*

dày be thick: *dày-dặn*

mau be rapid, prompt: *mau-mắn*

tròn be round: *tròn-trặn* be perfectly round

vuông be square: *vuông-vắn*

*Free morpheme of severely limited distribution.

-**ăn** (with long tone)

mò grope for [in dark or water]:
mò-mẫn grope for a long time

-**ăng** (with even tone)

nói to talk: *nói-năng*

lố be ridiculous in appearance:
lố-lăng

-**ăng** (with short tone)

sốt be hot: *sốt-sắng* be fervent

-**ăt**

quá exceed, surpass: *quá-quắt* be
very excessive

khuya be late at night: *khuya-
khoắt*

thêm to augment: *thêm-thắt*

dè be moderate: *dè-dặt* be
reserved

-**âm** (with short tone)

bụi dust: *bụi-bâm* be dusty

-**âm** (with long tone)

mò grope for [in dark or water]:
mò-mẫm

rà grope, feel one's way: *rà-rẫm*

rò grope, feel: *rò-rẫm*

sờ feel of, test by touch: *sờ-sẫm*
grope one's way

-**ân** (with long tone)

dờ be indolent: *dờ-dẫn* be slow,
stupid

mê be unconscious: *mê-mẫn* be
bewitched

-**âp**

ngượng be clumsy: *ngượng-ngập*

rầm make a heavy noise: *rầm-rập*
be noisy

-**ây** (with short tone)

động to move: *động-dậy*

-**e** (with even tone)

hăm threaten: *hăm-he*

lỏng be fluid: *lỏng-le* be very fluid

rụt withdraw, pull back: *rụt-rè* be
retiring, timid

màu (S) color: *màu-mè* (S) flavor;
beautiful appearance

nhắn send a message by someone:
nhắn-nhe

-**e** (with long tone)

mát be cool: *mát-mẻ*

sạch be clean: *sạch-sẽ*

mạnh be strong: *mạnh-mẽ*

vui be pleasant: *vui-vẻ*

chặt be tight: *chặt-chẽ*

đẹp be beautiful: *đẹp-đẽ*

mới be new: *mới-mẻ*

nhỏ be small: *nhỏ-nhẻ* be soft [of
voice]

suôn (S) go smoothly: *suôn-sẻ*

sạch-nhách (S) be completely
clean; all finished, exhausted
(7.54): *sạch-nhách sạch-nhẻ* (S)

-**em** (with short tone)

gói to wrap up, package: *gói-ghém*

-**en** (with even tone)

nhỏ be small: *nhỏ-nhen* be pretty

rối be mixed up, tangled: *rối-ren*
be in confusion, disorder

-**eo** (with even tone)

bủng be jaundiced: *bủng-beo*

ngặt be severe, stern: *ngặt-nghèo*
be very difficult

nhăn be wrinkled, shriveled: *nhăn-
nheo*

phì exhale: *phì-phèo* inhale and
exhale, puff, smoke

răn be wrinkled, shriveled: *răn-reo*

-**eo** (with short tone)

ngoắt turn around quickly: *ngoắt-
ngoéo* be sinuous; complicated,
tricky

tru to howl: *tru-tréo* yell

ưỡn to stick out [of part of body]:
ưỡn-ẹo wriggle, swing hips

-eo (with long tone)

bạc be ungrateful: *bạc-bẽo*

lạnh be cold: *lạnh-lẽo* be very
cold

trắng be white: *trắng-trẻo* be very
white

trong be clear, transparent: *trong-trẻo* be very clear, unclouded

lỏng be loose, not tight: *lỏng-lẻo*

-ê (with even tone)

rủ invite, urge: *rủ-rê* inveigle

dầm to dip, soak: *dầm-dề* be
soaked, drenched

não suffer, be sorrowful: *não-nề*
be very sad

nặng be heavy: *nặng-nề* be very
heavy

no be replete: *no-nê* be very full
from eating

-ê (with long tone)

ngạo mock, scoff at: *ngạo-nghễ* be
arrogant

-êch

khờ be gullible, naive, dull: *khờ-khệch* be dull, stupid

ngờ to doubt, be suspicious: *ngờ-nghệch*

-ênh (with even tone)

hớ be inexperienced, imprudent:
hớ-hênh be indiscreet

-êt

mê be unconscious; infatuated:
mê-mết be very enthusiastic

rõ be clear: *rõ-rệt* be very clear

sợ be afraid: *sợ-sệt*

-i (-y) (with even tone)

ầm be noisy: *ầm-ì* (or *ầm-ỳ*) be a
prolonged weak noise

sân be angry: *sân-si* be quarrel-some

-i (-y) (with short tone)

nhảm be outside the regular order
of things: *nhảm-nhí*

xấu be bad; ugly: *xấu-xí* be very
ugly

mông dream: *mộng-mị*

-i (-y) (with long tone)

cũ be old: *cũ-kỹ* be [rather] old

ầm be noisy: *ầm-ĩ (ầm-ỹ)*be a very
loud noise

rên to groan: *rên-rĩ*

rầu be very sad: *rầu-rĩ*

sắp be all the way up to: *sắp-sỉ*
be nearly, approximately

-ia (with short tone)

chặt be tight: *chặt-chịa*

độc be poisonous; cruel: *độc-địa*
be cruel

tròn be round: *tròn-trịa* be perfect-ly round

-iêm (with short tone)

giấu to hide: *giấu-giếm*

-in (with short tone)

ru to rock [cradle]: *ru-rín* sing a
lullaby

-inh (with long tone)

tròn be round: *tròn-trĩnh* be round-ish, plump

khờ be gullible, naive, dull: *khờ-khĩnh*

bướng be headstrong, stubborn:
bướng-bỉnh

ngộ be strange; cute: *ngộ-nghĩnh*

tươi be gay, merry: *tươi-tỉnh* be
joyous

-ip

rộn be noisy, disorderly: *rộn-rịp* be
bustling, busy

-it

rối be mixed up, tangled: *rối-rít* be
perplexed

-it (continued)

chẳng to tie up: *chẳng-chịt* be intertwined

hôn to kiss: *hôn-hít*

bận be busy: *bận-bịt*

-iu (with even tone)

nâng pick up and support: *nâng-niu* pamper

phẳng be even, level, smooth: *phẳng-phiu*

-iu (with short tone)

bận be busy, occupied: *bận-bịu*

mắc be caught in: *mắc-míu*

quăn be curled: *quăn-quýu* be twisted

nũng be wheedling: *nũng-nịu*

-iu (with long tone)

tục be vulgar, obscene: *tục-tĩu*

-o (with even tone)

hay be good, well done: *hay-ho*

gầy be thin: *gầy-gò*

rủi be unlucky: *rủi-ro*

thơm be sweet-smelling: *thơm-tho*

thẹn be ashamed: *thẹn-thò*

líu be tongue-tied, embarrassed: *líu-lo* jabber, speak indistinctly

-o (with short tone)

răn be wrinkled: *răn-ró* be very wrinkled

vẹo be twisted, crooked, distorted: *vẹo-vọ*

méo be out of shape: *méo-mó*

-o (with long tone)

mắt (S) be expensive: *mắt-mỏ* (S)

xin to beg for: *xin-xỏ* bother with requests

-oc

gan be courageous: *gan-góc*

mời invite: *mời-mọc*

-oi (with even tone)

hẹp be narrow; stingy: *hẹp-hòi* be stingy

hẳn be thorough, complete: *hẳn-hoi* be correct, proper

ít be a small amount: *ít-oi* be a very small amount

mặn be salty: *mặn-mòi*

-oi (with long tone)

cứng be hard, stiff: *cứng-cỏi* be firm

lọc to filter: *lọc-lõi* be experienced

-om (with long tone)

nhẹ be light [in weight]: *nhẹ-nhõm* be very light [in weight]

nhắc to recall: *nhắc-nhỏm* to recall frequently

-on (with short tone)

hay be good, well done: *hay-hón*

-ong (with short tone)

riết pull tight; be stingy: *riết-róng* be stingy

-ong (with long tone)

gắt be violent; grumble: *gắt-gỏng* lose one's temper

ghét to hate, detest: *ghét-gỏng*

-ot

nặn to model [e.g., with clay]: *nặn-nọt*

nhảy to jump: *nhảy-nhót* to jump around

trồng (S) to plant: *trồng-trọt* (S) to cultivate

sai be false, wrong: *sai-sót*

nắn to put back into shape: *nắn-nót* to form carefully

-ô (with even tone)

lõa be naked: *lõa-lồ*

xì leak out; fizzle [out]: *xì-xồ* talk incoherently and be unable to understand

-ô (with short tone)

rầm be noisy: *rầm-rô*

-ôc

gậy stick, cane: *gậy-gộc* sticks (coll.)

-ôi (with even tone)

nắng to be warm, sunny: *nắng-nôi*

-ôi (with short tone)

bực be displeased, annoyed: *bực-bội*

lầy be swampy, miry: *lầy-lội* be muddy

nhức to ache: *nhức-nhối*

-ôn (with short tone)

thiếu to lack, be insufficient: *thiếu-thốn* lack money

-ôt

hoảng be afraid: *hoảng-hốt* be terrified

dại be stupid, foolish: *dại-dột* be very stupid

hư to spoil, break down: *hư-hốt* deteriorate

-ơ (with even tone)

xác be poor: *xác-xơ* be destitute

lẳng be flirtatious: *lẳng-lơ*

gật to nod: *gật-gờ* to balance, nod back and forth

-ơ (with short tone)

bắt to seize, arrest: *bắt-bớ* to arrest

-ơ (with long tone)

gặp to meet: *gặp-gỡ* encounter unexpectedly

nhắc to recall: *nhắc-nhở* to remind [of something]

-ơi (with even tone)

vẽ draw, sketch: *vẽ-vời* create, invent

-ơi (with short tone)

nghĩ think: *nghĩ-ngợi* think, be pensive

phất to wave: *phất-phới* to flutter

-ơm (with short tone)

nhác be lazy, negligent: *nhác-nhớm*

lì be stubborn: *lì-lợm*

-ơn (with short tone)

đau be painful; sorrowful: *đau-đớn*

-ơt

hời be inexpensive: *hời-hợt* be frivolous

non be tender, young: *non-nớt* be very tender, young

rã be broken up, dispersed: *rã-rợt* be completely broken up

-u (with even tone)

gật to nod: *gật-gù* nod one's head with contentment

-ua (with even tone)

gầy be emaciated: *gầy-gùa*

sớm early: *sớm-sua*

-ua (with short tone)

giãy (or *giẫy*) to struggle: *giãy-giụa* (or *giẫy-giụa*)

nhầy be viscous, gluey: *nhầy-nhụa* be covered with sticky substance

nhớp be dirty, disgusting: *nhớp-nhúa*

sặc give off strong odor: *sặc-sụa* smell of, reek

-ua (with long tone)

sáng be bright, shine: *sáng-sủa*

-uc

nhịn put up with, endure: *nhịn-nhục*

-ui (with even tone)

sần be rough: *sần-sùi*

-ui (with short tone)

gần be near, beside: *gần-gụi*

nhẵn be smooth: *nhẵn-nhụi*

-ui (with long tone)

đen be black; unlucky: *đen-đủi* be unlucky

ngắn be short: *ngắn-ngủi* be very short

gần be near, beside: *gần-gũi*

- um (with short tone)

dè be moderate: *dè-dụm* economize

- un (with short tone)

măm chew into small pieces with
front teeth: *măm-mún* be in
tiny pieces

- ung (with even tone)

nhớ to remember; miss: *nhớ-nhung*
to miss

lạ be strange: *lạ-lùng*

não suffer emotionally: *não-nùng*
be sorrowful

lạnh be cold: *lạnh-lùng* be cold,
indifferent

- ung (with short tone)

nao be stirred, moved: *nao-núng*

rẻ be inexpensive; despicable:
rẻ-rúng belittle

làm do, make; work: *làm-lụng* to
toil

- ut

côi be orphaned: *côi-cút*

lẫn to hide: *lẫn-lút*

- ư (with even tone)

lắc shake from side to side: *lắc-*
lư swing, sway

trù be undecided, vacillate: *trù-*
trừ

- ưa (with even tone)

say be drunk: *say-sưa*

- ực

cùng end; be destitute: *cùng-cực*

náo make noise: *náo-nức* be
excited

rộn be noisy, disorderly: *rộn-rực*
be enthusiastic

- ươi (with short tone)

rách be torn: *rách-rưới* be ragged

dã to sap strength: *dã-dượi* be worn
out, tired

rũ droop: *rũ-rượi* droop, be dis-
heveled

7.57. Contrasting forms are common among these derivatives. Sometimes there seems to be little difference in meaning, but often the connotations or even the principal references are entirely different. The following examples furnish some notion of this variety. (Forms without glosses have meanings very similar to those of immediately preceding forms.)

chặt be tight:
  chặt-chẽ (7.56)
  chặt-chịa (7.56)
cứng be hard:
  cứng-cáp (7.56)
  cứng-cát (7.56)
  cứng-cỏi be firm (7.56)
dễ be easy:
  dễ-dãi be easy-going, generous
    (7.52)
  dễ-dàng be easy (7.56)

khát be thirsty:
  khao-khát (7.55)
  khát-khao (7.56)
khờ be gullible, naive, dull:
  khù- khờ be slow-witted (7.55)
  khờ-khạo be gullible, naive, dull
    (7.56)
  khờ-khệch be dull, stupid (7.56)
  khờ-khĩnh be gullible, naive, dull
    (7.56)

mò grope for [in dark or water]:
> *mò-mẫm* (7.56)
> *mò-mẫn* grope for a long time
> > (7.56)
> *lò-mò* grope feverishly (7.53)
> *tò-mò* be curious, want to know
> > all (7.53)

nhỏ be small:
> *nhỏ-nhắn* (7.56)
> *nhỏ-nhẻ* be soft of voice (7.56)
> *nhỏ-nhen* be pretty (7.56)

rối be mixed up, tangled:
> *rắc-rối* be complicated, intricate
> > (7.55)
> *rối-rít* be perplexed (7.56)
> *rối-rắm* be complicated (7.56)
> *rối-ren* be in confusion, disorder
> > (7.56)

rộn be noisy, disorderly:
> *rộn-rã* be vehement (7.56)
> *rộn-ràng* bother, disturb (7.56)
> *rộn-rịp* be bustling, busy (7.56)
> *rộn-rực* be enthusiastic (7.56)

rời come unstuck:
> *rời-rã* (7.56)
> *rời-rạc* be discontinuous, in-
> > harmonious (7.56)

sạch be clean:
> *sạch-sẽ* (7.56)
> *sạch-nhách* be completely clean;
> > all finished, exhausted (7.54)
> *sạch-nhách sạch-nhẻ* (7.56)
> *sạch-quách* be completely clean;
> > cleaned out, all gone (7.54)
> *sạch-sành-sanh* be very clean (7.51)

tròn be round:
> *tròn-trặn* be perfectly round (7.56)
> *tròn-trịa* (7.56)
> *tròn-trĩnh* be roundish, plump (7.56)

vặt be miscellaneous:
> *vặt-vạnh* (7.56)
> *vặt-vãnh* (7.56)

7.58. Problems. Just what the origin of these extremely varied formations may have been remains a difficult question. The surface of the modern language shows dissyllabic reduplicative elements of four different internal structures:

(1) **single morphemes:**
> *nấn-ná* procrastinate
> *nhí-nhảnh* be lively, sprightly
> *sột-sạt* rustle [paper or cloth] (also *sột-soạt*)
> *khắt-khe* (or *khe-khắt*) be stern
> *chu-chéo* to yell
> *đủng-đỉnh* go slowly, leisurely
> *thình-lình* be sudden
> *thỉnh-thoảng* from time to time
> *lôi-thôi* be complicated
> *đột-ngột* be sudden, unexpected

(2) **derivatives** (like those cited in the preceding sections)

(3) **compounds and pseudo-compounds:**

    xéo-xẹo be indirect, not quite straight (*xéo* be slanting, oblique, *xẹo* id.)

    tréo-trẹo be completely intertwined (*tréo* be crossed, at an angle, *trẹo* be off natural position, dislocated, out of joint)

    cầy-cấy engage in farming (*cầy* to plow, *cấy* transplant)

    bộn-rộn be troubled, agitated (*bộn* be in a mess, disorderly, *rộn* be noisy, troublesome, disorderly)

    tê-mê give oneself to an activity uninhibitedly (*tê* be anaesthetized, in a stupor, *mê* be unconscious; infatuated)

    dẻo-dai be pliable and durable (*dẻo* be soft, pliable, *dai* be durable)

    khẩn-khoản insist [in inviting] (*khẩn* be earnest, *khoản* insist)

    sửa-soạn prepare (*sửa* prepare, *soạn* id.)

    rải-rắc sow, disseminate (*rải* distribute, sow, *rắc* sow)

    mốc-meo be mildewed (*mốc* be mildewed, *meo* id.)

    khôn-khéo be smart, artful (*khôn* be clever, shrewd, *khéo* be skillful)

    trần-truồng be naked (*trần* be half naked, *truồng* be naked)

    ngu-ngốc be stupid (*ngu* be stupid, *ngốc* id.)

    béo-bở be advantageous (*béo* be fat, *bở* be profitable)

    lếu-láo be insolent (*lếu* be insolent, negligent, *láo* be insolent)

    đần-độn be stupid (*đần* be stupid, *độn* id.)

    chùa-chiền temples (coll.) (*chùa* Buddhist temple, *chiền* pagoda)

(4) **phrases:**

    dễ dạy be obedient, docile (*dễ* be easy, *dạy* teach, instruct)

    óng ánh be shiny (*óng* be shiny, *ánh* ray, beam)

    con cái female child (*con* child, *cái* female; cf. the apparent derivative *con-cái* children, -*ai* [with short tone])

    rõ rồi be already clear (*rõ* be clear, *rồi* be completed, over with)

The fourth category is generally quite separate from the first three—forms which are in syntactic relationship and happen to have some element in common seem easy for native speakers to separate from sequences having more intimate internal relationships. Of the examples cited above only *óng ánh* seems somewhat unclear—it may perhaps be a compound. However, to decide among the other three possibilities for many individual forms is

exceedingly difficult. For example, *thong-thả* 'be free, act leisurely' may
be a single morpheme, unanalyzable; it may contain the element *thong*
which recurs in *thong-dong* 'be at one's ease' (which otherwise appears unanalyzable; it may involve a riming suffix beginning with *d-*); it may be a
pseudo-compound containing this bound element *thong* and the free form *thả*
'throw; release, set free.'

A more complicated case is that of words meaning 'immense.' The following dissyllabic forms appear in the material studied:

> *mang-dương* be immense, huge
> *mang-mang* be immense, vast
> *mênh-mang* be immense, infinite
> *mênh-mông* id.
> *mông-lung* id. (*lung* be wicked; very, very much)
> *mông-mênh* id.
> *mông-quạnh* be vast and deserted (*quạnh* be solitary, deserted)
> *minh-mông* be immense, infinite

The constituents *mang, mênh, mông, minh* are each listed in Thanh Nghị
1952 with the notation *khd.* (*không dùng một mình* 'not used alone'); that is,
they are presumably bound forms. From the forms recorded it seems impossible to arrive at a clear base for the several forms as derivatives. The
Chinese borrowed elements which may possibly be involved are: *dương*
ocean, *mang* water overflowing, *mang* large, *minh* dark, hidden, *mông* dark,
obscure. However, it is noteworthy that Đào duy Anh 1951 gives rather different glosses for the complex elements, which may only be homonymous
Chinese borrowed forms:

> *mang dương* 'mênh mông lai láng' ('immense, overflowing, full')
> *mang mang* 'xa xuôi; mỏi mệt' ('distant; tired')
> *mang mang* (with the character glossed 'large') 'xa xuôi; mỏi mệt;
>   không biết gì; nhiều lắm (' ... ignorant; a great deal')
> *mang mang* (with the character glossed 'busy') 'việc nhiều bận rộn'
>   ('having many things to do, busy')
> *minh mông* 'mô hồ không rõ' ('imprecise, unclear')
> *mông lung* (with character glossed 'dark') 'che lấp cả' ('conceal
>   completely')
> *mông lung* (with character not separately glossed) 'lúc mặt trời
>   chưa mọc, trời còn tối' ('before sunrise, sky still dark')
> *mông lung* (with character not separately glossed) 'lúc mặt trời
>   gần lặn' ('close to sunset')

Đào duy Anh 1951 also lists three forms *mông mông*:

> (with character glossed 'drizzle') 'mưa dâm dâm' (presumably
>   a misprint for *mưa dầm dầm* 'a rather persistent rain')

(with character not separately glossed, refers only to this form)
'không rõ ràng' ('not very clear')
(with character glossed 'dark') 'mờ tối; phiền; thịnh' ('dim,
dark; disturb, bother; flourishing, a large amount')

This case is exemplary of the kind of problem involved in a careful interpretation of the material. It is obvious that a great deal of philological
study is often necessary to arrive at an understanding of the interrelationships of forms.

It might be speculated that in the dim past compounds and phrases which
involved alliteration, rime, or other similarities were considered of high
literary merit. On the basis of many such forms, new derivatives might have
been formed which resembled such compounds and phrases, but which contained elements that were by themselves meaningless. In this way reduplicative derivative patterns may have been born. Single-morpheme forms may
involve either the loss of the base as an individual recurrent element or
the imitative creation of new dissyllabic elements on the analogy of patterns already found.

On the other hand, it may be argued that at an earlier stage of the language there was an elaborate morphological system, involving many types
of chameleon affixes with more or less consistent meanings. These may or
may not have been related historically to a variety of onomatopoetic and
other single-morpheme forms of reduplicative type. Modern compounds,
pseudo-compounds, and phrases of reduplicative appearance may have been
partly coincidental, partly coined on the basis of their resemblance to the
derivatives. Or, possibly, many monosyllabic morphemes which are free in
the modern language, and thus appear now as elements in compounds or
phrases, may originally have been bound elements in earlier derivatives.
(A similar development of monosyllabic elements from dissyllabic originals
may well have taken place with nonreduplicative materials as well. The
great number of compounds and pseudo-compounds containing synonymous
elements would seem to support such a theory. See 6.24, 6.32.)

A third possibility is that reduplicative patterns may have been borrowed along with some large-scale borrowing of forms from other languages of
the area, with subsequent imitative extension. In this connection it should
be noted that the wholesale borrowing of dissyllabic forms from Chinese
seems not to have included many such elements. However, the Chinese
borrowed material enormously complicates the investigation of reduplicative forms.

A meaningful solution to this puzzle can be hoped for only after very
extensive analysis of the variety of materials involved. On the basis of
the limited examination which has been possible, the second explanation

seems to me most likely. This opinion takes into consideration the diversity of the forms involved, the lack of consistent correlation between form and meaning among the derivatives, the existence of multiple contrasting forms from the same bases, and the regularity of tonal patterning for most of the material. This view seems to fit best with the suggestions about the history of the language which have been published (esp. Maspero 1912, Haudricourt 1954).

7.6. Productive Emphatics are similar to the forms described in 7.5, but they have a consistent correlation between form and meaning and new forms seem to be coined readily. The first type involves a chameleon tonal prefix which adds a connotation of attenuation; the formation seems general for the language as a whole. The second is apparently limited to the southern dialect: a chameleon alliterative suffix adds a heavy touch of irony or scorn to the meaning of the base.

7.61. Attenuative Emphatics are slightly more picturesque and stylistically more vivid than simple attenuatives formed with the perfect chameleon affix (7.43). The prefix has the even tone of the same register as the base, except that the very few bases in the material with *ngã* tone have derivatives with *ngang* tone in the prefix (where *huyền* would be expected in keeping with the regular alternation types). It is noteworthy in this connection that some informants pronounce these forms with a *huyền* tone (especially southern speakers). It is particularly interesting that this distinction between bases with *hỏi* and *ngã* tone should be made in the south where the tones themselves have fallen together. Derivatives from bases with even tones are homonymous with the corresponding simple attenuatives.[2]

> *biệt* disappear, be lost: *biền-biệt* lose track of, lose sight of
> *bớt* diminish: *bơn-bớt* be somewhat less
> *cụt* be short: *cùn-cụt* be rather short
> *mét* be pale: *men-mét* be rather pale
> *ngót* taper off, become less: *ngơn-ngót* taper off somewhat
> *phớt* be light [of color]: *phơn-phớt* be rather light
> *sạch* be clean: *sành-sạch* be rather clean
> *sệt* be viscous: *sên-sệt* be somewhat viscous

[2] Another way of describing the circumstances would be to say that for bases with even tones there is a single attenuative formation, while for bases with short and long tones there are two possibilities—derivatives with tonal prefix are slightly more emphatic and picturesque than those with perfect chameleon affix. The derivatives discussed here might of course also be considered as based on simple attenuatives, with a first-syllable tonal superfix. However, the over-all pattern of derivatives in the language weighs against such a description. Other derivatives with dissyllabic bases are tetrasyllabic (cf. 7.7), and there are virtually no other instances of derivative superfixes (the anaphorics discussed in 7.3 are the only possible parallel).

cứng be tough: *cưng-cứng* be somewhat tough
ánh ray of light: *anh-ánh* be rather luminous
giợn tremble with fear: *giờn-giợn* be rather fearful
khá be rather good: *kha-khá* be rather mediocre
lạnh be cold: *lành-lạnh* be a bit cold
nhẹ be light [in weight]: *nhè-nhẹ* be rather light [in weight]
khẳm be full, loaded to capacity: *khăm-khẳm* be fairly full
lỏng be fluid, liquid: *long-lỏng* be somewhat fluid
nhỏ be small: *nho-nhỏ* be rather small
rõ be clear: *ro-rõ* be rather clear
sẽ be soft, gentle [of voice]: *se-sẽ* be rather soft, gentle [of
voice]

7.62. Ironic Emphatics (S) are formed with an alliterative chameleon suffix with the key shape **- iêc** [-iặk] and *sắc* or *nặng* tone according to the regular pattern. This affix adds a high emotional coloring to the meaning of the base; it generally suggests annoyance, disapproval, disinterest (perhaps feigned), irony, disparagement, and the like, on the part of the speaker, or in some instances simply a refusal to assume any responsibility in the matter at hand. These derivatives are apparently heard only in the southern dialect area, and are highly colloquial, seldom written. (This formation is extremely common with polysyllabic bases; see 7.75.)

Không có **điện-điệc** *gì đâu.* No electricity at all! (annoyed)
Không có **sách-siếc** *gì đâu.* There are no books worth anything.
Trong nhà ông đó không có tủ ghế **bàn-biệc** *gì đâu.* In his house
there's no furniture at all!
Trong nhà ông đó không có **bàn-biệc ghế-ghiếc** *gì hết.* In his
house there are no tables or chairs at all! (compound of two
derivatives; cf. 7.8)
Tôi mắc công việc nhiều quá, **rồi-riệc** *gì mà đi chơi.* I'm terribly
busy with many things, never have time to go out for a good
time.
Cuốn sách cuốn siếc *đây nè,* **lấy-liếc** *gì lấy đi!* If you want
this damned book, then take it! (angry)
Người đó không có **đau-điếc** *gì đâu!* That person's not sick at
all [he just says he is to attract attention]!

7.7. Derivatives with Polysyllabic Bases are fairly common. However, they belong to the rhetorical phase of usage rather than to the language of everyday conversation. There are few enough examples in the material studied so that the analysis reflected here may need modification in the

light of new forms. In general the resulting forms consist of four syllables, but there are also some of six syllables (cf. the much rarer three-syllable derivatives formed on monosyllabic bases). For the most part the forms may conveniently be described in the same framework as that provided for non-productive emphatics (7.5), although no vocalic affixes are evidenced and there are no riming suffixes. Some of the forms have been listed as examples of formations in that section. They share with the simpler forms a similar variety of meanings and a similar number of contrasting forms from the same bases. These forms are grouped under the heading **dramatics**. They add to the basic meaning of their bases strong dramatic overtones. Glosses have been supplied only in cases where the meaning of the derivative differs in some other way from that of its base. The few apparently productive formations are discussed in 7.75. Again, as in 7.5, some marginal material which is problematic in various ways has been omitted (for some discussion of this see Emeneau 1951: 5.5.7.2, 5.5.7.4, 5.5.7.6).

7.71. Dramatics with Tonal Affixes demonstrate the common patterns found in emphatics and some analogous ones. In the majority of cases both prefixes and suffixes of the same shape were recorded with no apparent gross difference in meaning. Six-syllable forms, which seem to be rather bombastic and are seldom used, combine the same elements in various orders. The following examples are representative of the material as a whole, which is limited. In each case the affixal syllables both have the characteristic tone; the only other difference from the base syllables are automatic (morphophonemic) alternations described in 7.13.

Hỏi tone

> bối-rối be troubled, upset, perplexed: bối-rối bối-rối, bối-rối bối-rối
>
> lôi-thôi be complicated: lôi-thôi lôi-thôi, lôi-thôi lôi-thôi
>
> lộp-cộp [sound of wooden sandals] clop-clop: lộm-cộm lộp-cộp, lộp-cộp lộm-cộm
>
> còm-ròm be emaciated: cỏm-rỏm còm-ròm, còm-ròm cỏm-rỏm

Even tone of same register:

> bải-hoải be nervously upset: bai-hoai bải-hoải, bải-hoải bai-hoai

Even tone of opposing register:

> bối-rối be troubled, upset, perplexed: bồi-rồi bối-rối, bối-rối bồi-rồi
>
> lôi-thôi be complicated: lồi-thồi lôi-thôi, lôi-thôi lồi-thồi
>
> lộp-cộp [sound of wooden sandals] clop-clop: lôm-côm lộp-cộp, lộp-cộp lôm-côm
>
> còm-ròm be emaciated: com-rom còm-ròm, còm-ròm com-rom

Short tone of opposing register:

> *phục-phịch* be fat and clumsy: *phúc-phích phục-phịch, phục-phịch phúc-phích*
>
> *rút-rít* move around a great deal: *rụt-rịt rút-rít, rút-rít rụt-rịt*
>
> *bại-hoại* be corrupted: *bái-hoái bại-hoại, bại-hoại bái-hoái*

Six-syllable combinations:

> *bổi-rổi bồi-ròi bối-rối, bối-rối bồi-ròi bổi-rổi, bổi-rổi bối-rối bồi-ròi, bồi-ròi bối-rối bổi-rổi, bối-rối bồi-ròi bổi-rổi, bổi-rổi bối-rối bồi-ròi*
>
> *lổm-cổm lôm-côm lộp-cộp, lộp-cộp lổm-cổm lôm-côm,* etc.

7.72. Dramatics with Riming Affixes are relatively rare. No suffixes have been observed, and only prefixes with *l-* and *t-* were recorded. In these forms the prefix appears in interlocking order with the syllables of the base: the first syllable of the four-syllable form is the first syllable of the prefix, followed by the first syllable of the base; then comes the second syllable of the prefix, followed by the second syllable of the base.

> *quýnh-quáng* be careless: *lính-quýnh láng-quáng*
>
> *túng-tíu* be reduced to poverty: *lúng-túng líu-tíu* be caught in a situation without recourse
>
> *mò-mẫn* grope for a long time: *tò-mò tẫn-mẫn*

7.73. Dramatics with Alliterative Prefixes are most common in the material studied, except for the productive formation described in 7.75. In the four-syllable forms the prefix reproduces the base exactly through the initial of the second syllable, replacing the vowel and final of that syllable with the even tone of the same register.

-a (with even tone)

> *khóc-lóc* weep, cry: *khóc-la khóc-lóc*
>
> *ky-cóp* collect bit by bit: *ky-ca ky-cóp*
>
> *lung-thung* be too big [of clothes]: *lung-thà lung-thung*
>
> *dủng-dỉnh* go slowly, leisurely: *dủng-da dủng-dỉnh*
>
> *õng-ẹo* behave affectedly: *õng-à õng-ẹo*
>
> *dỏng-dảnh* be difficult, exacting: *dỏng-da dỏng-dảnh*
>
> *nhí-nhảnh* be lively, sprightly: *nhí-nha nhí-nhảnh*

7.74. Dramatics with Alliterative Suffixes only vaguely suggest the enormous variety of the formations with monosyllabic bases. In the tetrasyllabic forms the suffix reproduces the base exactly through the initial

175

of the second syllable, replacing the vowel, final, and tone of that syllable
with one of the elements reported in 7.56. (Note that the tone register of
the suffix depends on the tone of the second syllable of the base.)

> sạch-nhách be absolutely clean: sạch-nhách sạch-nhẻ
> trong-sạch be clear: trong-sạch trong-sẽ
> cụt-ngủn be very short: cụt-ngủn cụt-nghỉu
> thấp-xủn be very short: thấp-xủn thấp-xỉu
> nhớt-nhợt be very viscous: nhớt-nhợt nhớt-nhọ
> trụi-lủi be completely denuded: trụi-lủi trụi-lơ
> xa-lắc be very distant: xa-lắc xa-lơ

Many of the bases here are compounds or pseudo-compounds; of the ones
cited above only sạch-nhách and nhớt-nhợt are derivatives. The same patterns extend to phrases (see 7.8).

7.75. Productive Derivation with Polysyllabic Bases involves the
chameleon alliterative suffix - iêc, limited to the southern dialect. It might
well be expected that the productive attenuative affix (7.61) would form
derivatives on polysyllabic bases, but no such forms occur in the material.

> khóc-lóc weep, cry: khóc-lóc khóc-liếc be a cry-baby
> Đừng khóc-lóc khóc-liếc hoài như thế! Don't be such a cry-baby
> all the time!
> Người đó không khóc-lóc không khóc-liếc gì đâu. That person
> won't weep at all [don't be ridiculous].
> Em đó hay khóc-lóc hay khóc-liếc, không bao giờ nín. That
> child cries continuously, never stops.

Note the interlocking order in the last two examples. This shows the extension of the principle of reduplicative derivatives based on polysyllabic
forms to phrases (see 7.8).

7.8. Derivatives and Phrase Structure. The same vagueness of the line
separating words from phrases which we have noted in connection with
compounds and pseudo-compounds (6.1) can be observed in derivative
formations as well. Many of the derivatives described in the preceding sections occur in prose more often than not in interlocking order with the immediately preceding word and its repetition.[3] In the case of alliterative
suffixes there is no formal difference between the resulting sequence of
forms and similar sequences involving derivatives based on other derivatives or compounds or pseudo-compounds. Examples with the ironic suffix
-iêc are extremely common in southern speech.

---

[3] We might expect cases when it is rather the word following the derivative that is involved, but examples are lacking in the material.

Cuốn sách cuốn siếc *đây nè, lấy-liếc gì lấy đi!* If you want this
damned book, then take it!
Người đó **không đau không điếc** *gì đâu!* That person's not sick
at all [he just says he is to attract attention]!
In some cases, this interlocking order is the only one possible. This suggests that the syntactic relationships involved are somewhat closer in such
cases. The first example above involves such a sequence: when the classifier *cuốn* is used with *sách-siếc* it is always repeated between the two
syllables of the derivative. In other cases, where this construction is optional, the interlocking order achieves a more emphatic or picturesque
effect.

There are also differences between compounds or phrases made up of
derivatives and derivatives based on phrases or compounds: *bàn-ghế bàn
ghiếc* 'any old kind of furniture' is a derivative based on the compound
bàn-ghế 'furniture'; *bàn-biệc ghế-ghiếc* is a phrase or compound made up
of derivatives. The phrase means something like 'any old tables and
chairs'; the compound means something barely distinguishable from the
preceding example—here there is a heavier emphasis on disapproval of the
items composing the furniture, while in *bàn-ghế bàn-ghiếc* there is more
emphasis on disapproval of the furniture as a whole.

Further examples of derivatives of various sorts in interlocking order
with preceding repeated elements follow.
Việc đó tôi làm **không lính không quýnh** *gì, tự-nhiên.* (S) I took
care of that matter myself without fearing anything.
Người đó làm việc **hay lính hay quýnh** *quá, nên không được gì
hết.* (S) That fellow works with such a fearful attitude that he
can't do anything.
Ông làm ơn nói **cho rành cho rẽ** *ra đặng tôi hiểu cho rõ.* (S) Please
speak very distinctly [separating words] so that I can understand clearly.
Ông ăn **thật no thật nê** *đi, rồi sẽ làm.* (S) Go ahead and eat
really heartily, then work afterwards.
Ông **ăn no ăn nê** *đi!* Eat heartily
Người đó **ngủ mê ngủ man** *như chết.* (S) That person is sound
asleep—dead to the world.
Nó **đi chậm đi chạp** *quá.* It [a child or animal] walks very slowly.
Việc đó làm cho tôi **phải bùi phải ngùi** *luôn-luôn.* (S) That [sort
of] thing makes me feel melancholy all the time.
Cái áo nầy thợ may cắt **cho cụt-ngủn cho cụt-nghỉu.** This tunic
the tailor cut terribly short.
Thằng nhỏ nầy **thấp lùn thấp xủn** *quá đỗi.* (S) That child is
short beyond imagination!

Công việc đó làm **cho bai-hoai cho bải-hoải** *mọi người.* (S) That affair enervated everyone.

Người đó không **có đất có đai** *gì hết.* (S) That person has no land whatsoever.

Cái đó **không bứ không bự** *gì.* (S pop.) That's not big at all.

Cái ruột xe đó **không xẹp không lép** *chút nào.* (S) That inner tube isn't at all deflated.

Tôi có một số tiền **rất cỏn rất con.** I have a very small sum of money.

Hãy **làm lia làm lịa** *đi!* Go ahead and get it done quickly!

Because of this difficulty in drawing the line between derivatives and phrases involving them, it is sometimes difficult to determine whether a given sequence is a complex derivative (that is, based on another derivative or compound) or an instance of a phrase involving one or more derivatives. A few examples of questionable cases follow:

xéo-xẹo xéo-xọ 'be very deformed' may be a phrase containing the compound *xéo-xẹo* id. and the derivative *xéo-xọ* id.; or it may be a complex derivative based on *xéo-xẹo.*

khóc-la khóc-lết 'drag oneself along crying' may be a phrase containing *khóc* 'weep' and *la-lết* 'drag oneself along' (derivative based on *lết,* or possibly a compound containing *la* 'cry out'); or it may be a derivative based on *khóc-lết* 'drag oneself along crying.'

It is interesting to note that derivatives of the type described in 7.61 (attenuative emphatics) do not occur in interlocking order.

Anh ấy chưa làm việc nhiều, nhưng **hơi mền-mệt** *rồi.* He hasn't been working long but he's a bit tired already.

There are also some derivatives which only rarely appear in interlocking order. It has not been possible to identify any controlling factors.

CHAPTER 8

Substantival Elements

8.1. Substantives. There are two sets of markers (5.63) which help identify substantival elements. They are **plural markers** (appearing as restrictive complements) and **demonstrative markers** (appearing as descriptive
complements).

PLURAL MARKERS (8.2)

những plural

các plural (all of a given set)

mọi every

mỗi each

từng each (in turn)

DEMONSTRATIVE MARKERS (8.5)

nào which(ever)

này (S nầy) this

nọ that, (an)other

ấy [the one] just referred to

nấy this [one] just mentioned

All those words which are found in some instances directly following a
sentence initial plural marker and/or which occur as head with a demonstrative marker as complement are **substantives.**

Mỗi **người** ... Each person ...

Mỗi **sáu** *người* ... Each six people ...

Mỗi **trăm** *người* ... Each hundred people ...

Mỗi **mấy** *người* ... Each few people ...

Những **chó** ... Dogs ...

Những **con** *chó* ... The dogs ...

Những **gì** ... Things ...

sữa *này* this milk

trong *ấy* Inside there

A phrase containing a substantive as center (5.62) is a **substantival
phrase.** Such phrases are formed by various subtypes of the three basic
construction types (5.61): they are called **substantival constructions,**
and are discussed in detail in 8.3.

179

8.2. Plural Markers convey, in addition to the notion of plurality, some special connotations. We have used their occurrence at the beginning of sentences to define substantives, but they are all common in other positions as well.

Những 'some, several [of the same category]' has a slightly literary flavor and is less common than **các** in ordinary speech. **Các** implies that all of a given set of entities are involved, while **những** suggests that only certain of the total possible number are referred to.

> **Những** *cái đèn trong nhà nầy tối quá.* (S) [Some of the] lights in this house are terribly dim.

> **Các** *cái đèn trong nhà nầy tối quá.* (S) The lights in this house are terribly dim [all of them].

> *Như vậy* **các** *ông đến nơi thì gặp* **những** *ngày cuối năm âm-lịch.* In this way they ["the gentlemen"] [would] arrive there [and] run into some of the final days of the year [according to] the moon calendar.

> **Những** *làn sóng lớn bị tầu cắt đôi, đập vào hai bên mạn tầu, tung lên* **những** *bọt trắng-xóa.* Large waves were cut in two by the ship, [they] struck against the two sides of the ship [and] threw up bubbles of glistening white spray.

> *Anh ấy ăn* **những** *tám bát cơm.* He ate some [i.e., as many as] eight bowls of rice.

> *Ngoài cửa là dẫy nhà đồ-sộ, một bên thì bầy* **những** *ảnh* **các** *tài-tử và* **những** *ảnh chụp* **các** *đoạn phim đã quay.* Outside [the door] was a row of imposing buildings, on one side [there were] displayed some portraits of the actors and some shots from completed films. ["...portion film already turn"]

It has been asserted (e.g., Lê văn Lý 1948, p. 174) that **các** serves to distinguish second person reference (the persons addressed) from third person reference (forms pluralized with **những**). This formulation is misleading, since **các** often appears pluralizing forms referring to third person entities (as in the second example above). **Những** is uncommon in conversation; moreover, in addressing persons a speaker almost inevitably includes all of a certain category in his reference. Thus **những** would hardly be expected in direct address.

The three remaining forms all carry some connotation of individuality of the entities pluralized; they differ in emphasis. **Mọi** 'every' stresses the totality of the category referred to. Jones and Thông 1960 notes (p. 190) that with words denoting units of time *mọi* refers to past time. Presumably this is simply a consequence of the connotation of totality or completeness which it bears. The notion 'every item of a complete set' must presume that the set is a closed class, thus naturally referring to something in the

180

past. **Mỗi** 'each' emphasizes rather the identity of individual members of the class. **Từng** 'each (in turn)' adds the notion of individual entities following one another rather than engaged in concerted activity.

Mọi *năm các bạn lên Đà-lạt ở hai tuần nghỉ mát.* Every year the friends went up to Dalat for their two-week vacation.

Tôi sẽ lo **mọi** *việc.* I'll take care of everything.

Tôi sẽ lo **mỗi** *việc* **mỗi** *lúc.* I'll take care of one thing at a time.

Hôm qua **mọi** *người có mặt.* Yesterday everybody was present.

Hôm qua **mỗi** *người có mặt đều cho tiền.* Each person present yesterday gave money.

Từng *gia-đình một đi bỏ phiếu.* Family by family they went to cast [their] votes.

Từng *ba người một chạy thi.* Three by three they ran races.

Công-an đi đến **từng** *nhà mà điều-tra.* The police went from house to house investigating.

Phrases with **mỗi** are nearly always followed by phrases later in the sentence in which a specific quantity or individual item is mentioned. In cases where a speaker does not wish to mention such a specific quantity, he uses a different kind of expression, with an indefinite word and either **cũng** 'likewise' or **đều** 'equal(ly)' (see 14.2).

Mỗi *ngày tôi ăn hai quả trứng.* Each day I eat two eggs.

Ngày **nào** *tôi* **cũng** (or **đều**) *ăn trứng.* Every day I eat eggs.

Expressions with **từng** are regularly closed by the word **một** 'one' as a final descriptive complement when they come first in the sentence (as focal complements, cf. 10.1-2). This usage is also common in other positions. For further discussion and examples see **từng** in Appendix A.

8.3. Substantival Phrase and Word Classes.

All three of the basic construction types are well represented in phrases having a substantive as center (5.62). These constructions are discussed in the following sections, together with the special features which make clear the different grammatical functions of the various subtypes of substantives.

8.31. Numerative Phrases

are formed by a restrictive construction with a substantive or substantival phrase as head. The first element of such phrases (the restrictive complement) is the **numerator**; it is often itself a numerative phrase, although other phrase types also occur in this position (8.32-33).

The plural markers are **numerators**. Substantives which serve as numerators are **numerals** (8.4). Other substantives are **nominals** (8.6).

There are certain kinds of phrases in which a numeral appears as head: these are **numeral phrases** (distinct from numerative phrases, as defined above: some numeral phrases are also numerative phrases, formed with the restrictive construction, but others have a coordinating construction). The more complicated numbers involve such numeral phrases (cf. 8.45). A **nominal phrase**, on the other hand, has a nominal as head (for examples, see 8.34).

NUMERALS

> **sáu** *người* six people
> **trăm** *năm* a hundred years
> **nửa** *giờ* half an hour

NUMERAL PHRASES

> *hai trăm* two hundred (numerative)
> *năm sáu* five or six (approximative, with coordinating construction)
> *mười hai* twelve (additive, with coordinating construction)

A few nonsubstantives occur as numerators. The most common are quantifiers (9.53). However, not all restrictive complements of substantives are numerators (see 8.35).

8.32. Approximative Phrases have two or more heads in a coordinating construction. These heads are generally numerals denoting successively larger quantities. Such phrases most commonly serve as numerators (8.31).

> *Sáng nay có* **ba bốn** *người đến hỏi thăm.* This morning three or four people came to inquire.
> *Tôi có thể tới trễ* **năm mười** *phút được không?* If I should arrive five or ten minutes late, will it be all right?
> *Nhớ lúc rượu ngon năm bảy chén ...* Remembering the occasion of five or [six or] seven glasses of good wine ...–Tản-Đà
> *Sau lưng theo* **một vài** *thằng cỏn con.* Behind him ["behind back"] followed a few ["one or a couple"] small boys.

Note in the second example that **năm mười** means 'five or ten', as opposed to **năm mươi** 'fifty', a numerative phrase with **năm** as numerator (8.31). ((For the special allomorph **mươi** see 8.43.)

This construction appears occasionally with focuses (10.4) as heads.

> **Mai mốt** *ông đó lên Đà-lạt.* (S) Tomorrow or the next day he's going up to Dalat.

8.33. Additive Phrases are other substantival phrases formed by a coordinating construction. Like approximative phrases they involve two or more heads; when the heads are numerals, the earlier ones denote quantities larger than the later ones. In phrases containing nominals, the first head often denotes a larger or more important entity than the second, and so on. But there are phrases where there is little indication of any priority for any of the heads. As is the case with phrases of similar function in English and other languages, there are a number of common expressions with a fixed order, while other collocations of heads are found in different orders. Phrases of various other constructions are common as heads.

VARIABLE

 cam, quít, chuối oranges, tangerines, and bananas
 cam, chuối, quít oranges, bananas, and tangerines

FIXED

 ông bà Mr. and Mrs., a gentleman and a lady (his wife)
 vợ chồng husband and wife ["wife husband"]
 cha con father and son
 hai đồng rưỡi two and a half piastres
 ba trăm sáu mươi bảy three hundred sixty-seven

  Hai vợ chồng *lấy vàng đưa về làm giàu làm có, ăn tiêu sung-
  sướng.* The two of them, husband and wife, took the gold home, it made them rich and they spent it happily.

  Các ông các bà *là ai?* Who are you people ["plural gentleman plural lady"]?

  Đêm ngày *tôi thường cầu-nguyện để xin Thượng-đế cho cha tôi sinh mấy đứa em nữa để chúng nó chơi với tôi cho vui.* Night and day I (often) pray (in order to beg) God to let my father give birth to some younger brothers and sisters so they [could] play with me and [we all would] have a good time.

8.34. Descriptive Phrases are extremely common with a nominal or nominal phrase as head. Complements are of the most varied sorts: nearly every type of phrase and a great many individual word types appear as descriptive complements to nominal heads.

  người bạn a friend ["person friend"]
  số mười number ten
  số mười hai number twelve
  cái bàn the table ["object table"]
  tiếng Việt-nam the Vietnamese language
  cha tôi my father ["father I"]
  nhà tôi ở the house I live in
  nhà thương hospital ["building be-wounded"]
  nhà thương-binh military hospital ["building wounded-soldier"]
  hôm nay today ["day now"]
  áo mưa raincoat ["tunic rain"]

As can be seen from the examples above, descriptive complements regularly make more specific the reference of their heads. This has to do with important differences in the class meanings of different types of nominals (8.6).

Complexes (5.62) with descriptive construction and nominals as centers are common, especially two or three layers deep.

> *người bạn tôi* my friend
>
> *nhà thương-binh Đà-lạt* the Dalat military hospital
>
> *cột ăng-tên vô-tuyến truyền-hình ở các làng Mỹ* television antennas in American villages ["pole antenna without-wire transmit-picture located plural village America"]

Demonstrative markers serve primarily as descriptive complements, and in general they are outermost in substantival descriptive complexes. For details see 8.5.

8.35. Other Substantival Phrases are restrictive phrases with a complement other than the usual numerators (8.31). These restrictive complements are to be separated from numerators on the basis that they occur on occasion with heads consisting of numerative phrases in which the numerator is a plural marker or a numeral. The most common of these restrictive complements are prepositive particles (11.82) and predicative markers (see 9.1), but negatives are also found in this use (9.4).

> **như** *các bạn của ông Lâm* like Mr. Lâm's friends; **như** *cha tôi* like my father (prepositive particle)
>
> *Họ* **là** *các người cùng làm một sở với tôi.* They are the people who work in the same office I do. (predicative marker)
>
> *Bây giờ* **đã** *hai giờ.* It is already two o'clock now. (predicative marker)
>
> **không** *ai* no one; **không** *mọi ngày* not every day (negative)

8.4. Numerals are substantives which occur as numerators. Some numerals also occur as heads of numerative phrases; they are **multiple numbers** (8.43). Others do not occur in this position; they are **unit numbers** (8.41). One unit number has a special limited distribution: **mấy** 'an unspecified number (generally less than ten)' serves as a numerator like other unit numbers and occurs in most other positions as they do, but in additive phrases it occurs only as the final head or as the numerator of a nonfinal head which is followed by heads containing recurrences of **mấy**. This is the **indefinite number** (8.42).

8.41. Unit Numbers are numerals which do not occur as heads of numerative phrases. They appear as simple numerators (8.31), as heads in approximative phrases (8.32), as the final head in additive phrases (8.33), and as descriptive complements (8.34). In these positions some unit numbers have special forms, which are listed below. There is also a good deal of dialectal variation in the use of numbers. The most important variants in current use are included in the list. Those which are geographically determined are shown in parentheses after the form regarded as standard. Some variants appear to be optional (further study may well reveal that many or all of these have distributions determined by geographical region or social class): these are listed separated by diagonals, with the most common form first; geographical identification is included in parentheses where it is determinable. The special forms have limited distributions which are only suggested by the column headings; these distributions are detailed in the discussion following the list.

BASIC FORM	FINAL ADDITIVE HEAD	DESCRIPTIVE COMPLEMENT
một one	*mốt*	*nhất* (S *nhứt*)
hai two		*nhì/hai*
vài a couple, two or three, a few		
ba three		
bốn four	*bốn/tư* (N)	*tư*
năm five	*lăm/nhăm* (N)	
sáu six		
bảy (S *bẩy*) seven		
tám eight		
chín nine		

Một occurs as final additive head in *mười* **một** 'eleven', *một trăm* **một** 'one hundred one', *một ngàn* **một** 'one thousand one', *một giờ* **một** 'one hour and one minute; one minute past one'; but elsewhere we find **mốt**: *hai mươi* **mốt** '21', *ba mươi* **mốt** '31', *một trăm* **mốt** '110', *một ngàn* **mốt** '1,100', *một đồng* **mốt** '1.1 piastre', etc.

The special forms as descriptive complements occur after **thứ** 'ordinal designator, - th' (8.45), **phần** 'fractional denominator' (8.44), and in a few other cases. They do not occur after the general categorical **số** 'number', which is used most commonly to introduce numbers as descriptive complements. **Thứ nhì** has a more literary flavor than **thứ hai** 'second.' However, only **thứ hai** occurs as the form meaning 'Monday' (second day of the week).

As an alternate for **bốn** as final additive head, **tư** occurs after *mười* (8.43) in *mười* **tư** 'fourteen', and is quite common in higher numbers: *hai mươi* **tư** '24', *ba mươi* **tư** '34', etc. However, **bốn** is also common in this use throughout the country, and is the regular form in the south.

Lăm replaces **năm** everywhere after *mười* and *mươi* (8.43): *mười* **lăm**

'15', *hai mươi* **lăm** '25', etc. In the north **nhăm** is also heard beginning
with *hai mươi* **nhăm** '25' (but **nhăm** is not used after *mười* in the expression
for 'fifteen'). Both of these forms are often replaced by **rưởi** 'and one half'
(8.43): *một trăm* **rưởi** '150', *hai ngàn* **rưởi** '2,500' ["a hundred and a half",
"two thousand and a half"].

   Một has a number of special uses which set it apart from other numerals.
Note, for example, its appearance in expressions with **từng** (8.2 end). Only
one case, however, is of special consequence: this is the fact that nominals which are not numerated by other numerals do appear on occasion with
một as numerator (cf. 8.6).

   Anh sống một đời giản-dị và chết đi không nhớ tiếc **một** *ai*. He
      lived a simple life and died not recalling with regret a single
      person [i.e., he died happily].

It is also clear that **một** has a far less specifically numerical value than
other numbers. In many contexts it functions much like the indefinite article in English. In some cases it emphasizes the notion of identity: 'one
and the same.'

   Anh tự nghĩ anh là **một** *người sung-sướng*. He considers himself a
      happy person.

   Hai ông cùng có chung **một** *ý-tưởng*. The two men both had the
      same idea.

   *Từ trước đến nay, người ta vẫn tin rằng ch, nh, cuối trong các
      tiếng anh, ách, ênh, ếch, inh, ích là* **một** *với ch, nh đầu trong
      cha, nha...* (From an earlier period) up to the present time
      people still believe that final *ch, nh* in the words *anh, ách,
      ênh, ếch, inh, ích,* are identical with initial *ch, nh* in *cha, nha...*

8.42. The Indefinite Number. **Mấy** 'an unspecified number (generally
less than ten)' has the regular semantic range and variety of uses of indefinites (14.2). In additive phrases it occurs only in the final head or in
a nonfinal head which is followed by heads containing recurrences of **mấy**.

   mấy *ngàn* **mấy** *trăm* **mấy** *mươi* **mấy** a few thousand odd
   hai mươi **mấy** twenty-odd
   mấy *trăm* a few hundred
   mấy *người?* how many people?

8.43. Multiple Numbers are numerals which occur as heads of numera-
tive phrases. They are listed below, with special forms and dialectal variations noted.

BASIC FORM	SPECIAL FORMS AND VARIANTS
nửa half	*rưỡi* (second head in additive phrase with a numeral as first head)
	rưỡi (second head in additive phrase with a non-numeral as first head)
mười ten	*mươi* (head of numerative phrase)
trăm hundred	
ngàn thousand	*nghìn* (N)
vạn ten thousand	*muôn* (S)
úc hundred thousand	
triệu million	
tỷ billion	

Numbers larger than **vạn** (S **muôn**) are seldom used. In many local dialects the distinction between **rưỡi** and **rưỡi** has disappeared—**rưỡi** occurring in all cases. There is frequent confusion in print because of this. (Of course, in the dialects where *hỏi* and *ngã* tones have coalesced the forms cannot be distinguished in any case.) **Muôn**, in addition to being a southern dialectal form, also occurs frequently in poetry.

The word **chục** (a classifier, 8.61) basically refers to ten items considered as a group or collection. However, in colloquial speech in many areas it virtually replaces **mươi** in the designation of approximately even groups of ten.

> *hai* **chục** 'group of (about) twenty' replacing *hai* **mươi** 'exactly 20'
> *bốn* **chục** 'group of (about) forty' replacing *bốn* **mươi** 'exactly 40'
> *năm* **chục** *rưỡi* 'group of 55'

8.44. Other Numerators

8.44. Other Numerators are a few nonsubstantives (cf. 9.53 and 11.82) and phrases of various sorts. The more complex numbers have numerators which are themselves numerative phrases (8.31) or additive phrases (8.33) or combinations of the two. Approximative phrases (8.32) also occur. Some complex numerators involve phrases containing non-numerals.

Fractions smaller than one half are phrases with the general categorical (8.62) **phần** 'part' as ultimate head. At simplest, **phần** is followed by a descriptive complement denoting the denominator, and no numerator is stated. In the more complex forms the phrase with **phần** becomes the head of a numerative phrase. With the word for 'hundred' the form also designates percentages.

phần *tư* a fourth	*hai* **phần** *ba* two thirds
phần *mười* a tenth	*sáu* **phần** *mười* six tenths
phần *trăm* a hundredth; percentage	*chín* **phần** *ba mươi hai* 9/32
một **phần** *tư* one fourth	*tám mươi lăm* **phần** *trăm* 85/100; 85 percent

In southern colloquial usage the general categorical **góc** 'corner' replaces **phần** in the more frequently used fractions (involving low numbers).

> *một* **góc** *tư* one fourth
> *hai* **góc** *ba* two thirds

8.45. The Number System is based on decimal distinctions.

The unit numbers represent quantities less than ten; multiple numbers denote groups beginning with ten and increasing by a factor of ten: hundreds, thousands, ten thousands, hundred thousands, millions, billions. The higher numbers consist of additive phrases in which each head denotes a successively lower level in this decimal system. Unless some device makes it clear that something else is to be understood, the final head in such phrases refers to the next lower level in the system. Thus *hai trăm hai* means 220, *hai ngàn hai* means 2,200 (2,020 is *hai ngàn hai mươi*), and so on. The prepositive particle (11.81) **lẻ** (N **linh**) signals that one or more levels are skipped: *hai ngàn* **lẻ** (or **linh**) *hai* '2,002', *hai trăm* **linh** (or **lẻ**) *hai* '202', etc. Actually the phrase *hai ngàn hai* is ambiguous. Although it usually would be understood to mean '2,200', it could be understood as '2,002.' It is thus much like the American English usage *seventeen (thousand) five* meaning 17,500, which could also be understood as 17,005 (or, without the word *thousand*, as 1705). After **linh** and **lẻ** only the basic forms of unit numbers are found.

There are two common abbreviated (contracted) forms in the spoken language which are sometimes also written: **hăm** for *hai mươi* (before another additive head), **băm** for *ba mươi* (similarly).

> **hăm** *mốt* 21, **hăm** *chín* 29, **băm** *hai* 32, **băm** *bảy* 37

Beginning with the forties the word *mươi* is often simply omitted in rapid speech before a following additive head (these forms are also occasionally written).

> *bốn hai* 42, *năm ba* 53, *sáu tám* 68, *bảy tư* 74, etc.

There are a number of cases of alternate forms in current use. The overall system is outlined below. It is interesting to note that there seems to be no primary word for zero; where this concept is discussed it is designated **số không** 'empty (or perhaps "negative") number.'

0	*số không*	6	*sáu*
1/2	*nửa, rưỡi, rưởi* (8.43)	7	*bảy* (S *bẩy*)
1	*một, mốt* (8.41)	8	*tám*
2	*hai, nhì* (8.41)	9	*chín*
3	*ba*	10	*mười*
4	*bốn, tư* (8.41)	11	*mười một*
5	*năm, lăm* (N *nhăm*) (8.41)	12	*mười hai*

13 *mười ba*

14 *mười bốn, mười tư* (8.41)

15 *mười lăm*

16 *mười sáu*

17 *mười bảy* (S *mười bẩy*)

18 *mười tám*

19 *mười chín*

20 *hai mươi, đôi mươi, hai chục*

21 *hai mươi mốt, hăm mốt*

22 *hai mươi hai, hăm hai*

24 *hai mươi bốn, hăm bốn, hai mươi tư, hăm tư*

25 *hai mươi lăm, hăm lăm* (N *hai mươi nhăm, hăm nhăm*)

30 *ba mươi, ba chục*

31 *ba mươi mốt, băm mốt*

34 *ba mươi bốn, băm bốn, ba mươi tư, băm tư*

35 *ba mươi lăm, băm lăm* (N *ba mươi nhăm, băm nhăm*)

40 *bốn mươi, bốn chục*

41 *bốn* (*mươi*) *mốt*

49 *bốn* (*mươi*) *chín*

50 *năm mươi, năm chục*, occasionally *nửa trăm*

55 *năm* (*mươi*) *lăm* [N *năm* (*mươi*) *nhăm*]

60 *sáu mươi, sáu chục*

64 *sáu* (*mươi*) *bốn, sáu* (*mươi*) *tư*

70 *bảy mươi, bảy chục* (S *bẩy mươi, bẩy chục*)

80 *tám mươi, tám chục*

90 *chín mươi, chín chục*

100 (*một*) *trăm, mười mươi*

101 *một trăm* (*lẻ*) *một* (N *một trăm linh một*)

102 *một trăm lẻ* (or N *linh*) *hai*

104 *một trăm lẻ* (or N *linh*) *bốn*

105 *một trăm lẻ* (or N *linh*) *năm*

110 *một trăm mốt, một trăm mười*

111 *một trăm mười một*

115 *một trăm mười lăm*

120 *một trăm hai* (*mươi/chục*)

121 *một trăm hai mươi mốt, một trăm hăm mốt*

150 *một trăm năm* (*mươi/chục*), *một trăm rưởi*

200 *hai trăm*

500 *năm trăm* occasionally *nửa ngàn* (N *nửa nghìn*)

1000 (*một*) *ngàn* [N (*một*) *nghìn*], *mười trăm*

1001 *một ngàn* (*lẻ* or N *linh*) *một* [N *một nghìn* (*linh* or *lẻ*) *một*]

1010 *một ngàn mười* (N *một nghìn mười*)

1100 *một ngàn mốt, một ngàn một trăm* (N ...*nghìn*...)

10,000 (*một*) *vạn* [S (*một*) *muôn*], *mười ngàn* (N *mười nghìn*)

100,000 (*một*) *ức, mười vạn* (S *mười muôn*)

1,000,000 (*một*) *triệu*

10,000,000 (*một*) *tỷ*

One of the forms cited above merits a special note. *Đôi mươi* is a descriptive phrase: 'a pair of tens.' *Đôi* 'couple, pair' is a general categorical (8.62). However, it must be recognized that this expression involves a special case of *mươi* as a complement; otherwise it occurs only as head of numerative phrases with unit numbers. For this reason *đôi* might be regarded as a kind of numeral, although it also occurs in positions (e.g., with a demonstrative marker as descriptive complement) where no other numeral occurs.

Sino-Vietnamese numerical forms are frequent in literary texts. They combine with other pseudo-bases (5.55) of Chinese origin. The basic forms are shown below with enough examples to make the system clear. Note that the elements meaning 'one', 'two', 'four', and 'ten thousand' appear in (or are very similar to related forms in) the regular system.

1	*nhất* (S *nhứt*)	11	*thập nhất* (S *thập nhứt*)
2	*nhị*	22	*nhị thập nhị*
3	*tam*	33	*tam thập tam*
4	*tứ*	400	*tứ bách*
5	*ngũ*	555	*ngũ bách ngũ thập ngũ*
6	*lục*	6000	*lục thiên*
7	*thất*	7143	*thất thiên nhất bách tứ*
8	*bát*		*thập tam*
9	*cửu*	80,000	*bát vạn*
10	*thập*	90,700	*cửu vạn thất bách*
100	*(nhất) bách*		
1000	*(nhất) thiên*		
10,000	*(nhất) vạn*		

8.46. Other Uses of Numerals and Numeral Phrases. Both individual numerals and approximative and additive numeral phrases are common as descriptive complements. First of all, the equivalents of English ordinal numbers are formed as descriptive phrases with the ordinal general categorical (8.62) **thứ** as head (for special allomorphs, see 8.41).

thứ nhất (S *thứ nhứt*) first	*thứ mười* tenth
thứ nhì second	*thứ mười một* eleventh
thứ ba third	*thứ mười lăm* fifteenth
thứ tư fourth	*thứ ba mươi* thirtieth
thứ năm fifth	*thứ một trăm năm mươi hai* 152d

Another common descriptive complement position for numerals is after the general categorical **số** 'number.' Descriptive phrases of this sort handle most instances where specific cardinal numbers are called for.

đường Lê Lợi số 182 (read: *một trăm tám mươi hai*) 182 Lê Lợi Street
số 31 (read: *ba mươi mốt*) No. 31

Numerals appear as complements in predicative descriptive phrases (9.62) as well as in their substantival counterparts.

Chia ra làm ba. Divide [it] into three [parts].

Xưa có người học trò rất thông-minh. Học **một** *biết* **hai,** *tính lại chăm học.* Long ago there was a very intelligent student. He learned very quickly; moreover he was by nature studious. ["Formerly exist person student (*học trò*) very intelligent. Study one know two, character contrary-to-expectations diligent know two, character contrary-to-expectations diligent study."]

8.5. Demonstrative Markers are manner focuses (10.45; see also 7.23)

which are far more frequent as descriptive complements to nominals and nominal phrases (8.31, 8.6). In descriptive complexes (8.34) a demonstrative marker usually appears as outermost complement.

nào whichever (indefinite, see 14.2)
này (S **nầy**) this
nọ (an)other, that
ấy just mentioned or referred to

Phải của trời cho thì đứa **nào** *lấy được.* [If it's] really given by heaven, then whoever could take it [away]!

Những chiếc phi-cơ **này** *bay nhanh quá.* These (several) airplanes are flying very fast.

Đi qua một cổng to lại đến một cổng nữa, từ cổng **nọ** *đến cổng kia là những ngôi nhà mái cong.* Passing by one large main entrance [and] coming to yet another, [one sees that] between those main entrances are sumptuous buildings with curved roofs. ["go pass one main-entrance large contrary-to-expectations arrive one main-entrance in-addition, from main-entrance that arrive main-entrance yonder identificational-marker plural sumptuous-structure building roof be-curved"]

Nó còn bán cái xác chết **ấy** *cho ai được mà bác sợ?* Who in the world else do you suppose he can sell that dead body to? (So what are you worried about?) ["he remain sell object corpse die just-referred-to give whoever possible descriptive-marker father's-elder-brother be-afraid?"]

nhà **này** this building
nhà thương **này** this hospital
nhà thương-binh **này** this military hospital ["...wounded-soldier..."]
nhà thương-binh Đà-lạt **này** this Dalat military hospital

Occasionally there are descriptive complements appearing as outer elements beyond demonstrative markers; they are most often clauses, sometimes introduced by the subordinating particle *mà* (11.52 and Appendix A).

Cái nhà trắng ấy **mà ông đứng đây thấy** *là của ông Lâm.* That white house that you [can] see [from a position] standing here is Mr. Lâm's.

8.6. Nominals are those substantives which do not occur as (single-word) numerators (8.31). (Some of them do occur as parts of phrases serving as numerators; cf. 8.44.) On the other hand, they are frequently heads of descriptive phrases, where numerals do not occur.

Categoricals. Some nominals occur freely as heads of numerative phrases, with all kinds of numerators. They are categoricals, of two subtypes—**general categoricals** (8.62), which occur as single-word descriptive complements; and **classifiers** (8.61), which do not.

General categorical: **người** person

> *hai người* two people
>
> *Không nên đánh người.* [One] shouldn't hit people.

Classifier: **quyển** volume (speaking of books)

> *hai quyển* two volumes
>
> *Tôi lấy một quyển.* I'll take one volume.
>
> *Tôi lấy quyển ấy.* I'll take that volume.

In the last two examples *quyển* is part of a phrase serving as descriptive complement, but it does not occur in this position by itself.

Nouns. Other nominals do not appear as head when a numeral (except *một*; cf. 8.41 end) is numerator. They are **nouns,** of several subtypes, depending on certain other special features of distribution. **Relator nouns** (8.63) are not numerated at all. **Mass nouns** (8.64) are not preceded by any of the usual numerators, but commonly appear with quantifiers (9.53) in that function (cf. 8.31). **Indefinite nouns** (8.65) are numerated with *những* (and occasionally with *một*). Others are **item nouns** (8.66), which occur with all kinds of numerators except numerals (other than *một*).

Relator noun: **trong** interior, the inside of something

> *trong ấy* inside that, inside there

Mass noun: **sữa** milk

> *sữa ấy* that milk
>
> *nhiều sữa* a lot of milk
>
> *ba cốc sữa* three glasses of milk

Indefinite noun: **ai** who(ever)

> *những ai* what(ever) persons

Item noun: **bàn** table

> *bàn ấy* that [sort of] table
>
> *những bàn* tables
>
> *các bàn* the tables
>
> *mỗi bàn* each table
>
> *hai cái bàn* two tables (*bàn* is descriptive complement to classifier *cái*; the phrase *cái bàn* is head of numerative phrase)

192

There are important differences in the class meanings of different kinds of nominals. Categoricals refer to general classes or categories of things, while nouns refer to more specific kinds of things. On the other hand, categoricals generally designate particular individual items (although they do not describe them specifically), while nouns (at the same time that they describe items more specifically) are vague about the exact number of items involved and about which ones are referred to. Thus in the phrase *cái bàn* 'the table', *cái* 'object' makes clear that one particular object is involved, although it does not specify what kind of object; *bàn* 'table', on the other hand, describes a specific sort of object, but by itself it might refer to any number of tables, or tables in general, but none in particular. It is especially important for English speakers to keep in mind that Vietnamese nouns do not in themselves contain any notion of number or amount. In this respect they are all somewhat like English mass nouns such as *milk, water, flour,* etc.

8.61. Classifiers are categoricals which do not occur as single-word descriptive complements. They are most common as heads in descriptive phrases. In many instances a classifier is head of a descriptive phrase which in turn is head of a numerative phrase. In fact, this is perhaps the most typical of all Vietnamese substantival structures—a numeral as numerator with a head consisting of a classifier complemented by a following noun (e.g., *một* con *chó* a dog, *ba* cái *ghế* three chairs). In this position a classifier is nearly always accompanied by weak stress.

Classifiers have an important class meaning: while they usually refer to rather general categories of objects or concepts, they are specific in identifying single, individual units; without a preceding number to specify a given quantity the meaning is clearly one unit. (In this they are much clearer than general categoricals [8.62].)

One classifier is distinguished from all the rest in that it is found as head of descriptive phrases in which the complement is itself a descriptive phrase with another classifier as head; this is cái, the general classifier. In such phrases, where *cái* is followed by another classifier (any one but *cái* itself), there is often a connotation of deprecation, especially if persons are referred to.

Most other classifiers typically go with a particular group of nouns, thus setting off subclasses of classified nouns. To some extent there is apparent logic in these classifications, but there are often anomalous items which can be explained only in fanciful terms. This usage in Vietnamese is not unlike a far less extensive classification system in English, where we say, for example, *a flock of sheep, a herd of cattle, (so many) head of cattle* (note that *cattle* really has no singular), *a school of fish,* and so on. In Vietnamese the system is simply much more extended; it embraces all nouns in the language.

The following list sets forth a few common classifiers together with the general categories they serve and some examples. Many of the examples are from Emeneau 1951 (pp. 100-113), and Nguyễn đình Hòa 1957a. They all have been rechecked, some reanalyzed, and a number have been glossed differently. Note that many words listed as classifiers by other grammarians do not appear here because they are, rather, general categoricals (8.62) in terms of this analysis.

bộ set (with things made up of more or less specific parts, composite entities): *bộ bài* pack of cards, *bộ bàn ghế* set of table and chairs, *bộ lòng* giblets, innards, intestines, *bộ máy* machine (also *ổ máy*), *bộ ngực* chest [part of body], *bộ óc* brain(s), *bộ quần-áo* suit (of clothes), *bộ râu* moustache (cf. *râu* facial hair), *bộ ruột* intestines, *bộ xa-lông* living room furniture (cf. Fr. *salon* living room), *bộ xương* skeleton (*xương* bone)

bức flat rectangular object (with relatively thin, flat rectangular objects, of fairly large size): *bức ảnh* (large) photograph, *bức màn* curtain, window shade, *bức phên* wall of bamboo or leaves, *bức sáo* bamboo blind, *bức tường* wall (brick, stone or solid wood), *bức tranh* painting, *bức vách* wall (wood or mud)

cặp couple, pair (with items occurring in sets of two, naturally connected or inseparable; cf. *đôi* 'separable pair', a general categorical): *cặp mắt* eyes, *cặp mắt kính* pair of glasses, spectacles, *cặp ngà* [elephant's] tusks, *cặp vợ chồng* married couple (also **đôi** *vợ chồng* married couple), *cặp bản lề* hinge

chiếc individual item (with things which usually come in sets of two or more; extended to a large number of manufactured or constructed items, of which there are generally produced a great number more or less the same): *chiếc đũa* chopstick, *chiếc giày* shoe, *chiếc ngà* [elephant's] tusk, *chiếc tất* sock, stocking; *chiếc cầu* bridge, *chiếc chiếu* mat, *chiếc đò* small boat, *chiếc ghe* junk, sampan (in northern Viet Nam speakers tend to avoid this form because of its proximity to *cái ghe* vulva), *chiếc lá* leaf, *chiếc nhẫn* ring, *chiếc máy bay* airplane, *chiếc tàu* ship, *chiếc thuyền* junk, sampan, *chiếc xe* vehicle, *chiếc chiến-xa* armored vehicle

In the many cases where *chiếc* contrasts with some other classifier it stresses the notion of an individual item separated from the set, series, mass production line, or category of which it is usually considered a part.

con living being (impersonal) (with animals, with human and supernatural beings in a few instances without personal reference, and with a number of other words): *con bò* bull, ox, cow, *con bọ* insect, *con bê* calf, *con cua* crab, *con cọp* tiger, *con chó* dog, *con ếch* frog, *con gà* fowl, chicken, hen, *con nhện* spider, *con giun* earthworm, *con mèo* cat, *con vật* animal; *con người* human being, *con bạc* gambler, *con buôn* merchant, *con hát* actor, *con tin* hostage, *con ma* ghost, *con quái* monster, *con quỷ* devil, evil spirit; *con bài* playing card, *con chèo* oar, *con cò* (S) postage stamp, *con cò* trigger, *con cờ* chessman, *con dao* knife, *con dấu* seal, stamp, *con đê* dike, *con đường* road, street, *con mắt* eye, *con người* pupil (of eye), *con mực* stick of Chinese [solid] ink, *con quay* (spinning) top, *con sào* pole (for punting), *con số* digit, figure, number, *con sông* river, *con súc-sắc* die, dice, *con tầu* (S) boat, ship, *con tem* postage stamp (cf. Fr. *timbre*), *con thuyền* boat, craft, *con thoi* shuttle, *con tơ* hank, skein of silk

cơn sudden violent state (with states of weather, emotions, and bodily conditions which are sudden and more or less violent): *cơn bão* typhoon, *cơn giận* fit of anger, *cơn gió* gust of wind, *cơn giông gió* heavy wind storm, *cơn mưa* squall (with rain), shower, *cơn nắng* burst of sunlight [on a dark day], *cơn rét* sudden fever chill, *cơn sốt* sudden fever wave

củ bulb, tuber (with roots used as food): *củ cà-rốt* carrot (cf. Fr. *carotte*), *củ hành* onion, *củ khoai* (sweet) potato, *củ lạc* peanut, *củ sánh* manioc, *củ tỏi* garlic

cuộc entity involving interaction (generally competitive) (with games, contests, meetings, parties, struggles): *cuộc cờ* game of chess, *cuộc chiến-tranh* war, *cuộc đời* life, *cuộc hòa-bình* peace, *cuộc hội-đồng* committee meeting, *cuộc cách-mạng* revolution, *cuộc săm-banh* champagne party, (cf. Fr. *champagne*) *cuộc tuyển-cử* election

cuốn (N **quyển**) volume, fascicle (with books of various sorts): *cuốn sách* book, *cuốn chuyện* novel, *cuốn nhật-ký* diary, *cuốn cổ* account book, register, pocket notebook, *cuốn sử(-ký)* history (in annal form), *cuốn tự-vị* dictionary, *cuốn vở* exercise book

đám mass, compact item (with entities characterized by a rather amorphous mass of individual similar parts): *đám bụi* cloud of dust, *đám cháy* fire, conflagration, *đám cỏ* field, meadow (*cỏ* grass), *đám đất* plot of land, *đám đồng* cultivable field, *đám ma* funeral (procession) (cf. *ma* ghost, spirit of dead person), *đám mây* cloud, *đám nương* field for dry cultivation, *đám người* crowd of people, *đám ruộng* field for wet cultivation, *đám rừng* jungle, forest, *đám vườn* garden

hòn rock, stone (with stones, stonelike objects and islands): *hòn cù lao* island (in a river or lake), *hòn đá* stone, *hòn đảo* island (in the sea), *hòn kim cương* diamond, *hòn nước đá* piece of ice (*nước đá* is a descriptive phrase, literally "water [which is like] stone"), *hòn ngọc* precious stone, *hòn sỏi* pebble; note *hòn gạch* piece of (broken) brick, in contrast to *viên gạch* a brick

tấm rectangular flat piece of material (with cloth, boards, and various other materials in more or less rectangular shapes) (generally connotes something smaller than *bực*): *tấm bảng* placard, blackboard, *tấm da* hide (*da* skin), *tấm địa-đồ* map, (also classified with **bản** 'something printed'), *tấm gấm* tapestry, *tấm gương* mirror, *tấm gỗ* flat piece of timber, *tấm hình* photograph, drawing or painting of a person (cf. *cái hình* likeness, appearance, image), *tấm kính* pane of glass, *tấm lưới* net, screen (cf. *cái lưới* spider web; net, screen), *tấm lụa* bolt or piece of silk, *tấm thiệp* (or *thiếp*) visiting card, *tấm vải* bolt or piece of cotton, *tấm ván* plank, board

tờ sheet of paper, document (with blank paper and a variety of unbound written and printed items): *tờ giấy* sheet of paper, *tờ giấy bạc* currency note (*bạc* silver), *tờ báo* newspaper, journal, *tờ giao kèo* contract, *tờ lý-lịch* curriculum vitae, *tờ lịnh* written order, *tờ hiệp-ước* treaty, pact

trái fruit; roundish object (with fruits of various plants and relatively small roundish objects; replaced in the north by the general categorical **quả**): *trái cam* orange, *trái bưởi* pomelo [large grapefruit-like fruit], *trái chuối* banana, *trái dưa* melon, cucumber, *trái dứa* (S *trái thơm*) pineapple, *trái dừa* coconut, *trái xoài* mango; *trái bôm* bomb, *trái đồi* hill, *trái núi* mountain (latter two also with *cái* or the general categorical *ngọn*), *trái tim* heart, *trái đất* the earth, globe, *trái cật*, *trái thận* kidney

The classifier **thứ** 'kind, sort' is used with a large variety of words; it does not seem limited in any obvious way, as are most other classifiers. One might logically expect it to be a general categorical, but grammatically it belongs here since it does not occur as a descriptive complement.
thứ cá kind of fish, *thứ cây* kind of plant, *thứ hoa* kind of flower, *thứ nhà* kind of building, *thứ tiếng* kind of sound, *thứ xe* kind of vehicle

In modern Vietnamese the general classifier **cái** is coming to be used more and more at the expense of other specific classifiers, especially with nouns denoting inanimate objects which in traditional usage go with one of the rarer classifiers. Phrases with *cái* are less colorful and interesting than corresponding phrases with the more specific classifiers.

The phenomenon of classification extends beyond the elements identified by classifiers in this system. In many instances general categoricals serve much the same function (8.62). Both classifiers and general categoricals are frequently complemented by words other than nouns—sometimes by other substantives, and frequently by verbals (9.5) or complete predications.

Tàu càng vào gần Sáu-kho thì càng lắm thuyền, **thứ** *to* **thứ** *nhỏ,* **cái** *đi vào* **cái** *đi ra.* The nearer the boat got to Sáu-kho the

more junks there were—some large, some small, some coming
in, some going out. (*thứ to* a large kind, *thứ nhỏ* a small
kind, *cái đi vào* one going in, *cái đi ra* one going out)

8.62. General Categoricals occur as single-word descriptive complements.
They also appear as heads of descriptive phrases with a wide variety of
complements. Like classifiers, general categoricals usually refer to a
single entity, but this reference is less specific and definite, except where
a restrictive complement (i.e., a numerator) makes it clear. Like classifiers,
too, they refer to entities as members of general classes rather than as
specifically characterized concepts.

người person
>   *hai người* two people, *người đánh cá* fisherman (*đánh cá* catch
>   fish), *hai người đánh cá* two fishermen
>   *Không nên đánh người* [One] shouldn't hit a person (or people).
>   (descriptive complement to verb; see 9.62)
>   *con người* human being (descriptive complement to classifier)

While classifiers constitute a rather small class of words which tend to
be relatively colorless, categoricals include a great number of words which
are translated by English nouns; they are generally more specific than
classifiers in reference to type, more descriptive, more colorful. They
furnish the wide variety of units of measure for the generalized entities
designated by nouns; they also have as descriptive complements a host of
other elements ranging from substantival and verbal phrases to whole
clauses.

Many general categoricals are common as descriptive complements to
classifiers. In this position they seem to function very much like classified
nouns. This feature of structure suggests for at least these general categoricals a status intermediate between that of classifiers and that of nouns.
It also makes it seem likely that the position directly after a numeral contrasts with the position once removed from the numeral in precisely the
terms that classifiers have been described as contrasting in class meaning
with nouns (8.61). There are a good many examples showing that the same
general categorical serves to designate a specific item (especially a container) when it appears as descriptive complement to a classifier. When it
occurs directly after a numeral, however, it designates rather the quantity
or amount generally contained in the item involved.

>   *hai cái hộp sữa* two milk cans: *hai hộp sữa* two cans of milk
>   *mười cái chai* ten bottles: *mười chai rượu* ten bottles of wine

Sometimes the reference differs in other ways as well, the position directly
after the numeral generally connoting a more technical kind of entity.

năm cái đèn five lamps: *năm đèn* five tubes (for a radio)

ba cái nhà three houses: *ba nhà chợ* three market stalls

In connection with this apparent designation of function by position, it
should be noted that verbals (9.5) are common as descriptive complements
to general categoricals. Often the resulting phrases seem very similar to
phrases containing nouns as complements.

người bạn a friend

người sinh-viên a student

người lớn an adult (verb)

người mua the buyer (verb)

General categoricals include the following important semantic groups:
kinship terms, a number of other terms of reference for human beings, containers, grades and classes, meals and dishes, various measuring units
(of time, space, money, quantity), items of discourse (sound, word,
sentence). The following list is suggestive rather than in any sense
exhaustive.

HUMAN REFERENCE TERMS
(see also 13.2)

anh elder brother; male familiar or inferior

chị elder sister; female familiar or inferior

em younger brother or sister; child (non-adult human)

bà grandmother; female rating respect

ông grandfather; male rating respect

cha father

mẹ mother

con child (offspring)

cháu grandchild, niece, nephew

cậu mother's brother

chú father's younger brother

bác father's elder brother or his wife

mợ aunt (uncle's wife)

cụ great-grandparent: person rating great respect

HUMAN REFERENCE TERMS (continued)

người person

ngài person rating highest respect short of king or emperor (cabinet minister, president, etc.)

thợ artisan, workman of a particular trade

CONTAINERS

hộp box, can, jar

chai bottle

lọ vial, small bottle

cốc (N) glass (S *ly*)

bát (N) bowl (S *chén*)

chén (N) cup (S *tách*)

thùng barrel, cask, keg, packing case, carton

ấm kettle, (tea)pot

giỏ market basket

bao bag; envelope

GRADES AND CLASSES

bậc category, rank; step [of stair stairs], rung [of ladder]

loài kind, species [of beings]

loại kind, sort (L)

hạng [socially, economically or qualitatively determined] clas

lớp class [group of students]

TIME UNITS (see also 14.5)

bữa day (also 'meal')

khi time [brief extent]

lần time, instance

giờ hour

phút minute

giây second

hôm day [time when]

ngày day [one of a series]

buổi portion of a day

đêm night

mùa season

tháng month

tuần(-lễ) week

năm year

tuổi year (of age)

SPATIAL UNITS

chỗ place

làng village

thành city (wall, fortification); city

phố street

lớp layer, stratum

gian interval, space [between two pillars of old-style house]

gang span [distance measured by spread of thumb and middle finger]

phòng room

châu continent

nước country, state

sở office, service, place where one works

SPATIAL UNITS (continued)

trời (N *giời*) heaven, sky

góc angle, corner

mẫu acre (one and one-third English acres)

tấc decimeter

cây số kilometer

sào one-tenth of a *mẫu*

thước meter

vườn garden

bờ edge, border

UNITS OF QUANTITY AND VALUE (see also 14.6)

đồng piastre [sometimes extended to basic unit of other currencies]

cắc dime (one-tenth of piastre)

giác (N) (L *hào*) dime (one-tenth of piastre)

xu cent (one-hundredth of piastre)

giá price

cân pound (approximately one and one-third pounds avoirdupois); (also used loosely for 'pound' and 'kilogram')

đôi pair (of separable items) (cf. classifier *cặp* pair of inseparable items)

giọt drop (of liquid)

ki-lô kilogram

lượng ounce (one-sixteenth of a *cân*)

số number, sum (of money)

món dish, course (in a meal); specific amount (of money)

UNITS OF LANGUAGE (see also 5.57)

chữ (written) word, character, letter

tiếng (spoken) word (also 'sound, noise; language')

câu sentence, clause

lời (spoken) word, phrase, saying

loại-từ word class

The very important general categorical **của** 'possession, belonging, property' has been widely designated as a verb, presumably because of its frequent appearance in expressions identifying the owner of something or the responsible party in some matter. The predicates involved are often of the substantival type (9.11), and **của** appears in a position where a verb might be expected. Since it is less frequent in unequivocal substantival positions, it is not surprising that it has been mistaken for a verb-like word. Note, however, that negation of these expressions establishing ownership or responsibility involves the expression **không phải** (14.33). (See also Appendix A.)

> *Cái này* **của** *tôi.* This belongs to me. ["object this possession I"]
>
> *Cái này* **không phải của** *tôi.* This doesn't belong to me. ["object this not true possession I"]
>
> *Tôi bị nhà tôi cháy, nên mất* **của** *hết.* My house burned, so I lost all my belongings.

Descriptive phrases with *của* as head are extremely common as descriptive complements to other nominals.

> *quyển sách* **của tôi** my book ["volume book possession I"]
>
> *mấy lời tỏ ý khen ngợi* **của thày giáo** a few words of congratulation from the teacher ["however-many words express idea commend praise possession master instruct"]

It needs to be recognized that many such occurrences of *của* involve quite complex descriptive complements, and there are a good many signs that the word is fast passing to the status of a prepositive particle (11.81).

> *Các ông các bà là ai? Nếu có phải là chủ* **của các hàng-hóa này** *thì cứ để cho tôi dùng, sau này tôi giàu có, tôi sẽ đem tiền lại giả.* Who are you ladies and gentlemen? If it's true [you are] the owners of these pieces of merchandise, then go ahead, let me use [them]; later on I'll be wealthy, [and] I'll bring the money back and pay.

8.63. Relator Nouns never occur as heads of numerative phrases. They occasionally appear as heads of restrictive phrases in which the complement is not a numerator (8.35). Many of the members of this small class appear superficially to resemble the prepositions of languages like English or French. This has to do with the fact that they all express position (in space or time) or some vaguer dimension in relation to something else. Although many expressions containing these words are best translated by prepositional phrases in English, the understanding of their basic nominal meanings will help remove some of the puzzling aspects of their uses.

Emeneau 1951 (e.g., p. 51) and Jones and Thông 1960 (e.g., p. 139) treat
most of these words as verb-like elements. For a discussion of this problem
see Martini 1958. Note that he specifically mentions the possibility of considering them nominal entities (p. 341). Following is a complete list of the
relator nouns which have been identified in the material studied. There may
well be others.

bằng a demonstrated quantity or proportion
dưới place at bottom or beneath
giữa place between
ngang place across or opposite (directly in line with a particular referent)
ngoài place outside, quantity beyond
quanh place surrounding
sau place behind or time after
trên place on top, above, or high in or on
trong place inside, time within which, or total capacity
trước place in front or time before

Bằng *ấy dủ chưa?* Is that enough? ["proportion just-referred-to
be-enough not-yet?"]

Cột to **bằng** *nào?* How big are the pillars?

dưới *triền núi* at the foot of the mountain

Để cả **dưới** *gầm phản.* Put [them] all in the space under the camp
bed. ["to-place inclusive-particle place-at-bottom space-
beneath wooden-camp-bed"]

Con mèo ở **dưới** *cái bàn.* The cat's under the table.

Lính cảnh-sát đứng ở **giữa** *đường.* The policeman is standing in
the middle of the street.

giữa *giời* right out in the open

Ngang *đường có một cây lớn.* (S) There's a big tree across the
road.

Cái nhà đó **ngang** *nhà tôi.* (S) That house is opposite mine.
(Substantival predicate, 9.11)

Ngoài *vườn từng đàn bươm-bướm lượn* **quanh** *hết khóm hồng này
lại đến cụm cúc kia.* Out in the garden various kinds of butter-
flies were flitting all around from this clump of roses to that
cluster of chrysanthemums. ["place-outside garden each-in-
turn group butterfly flit place-surrounding be-all clump rose
this resuming arrive cluster chrysanthemum that"]

ngoài *ba vật này ra* besides [i.e., in addition to] these three
things

Họ xúm đông **quanh** *cái xe buýt.* The crowd gathered around the bus. ["they gather-in-crowd be-in-crowds place-surrounding object vehicle bus"]

Sau *này tôi giầu có, tôi sẽ đem tiền lại giả.* After this I'm going to be rich, I'll bring the money back and pay.

Trên *cây khế mấy con chim vừa nhảy-nhót tìm sâu vừa ríu-rít hót.* Up in the carambola tree a few birds were hopping around looking avidly [for fruit] and chirping away.

Anh ấy đi dường **trên.** He went by the upper road.

Tôi để quyển sách **trên** *bàn.* I put the book on a table.

Trong *hai người ấy, ai giầu hơn?* Of those two people which is wealthier?

Như thế chúng ta tới Hà-nội **trước** *tết nhiều.* This way we'll arrive in Hanoi a long time before the [New Year] holiday.

Trước *cái nhà kia có mấy cây chuối.* In front of the other house there were a few banana trees.

8.64. Mass Nouns are generally numerated only by quantifiers (9.53). Like relator nouns they also occasionally appear as heads of non-numerative restrictive phrases (8.35). This class includes the great majority of words denoting substances which are not measurable or are measured only in arbitrary quantities, entities without typical shape or size, qualities and abstractions of various sorts. A few examples are *nước* water, liquid (cf. general categorical *nước* country), *dường* sugar (cf. item noun *dường* road, street), *sữa* milk, *gạo* husked rice, *cơm* cooked rice, *lúa* rice growing, *trà* (N *chè*) tea, *tiền* money, *vàng* gold, *lụa* silk, *cỏ* grass, *củi* firewood, *đông* winter, *xuân* spring, *hạ* (or *hè*) summer, *thu* autumn, *thì giờ* time (in general) (reinforcing pseudo-compound, 6.32).

Mời ông xơi **cơm** *nữa.* Please have some more rice.

Cám ơn ông, tôi đã ăn nhiều **cơm** *rồi.* Thanks, I've already eaten a lot of rice.

Cơm *này ngon lắm.* This rice is delicious.

Thì giờ *thấm-thoát mới ngày nào dân-chúng Hà-thành đang rộn-rịp sửa-soạn đón* **xuân** *thì hai ông Dong và Vỹ đến, nay mùa* **xuân** *đã qua, mùa* **hạ** *đã đến và cũng đã sắp hết.* Time had flown [so] fast [it seemed] only a few days [before] that, with the populace of the city of Hanoi busy getting ready to greet spring, the two fellows Dong and Vỹ had arrived; now spring had already passed, summer had come and very soon would be over.

202

Mass nouns appear with various categoricals as measures. General categoricals are most common, although some classifiers also occur.

ba cốc **sữa** three glasses of milk

chín hộp **sữa** nine cans of milk

hai bát **cơm** two bowls of rice

mười lăm ki-lô **gạo** fifteen kilos of [husked] rice

một cơn **mưa** a squall (with rain)

Although the classification system (8.61) is mainly effective in connection with the item nouns (8.66), it does touch on mass nouns. For example, the seasons regularly appear as descriptive complement to the general categorical **mùa** 'season': mùa đông 'winter', mùa xuân 'spring'.

There are exceptions to the general limitations on numerators of mass nouns. Occasionally the plural marker **những** and the number **một** appear with them, much as in English one sometimes hears such expressions as *a milk of fine quality, French wines*, etc.

những rượu có tiếng của nước Pháp famous French wines

một lụa thanh-nhã a fine ["elegant"] silk

With the names of the seasons the plural marker **mỗi** 'each' and the indefinite numeral **mấy** are also found. The resulting phrases are often poetic in flavor (as are phrases where these words are numerated by một and những), and in them the season frequently refers by synecdoche to the year as a whole.

những đông lạnh-lẽ, **những** xuân đầy hoa cold winters and flower-
    filled springs

một hè nóng nực, một vùng khô-khan a sweltering summer, an arid
    region

mỗi xuân each spring (i.e., each year in the spring)

mấy thu a few autumns (i.e., a few years)

8.65. Indefinite Nouns generally occur as heads of numerative phrases only when the numerator is the plural marker những. They are also set apart from other nouns by the fact that they are not frequently heads of descriptive phrases in general and do not appear at all with demonstrative markers as descriptive complements. They are three: **gì** anything, something, what(ever), **chi** anything, something, what(ever) (polite), **ai** anyone, someone, who(ever)

Gì có cánh đều bay được. (S) Whatever has wings can fly.

Những **gì** trong thùng tôi cũng không biết. Whatever things [may
    be] in the crate I don't know.

Ai nói bây giờ? Who's going to talk now?

Ở Đà-lạt **những ai** *trồng rau đều trúng lắm.* (S) In Dalat those who grow vegetables are all prosperous.

Xin lỗi ông, ông nói **chi?** (S) I beg your pardon, what did you say?

On very rare occasions they appear with the number **một** 'one' as numerator (cf. 8.41) with a force something like 'a single, even one'.

Anh sống một đời giản-dị và chết đi không nhớ tiếc **một ai.** He lived a simple life and died not recalling with regret a single person (i.e., he died happily).

8.66. Item nouns constitute the largest number of substantives in the lexicon. They differ from other nouns in occurring with all the plural markers, as well as with quantifiers (9.53) as numerators. In general they denote entities of rather specific shape and size, and they are measured as individual items (through the use of categoricals), rather than in arbitrary amounts, as are mass nouns. On the whole, it is with these item nouns that classifiers are characteristically found. For some notion of the extensive system of subclasses of item nouns in their relationships to classifiers, see 8.61. For the most part the various combinations of nouns and classifiers must simply be learned. A few examples of item nouns follow:

> *bàn* table: *cái bàn* the table, *hai cái bàn* two tables
> *ghế* chair: *các ghế* the chairs, *bốn cái ghế* four chairs
> *giấy* paper: *một tờ giấy* a (piece of) paper, *những giấy* papers
> *sách* book: *nhiều sách* many books, *mấy quyển sách* a few books
> *chó* dog: *mỗi chó* each (kind of) dog, *mỗi con chó* each (individual) dog

Although item nouns refer to quite specific kinds of entities, they do not themselves designate specific individual items. Reference of this sort is accomplished by the categorical to which the noun appears as descriptive complement. In addition, the reference of item nouns is vague as to number: *sách* may mean a book or several books or books in general. In many cases, however, an unclassified noun does refer to a specific item that is clear in the context. Note the varying reference of *tầu (hỏa)* 'train' in the following passage:

Tầu *chuyển bánh và bắt đầu từ-từ chạy ra khỏi ga, ông Vỹ hỏi:—*Tầu *chạy chậm như thế này thôi à?*

Người hành-khách: Vâng, **tầu hỏa** *chúng tôi chỉ chạy từ 30 đến 35 cây số một giờ.*

The train [the one the passengers were on] started up and began to move slowly out of the station; Mr. Vỹ asked: "The train only runs this fast, eh?"

Passenger: "Yes, our trains [those in Viet Nam in general] run only from thirty to thirty-five kilometers an hour."

That item nouns denote very specialized entities from one point of view while remaining vague from another is well demonstrated by the case of botanical items. The words which specify the species are item nouns, but only classifiers or general categoricals make entirely clear whether the plant or tree, the flower, or the fruit is referred to.

> *chuối* banana: *cây chuối* banana tree, *trái* (or *quả*) *chuối* banana (fruit)
>
> *cam* orange: *một cây cam* an orange tree, *hai trái* (or *quả*) *cam* two oranges (fruit), *mấy* (*cái*) *hoa cam* a few orange blossoms
>
> *hồng* rose: *năm cây hồng* five rose bushes, *hai* (*cái*) *hoa hồng* two roses (flowers)

This is much the same as the use in English of certain words like *walnut* now to designate the nut itself, sometimes to refer to the tree, and very often to specify the kind of wood of which something is made. The Vietnamese classification system allows somewhat more range.

As with certain other nouns there are occasional occurrences of item nouns numerated by the number **một** 'one'; in these cases the forms convey the notion 'a kind of, one sort of.'*

> **một** *chó tốt đẹp* a handsome (breed of) dog
>
> **một** *cam ngon ngọt* a good, sweet (kind of) orange

---

*Some linguists consider this phenomenon to be ideolectic.

CHAPTER 9

Predicative Elements

9.1. Predications. The head (5.43) of an independent sentence (5.41) is a **predication**.[1] Many independent sentences contain two or more heads; each is a predication. Each such predication either is itself a **predicate**, or else contains one or more predicates as heads. Predicates are of three kinds, identified in the terms defined in the following paragraphs.

The word **là** 'be, which is (are), that is, namely' is an **identificational marker.** It occurs as restrictive complement signalling that its constitute is identified with some immediately preceding element. Such phrases are **identificational predicates.** They are of extremely varied structure: *là* occurs with nearly all phrase types and a large number of individual word types. Because of this diversity of structure identificational predicates will be treated at length after the discussion of other predicate types and their elements (9.7).

The words **đã** 'anterior' and **sẽ** 'subsequent' are **tense markers.** They occur as restrictive complements in phrases which are thus marked as **temporal predicates.** (*Đã* also occurs as a descriptive complement: see Appendix A.) Each temporal predicate is paralleled by a similar sequence differing only in the absence of a tense marker; such sequences are **unmarked predicates.** In addition there are a number of sequences which are the same in structure as (but are not paralleled by) predicates containing *đã* or *sẽ*; it is convenient to regard them also as (unmarked) predicates. In most instances nonoccurrence of parallels with *đã* or *sẽ* is a matter of logically unlikely situations. Rigorously we might well not admit such elements to the class of predicates. In practical terms, however, these

---

[1] Actually there occur some very short independent sentences which do not constitute predications. These are forms which do not combine with other linguistic elements in the regular constructions or at best appear in such combinations only as complements, not as heads (interjections and exclamative substitutes, 11.2). Such elements are excluded in this definition of predication.

sequences are identified by their structural similarity to regularly defined predicates. Temporal and unmarked predicates are generally heads of the larger elements of which they form one part. However, they also occur as complements, especially in descriptive (following) position. In many cases, especially when they are comparatively long, they are emphatically marked by the identificational marker *là*.

Temporal predicates are of two types, depending on their structure: those consisting of a substantival phrase are **substantival predicates**; others are **verbal**. Unmarked predicates are of the same two types. In the following examples pertinent predicates are in boldface type.

IDENTIFICATIONAL PREDICATES:

Ông ấy **là lính.** He's a soldier.

Ông Lewis và ông Johnson **là hai sinh-viên Mỹ.** Mr. Lewis and Mr. Johnson are two American students.

Cũng như các sinh-viên khác, hai ông được giáo-sư cho tên Việt **là Lê Vỹ và Trần Dong.** Like the other students, the two of them were given Vietnamese names by the teacher— Lê Vỹ and Trần Dong.

Hai ông **là bạn thân** *và cùng có chung một ý-tưởng* **là đi sang Việt-nam du-lịch.** The two fellows were close friends, and they both had the same idea—to take a trip to Viet Nam.

TEMPORAL PREDICATES:

Tháng tới tôi **sẽ hai mươi lăm tuổi.** Next month I'll be twenty-five years old. (substantival)

Tôi **sẽ đi.** I'll go. (verbal)

Chị ấy **đã quên.** She's forgotten. (verbal)

UNMARKED PREDICATES:

Tôi **hai mươi lăm tuổi.** I'm twenty-five years old. (substantival)

Tôi **đi.** I'm going. (verbal)

Chị ấy **quên.** She forgets. (also 'She's forgotten' or 'She'll forget.' Temporal reference in such sentences is clear only in context; see 9.3.) (verbal)

In intimate conversation there occur occasional independent sentences of types which otherwise appear only as dependent sentences (5.41). Since they are relatively rare they need not concern us here, but in theoretical terms they present a problem. For example—

Chum vàng đâu? Where's the pot of gold?

Chum vàng đây rồi. The pot of gold is already here.

beside more usual independent sentences with the same general meaning—

Chum vàng ở đâu?

Chum vàng ở đây rồi.

It is not clear how these are best treated, but it is possible that they contain a third type of unmarked predicate which might be called **locational** and defined as consisting of a place demonstrative (7.22). Such sentences in the spoken language are similar to elliptical sentences of colloquial English like *Been dancing? Finished yet?* which occur as opening speeches but obviously presume a clearly defined (non-linguistic) context. These unusual predications will not be considered further here.

9.11. Substantival Predicates are temporal or unmarked predicates consisting of substantival phrases—numerative or descriptive—and these phrases are themselves often composed of smaller phrases of the various sorts described in Chapter 8. Of numerative phrases only those containing a numeral as numerator occur commonly, but a wide variety of descriptive phrases are found.

> **Mấy giờ rồi?** What time is it (already)?
> *Em ấy* **mấy tuổi?** How old is that child?
> *Cái này* **của ai?** Whose is this?
> *Thế cột* **bằng nào?** Then how large are the pillars [supporting the house]?
> *Ông ấy* **thầy thuốc.** (S) He's a doctor.

9.12. Verbal Predicates are temporal or unmarked predicates which are not substantival phrases. They vary from single words to long phrases of complicated structure. Words which occur singly as heads of verbal predicates are **predicatives**. Independent words which are not substantives (8.1) and which occur between a tense marker and the predicate center are also predicatives.

> **Sẽ đi.** [I, you, he, they, etc.] will go. (reference clarified only by context)
> **Hiểu.** [I, you, he, etc.] understand.
> *Tôi* **hiểu.** I understand.
> *Tôi* **không hiểu.** I don't understand.
> *Ông ấy* **sẽ đi Sài-gòn.** He will go to Saigon.

In the above examples the words *đi* 'go', *hiểu* 'understand', and *không* 'not' are predicatives.

9.2. Predicatives are words which occur as heads of verbal predicates and independent words (not substantives) which occur between a tense marker and the predicate center. They belong to two subclasses: **verbals** (9.5), which occur as heads of descriptive phrases; and **negatives** (9.4), which do not.

208

Ông ấy sẽ **không đi.** He won't go.
Tôi **chưa hiểu.** I don't understand yet.
Tôi đã **hiểu.** I've (already) come to understand.
Đi *Sài-gòn.* [I'm] going to Saigon.
Tôi **hiểu** *câu này.* I understand this sentence.

In the above examples, the words *không* 'not' and *chưa* 'not yet' are negatives; *đi* 'go' and *hiểu* 'understand' are verbals.

9.3. Tense Markers.

Without specific indications to the contrary a sentence refers to the **basic time** of the context—that is, the time which has been made clear in the context up to that point. The principal predicate of a sentence often denotes an action or state which begins or is about to begin during the basic time. The tense markers announce or emphasize a situation obtaining at a time different from this basic time. **Đã** 'anterior' identifies an action or state at least the beginning of which precedes the basic time; **sẽ** 'subsequent' identifies an action or state which begins later than the basic time. In more complicated circumstances a subordinate marked predicate often modifies the temporal reference in relation to the principal marked predicate.

Bây giờ các ông chỉ còn đặt chương-trình cuộc hành-trình nên đi bằng cách gì, tầu bay hay tầu thủy; các ông **sẽ đi bao lâu** *và* **sẽ đi vào độ nào.** *Sau khi bàn tính và hỏi các điều cần biết ở sứ-quán Việt-nam tại Hoa-thịnh-đốn, hai ông quyết-định đi du-lịch sáu tháng. Cuộc hàng-trình* **sẽ khởi-hành** *sau ngày các ông* **đã ăn mừng xong** *lễ Chúa Giáng-Sinh năm nay.*

Now they had only to make plans for the trip—how they should go, by plane, or by ship; **how long** they **would go for** and **what time** they **would start out.** After talking things over and requesting necessary information at the Vietnamese Embassy in Washington, the two of them decided to travel for six months. The trip **would begin** following the day they **finished celebrating Christmas this year.**

Predicates marked by tense markers appear in boldface type in the text and corresponding translation. Actually, the predicate beginning *sẽ khởi-hành...* comprises all the rest of the sentence; the final predicate indicated (*đã ăn mừng ...*) is contained within it as the head of a sequence which serves as complement to *ngày*. In this latter case the *đã* predicate refers to a state of affairs preceding that of the main predicate (which is marked by *sẽ*), although both are later than the basic time of the passage.

In this way the tense markers substitute for the system of verbal tenses familiar to speakers of Western languages. There are cases where *đã* in-

troduces a kind of hypothetical predicate with past reference (roughly
equivalent to a conditional in English).

>*(Nếu) ông nói với tôi sớm hơn thì tôi* **đã săn sóc đến việc ông.**
>If you had told me [about it] earlier I would have taken care
>that business of yours.

>*(Nếu) ông thầy thuốc không đến tôi* **đã chết rồi.** If the doctor
>hadn't come I'd be dead already.

Due to the lack of specificity about temporal references the device
known as the *historical present* in Western languages is less obvious in
Vietnamese. However, there are many cases where the focal elements (see
Chapter 10) that generally specify present time appear in the telling of a
story. Such cases are probably best considered instances of a similar historical or narrative present (referring to the past) for Vietnamese.

>*Hai người nói chuyện vui-vẻ không còn nhớ gì đến thì-giờ. Trời
>hôm* **nay** *nắng ấm đẹp quá...* The two people talk pleasantly
>[and] no longer remember (anything about) time. The weather
>today is sunny and warm, very lovely...

9.4. Negatives are predicatives which do not occur as heads of descriptive phrases. Typically they are restrictive complements but in dependent
sentences (especially in responsive utterances, 5.41) they are common as
heads of restrictive phrases. In no case, however, do they appear as head
with another negative as restrictive complement.

There is a partially consistent pattern in the semantic coverage of these
forms, as shown below.

SEMANTIC COVERAGE	MILD	EMPHATIC
Denial	*không* not	*chẳng* (or *chả*) definitely not
Prohibition	*chớ* better not	*đừng* don't
Delay		*chưa* not yet
Contradiction		*nào* on the contrary, not

The form **chẳng**, as well as being stronger than **không**, sometimes also
suggests impossibility or a wish to the contrary. As second head in choice
questions (9.67) it has the special allomorph **chăng** (with *ngang* tone).
Chả seems to be a less frequent variant; it is not found as second head
in choice questions (9.67, 13.32). Some sources cite it as an abbreviated
form of *chẳng.* Both words have a somewhat more literary flavor than
không.

The prohibitives **chớ** and **đừng** are rare with preceding tense markers,
and it may be that they would be better treated structurally as preverbs
(11.72). Because of their semantic connection with other negatives it has

seemed most useful to handle them here. **Chớ** should not be confused with the coordinating particle (11.51) and the final particle (N *chứ*) (11.4), although the meanings of the three forms seem related (see Appendix A). The form **nào** is relatively rare.

> *Tôi* **không** *hiểu.* I don't understand.
>
> **Chẳng** *thấy gì hết.* Can't see a thing.
>
> *Nó* **chả** *hát.* He won't sing.
>
> **Chớ** *uống rượu.* You shouldn't drink alcoholic beverages.
>
> *Anh* **đừng** *sợ.* Don't be afraid.
>
> *Sông sâu* **chớ** *lội, đò đầy* **chớ** *đi.* [When the] river is deep, better not swim; [if the] ferry is full better not go [aboard].–Folk saying.
>
> *Mời ông lại nhà chúng tôi xơi cơm. Ông sẽ* **đừng** *làm khách.* Please come to our house for a meal. [And] don't stand on ceremony.
>
> *Ông ấy* **chưa** *về.* He hasn't returned home yet.
>
> *Tôi đã* **nào** *ngủ.* I certainly didn't sleep [contrary to what you suggest].

The negatives **không, chẳng** and **chưa** are fairly common as restrictive complements to substantives and substantival phrases, although this is clearly a secondary function.

> *Ông ấy* **không** *tiền.* He has no money.
>
> **Không** *ai thấy con chó ở đâu?* No one has seen where the dog is.
>
> **Chẳng** *chè,* **chẳng** *chén sao say./* **Chẳng** *thương,* **chẳng** *nhớ sao hay đi tìm?* No drink, no cup, how [can one] be drunk?/ [If you] don't love, don't recall nostalgically, why so often [do you] go looking [for someone]?–Folk saying.
>
> *Bây giờ* **chưa** *ba giờ.* It's not three o'clock yet.

Negatives appear as heads in secondary main clauses (12.21), in minor sentences (12.42), and in second position in phrases with coordinating construction (choice questions; see 9.67).

> *Ông đi chợ, còn tôi* **không.** You're going to market, but I'm not.
>
> *Anh làm xong* **chưa**?-**Chưa.** Have you finished [it] yet?–No.

9.5. Verbals

are predicatives which occur as heads of descriptive phrases. They are also common with negatives (9.4) as restrictive complements. A few have special distributions which set them apart from the great majority. The **definitive** (9.51) never has another verbal as descriptive complement. Similarly, **comparatives** (9.52) have non-verbals as descriptive complements, but of verbals generally only the definitive appears. **Quantifiers** (9.53) have comparatives and the definitive (as well as certain non-verbals) as descriptive complements, but no other verbals. A few verbals serve frequently as restrictive complements of other verbals: they are **auxiliaries** (9.54). These special subclasses aside, the great majority of forms in the class are **verbs** (9.55). A phrase with a verbal as head is a **verbal phrase** (see 9.6).

9.51. The Definitive. Rồi 'to be over and done with' is a verbal which occurs with non-verbals as descriptive complements, but never has another verbal as partner in such constructions. Actually, it appears less frequently as predicate center than as a descriptive complement in predicates with other predicative elements or substantival elements as heads. In this very common use it marks a terminated action or condition.

> *Tôi* **rồi** *việc đó, tôi làm việc khác.* (S) [When] I finish this business I'll do something else.
> *Việc này đã* **rồi.** This matter is over and done with.
> *Việc kia chưa* **rồi.** The other business isn't finished yet.
> *Ăn* **rồi.** [We've] already eaten.
> *Mấy giờ* **rồi?** What time is it (already)? (i.e., What time has it gotten to be ?)
> *Anh ta lấy đầy túi* **rồi** *lại cưỡi lên mình chim mà về.* He filled the pouch, then again mounted astride the body of the bird to return.

9.52. Comparatives are verbals which occur with non-verbals as descriptive complements, but of verbals generally only the definitive *rồi* appears. They are themselves often descriptive complements of other verbals. Two words have been identified as members of this class.

hơn be greater, more (than)
> *Tiền Việt-nam* **hơn** *rồi.* Vietnamese currency is worth more [now].
> *Tiền này* **hơn** *tiền của tôi.* This [sum of] money is greater than mine.
> *Ông ấy ốm* **hơn.** He is sicker.

quá exceed, be excessive
> *Ông ấy* **quá** *tôi.* He surpasses me [in doing something].
> *Đẹp* **quá.** [It's] exceedingly beautiful.

Note that with comparatives the amount by which something exceeds is expressed by a (following) descriptive complement.

> *Cô Lan mua* **hơn** *cô Hồng* **bốn quả cam.** Miss Lan bought four more oranges than Miss Hồng. ["young-lady Lan buy more-than young-lady Hồng four fruit orange"]

A special exception to the general observation on the distribution of comparatives is that **hơn** appears with the verb **hết** 'be completely finished, all used up' (see Appendix A) as descriptive complement. The resulting phrases translate superlatives of western languages.

    Cô ấy đẹp **hơn hết**. She's the prettiest (of all).

9.53. **Quantifiers** are verbals which occur with certain non-verbals (notably the contained postpositive particle **lắm** 'to a great extent, very much', 11.82) and with the definitive and comparatives as descriptive complements. Four words have been identified as members of this class; there may be others. All are common themselves as descriptive complements.

nhiều be a large amount, much, many

    Bạn tôi **nhiều**. My friends are many.

    Ở đây người **nhiều** *quá*. There are a great many people here.

    Em ấy khóc **nhiều**. That child cries a lot.

    Ông ấy làm việc **nhiều**. He works a lot.

    Tiền ấy **nhiều** *rồi*. That's already a great deal of money.

ít be a small amount, little, few (cf. *ít* seldom 9.54)

    Bạn tôi **ít**. My friends are few.

    Ở đây người **ít** *lắm*. There are very few people here.

    Tôi học **nhiều**, *anh ấy học* **ít**. I study a lot, he studies little.

    Tiền **ít** *rồi*. There's little money [left] already.

đông be many together, in a crowd (generally connoting people)

    Thành-phố này **đông** *dân-cư lắm*. This city is very crowded. ["city this be-in-crowds citizen great-extent"]

    Họ **đông** *con lắm*. They have too many children.

    Làm gì mà **đông** *thế này?* What brought this crowd here? ["do whatever descriptive-complement-marker be-in-crowds fashion this?"]

    Họ xúm **đông** *quanh cái xe buýt*. The crowd gathered around the bus. ["they gather-in-crowd be-in-crowds place-surrounding object vehicle bus"]

đầy be full [of], filled [with]

    Cái hộp này **đầy** *rồi*. This box is already full.

    Chai **đầy** *rượu*. The bottle is full of wine.

    Mày **đầy** *giỏ cá, tao* **đầy** *giỏ tôm*. You have a basket full of fish, I have a basket full of shrimp. (familiar)

    Anh ta lấy **đầy** *túi rồi lại cưỡi lên mình chim mà về*. He filled the pouch, then again mounted astride the body of the bird to return. ["...take full..."]

The first three words occur rather frequently as numerators (8.31); đầy has not been observed in this function. Numerative phrases appear in boldface in the following examples.

> *Thư-viện này có* **nhiều sách** *Việt-nam.* This library has many Vietnamese books.

> *Còn* **ít đường** *lắm.* There's very little sugar left.

> **Đông người** *đến buôn bán.* Lots of people came to do business.

Of the four, **đông** and **đầy** resemble verbs (9.55) more than the other two: they have a wider range of substantival expressions appearing with them as descriptive complements.

Nhiều frequently serves as descriptive complement to the proportion demonstratives (7.24) **bao** 'to what(ever) extent' and **bấy** 'to that extent' (more rarely, and in literary usage, to **bây** 'to this extent'). In these positions it has an allomorph with *ngang* tone: **nhiêu**.

> *Có* **bao nhiêu,** *xài* **bấy nhiêu.** Whatever [you] have [you] spend.

9.54. Auxiliaries are verbals which occur as restrictive complements of other verbals. They differ from negatives (9.4) in that they do occur as predicate centers in independent sentences (5.41) and in that they do occur as heads of descriptive phrases. They also appear with negatives as restrictive complements. The following verbals have been identified as members of this class; more extensive analysis may well reveal others. In order to give a more specific notion of the semantic content of these words they are glossed first in a general way, then, following a semicolon, with an English equivalent which suggests their range as restrictive complements.

bớt diminish; be less

> *Họ* **bớt** *cho tôi năm phần trăm.* They gave me a five percent discount. (More literally: "They diminished for me [by] five percent." For use of *cho* see 9.66.)

> *Lúc nầy tôi* **bớt** *đi Sài-gòn rồi.* (S) Now I go to Saigon less.

có exist; be definitely

> *Ở Việt-nam* **có** *hai mươi chín triệu mấy ngàn người.* In Viet Nam there are twenty-nine million-odd people.

> *Ông Hiền* **có** *nhà không?* Is Mr. Hiền at home? ["gentleman Hiền exist (with respect to his) house (or) not?"]

> *Tôi nói chắc ông khó tin, nhưng* **có** *đi sâu vào xã-hội Việt-nam thì mới thấy rõ.* [What] I say you probably find hard to believe, but [if you] go deeper into Vietnamese society, then (only) [you'll] see [it] clearly.

> **Có** *hai người đến đây hỏi thăm.* There were two people [who] came here inquiring. (Here *có* is predicate center; the predicate *có hai người* has the balance of the sentence as descriptive complement.)

còn remain, be left; still

> *Đường* **còn.** There is still [some] sugar left.
>
> *Anh ấy* **còn** *ở Hà-nội.* He's still in Hanoi.
>
> *Đời sống hằng ngày của thủ-đô Hà-nội hãy* **còn** *rời-rạc.* The everyday life of the capital Hanoi is still disrupted.

gần be close, near; nearly, almost

> *Làng ấy* **gần** *lắm.* That village is very near.
>
> *Tôi* **gần** *đi Sài-gòn.* I'm on the point of going to Saigon.
>
> *Tôi* **gần** *muốn khó ở.* I'm almost sick. (Note that *muốn* 'wish, want, feel like' is often used to indicate immediacy of an undesirable condition.)

hết be completely finished, used up; no longer (cf. Appendix A)

> *Đường* **hết** *rồi.* The sugar is all used up.
>
> *Lúc nầy tôi* **hết** *đi Sài-gòn.* (S) I no longer go to Saigon now.

lâu be a long time; (already) for a long time (rare as a main predicate center)

> *Trăm năm thì* **lâu** *lắm.* A hundred years—that's a long time!
>
> *Ông ấy* **lâu** *ở Đà-lạt rồi.* He's been away from Dalat for a long time. (Cf. with descriptive phrase, 9.62, *Ông ấy ở Đà-lạt* **lâu** *rồi.* He's lived in Dalat for a long time already.)

ít be infrequent, uncommon; seldom (cf. *ít* little 9.53)

> *Dịp nói chuyện với bạn thì* **ít** *lắm.* Opportunities to talk with friends were very infrequent.
>
> *Tôi* **ít** *đi Sài-gòn.* I seldom go to Saigon.
>
> *Sinh-viên ấy* **ít** *học.* That student seldom studies.

mau be fast, quick; soon

> *Xe lửa nầy* **mau** *lắm.* (S) This train is very fast.
>
> *Mực này* **mau** *khô.* This ink dries quickly.
>
> *Chúng ta* **mau** *đi đi!* Let's get on our way soon.

In northern speech *mau* is most common as auxiliary; as predicate center it is replaced by **nhanh** 'be rapid.' Note that *mau* often conveys the notion 'status soon to change:'

> *Ông ở đây lâu* **mau?** How long are you here for? ["gentleman located here long-time (or) soon (depart)"]

nên be appropriate; necessarily, must, obliged to (cf. Appendix A)

> **Nên** *chăng?* Is it appropriate?
>
> *Chúng ta* **nên** *tập thể-thao.* We should have physical exercise.

thật be real, true; really, truly (S **thiệt**)

> *Câu truyện nầy* **thật.** This story is true.
>
> *Câu truyện nầy* **thật** *lý-thú.* This story is really interesting.
>
> *Con chó đó* **thiệt** *dữ* (S) That dog is really vicious.

thêm to add, increase; more, in addition

> *Ông cho tiền ít quá! Xin ông* **thêm** *một chút đi!* You've given [me] very little money. Please add a little more.
>
> *Tiếng âm-nhạc du-dương ở góc phòng do một máy phóng-thanh tung ra càng làm cho câu truyện ba người* **thêm** *vui-vẻ.* The sound of harmonious music produced by a loudspeaker in the corner of the room made their (the three people's) stories still more pleasant.

thường be common, frequent, ordinary; often, usually

> *Ông ấy* **thường** *lắm.* That man is very ordinary [i.e., he has nothing in particular to recommend him].
>
> *Tôi* **thường** *đi Sài-gòn.* I often go to Saigon.

The auxiliary **có** is especially important. It is in many ways similar to the English auxiliary verb *do*: it is less frequent in ordinary affirmative sentences, and in those cases it denotes a kind of emphasis of the verb it precedes; it is almost indispensable in interrogative sentences, just as *do* is in English. In negative sentences it frequently occurs, but not as frequently as *do* in English. It is this **có** which appears as the short affirmative answer. (Cf. also the use of **có phải** in questions, 13.32.)

> *Ông* **có** *đi không?*–**Có.** Are you going?–Yes.
>
> *Tôi không* **có** *đi.* I'm *not* going. (less common than *Tôi không đi.*)
>
> *Các ông các bà là ai? Nếu* **có** *phải là chủ của các hàng-hóa này thì cứ để cho tôi dùng, sau này tôi giầu có, tôi sẽ đem tiền lại giả.* Who are you ladies and gentlemen? If it's true [you are] the owners of these pieces of merchandise, then go ahead, let me use [them]; later on I'll be wealthy, [and] I'll bring the money back and pay.
>
> *Hôm qua tôi* **có** *đi săn.* Yesterday I did go hunting.
>
> *Sáng mai* **có** *đi thì đi!* Tomorrow morning if you [insist on] going, then go ahead.
>
> *Nó* **có** *gõ, cũng đừng* **có** *mở.* Even [if] he raps, don't open [the door].

In a specialized usage, a predicate with **có** as center followed by a substantival element as descriptive complement (9.62) appears as a descriptive complement itself with the meaning 'just this and nothing more, only...'

> *Tôi lấy* **có** *một cái bánh.* I'll take just one cake.
>
> *Nó làm* **có** *hai ngày.* He's worked only two days.

It has been suggested (e.g., Bulteau 1950, p. 125; Jones and Thông 1960, pp. 133-34) that *có* is used to specify action in past time. It seems more likely that anterior reference in the cases involved is rather either clear from the context or specified by some other means, while *có* has the emphatic function described here.

As a predicate center **có** very frequently corresponds to the English verb *have*, and for this reason it is generally translated in this manner. However, an understanding of the structure of Vietnamese predicates and their complements (9.62-63 and especially 10.5) makes clear that the gloss 'be [definitely] existent' is more suggestive of the basic meaning.

The auxiliary **còn** is important as a predicate center with a descriptive complement announcing an additional (often contrary) factor. And it often signals the final item in a series.

> **Còn tôi** *không muốn đi.* As for me, I don't care to go. ["remain I not want go"]
>
> *Chuyến thứ nhất thì bảy giờ sáng. Chuyến thứ nhì thì mười hai giờ trưa.* **Còn chuyến thứ ba** *thì tám giờ chiều.* The first [train] is at seven in the morning. The second is at twelve noon. And the third is at eight in the evening.
>
> **Còn việc làm chiếu,** *nên hỏi ông Nam.* On the matter of making mats better ask Mr. Nam.

9.55. Verbs are verbals which do not appear as restrictive complements and do occur as heads of descriptive phrases with a variety of verbal descriptive complements (i.e., in addition to the definitive, 9.51, and comparatives, 9.52). Several features of Vietnamese verbs are quite different from what we call verbs in English. The class does include a great majority of words which may be translated by English verbs. However, it also includes a very large number of forms which are most conveniently rendered by English adjectives following some form of the verb *be*: thus *Tôi mệt* means 'I am tired', *Ông ấy già* 'He is old', and so forth. The meaning 'be' represents an integral part of the semantic range of this sort of verb.

An important way in which Vietnamese verbs differ from English verbs is that they do not in themselves imply a clear notion of "voice" in the grammatical sense. In English a (transitive) verb must be either active or passive. No such distinction is necessary in Vietnamese. As a matter of fact, the actor and the goal or object of Vietnamese verbs are regularly not formally marked; these relationships are generally clear from the context, and if they are not there are ways in which they can be made clear; the point is that they need not be, and in the vast majority of Vietnamese sentences such clarifying devices are not used. The device which indicates that a preceding focal complement (10.2) is actually a goal or object of the action we shall call the **logical passive;** expressions of this sort are discussed in connection with verbal phrase types (9.64). Following are some examples of verbs which demonstrate the lack of specific distinctions of voice.

Làm việc này *rồi.* [We've] already done this.

Việc này làm *rồi.* This has already been done.

Những bức vẽ này thường dán *ở cửa ra vào.* These drawings are often pasted on entrances and exits.

Hai thằng trộm vội ra bờ ruộng và khiêng chum vàng về nhà định mở ra chia nhau. **Nhưng vàng chả thấy** *đâu chỉ* **thấy toàn là rắn độc.** The two robbers hastened out to the edge of the field and brought back home the pot of gold [carrying it between them], determined to open [it] up and divide [it] between them. But no gold was to be seen anywhere; [they] only saw [that] it consisted entirely of poisonous snakes.

Ông ấy **cất nhà** *ở gần trường học.* He's building a house near the school.

Hai cái nhà kia cất *gần nhau cùng trên một miếng đất.* Those two houses are built close together on the same lot.

Anh ấy **dùng một chữ ít lễ-phép.** He used a word that was not very polite.

Chữ này không dùng *một mình.* This word is not used by itself.

Vietnamese verbs are in themselves also timeless.. They establish only the fact that a particular action, series of actions or state of affairs is in effect. They depend entirely on the linguistic and situational context for their reference to relative time (see also 9.3). However, we may distinguish semantically two types of verbs:

(1) **momentary action verbs**, referring to specific actions which take a more or less definable amount of time: *đi* go, *làm* do, make, *hát* sing, *ở* be located, stay, *ăn* eat, *uống* drink, *đánh* hit, *đọc* read, *ngồi* sit, *đậu* moor a boat

(2) **extended state verbs**, referring to states of affairs, attitudes, feelings, wishes, mental processes, etc., which extend over an indefinite period of time: *khó* be difficult, *tốt* be good, attractive, *hay* be interesting, attractive, appealing, *xấu* be bad, ugly, *biết* know, *hiểu* understand, *đúng* be correct

Extended state verbs when not specifically marked for temporal reference in some way, refer to states obtaining at the basic time of the context. Momentary action verbs operate in the same way in narrative contexts, but in conversational situations those which are not otherwise temporally distinguished refer to the immediate future.

NARRATIVE SITUATION

Trương-Tri là tên của thanh-niên làm nghề thuyền chài. Anh này có một giọng hát rất hay, nhưng mặt thì rất xấu. Ngày ngày sau khi đánh cá xong, anh thường đậu thuyền ở một ngã ba sông dưới hàng cây dương-liễu xanh-xanh.	Trương-Tri was the name of a young fisherman. He had a splendid way of singing, but a very ugly face. Every day after he finished fishing he would moor his boat at a fork in the river under a row of pale green willows.

CONVERSATIONAL SITUATION

Bà Lan drops by the house of her friend Bà Hồng. They meet outside and talk for a few minutes about both families' health. Then, as Hồng invites Lan inside, Lan says—

Lan: *Chị đi chợ không?*	Are you going to market?
Hồng: *Không. Tôi ở nhà. Chị uống nước không?*	No. I'm going to stay home. Will you have some tea?
Lan: *Có. Cám ơn chị. À chị biết không? Cô Kính lấy chồng.*	Yes, thanks. (Changing subject:) Do you know that (Miss) Kính is getting married?
Hồng: *Tôi nghe nói rồi. Có đúng à?*	I heard (someone) say (so). It's true, is it?

Extended state verbs rather often carry a connotation of augmentation, increase. It may well be that this is the counterpart of the momentary action verb's reference to the immediate future.

> *Ba người cùng ngẩng mặt lên xem đoàn phi-cơ bay* **cao, cao** *mãi.*
> The three people (together) raised [their] faces (upward) to watch the group of airplanes flying higher, ever higher.

In any case, this feature is clearly utilized whenever two or more entities are compared: the extended state verb designates which of the entities is most endowed with the quality involved.

> *Hai cái bàn này, cái nào* **dài?** [Of] these two tables, which [one] is longer?
> *Các quả kia, thứ nào* **ngon?** [Of] those fruit, which are the tastiest?

There seems to be no formal way to distinguish momentary action verbs from extended state verbs. In general, the latter include those forms which appear after the preverb *rất* 'very', but in the long run this appears to be an inadequate criterion for separating them from other verbs. It is likely that further research will reveal some formal subclasses of verbs. This problem has been studied in some recent Soviet publications: Bystrov 1961 separates from verbs a class of adjectives, which do not occur after the prohibitives *đừng* and *chớ* (p. 4). Stankevič 1961a studies the question in detail and is responsible for the specific distinction cited by Bystrov, as well as some other differences between his verbs and adjectives. However, these categorizations seem to rest on quite tenuous non-occurrences and some rather rare forms. For example, he identifies a 'sign of the past tense' *từng*, after which his adjectives do not appear (p.45). Actually, this seems to be rather a verb meaning something like 'to experience, have an experience', and following elements are descriptive complements (9.62). Considerable further work is needed.

It is important to note that the familiar dichotomy of English verbs between those which "take objects" and those which do not is absent in Vietnamese. Logical goals and objects are discussed in 9.63. Here it will suffice to cite a few examples involving elements similar to goals or objects with verbs whose English counterparts are intransitive. In Vietnamese these elements are descriptive complements.

Tôi đi **Hà-nội.** I'm going to Hanoi.

Ông xa **nhà.** You're far from home.

Tôi buồn **ông.** I [feel] sorry for you. ["I sad gentleman"]

This feature is, of course, consistent with the lack of specific active-passive reference in Vietnamese verbs (see above).

Vietnamese verbs lack the "modal" distinctions which characterize verbs in many Western languages. This means that there are no such forms as infinitives, subjunctives, and so forth. It is particularly important to note in this connection that commands and injunctions (which in many languages make use of a special imperative form) are not markedly distinguished from statements and questions. They occur with and without focal complements specifying the person (resembling subjects in English; cf. 10.5); those without are generally somewhat less polite.

Anh lấy cái va-li này. Take this suitcase. (polite to servant)

Lấy cái va-li này. Take this suitcase. (less polite)

In other contexts the first example might mean 'You'll take this suitcase', 'You took this suitcase' or 'He took this suitcase.' The second example has an even wider range of meanings in other contexts, including, for instance, also 'I'll take this suitcase', 'Let's take this suitcase', etc. In other words, the identification of a sentence as expressing a command in such cases depends entirely on the context. Or, to state it another way, Vietnamese does not distinguish commands and injunctions from statements. Even the preverb **hãy** (11.72 and Appendix A), which is often cited as a mark of the imperative, is ambiguous: it frequently has the force 'one should...', 'let's be sure to...'

Hãy *đi sớm.* Better go early. *or* Let's go early.

However, the prohibitives **đừng** and **chớ** often correspond to English negative imperatives, and the momentary action verb **đi** 'go' appears as a descriptive complement (9.62) with the force 'go ahead...'

> **Chớ** *uống rượu.* [You] shouldn't (*or* Don't) drink alcoholic beverages.
> *Anh* **đừng** *sợ.* Don't be afraid.
> *Anh nói* **đi***!* Go ahead and talk.

Verbs are extremely common as descriptive complements, both in substantival and verbal phrases.

SUBSTANTIVAL

> *người* **to** a big person
> *nhà* **nhỏ** a small house
> *nhà* **ở** a residence ["building to-live-in"]
> *chuyến* **đi** *chuyến* **đến** departures and arrivals (e.g., of trains)
>   ["scheduled-run go scheduled-run arrive"]
> *bàn* **ăn** dining table ["table eat"]

VERBAL

> *khó* **hiểu** difficult to understand
> *ăn* **sống** eat [something] raw ["eat be-alive"]
> *chạy* **đi** set out, start up (speaking of vehicle or machine)
>   ["run go"]
> *muốn* **học** want to study
> *nói* **giỏi** say [something] well

9.6. Verbal Phrases.

Predicatives enter into a variety of constructions. Their relationships are not so well understood as those of substantives, and some of the apparent subtypes of verbal phrases cannot be clearly justified on formal grounds. However, it is important to present the patterns which emerge in order to afford a better picture of the structure of predicates, even though certain difficult formal points may need revision in the light of further research.

The distinction between subordinating and coordinating constructions is clear, and **restrictive phrases** (9.61) are easily distinguishable from **descriptive phrases** (9.62-64). The difficulties arise with the separation of different types of coordinate phrases. To some extent the difficulties stem from the lack of a firm criterion for defining extended state verbs as a class apart from momentary action verbs (9.55), but there are other problems as well. However, one type of coordinate phrase is set apart by its usual intonational accompaniment: **alternative phrases** (9.67) have two heads (expressing semantically opposite points of view), most often with sustaining intonation (5.34) accompanying the second head. In other coordinate phrases the two or more heads represent either several actions or states obtaining at the same time (**coterminous phrases,** 9.65), or situations which follow one another (**sequential phrases,** 9.66). The latter are by far the more common, and it may well be that only logical differences of meaning separate the two.

Predicates are themselves often the heads of restrictive phrases formed by the focal construction (Chapter 10). Focal complements are distinguished from restrictive complements within predicates in that they precede the position of tense markers (see definition of predicates in 9.1).

9.61. Restrictive Phrases contain a single predicative or a verbal phrase as head and as complement a negative (9.4), an auxiliary (9.54), or one of certain kinds of particles (11.7-8) (including predicative markers, 9.1). In a few instances complex complements appear, usually themselves restrictive phrases containing a prepositive particle (11.81). In the following examples complements appear in boldface and are identified in parentheses.

> *Tôi* **sẽ** *đi.* I'll go. (tense marker)
> *Tôi* **chưa** *đi.* I haven't gone yet. (negative)
> *Tôi* **ít** *đi.* I seldom go. (auxiliary)
> *Tôi* **vừa** *đi.* I just left. (preverb)
> *Tôi* **cũng** *đi.* I'm going too. (prepositive particle)
> *Tôi* **rất** *vui.* I'm very happy (preverb)
> *Tôi* **rất ít** *đi.* I very seldom go. (restrictive phrase *rất ít*)
> *Ông ấy* **đã không có** *ốm nhiều.* He's already *not* very sick now.
> (restrictive complex with successive complements *đã, không, có*; and the descriptive phrase *ốm nhiều* as center)

9.62. Descriptive Phrases contain a verbal or verbal phrase (9.5) as head; complements are other verbals and verbal phrases, substantives and substantival phrases (Chapter 8), certain focuses (10.4), certain particles (11.7-8), and sometimes entire clauses (9.8).

> *Ông ấy ốm* **nặng.** He's seriously ill. ["gentleman just-referred-to ill heavy"] (verb)
> *Đi* **không được.** Can't go. (verbal restrictive phrase)
> ...*đi* **sâu vào xã-hội Việt-nam**... [if you] go deep into Vietnamese society (*đi* 'go' as head; complement: *sâu vào xã-hội Việt-nam*, verbal descriptive phrase, consisting of verb *sâu* 'be deep' and complement *vào xã-hội Việt-nam*, verbal descriptive phrase, in turn consisting of verb *vào* 'enter' and complement *xã-hội Việt-nam* 'Vietnamese' society', substantival phrase)

Ông ấy ngắn **tay.** He has short arms. (substantive)

Chị ấy đau **bụng.** (S) She has a stomach ache. (substantive)

Lý-thú **lắm.** Very interesting. (postpositive particle)

Hay **quá!** Marvelous! (comparative)

Vì thế mà người ta tin là đã có duyên-kiếp lấy nhau thì thế nào cũng phải kết-hợp một lần không sao tránh được. And so it is that people believe that if two people are destined to be lovers they must in any case unite at least once—there's no way to avoid it. (The clause beginning with the identificational marker *là* is complement to the verb *tin* 'believe.')

Chợ vắng **người.** The market is empty of people. (general categorical)

Nó giàu **của** *nhưng nghèo* **con.** He's rich in possessions, but poor in children [i.e., he has many inanimate possessions but few children]. (general categoricals)

Cái nhà này cất **tốn tiền lắm.** This house cost a lot of money to build. (Complement is itself a verbal descriptive phrase with the head *tốn tiền* and the postpositive particle *lắm* as complement. *Tốn tiền* is also a descriptive phrase with the extended state verb *tốn* 'be costly' as head, and the mass noun *tiền* 'money' as complement.)

Tôi thả con mèo ra ngoài, lạnh nó **lắm.** I let the cat out of doors; [it was] very cold for it. (The final predicate has the head *lạnh nó* with the complement *lắm*; *lạnh* 'be cold' has the complement *nó* 'it', a pronoun, 10.43.)

Mặt trời lặn, mau đỏ **đèn.** [When] the sun goes down lamps are quickly lighted. ["face sky dive, soon be-red lamp"]

Tôi không thích **lạnh ở Đà-lạt.** I don't like the cold [weather] in Dalat. (Descriptive complement *lạnh ở Đà-lạt* is itself a verbal descriptive phrase with head *lạnh* 'be cold', and, in turn, the verbal descriptive phrase *ở Đà-lạt* as complement.)

Xe lửa đến **sớm ba phút.** The train arrived three minutes early. (The descriptive complement *sớm ba phút* is itself a verbal descriptive phrase with the head *sớm* 'be early' and the complement *ba phút* 'three minutes', a numerative phrase.)

Some descriptive phrases of this type seem to appear primarily or only as focal complements (10.2).

Thường ngày *tôi đi chợ.* I go to market daily. ["be-common day I go market"]

Thường khi *tôi thích ăn ở ngoài.* I usually prefer to eat out.

Probably the most common complements are substantives and substantival phrases. Many of these seem from the English point of view to be
goals or objects (see 9.63). Of verbals, the definitive (9.51), comparatives
(9.52) and quantifiers (9.53) are very common. Of verbs, extended state
verbs are probably most common complements to momentary action verbs:

> *đi* **chậm** go slowly
> *hiểu* **rõ** understand clearly
> *ăn* **ngon** eat [things that are] tasty; make good eating
> *bán* **rẻ** sell cheaply

Less frequently a momentary action verb is found as complement to an
extended state verb:

> *khó* **nói** difficult to say
> *dễ* **thương** lovable ["easy to-love"]
> *muốn* **làm** want to do [something]

Rather rarely a momentary action verb appears as complement to another
momentary action verb:

> *hỏi* **thăm** to inquire ["ask-questions to visit," i.e., 'to ask for
> information while visiting']

Descriptive complements generally involve an obvious or not very
startling contrast with preceding complements which are restrictive (focal
complements, 10.2). They offer more specific or detailed information about
the head, but do not in principle limit it. However, there are a few cases
in which some special contrasts are involved. In reference to time and
space, descriptive complements suggest expansion, extension, duration—
in contrast to focal complements, which signal points in time or space
(10.21).

> *Mỗi ngày tôi làm việc* **tám giờ**. I work eight hours each day.
> Cf. (with focal complement) *Mỗi ngày* **tám giờ** *tôi làm việc*. I
> [begin] work at eight o'clock each day.
> *Xe sẽ phải lên giốc* **ba cây số nữa**. The car has to climb a
> slope for three more kilometers. Cf. (with focal complement)
> **Ba cây số nữa** *xe sẽ phải lên giốc*. Three kilometers further
> on the car has to climb a slope.

Without other indications to the contrary, descriptive complements specifying time refer to the past, while similar focal complements refer to the
future (10.22).

> *Ông đi* **hôm nào?** What day did you go? Cf. (with focal complement)
> **Hôm nào** *ông đi?* What day are you going to go?

The extended state verb with a substantive as complement is sometimes considered in traditional grammar as a sort of preceding modifier with
special idiomatic meaning (e.g., Trần trọng Kim *et al* 1950, p. 88). It seems

clear, however, that even these cases are better understood in the terms described here (i.e., the following substantive is complement to the verb, which is head), and the idiomatic meanings are simply the result of specialization.

> *mặt đẹp* a beautiful face: *đẹp* **mặt** be glorious, honored (esp. in *làm đẹp mặt* do honor to) ["beautiful of face"]
>
> *người lớn* adult, grownup: *lớn* **người** (be) a tall person ["large of person"]
>
> *tay mát* a cool hand: *mát* **tay** be skillful ["cool of hand"]
>
> *răng trắng* white teeth: *trắng* **răng** be still young ["white of tooth"]
>
> *người đúng* a "correct" person (i.e., meritorious): *đúng* **người** the very person [I wanted to see] ["correct as to person"]

There are cases where it might appear that a "subject" (from the English point of view) appears following its predicate. These are rather verbal descriptive phrases of the same type.

> *Người chồng thật là dầu-dĩ, lúc vắng* **vợ** *thì hết sức lấy lời ôn-tồn nói với me, lúc vắng* **mẹ** *thì nghiêm-nghị khuyên-can vợ.* The husband was really worried; when [his] wife was out he put a lot of effort into talking kindly with [his] mother; when [his] mother was out he was stern in warning [his] wife. (*vắng vợ* "deserted from the point of view of the wife," *vắng mẹ* "deserted from the point of view of the mother")
>
> *Cái xe máy dầu của tôi hôm trước hư, chết* **máy.** (S) My motor-bike went out of commission the other day—the motor died. ["object vehicle machine oil possession I day time-before spoil, die machine"]
>
> *Đau* **con mèo.** (S) The cat's hurt.

Phrases of this type are frequent as descriptive complements to the verb **làm** 'do, make'; the result is a kind of causative expression, with the overtone 'unintentional.'

> *Tôi làm* **chết máy.** (S) I killed the motor.
>
> *Tôi làm* **đau con mèo.** (S) I hurt the cat [unintentionally].
>
> *Chị ấy làm* **vỡ cái đèn.** She broke the lamp.

(A causative expression with intentional implication involves the sequential construction; phrases have second heads which are descriptive phrases headed by the verb **cho** 'give'; cf. 9.66.)

9.63. Logical Goals and Objects.

In a large majority of the cases where a verbal is complemented by a following substantive or substantival phrase it will appear from the English point of view that it is a matter of verb and object or goal. However, it is especially important to realize that in the over-all scheme of Vietnamese grammar this English category has no real counterpart. There seems to be no difference in structure between a phrase which is translated in English by a verb plus an object and one which is translated as an adjective or sometimes a verb with some kind of modifier. Thus *đi Sài-gòn* 'go to Saigon', *ăn cá* 'eat fish', *hỏi ba câu* 'ask three questions' and *làm gì?* 'what [are you] doing?' have exactly the same structure as *ngắn tay* 'short of arm', *ăn cao-lâu* 'eat [at] a restaurant', *nói ba lần* 'say [it] three times', *đi đường này* 'go [by] this street (*or* this way)', *lâu ngày* 'for a long time [in terms of days passing]', *làm lính* 'be a soldier' (more literally 'act as a soldier'), *xin lỗi* 'beg pardon' ["beg (from point of view of) error"], *buồn gì?* 'what [are you] sad about?', *xa nhà* 'far from home', *tốt đôi* 'making a good pair', *vui tai* 'pleasing to the ears', *vui tính* 'pleasant by nature', and so on. In each case the phrase is an expansion (5.42) of the verbal and this verbal is thus the head of the phrase; when this aspect of the system is understood and is considered together with another difficult matter—the lack of a grammatical subject (in the English sense) for predications (cf. 10.5)—a much deeper insight into the structure of the language is achieved. The opposition of subject and object—so important in English—is simply not part of the Vietnamese system. This fact is clearly connected with the lack of grammatical "voice" connotations in the verb (9.55, 9.64).

This understanding of the relationship of verbals with following substantival complements makes clear the central meaning of the important auxiliary **có** 'be (definitely) existent' (9.54) and unites its many (superficially varied) uses.

Đây **có** *nhiều người.* There are many people here.

Việt-nam **có** *nhiều người.* Viet Nam has many people.

Ở Việt-nam **có** *nhiều người.* In Viet Nam there are many people.

Hành-khách không ai được lên bờ vì đang **có** *cuộc đình-công của các phu khuân vác làm ở bến tàu.* None of the passengers got to go ashore because there was a strike by the coolies working at the dock.

Hai ông **có** *thể cho tôi biết tên các vị ấy được không?* Could you two let me know the names of those (distinguished) gentlemen? (*thể* possibility, capacity)

Giáo-sư chúng tôi **có** *dặn là các bạn khác ở xa Hà-nội thì ba ông Thái, Cung hay Chỷ sẽ đưa chúng tôi đi thăm.* Our teacher did advise us that as for the other friends far from Hanoi, Mr. Thái, Mr. Cung or Mr. Chỷ would take us to visit [them].

Cuối mùa đông ở Bắc-Việt **có** *nhiều sương mù.* At the end of winter in North Viet Nam there is a great deal of fog.

Kìa, hai ông trông chỗ **có** *nhiều tầu, thuyền đỗ và* **có** *sáu cái kho hàng to kia là bến Sáu-kho đấy.* Way over there you two see the place [where] there are a lot of ships and small boats moored and there are six large warehouses—that's the port of Sáu-kho there.

Ăn **có** *nhai, nói* **có** *nghĩ.* For eating there is chewing, for talking there is thinking. (Rough equivalent of the American aphorism: 'Before opening mouth make certain mind is in gear.')

Ông Hiền **có** *nhà không?* Is Mr. Hiền at home?

The last sentence exemplifies a type often explained by grammarians as involving omission of the principal verb *ở* 'be located.' This may well be the historical explanation, but the phrase occurs frequently as it is and must be explained without resort to missing elements. If we were to allow missing elements there would be no end of them and we would very shortly have projected the prejudice of a foreign grammar onto the language. It must also be mentioned that there is a homonymous phrase meaning 'Does Mr. Hiền have a house?' although it is a less likely Vietnamese sentence.

Sometimes there are two descriptive complements which resemble goals or objects. In this case the second element complements the phrase consisting of the verbal head and the first complement. In its simplest form the sequence involves a first complement which generally identifies a personal beneficiary or agent, and a second denoting the concrete objects, abstract ideas, actions or states affected.

Cho tôi ba đồng. Give me three piastres. Cf. *Nói câu này ba lần.* Say this sentence three times.

Tôi cho anh xích-lô năm đồng. I gave the cyclo-driver five piastres.

Tôi muốn hỏi ông một câu. I want to ask you a question.

Ông làm ơn giúp tôi công việc này. Please help me with this task.

Here, as in other cases, the descriptive complement is often another verbal or verbal phrase.

Ông để tôi làm. Allow me to do [it].[2]

Ông ấy mời tôi đi xem hát. He invited me to go to a play. (In this sentence the second complement *đi xem hát* is a sequential phrase [9.66] of which the second head, *xem hát*, is also a verbal descriptive phrase with head *xem* 'watch' and complement *hát* 'sing, act on stage.')

[2] Sentences of this type have elsewhere (Gage and Jackson 1953, p. 13) been analyzed as containing a "pivot"—a word which is at the same time object of one verb and subject of another. The understanding of these elements as complements in a descriptive complex rather than as objects in the English sense removes the quandary.

Chị mua hai chục quả cam cho chúng tôi ăn quà sáng tuần sau.
Buy about twenty oranges for us to eat for breakfast next
week. (Here the two major predicates are in sequential construction [9.66]. *Mua* 'buy' has the single descriptive complement *hai chục quả cam.* The second predicate is a descriptive
complex with head *cho chúng tôi* 'give us' and complement *ăn
quà sáng tuần sau* 'eat [for] breakfast next week.' This latter
complement itself is a verbal descriptive phrase with head *ăn*
'eat' and complement *quà sáng tuần sau* 'next week's break-
fasts', a substantival descriptive complex [8.34].)
Such verbal descriptive complexes frequently involve more than two layers,
and the complement elements are often themselves constructed in the same
way or by means of the sequential construction (9.66).

*Người ta tin là khi hai người lấy nhau thì có một vị-thần ở trên
Giời lấy hai sợi chỉ hồng xe lại với nhau thành một sợi.* Some
believe that when two people are married there is a benevolent
spirit in heaven which takes the two strands of pink thread and
spins them together to make one. (The final clause of this
sentence begins *thì có một vị-thần...*, in which the particle
thì marks it as head of a focal phrase [10.24, 11.51]. Its head
is *có một vị-thần ở trên Giời* '[there] exists a benevolent spirit
located up in heaven', itself a verbal descriptive phrase with
complement *ở trên Giời* [of the same structure] and the head
có một vị-thần, again a descriptive phrase with head *có*, the
predicate center. The outermost descriptive complement is a
sequential phrase: *lấy hai sợi chỉ hồng xe lại với nhau thành
một sợi* '[who] takes the two strands of pink thread [and]
spins [them] with one another [so that they] become one
strand.' Its first head is the verb *lấy*, its complement a numerative phrase. The second head involves another descriptive
complex with the outermost complement *thành một sợi* 'become
one strand'; next is *với nhau* 'with one another'; innermost
complement is the postpositive particle *lại* 'close together'
[11.82, Appendix A]; and center of this predicate is *xe*
'spin.')

9.64. Logical Passive Expressions.

There are three common momentary
action verbs of very generalized meaning which most frequently appear
with a descriptive complement, often itself a clause:

bị suffer, undergo, be affected adversely by some action, state
or factor

228

do be accomplished, caused, effected by, be dependent on, the result of

được receive, get, obtain; be benefited by, affected favorably by some action, state or factor, be permitted (see also Appendix A)

Predicates containing one of these verbs as head and a clause as descriptive complement resemble English passive expressions and the phenomenon is so labeled in traditional grammars. However, it is important to remember that basically Vietnamese verbs are neither active nor passive (9.55). In the following examples the nature of descriptive complements (in boldface type) is indicated in parentheses.

Ông ấy bị **bệnh.** He has a disease. (general categorical)

Anh ấy bị **người ta đánh.** He has been beaten by someone. (clause)

Trong khi bị giam, Trê bị **khổ-sở,** *ăn uống thiếu-thốn, sáng bị* **đòn,** *tối bị* **tra.** While he was detained [in police custody], Catfish suffered hardships—his food and drink were entirely insufficient, by morning he was flogged, by night he was interrogated. (verbs)

Xe anh ấy bị **hỏng những gì?**—*Bị* **vỡ kính, vỡ đèn và hỏng cửa.** What was damaged on his car?—The windshield was broken, the lights smashed and the door damaged. (verbal descriptive phrases)

Tiếng âm-nhạc du-dương ở góc phòng do **một máy phóng-thanh tung ra** *càng làm cho câu truyện ba người thêm vui-vẻ.* The sound of harmonious music produced by a loudspeaker in the corner of the room made their (the three people's) stories still more pleasant. (clause)

Ông giàu do **sự làm lụng khó nhọc.** You are rich due to the fact that you toiled arduously. (substantival phrase, *sự* as head)

Xe ấy do **một cô gái lái.** That car is driven by a girl. (clause)

Ngày xưa ở Việt-nam việc hôn-nhân là do **ở bố mẹ kén chọn cho con cái.** In olden days in Viet Nam marriages depended on the parents' choosing for [their] children. (clause)

Sáng nay chị tôi được **thơ.** My [elder] sister got a letter this morning. (item noun)

Em được **mấy tuổi rồi?** How old are you? (speaking to child) (substantival phrase)

Hôm nay tôi được **bớt đau.** (S) I'm less ill today. (verbal predicate)

Tôi được **ăn.** I am permitted to eat. (verb)

Tôi được **ông thương-yêu** *vì tôi siêng-năng.* I am esteemed by you because I am diligent. (clause)

Tôi không được **đi.** I was not permitted to go. (verb)

9.65. **Coterminous Phrases** are coordinate phrases presenting two or more actions or states obtaining at the same time. Extended state verbs are most common as heads although momentary action verbs also occur. There is no formal way of separating such phrases from sequential phrases (9.66), and it may well be that only a semantic specialization is involved.

> *Mấy con chó con này* **tốt đẹp dễ thương.** These puppies are cute and lovable. ["indefinite-number animal dog offspring this good beautiful easy love"]

> *Chúng ta cùng nhau đi chợ.* **Chị mua rau cải, tôi mua thịt.** Let's go to market together. You buy vegetables, I'll buy meat.

> *Trước thì còn riêng các cụ bô-lão và quan-viên kỳ-cựu họp* **bàn mưu** **tìm kế,** *sau phải hội toàn dân cũng không ai có ý-kiến gì.* First separately the village notables and elder officials got together to discuss strategy, later they had to assemble the entire populace, and still no one had any [constructive] idea. (*Bàn tìm* 'discuss in quest of' is a coterminous phrase, appearing in interlocking order with the reinforcing compound *mưu-kế* 'strategy'; cf. 6.4.)

> *Các người ấy* **biết ăn biết nói.** Those people know how to get along. ["plural person just-referred-to know eat know speak"]

> *Thưa thầy tốt lắm ạ,* **nhà ngói năm gian, cột bằng lim, cửa** **bằng gụ và cột cũng khá to.** Oh, it's a very good one, sir— [it's a] five-section tiled roof house, ironwood pillars, hardwood doors—and the pillars are pretty good size.

> *Hai người* **nói chuyện vui-vẻ không còn nhớ gì đến thì-giờ.** The two people were conversing happily [and so] forgot completely ["no longer remembered anything"] about time.

That the dividing line between coterminous phrases and sequential phrases is impossible to draw clearly is exemplified by the following sentences, which could be analyzed as containing either.

> *Vì sức yếu nên* **nhờ cây gậy chống đi.** Because he is weak he has to walk leaning on his stick. ["because strength weak therefore depend-on stick cane lean-on go"]

> *Tôi* **đi ra về.** I'm going home. ["I go go-out return-home"]

9.66. **Sequential Phrases** are coordinate phrases presenting situations which follow one another. Heads vary from single verbals to lengthy clauses.

> *Ông ấy* **ở Sài-gòn ra Hà-nội** *thứ hai.* He left Saigon for Hanoi on Monday. ["gentleman just-referred-to located Saigon go-out Hanoi Monday"]

Tôi đi chợ mua đồ. I'm going to market to buy some things.
Ông chủ nhà thấy liễn hết cơm, vội gọi người nhà lấy thêm. Cơm đưa lên cậu Thanh lại tiếp-tục ăn và nói chuyện vui-vẻ như thường. The host saw that the serving dish was empty of rice [and] hastened to call the servant to get more. [When] the rice was brought Thanh again resumed eating and talking happily as usual. (*Ông chủ nhà thấy liễn hết cơm* is first head of a sequential phrase; the balance of the sentence is the second head. In the second sentence the first sequential head is *Cơm đưa lên*; the second head is again the balance of the sentence.)
Sometimes a cause-and-effect relationship is implied.
Muốn có ăn phải đi làm. [If you] want to have [anything] to eat, [you] have to go to work.
Muốn biết được thua phải đi hỏi. [If you] want to know [whether you] won [or] lost [you] have to go ask.
Tội-nghiệp cho anh ta, lúc trở về, trong khi bay qua bể, **chim bị nặng quá không cõng nổi,** *liền để anh theo với túi vàng rơi tõm xuống bể.* Unfortunately for him, on the way back, while flying across the sea, the bird found [its load] too heavy [and] could not carry [it], [so] promptly let him and the pouch of gold fall down into the sea. ["too-bad give elder-brother you-and-I, time return return-home, inside time fly cross sea, bird undergo heavy exceed not carry-on-back capably, directly leave elder-brother follow with pouch gold fall kerplop go-down sea"]

As can be seen from some of the above examples, this construction is exceedingly common, and it often appears where from the point of view of English usage we should expect some kind of subordinate clauses with adverbial elements clarifying the relationships. As common as the sequential construction is, it is not surprising that a number of high-frequency verbs appear with rather specialized meanings as second head in sequential phrases. In the following examples the basic meaning of each verb is covered first.

bằng be equal, even, flat; as...as (not to be confused with the relator noun *bằng* 'a particular quantity or proportion', 8.63; or the extended state verb *bằng* 'be the essential substance of'—*làm bằng gỗ* made of wood, *đi bằng máy bay* go by plane)
Hai phân-số ấy **bằng** *nhau.* Those two ratios are equal (to one another).
Cái ghế này to **bằng** *cái kia.* This chair is as big as the other one.

cho give; for the benefit of, that, for the fact that, so that, in order to

Ông làm ơn cho tôi hai đồng. Please give me two piastres.

Tôi sẽ làm cho ông. I'll do [it] for you.

Vợ ông chỉ biết khóc mà thương cho duyên-kiếp mình không ra gì, không hề oán-trách chồng. His wife was of such a personality [that she] only wept, regretting [the fact] that her predestination turned out to be so disappointing ["came to nothing"]; she never reproached [her] husband.

Tôi làm cho con mèo đau. (S) I hurt the cat [on purpose]. (cf. 9.62 end)

Tôi mài dao định giết mẹ đi cho rồi. I'm sharpening the knife [having] decided to kill mother off and get it over with.

Hai họ thường ngồi chung để nói chuyện cho dễ. The two families usually sit together to allow for easy conversation.

Chia hai bánh này cho đều. Divide these two cakes equally.

Tôi nghĩ cho ông ấy là một người học giỏi. I thought he was a good student.

Ông ấy đã bán nhà cho tôi. He sold me a house. (Note that in some contexts this means 'He sold a house for me.')

đến go to, arrive at; all the way to, up to; concerning

Lúc nào ông đến? When will you arrive?

Anh ấy làm đến hai giờ rưỡi. He worked up to two-thirty.

Chúng tôi nhớ đến cô. We remember you.

Tôi nghĩ đến anh đương làm việc này. I think about you doing this work.

Việc này thuộc đến ông Lâm. This matter concerns Mr. Lâm [superficially]. (cf. *về*)

đi go; away, completely [destroyed]

Tôi đi chợ. I'm going to market.

Xin anh đem cái va-li này đi. Please take this suitcase away.

Ấy là những giấy tờ cũ, nên hủy đi. Those are some old papers, it's appropriate to destroy them.

Tôi mài dao định giết mẹ đi cho rồi. I'm sharpening the knife [having] decided to kill mother off and get it over with.

lên go up; raising, increasing

Lúc nào ông lên Đà-lạt? When are you going up to Dalat?

Chúng ta mau lên, kẻo bị chết! We'd [better] hurry up, or else [we'll] be dead!

mất lose; use up, take; completely

Bà ấy mất hai trăm bạc. She lost two hundred [piastres] (in silver).

Làm việc này **mất** *mấy ngày?* How many days will it take to do this job?

Cái xe của Bính hỏng **mất.** Bính's car was a total loss.

Nếu ông không uống thuốc này thì ông chết **mất.** If you don't take this medicine you'll die.

ra go out; open, separate, changed

Con tầu càng **ra** *xa bờ càng chạy nhanh hơn.* The farther the ship got from the shore the faster it went. ["(classifier) ship the-more go-out far shore the-more run rapid more"]

Mở cửa **ra.** Open the door.

Chia **ra** *làm ba.* Divide [it] into three [parts]. ["divide go-out make three"]

Mây hóa **ra** *mưa.* The clouds were transformed into rain. ["cloud transform go-out rain"]

thấy perceive (used mainly as second head in sequential phrases referring to perception via one of the physical senses)

Tôi nghe **thấy** *tiếng người kêu.* I hear the sound of someone calling (*nghe* listen, hear)

Ở đây ngửi **thấy** *mùi hoa huệ.* Here [you can] smell the odor of lilies. (*ngửi* 'sniff')

Ông Vỹ rất mừng khi trông **thấy** *quyển sách ông cụ cầm tay là một quyển tiểu-thuyết Việt-nam.* Mr. Vỹ was very pleased when [he] saw [that] the book the old gentleman was holding in his hand was a Vietnamese novel. (*trông* 'look')

theo follow; after, according to, accompanying, along with

Có ba đứa **theo** *chúng ta.* There are three rascals following us.

Anh làm **theo** *mẫu này.* Make [it] according to this model.

Tội-nghiệp cho anh ta, lúc trở về, trong khi bay qua bể, chim bị nặng quá không cõng nổi, liền để anh **theo** *với túi vàng rơi tõm xuống bể.* Unfortunately for him, on the way back while flying across the sea, the bird found [its load] too heavy [and] could not carry [it], [so] promptly let him and the pouch of gold ["leave elder-brother follow with pouch gold"] fall down into the sea.

Mang **theo** *cơm với thịt.* Bring along [cooked] rice and meat.

vào go in; attached directly to, onto

Mời ông **vào.** Please come in.

Người ta cũng treo **vào** *cành đào một tờ giấy bùa.* They also hang an amulet onto the peach branch.

Sau này nhiều nhà không có cành đào thì họ vẽ cành đào **vào** *tờ giấy bùa.* Lately many families do not have a peach branch, so they draw a peach branch on a (paper) amulet.

về return home; toward, concerning, about

>*Mai tôi* về *nhà quê.* Tomorrow I'm going home to the country.
>*Làng tôi ở* về *phía tây một ngọn núi.* My village is situated to the west of a mountain.
>*Việc này thuộc* về *ông Lâm.* This matter concerns Mr. Lâm [intimately]. (cf. *đến*)
>*Bây giờ tôi nói* về *sử ký.* Now I'm speaking of history.

9.67. Alternative Phrases constitute for the most part choice questions—the most common form corresponding to English yes-or-no-answer questions. The first head is a verbal phrase (lengthy ones are common); the second head is always a single predicative, most often one of the negatives (9.4) **không** 'not', **chăng** (special form of *chẳng* 'definitely not' for this position), **chưa** 'not yet', or (in southern usage) **chớ** 'better not.' A few other verbals occur as second head: such a verbal is always diametrically opposite in meaning to that of the center of the first head. With the final head **không** the first head very often (but not invariably) has the auxiliary **có**; it is less frequent with other final heads. The final head is most often accompanied by sustaining intonation (5.34).

>*Ông đi* **không?** Are you going?
>*Ông* **có** *đi* **không?** Are you going? (This is a somewhat more insistent question than the preceding. Still more intricate shades of insistence in such sentences involve the differences in the stress pattern. The auxiliary *có* very often has weak stress, much like English *do*, but also occurs with heavier stresses.)
>*Ông* (**có**) *ăn* **chưa?** Have you eaten yet?
>*Ông biết* **chăng?** Do you know?
>*Thưa cụ, thế câu truyện bán nhà cụ định kể cho chúng tôi nghe có liên-quan đến việc làm rể* **không?** Well, sir, then does the story [about] selling a house [which] you have decided to tell us have a connection with the business of being a suitor?
>*Ông ở đây lâu* **mau?** (S) Will you be here long?
>*Ông sẽ ở đây lâu nữa* **thôi?** Will you stay here a good deal longer (or leave shortly)?
>*Ông đi Sài-gòn* **chớ?** (S) Are you going to Saigon?
>*Ông có biết nói tiếng tây* **không?** Do you (know how to) speak French? (*tây* 'west' has come to be a synonym for *Pháp* 'France')

Substantival and identificational predicates are not negated directly (cf. 14.3); similarly, an alternative question based on a substantival predicate has the verb **phải** 'be true, real, definite', nearly always preceded by the auxiliary **có** (cf. 13.32). *Phải* appears either directly before a predicative marker or in a position where a predicative marker could occur, or preceding one or more focal complements (10.2-3).

> *Thưa cụ, người thông-thạo pháp-luật cụ vừa nói* **có phải** *là trạng-sư* **không?** (Sir), is the person experienced with [matters of] law you just mentioned a lawyer?

> **Có phải** *Ông là người Mỹ* **không?** Are you an American?

> **Có phải** *bây giờ là mùa cưới* **không?** Is now the season for marriages?

Alternative questions often constitute the final head of a sequential phrase: the first head of the sequential phrase is a statement (often relatively long) which is then more or less summed up in a single verbal or brief verbal phrase followed by a negative.

> *Mai đi đám cưới* **có xa không?** Is the wedding we're going to tomorrow far away?

> *Hai ông có thể cho tôi biết tên các vị ấy* **được không?** Could you let me know the names of those gentlemen?

> *Năm nay hai bác ăn tết* **có to không?** Are you having a big New Year's celebration this year?

The latter device is used in the very familiar formula **...phải không?** the equivalent of the French *n'est-ce pas?* and similar English final question tags modeled on the verb (...isn't it?...don't you? etc.). The meaning of the Vietnamese formula is analagous: it indicates that the speaker expects his hearer to confirm what he has just said.

> *Cụ là người Việt,* **phải không?** You're Vietnamese, aren't you?

> *Ai đấy, tiếng ai nghe như tiếng cô Hồng* **phải không?** Who's there? Someone's voice sounds like Miss Hồng's—am I right?

Not all alternative phrases have sustaining intonation with the second head: choice questions with increasing and fading intonations are also common (cf. 5.3). In addition there are occasional alternative phrases which carry roughly the notion 'whether...or'—they are generally short and might be described as indirect questions embedded in longer phrases.

> *Muốn biết* **được thua** *phải đi hỏi.* [If you] want to know [whether you] won [or] lost [you] have to ask.

On occasion the second head in an alternative phrase is marked by the prepositive particle **hay** 'or' (11.81). The result is much like the alternative type question in English (*Are you going or not? Are you glad or sorry?*), whereas the regular Vietnamese alternative phrase corresponds to the average colorless question in English.

> *Xoài ngon không?* Is the mango good (tasting)?

Xoài ngon hay không? Is the mango good (tasting) or not?
Ông thích cơm Việt hay cơm Tàu? Do you prefer Vietnamese or
Chinese food?

9.7. Identificational Predicates are those introduced by the identifica-
tional marker **là** (9.1). Potentially any independent word or phrase in the
language may occur after *là* as such a predicate. It is thus marked specifically as a predicate which is to be identified with (considered in some way
the equivalent of) an immediately preceding item—either in the same speech,
or, occasionally, in the speech of another person. In rare circumstances it
may refer in a similar way to some element in the physical surroundings or
the sociocultural situation which has been identified in some nonlinguistic
way (for example, by pointing to or holding up an object, by exhibiting
surprise about a turn in the weather, etc.). In many cases the words of
phrases marked by *là* would not be predicates without it. In those cases
where *là* marks a temporal predicate special attention is called to the
identification of this predicate with the preceding element; such predicates
often appear in emphatic sentence-final position (12.62).

Identificational predicates are often heads of larger phrases; in these
cases they most often constitute the final element of a sentence, with
preceding (restrictive) complements (see Chapter 10). They also occur,
however, as descriptive complements; in this use they are sometimes non-
final, but the end of the identificational predicate is usually followed by
a pause.

IDENTIFICATIONAL PREDICATES AS HEADS

Ông Lewis và ông Johnson **là hai sinh-viên Mỹ.** Mr. Lewis and
Mr. Johnson were two American students.

Chỉ còn một tuần-lễ nữa **là tầu đi.** It's just one more week until
the boat leaves.

Điều mà các ông chú-trọng đến nhất **là đem theo máy ảnh và
máy quay phim đi.** The matter they paid the most attention
to was taking along a [regular] camera and moving-picture
camera.

Còn gì bằng **là hai ông đang đi sang Việt-nam du-lịch mà
được nghe một cụ già lịch-duyệt kể chuyện về Việt-nam.**
What could be better than that two gentlemen on their way to
Viet Nam for a trip should get to hear an experienced old
gentleman tell stories about Viet Nam!

Tôi hút thuốc **là tôi làm giàu cho hãng thuốc.** (S) I smoke [and
the result is] I make the tobacco companies rich. (sarcastic)

236

IDENTIFICATIONAL PREDICATES AS DESCRIPTIVE COMPLEMENTS

Cũng như các sinh-viên khác, hai ông được giáo-sư cho tên Việt **là Lê Vỹ và Trần Dong.** Just like the other students the two of them had been given Vietnamese names by the teacher—Lê Vỹ and Trần Dong.

Như vậy các ông đến nơi thì gặp những ngày cuối năm âm-lịch **là dịp dân-chúng rộn-rịp đua nhau sắm-sửa ăn tết.** In this way they would get there and experience ["then meet"] the last few days of the year [according to] the moon calendar, which is the occasion [when] the people are bustling, competitively preparing to celebrate the [New Year] holiday.

Vì thế mà người ta tin **là đã có duyên-kiếp lấy nhau thì thế nào cũng phải kết-hợp một lần không sao tránh được.** And so it is that people believe that if two people are destined to be lovers they must in any case unite at least once—there's no way to avoid it.

Vị thần ấy gọi **là ông Tơ-hồng.** That benevolent spirit is called Mr. Pink-Thread.

Tiếng Việt gọi cái này **là cái bàn.** [In] Vietnamese (language) [they] call this *cái bàn* [the table].

Con chó nầy tôi thích lắm, vì **là tôi dạy nó công-phu lắm.** (S) This dog I like a lot because I spent a lot of effort training him.

Tôi thích cái nhà này vì **là của tôi.** I like this house because it's mine.

Identificational predicates are not negated directly; the verb **phải** 'be correct, true' is introduced in the creation of corresponding negative sentences (cf. 14.33).

Tôi **không phải** *là người nghèo.* I'm not a poor person.

Similarly, **phải** is used in the choice questions created with the alternative construction (9.67).

Thưa cụ, người thông-thạo pháp-luật cụ vừa nói có **phải** *là trạng-*sư **không?** (Sir), is the person experienced with [matters of] law you just mentioned a lawyer?

Identificational predicates occasionally appear marked by a tense marker, making then temporal predicates with a *là* predicate as head.

Hôm nay **đã là mồng mười tết.** Today is already the tenth day of the New Year.

Because of this identificational (often equational) function the word *là* is termed the verb 'to be' in traditional Vietnamese grammar. As can be seen from the foregoing examples this view is somewhat misleading. The analysis presented here seems to cover all occurrences and provide a deeper understanding of sentence structure.

9.8. Uses of Predicates.

Like most other Vietnamese grammatical elements, predicates often occur as descriptive complements. However, more frequently a predicate is head of the next larger phrase of which it is a part.

> Ông Vỹ đang hút thuốc lá, mắt nhìn mấy con hải-âu bay theo tầu thì có một cụ già độ ngoài 60 tuổi tay cầm một cuốn sách đến xin ông một que diêm để hút thuốc lá. Vỹ was smoking a cigarette, (eyes) watching some seagulls flying after the ship, when an old man over sixty years old, holding a book in his hand, came and asked him for a match to light a cigarette.

In this example *đang hút thuốc lá* 'in the act of smoking a cigarette' (in which *đang* is a prepositive particle, 11.81) is head of the phrase *Ông Vỹ đang hút thuốc lá.* Similarly, *nhìn mấy con hải-âu bay theo tầu* 'watch some seagulls flying after the ship' is head of the phrase *mắt nhìn mấy con hải-âu bay theo tầu.* (Within this predicate there is the predicate *bay theo tầu* 'fly following the ship', which serves as descriptive complement to *mấy con hải-âu.*) *Cầm một cuốn sách* 'hold a book' is head of the phrase *tay cầm một cuốn sách.* In each of these cases the first element is a focal (restrictive) complement (10.1). The predicate (*thì*) *có một cụ già độ ngoài 60 tuổi tay cầm một cuốn sách* '(then) there was an old man (approximately) more than sixty years old holding a book in his hand' is a head, with the descriptive complement *đến xin ông một que diêm để hút thuốc lá* '[who] came [and] asked him for a match to light a cigarette.' (*Thì* is the isolating particle, 11.51, which often marks the heads of focal phrases, 10.24.) In turn *để hút thuốc lá* 'permit to smoke a cigarette' is a descriptive complement to *đến xin ông một que diêm.* Note that the phrase *tay cầm một cuốn sách* '[with his] hand holds a book' is a descriptive complement to *có một cụ già độ ngoài 60 tuổi* 'there was an old man (approximately) over sixty.'

A predicate, together with any complement it may have, viewed as one of the constituents of a sentence, is a **clause.** Clauses are discussed further as sentence constituents in 12.2.

Focal Elements

10.1. The Focal Construction forms restrictive phrases with predicates (9.1) as head or center (5.62). Various kinds of substantives, substantival phrases and even predicates occur as **focal complements** (in boldface type in the following examples).

Nhà *cháy rồi.* The house has burned already.

Bạn *đã làm cho tôi.* A friend did it for me.

Liễn *hết cơm.* There's no more rice in the serving dish.

Cơm *đưa lên.* Rice was brought up [i.e., from the kitchen to the table].

Người ấy *là bạn tôi.* That person is my friend.

Con chó *bị chết.* The dog died.

Hai ông ấy *học tiếng Việt-nam.* Those two gentlemen are studying Vietnamese.

Trên bàn *có nhiều cây bút chì.* On the table there are a lot of pencils.

Hôm qua *mưa to quá.* Yesterday it rained hard.

Thế-gian *còn nhiều kẻ hiếu-lợi hơn ta.* In the world there are still many people greedier than I. (arrogant)

Hai bên *cũng chưa có vợ có chồng.* Neither of them was married. ["two sides likewise not-yet exist wife exist husband"]

Ở bên nam *nóng lắm.* In the south it's very hot.

There are also single words occurring as focal complements which are neither substantives nor predicatives: they are **focuses** of several types, distinguished by the positions in which they occur (10.4).

Mai *đi Hà-nội.* Going to Hanoi tomorrow.

Tôi *sung-sướng lắm.* I'm very happy.

Sao *ông không đến nhà chơi.* Why don't you come to [my] house for a visit?

Đấy *ông thấy làng Phát-diệm.* Over there you see the village of
Phát-diệm.

Focal phrases occur as heads of larger focal phrases; often there are
several nested layers (5.62) of the construction—**focal complexes.**

Nay thiên-hạ chẳng ai làm việc nghĩa. Today no one in the world [is
concerned with] doing good deeds.

> *nay* present time (focal complement)
> *thiên-hạ chẳng ai làm việc nghĩa* in the world no one does good
> deeds (focal phrase)
> > *thiên-hạ* below heaven (attributive pseudo-compound; focal
> > complement)
> > *chẳng ai làm việc nghĩa* no one does good deeds (focal phrase)
> > > *chẳng ai* definitely not anyone (focal complement)
> > > *làm việc nghĩa* accomplish righteous works (predicate)

There are certain restrictions on the kinds of elements which occur in
some positions of focal complexes (see 10.3).

10.2. Focal Complements establish for their predicates points of reference in terms of the specific person, thing, or concept, the exact place,
the point in time, the precise quantity, the distinctive manner.

Cái này tôi *ăn được,* **cái này tôi** *mặc được,* **cái này tôi** *dùng
được,* **cái này tôi** *thích lắm.* This I can eat, this I can wear,
this I can use, this I like very much. (said by a person pick-
ing things up at market) (Each of the four parts of this sentence is a focal complex, containing first the focal complement
cái này 'this' and a smaller focal phrase with *tôi* 'I' as
complement.)

Từ nhỏ đến lớn ít khi *đi ra khỏi làng.* From [the time they are]
small till [they are] grown up [they] seldom go outside of
[their] village. (focal complex with two focal complements:
từ nhỏ đến lớn 'from small to big' and *ít khi* 'few times'; the
first is itself a focal phrase with the complement *từ nhỏ* and
the predicate *đến lớn* 'arrive at being big' as head)

Cái cột đồng ấy nay *đã mất mà* **Tây-hồ** *vẫn còn.* That bronze
pillar today is lost, but East Lake still exists. (focal complex with two complements: *cái cột đồng ấy* 'that bronze pillar'
and *nay* 'present time'; the second part of the sentence contains the predicate *vẫn còn* 'nevertheless remains' with the
focal complement *Tây-hồ* 'East Lake')

Hai ông Dong và Vỹ ngày *thì đi xem thành phố,* **tối** *về nhà cụ
Đàm đọc báo và nói chuyện với gia-đình cụ như người trong
nhà.* The two fellows Dong and Vỹ by day went to see the city,
in the evening returned to Mr. Đàm's house to read the news-

paper and talk with his family like [regular] people of the household. (contains two focal phrases, of which the first is a complex with complements *hai ông Dong và Vỹ* 'the two gentlemen Dong and Vỹ' and *ngày* 'day [time]'; the second contains the focal complement *tối* 'night, evening')

Nói *phải có người nói đi nói lại chớ bắt người ta nói một mình hoài!* (S) For a conversation [you] ought to have people talking back and forth, not make somebody talk alone all the time! ["speak ought exist person speak go speak come prohibit constrain someone speak alone continually"] (*nói* 'speak, talk' is focal complement)

Những gì trong thùng, tôi *không muốn khui ra.* [No matter] what things are in the crate, I don't want to open it. (focal complex with complements *những gì trong thùng* 'whatever things in large container' and *tôi* 'I')

Thế này *làm không được.* This way it's impossible.

10.21. Integral Emphasis.
In contexts where no specific reference indicates otherwise, focal complements denoting time or space emphasize the point in time or space at which something occurs, rather than the extent or duration. In this respect some focal complements contrast with descriptive complements containing the same elements, with the same internal structure but occurring after the predicate (9.62).

Ba giờ *đi Hà-nội.* At three o'clock [we're] going to Hanoi. Cf. (with descriptive complement) *Đi Hà-nội* **ba giờ.** [It takes] three hours to go to Hanoi.

Hai ngày nữa *tôi làm cho ông.* Two days from now I'll work for you. Cf. (with descriptive complement) *Tôi làm cho ông* **hai ngày nữa.** I'll work for you for two days more.

Ba cây số nữa *xe sẽ phải lên giốc.* Three kilometers further on the car has to climb a slope. Cf. (with descriptive complement) *Xe sẽ phải lên giốc* **ba cây số nữa.** The car has to climb a slope for three more kilometers.

10.22. Basic Future Reference.
Focal complements which are not specifically qualified temporally refer to a time later than the basic time of the sentence. In this respect they contrast with descriptive complements containing the same elements, with the same internal structure but occurring after the predicate (9.62).

Bao giờ *chị đi chợ?* When are you going to market? (e.g., speaking to female servant) Cf. (with descriptive complement) *Chị đi chợ* **bao giờ?** When did you go to market?

Hôm nào *anh làm xong?* What day will you finish [a particular job]? Cf. (with descriptive complement) *Anh làm xong* **hôm nào?** When did you finish?

10.23. Contextual Dependence of Reference. The basic meanings described in the preceding sections apply in cases where the context does not make the reference clear, but in many circumstances the previous speeches in a conversation or the preceding lines in a written passage set up the basis for identifying the reference of the focal complement. For example, a man has just told an acquaintance that he has made a trip to the the country, staying in a small village for several days. His acquaintance might well ask: **Mấy ngày** *ông ở làng?* How many days did you stay in the village? or **Hôm nào** *ông về Hà-nội?* When did you return to Hanoi?

Even more often· the predicate which is head of the focal phrase contains an element which controls the reference of the complement.

> **Thứ tư** *tôi đã làm xong.* On Wednesday I finished [a particular job].
>
> **Ba giờ** *chị ấy dương nói nói hoài, không bao giờ nín.* For three hours she kept talking and talking continually, never stopping.

It is also extremely common for the focal complement to contain within itself specific elements which signal its reference.

> **Hôm qua** *tôi đến thăm ông Nam.* Yesterday I went to see Mr. Nam.
>
> **Năm ngoái** *anh tôi sang bên Pháp.* Last year my [elder] brother went to France.
>
> **Ngày mai** *chúng ta đi xem hát đi.* Tomorrow let's go see a play.

10.24. Kinds of Focal Complements. All types of substantival phrases occur as focal complements.

NUMERATIVE

> **Hai ông** *đi đâu?* Where are the two of you going?
>
> **Các bạn** *đi cao-lâu ăn cơm.* The friends went to the restaurant to eat.
>
> **Nhiều khi** *tôi ăn ở ngoài.* I often eat out.
>
> **Hai bên** *cũng chưa có vợ có chồng.* Neither of them was married. ["two sides likewise not-yet exist wife exist husband"]

DESCRIPTIVE

> **Người ấy** *là bạn tôi.* That person is my friend.
>
> **Con chó** *bị chết.* The dog died.
>
> **Trên bàn** *có nhiều cây bút chì.* On the table there are a lot of pencils.

Beside focuses (10.4), various kinds of nominals are common as single-word focal complements. Of these, mass nouns, item nouns and general categoricals are most common; classifiers (by definition) do not occur at all.

ITEM NOUNS

Bạn *dã làm cho tôi.* A friend did it for me.

Liễn *hết cơm.* There's no more rice in the serving dish.

MASS NOUNS

Cơm *dưa lên.* Rice was brought [to the table].

Sữa *hết rồi.* There's no more milk.

RELATOR NOUNS

Trên *có nhiều người.* Up above there are a lot of people.

INDEFINITE NOUNS

Ai *biết?* Who knows?

GENERAL CATEGORICALS

Ông *đi đâu?* Where are you going?

Ngày *đi chơi,* đêm *ngủ ngon.* In the daytime [they] went out and had a good time, at night [they] slept well.

Nhà *cháy rồi.* The house has burned already.

A few predicates appear as focal complements, principally with certain verbs denoting location or position. (Predicates as focal complements are rare, because most often a predicate is itself a head and when followed by another independent predicate the sequential construction is usually involved.)

Ở bên nam *nóng lắm.* In the south it's very hot.

Gần chợ *có nhà cũ của ông Lâm.* Near the market there's an old house belonging to Mr. Lâm.

Đi xe *cũng được.* [You] can go by car, too. ["go vehicle likewise possible"]

Đỏ đèn, *tôi sẽ đến đây.* When the lights glow [i.e., in the evening] I'll come here.

Trời mưa *tôi thích ở nhà đọc sách.* When it rains I prefer to stay at home and read.

Examples in this category make clear that there is no possible sharp dividing line between the focal construction and the sequential construction (9.66). Many sentences seem to permit either analysis with slight possible difference in meaning. For example, in the last sentence cited above the analysis with a focal complement suggests that a particular time is in focus—the time when it is raining; considering this first element rather as the first head in a sequential phrase suggests that first it rains, then the speaker decides to stay at home. This overlap is important to note: the same feature is probably at the bottom of the future reference specialization in focal complements (10.22).

On many occasions focal complements are marked as such by a restrictive subordinating particle (11.52) such as **nếu** 'if', **vì** 'because'. Still more frequent is the marking of the head of a focal phrase by the isolating particle **thì** 'then, in that case' (11.51).

> **Khi** *thì ba người đàm-luận trong phòng ngồi chơi của tàu.* At times the three people had discussions in the lounge of the ship.

> **Sau khi cụ Đàm ăn sáng xong đi ra boong tầu** *thì gặp hai ông Vỹ và Dong.* After cụ Đàm ate breakfast and went out on the deck of the ship, [he] ran into the two fellows Vỹ and Dong.

> **Rừng** *thì rậm,* **đường lối đi lại** *thì khó-khăn.* The forest was dense, the routes of communication difficult.

Clauses are common as focal complements: see 12.23.

10.3 Focal Complexes

10.3 Focal Complexes show elements in certain rather consistent orders. Three general types are observed: those displaying the relative order **manner-time-place-topic**; those in which outer complements are more general and inner complements more specific; and those in which the outermost complement is the central topic of discussion for the sentence. Each type is discussed separately with examples in the following sections. These differences are largely semantic rather than formal; however, it seems useful to separate the semantic types involved in order to provide a better notion of the range covered by complexes of this sort.

10.31. Normal Order

10.31. Normal Order places a complement designating a topic in innermost position, one designating place in next outer position, one designating time at next level, and one designating manner in outermost position. In general, these relative positions are observable only in the comparison of many sentences containing complexes of two or three complements. Phrases with all positions filled are relatively rare. In particular, focal complements of manner are infrequent. This order is diagrammed:

MANNER	TIME	PLACE	TOPIC	PREDICATE
Như thế	hôm qua	tại chợ	tôi	*mua nhiều đồ.*

So it was that yesterday at market I bought a lot of things. [*như thế* 'thus' (manner), *hôm qua* 'yesterday' (time), *tại chợ* 'at market' (place), *tôi* 'I' (topic)]

> **Hôm nay tôi** *quên làm.* I forgot to do it today.

> **Vậy hôm nay** *nóng quá.* So [it is that] today it's very hot.

> **Ngày xưa ở Việt-nam việc hôn-nhân** *là do ở bố mẹ kén chọn cho con cái.* In the old days in Viet Nam the business of marriage depended upon the parents' choosing for the daughter.

244

10.32 Specializing Focal Complexes have as outermost (first) complement some general element which is more specifically identified by an inner complement.

Hai ông xem, **các bà và các cô Việt-nam môi** *lúc nào cũng đỏ mà không cần dùng sáp môi, chỉ nhai một miếng giầu là đủ môi đỏ cả ngày.* The two of you notice [that] Vietnamese women and girls [have] lips [which are] always red without needing to use lipstick, [they] just chew a portion of betel, which is enough [so that their] lips are red all day long. (The sequence *các bà và các cô Việt-nam môi lúc nào cũng đỏ...* is a focal complex with the outer complement *các bà và các cô Việt-nam* 'Vietnamese women and girls', followed by a more specific referent *môi* 'lips', followed by a temporal complement *lúc nào* '[on] whatever occasion'. The first two complements are emphatic topics; see 10.33.)

Ông ấy tánh *ưa sung-sướng.* (S) He's of a happy disposition. (focal complex with outer complement *ông ấy* 'he', followed by a more specific referent *tánh* 'personal character, disposition')

Trên lầu tại bàn viết tôi *có hai cây viết.* (S) Upstairs on my desk there are two pens. (outer complement *trên lầu* 'upstairs' followed by a more specific place referent *tại bàn viết tôi* 'on my writing table')

Người Việt-nam ai ai *cũng biết truyện này.* All Vietnamese know this story. ["Vietnamese people whoever whoever likewise know story this"]

Côn-trùng mỗi thứ *có một mình khác nhau.* Each kind of insect has a different body. ["insect each sort exist one body different reciprocally"]

10.33. Emphatic Topic Complexes have as outermost complement a word or phrase which identifies the principal topic of the sentence.

Cái nầy *tiếng Việt gọi chi?* (S) What is this called in Vietnamese?

Mỗi người lính nằm nhà thương binh Đà-lạt-*ông đó cho ba cuốn sách.* (S) To each soldier lying in the Dalat military hospital he gave three books.

Đi Sài-gòn, *tôi đi mỗi tuần ba lần.* As for going to Saigon, I go three times every week.

Such emphatic topics as outermost complements account for apparent irregularities in the normal order described in 10.31.

Hai ông Dong và Vỹ *ngày thì đi xem thành phố, tối về nhà cụ Đàm đọc báo và nói chuyện với gia-đình cụ như người trong nhà.* The two fellows Dong and Vỹ by day went to see the city, in

the evening returned to Mr. Đàm's house to read the newspaper and talk with his family like [regular] people of the
household.

Cái cột đồng ấy *nay đã mất mà Tây-hồ vẫn còn.* That bronze
pillar today is lost, but West Lake still exists.

10.4. **Focuses** are independent words which are neither substantives nor
predicatives and which occur by themselves as focal complements.

Focuses which appear in innermost (topic) position in normal order
(10.31) are **topic focuses.** They are further of two types: **proper names**
(10.41), which occur with a few types of descriptive complements; and
pronouns, which never occur as heads of descriptive phrases at all. Pronouns are subdivided into three classes: the **collective** (10.42), which
occurs as a restrictive complement (numerator) of certain other pronouns;
personal pronouns (10.43), which occur with the collective as numerator;
and **absolute pronouns** (10.44), which do not occur with the collective as
numerator.

Focuses which appear in outermost (manner) position in normal order
are **manner focuses** (10.45). Occurring between innermost and outermost
position in normal order are **locational focuses** (10.46), which are also
found as descriptive complements to verbs; and **temporal focuses** (10.47),
which do not serve as descriptive complements to verbs.

Like substantives, focuses occasionally occur in coordinate phrases,
with additive (8.33) or approximative (8.32) meaning.

Xưa nay *ai cũng nói chỉ có phải hay sai.* Since time immemorial
everyone says [things] are only [either] right or wrong. ["in
olden times (and) nowadays ..."]

Xưa kia *có hai người, người con giai tên là Văn-Mài, người con
gái tên là Thị-Mật.* Once upon a time there were two people, a
boy named Văn-Mài (Yam), a girl named Thị-Mật (Honey).
["long ago (and) far away ..."]

Mai mốt *ông đó lên Đà-lạt.* (S) Tomorrow or the next day he's
going up to Dalat.

10.41. **Proper Names** are topic focuses which appear as heads of descriptive phrases, although the kinds of complements which occur with
them are quite limited. Included are personal and place names, as well as
the designations of some other entities, such as supernatural beings and
holidays. They themselves appear frequently as descriptive complements.

Nguyễn Công-Trứ *vốn thích chơi-bời nên không để trí gì đến
sách-đèn.* Nguyễn Công-Trứ at heart liked to lead a carefree life, so did not apply himself at all to [his] studies.

Sài-gòn *hiện-đại là thành-phố dân-cư gần hai triệu người.* Modern
Saigon is a city of nearly two million inhabitants.
Tháng tới chúng tôi đi **Sài-gòn** *chơi.* Next month we [exclusive]
are going to Saigon on a pleasure trip.
Vị thần ấy gọi là ông **Tơ-hồng.** That benevolent spirit is called
Mr. Pink-Thread.
*Cuộc hành-trình sẽ khởi-hành sau ngày các ông đã ăn mừng xong
lễ* **Chúa Giáng-Sinh** *năm nay.* The trip is to begin after the
day the fellows finish celebrating Christmas this year.

Proper names are common as descriptive complements to nominals and
the whole phrase is then often head of a larger restrictive or descriptive
phrase. Such phrases replace individual proper names which might be
expected to appear themselves as heads in such circumstances, not only
where they are structurally impossible in the language (with numerals as
numerators or demonstrative markers as descriptive complements) but also
in cases where they are theoretically possible.
Ngày mai là ngày cưới **anh Trần Ngọc** *bạn học của tôi.* Tomorrow
is wedding day for Trần Ngọc, a school friend of mine.
Thủ-đô Hà-nội *thế-kỷ thứ mười chín...* The capital Hanoi of the
nineteenth century...
In this connection it is important to note that some place names, as well
as some titles of persons and designations of supernatural beings, are
simply substantives or substantival phrases and behave grammatically as
such.
Hồ Hoàn-kiếm *này ở ngay giữa thành phố Hà-nội.* This Lake of
the Returned Sword is right in the middle of the city of Hanoi.

10.42. The Collective chúng 'group of animate beings' occurs as restrictive complement in phrases with other pronouns as head. It serves to
pluralize these forms. (It is also found as restrictive complement in phrases
with certain general categoricals as head when they are used as substitutes
for first person pronouns; see 13.22, 13.24.) In fact, it is considerably
more common in this role as restrictive complement to these limited other
forms than as a simple focal complement.
Nếu ông muốn xem kỹ, tôi sẽ gọi một em lại, thường thì **chúng** *chỉ
bán cho hành-khách ở hạng tư thôi.* If you want to examine [one]
closely I'll call one of the youngsters over; usually they only
sell to passengers in fourth class [railway carriages].
Chúng *đã đi rồi.* They've gone already.
Chúng tôi *ở đây lâu lắm rồi.* We [exclusive] have lived here for
a long time.

Chúng ta *không thường gặp nhau.* We [inclusive] don't meet one another often.

Chúng con *làm xong rồi.* We [children] have finished it.

In a very few instances phrases consisting of *chúng* and a following pronoun head occur with a numeral as numerator.

Nay **hai chúng tôi** *cùng sang Việt-nam du-lịch.* Now the two of us [exclusive] are taking a trip to Viet Nam together.

It is important to note that *chúng* refers only to animate beings, primarily people. Thus, although **nó** (10.43) on occasion refers to things as well as people, **chúng nó** refers only to people or animals.

Tôi để **nó** *trên bàn.* I put it on the table [e.g., the book].

Tôi để **mấy quyển ấy** *trên bàn.* I put them on the table [the books].

10.43. Personal Pronouns occur with *chúng* as numerator. They may be tabulated in terms of persons and courtesy levels (13.1). In addition to their function as focal complements, they are extremely common as descriptive complements.[1]

TABLE 1. PERSONAL PRONOUNS

LEVEL	FIRST (Speaker)	SECOND (Hearer)	THIRD (Referent)	GENERAL
RESPECTFUL	tôi			
SUPERIOR	ta			
FAMILIAR				mình
ABRUPT	tao	mày bay (pl)	nó	

For the speaker in most polite situations the form **tôi** is appropriate; it seems to be the form which originally meant something like 'subject of the king.' There are no corresponding pronouns for the hearer(s) and referent(s); instead general categoricals or nouns are used (cf. 13.22). The plural form **chúng tôi** refers to the speaker and one or more other people, excluding the hearer. (It is also occasionally used by a speaker to refer to himself alone when he wishes to express still greater respect for the hearer than **tôi** alone suggests.)

Tôi **rất** *hân-hạnh được gặp ông.* I'm very pleased to meet you. ["I very have-honor receive-benefit meet gentleman"]

Thưa cụ **chúng tôi** *ăn quà sáng rồi ạ.* We've already had breakfast sir.

---

[1] The analysis presented here differs in certain respects from that of Emeneau 1950; see also 13.2.

Thưa ông, **chúng tôi** *chưa hiểu rõ ạ.* Sir, I don't yet understand
clearly. (e.g., servant speaking politely to employer)

Người Việt **chúng tôi** *rất chất-phác.* We Vietnamese (*or* Our Vietnamese people) are very simple.

On rare occasions (especially in old folk tales) **tôi** appears with a plural
exclusive meaning 'we, our family.'

Thưa ông **tôi** *ở đây đã ba đời. Ông tôi bị hổ cắn chết, bố tôi và
chồng tôi cũng bị hổ vồ và thiệt-mạng. Nay lại đến con tôi.*
Sir, we have lived here for three generations. My grandfather
was bitten to death by a tiger, my father and my husband were
both caught by tigers and lost their lives. Now it's happened
to my child too.

The form **ta** is used by speakers who assume a certain superiority over the
persons to whom or about whom they are speaking. It is also commonly
used by a person alone talking to himself.

Thế-gian còn nhiều kẻ hiếu-lợi hơn **ta.** In the world there are still
many people greedier than I. (arrogant)

Vả đây đường-sá xa-xôi, / Mà **ta** *bất động nữa người sinh nghi.*
Besides, [if] here on the road far from home I don't touch
[her] either, she'll become suspicious. ["besides here roads
be-distant, / but I not touch in-addition person produce
suspect"]—*Kim-Vân-Kiều*

Ta also appears with the meaning 'you and I.' This is precisely the meaning of the plural form **chúng ta** 'you and I, we [inclusive],' and we may
suspect that the contrast between *chúng tôi* 'we [exclusive]' and *chúng ta*
'we [inclusive]' arose from an earlier use where a person used *chúng tôi*
to designate himself and his colleagues humbly, but *chúng ta* to provide a
measure of respect for his hearer, if he was included.

Ta *về ta tắm ao ta, / Dù trong, dù đục, ao nhà đã quen.* We
go home and bathe in our own pool—whether it's clear or muddy,
[our] home pool is familiar [to us].—Folk saying

The abrupt forms **tao** 'I', **chúng tao** 'we (exclusive)', **mày** (or **mầy**)
'you', **chúng mày** (**chúng mầy**) 'you (pl.)', **bay** (or **bây**) or **chúng bay**
(**chúng bây**) 'you (pl.)' express either a deep familiarity between the
speaker and hearer or signal that the speaker considers the hearer grossly
inferior. In the latter use the forms are usually arrogant, and this connotation colors them generally so that they seem to be little used today in
most conversational situations.

Này mình ơi! Hôm nay **tao** *lại thấy chum vàng ở bờ ruộng rồi,* **tao**
mở xem hãy còn nguyên. Say, there! (farmer calling wife) Today
I saw the pot of gold already back again on the edge of the
[rice] field; I opened [it] to see [and it] was still all there.

Tao *không tha* mày *vì* mày *đã ăn cắp của người hàng xóm.* I won't
let you go because you stole something from a neighbor.
(deprecating)
Chúng mày *là đồ vô lại.* You're some kind of hoboes. (insulting)
Bây *ướt hết!* (S) You're all wet! (speaking to dogs)
Chúng bây *ướt hết!* (S) You're all wet, the whole bunch of you!
(speaking to dogs and emphasizing that they form a group)
Chúng tao *đi chợ về rồi.* We've been to market and gotten back
already. (deprecating)

Nó 'he, she, it, him, her' and chúng nó 'they, them' (referring only to
animate beings, cf. 10.42) carry the overtone that the speaker considers
himself unquestionably superior to the referent(s). These forms are at the
same time superior and familiar. In some circumstances there is a connotation of arrogance, but the forms are extremely common in situations where
there is no question of deliberately refusing to treat someone respectfully
and seem not to carry any general arrogant overtones, as do *tao, mày, bay*
(see above). They are used in referring to animals, children whose mention
does not demand any particular respect on the part of the speaker or hearer,
and unadmirable people of various sorts (criminals, objects of social humil-
iation, etc.). Nó in the singular is also used to refer to inanimate objects.

Nó *đi ra ngoài chơi.* He [a child] went outside to play.
Chúng nó *đánh nhau luôn.* They're always fighting. (e.g., speak-
ing of children)
Nó *không kính những người già.* He doesn't respect old people.
(Note that, perhaps as a result, he deserves no respect him-
self, in the mind of this speaker.)
Chúng nó *hỗn láo lắm.* They're extremely rude [impudent].
Con bò này sao nó *gầy thế.* This cow, why it is so thin?
Thằng kia, tôi bảo nó *làm việc ấy mà mãi* nó *không làm.* That
rascal—I told him to do that work and he still hasn't done it.
Tôi có thấy quyển sách ấy. Nó *đã cũ rồi.* I have indeed seen that
book. It's old already.
Tôi rất thích thứ hoa ấy; sắc nó *thanh mà hương* nó *dượm.* I like
this kind of flower; its color is pale but its fragrance is strong.

The pronoun mình is a familiar form which does not carry any connotation of arrogance, although its improper use (with someone whom one does
not really know well enough) may be offensive (see also 13.22). It is used
to refer to the speaker or hearer in a variety of circumstances; it signals
great intimacy. It is used especially often in calling one's spouse. In descriptive complement position it is very common in the meaning 'oneself,

himself, herself, myself, yourself.' **Chúng mình** is far less common but serves generally as a plural for **mình**. It most often means 'you and I.'

> *Này* **mình** *ơi!* Say, there! (farmer calling wife)
>
> **Mình** *nói đùa mà ai cũng tưởng thật.* I said [it] in jest but every-one took it seriously. ["self speak tease but whoever likewise think true"]
>
> **Chúng mình** *đi xem hát đi.* Let's go see a play.
>
> *Anh đánh nó, nó phải giữ* **mình.** You hit him, he has to defend himself.

Certain of the personal pronouns occur on rare occasions directly preceded by a numeral as numerator. However, such phrases are less common than corresponding ones with the pronoun serving as descriptive complement to a numerative phrase (consisting of the numeral with some appropriate categorical).

> *hai tôi* (rare) we two (usually husband and wife) (more common: *hai đứa tôi* we two, *đôi đứa tôi* the pair of us or *hai người chúng tôi* we two persons)
>
> *hai tôi đây* the two of us here
>
> *Nếu tiểu-thư thuận-tình thì chúng ta sẽ kết làm vợ chồng, bằng không thì với lưỡi kiếm này* **hai ta** *cũng chết.* If you (young lady of good family) consent, then we'll join together as husband and wife; if not, then with this sword the two of us will both die. (more common: *hai người chúng ta* we two persons)

10.44. Absolute Pronouns are pronouns which do not occur with *chúng* as numerator. A few, all signalling third person referents, are fairly common; the rest are primarily archaic and literary. It is beyond the purposes of this work to exemplify the latter, but they (marked L) are listed with the others in Table 2.

TABLE 2. ABSOLUTE PRONOUNS

	P E R S O N		
CATEGORY	FIRST (Speaker)	SECOND (Hearer)	THIRD (Referent)
GENERAL			người ta
FAMILIAR	min (L)	mi (L)	y, hắn nghỉ (L)
MASCULINE	qua (L)		va (L)
FEMININE	thiếp (L)	bậu (L)	
PLURAL	choa (L)		

251

In addition to these, there is the archaic form Trẫm 'I, we', used only by
a king or emperor to designate himself.

Người ta 'one, we, they, someone, people in general' has a wide variety
of uses resembling the French *on* or the German *man*.

> *Chừng nào cưới vợ làm cho* người ta *hay, đặng* người ta *sửa soạn*
> người ta *đi uống rượu chớ!* When [you] get married, let some-
> body know so people can set up a party! ["approximate-time
> whichever marry wife act give someone be-informed, permit
> someone make-preparations someone go drink wine contrary-to-
> foregoing"]

> Người ta *nói với tôi, ông qua bên Mỹ.* Someone told me you were
> going to America.

> Người ta *phải làm việc bổn-phận.* A person should do his duty.

The other two common third person forms, y and hắn, are probably used
far more frequently for male than for female referents. They are personal
and do not refer to inanimate objects. Of the two y is more common, and in the
the southern dialect area it is sometimes pluralized with *chúng*: in such
dialects it forms part of the personal pronoun system (10.43), replacing *nó*
in familiar reference to adult persons. It connotes more respect than *nó* but
less than *ông, bà,* etc.

> Y *có tiền nhiều.* He [or she] has a lot of money.

> *Lâu lắm tôi không gặp* y. I haven't run into him [or her] for a
> long time.

> *Miếng đất đó của* y, *nên* y *được phép bán, cất nhà.* (S) That
> piece of land belongs to him, so he has the right to sell [or]
> build a house.

> *Không nên chơi với* hắn. [You] shouldn't play with him [or her].

> Chúng y *ở gần bờ sông.* (S) They live near the bank of the river.

> *Hãy thong thả. Nhưng phải luôn để ý đến* hắn. Take it easy. But
> [you'd] better watch ["put mind to"] him all the time.

10.45. Manner Focuses appear in outermost position in normal order
(10.31) of focal complexes. They also occur as descriptive complements.
The class includes manner demonstratives (7.25) and reference demonstratives (7.23) and a few other forms. (It might be expected that *vầy* 'this
way, as follows' would appear in the category of manner demonstratives,
but there are no examples in the material. Its usual reference to an immediately following element may naturally exclude it from this position.)

MANNER DEMONSTRATIVE	REFERENCE DEMONSTRATIVE	OTHER FORMS
sao however	nào whichever	ấy just mentioned or referred to
	này (S nầy) this	kia that, there (more remote than đấy)
vậy that way	nọ that, (an)other	kìa that, there (more remote than kia)

Sao *cũng ráng gởi cho tôi.* (S) Whatever happens, try to send it to me anyhow.

Vậy *ông sẵn lòng cho.* So [in view of all just said], you be ready for [what you're expected to do]. ["that-way gentleman be-prepared intestines (i.e., feelings) give"]

Thưa cụ, hôm trước cụ dậy là phong-tục Việt-nam không cho phép con trai, con gái nói chuyện với nhau. **Vậy** *khi chúng tôi sang Việt-nam có được hân-hạnh gặp các cô, các bà không?* Sir, the other day you said that in Vietnamese custom permission isn't given for boys and girls to converse together. This being the case, when we get over to Viet Nam will [we] get to have the pleasure of meeting girls and [married] women?

Này *hai ông ạ, tôi trông thấy những vệt trắng trên trời kia sực nhớ đến truyện thi vẽ nhanh của trạng Việt-nam đi sứ Tầu ngày xưa.* There now, you two, I saw the white lines up in the sky there [and] suddenly remembered about the story 'Contest [to see who who could] Draw Fastest' [told about] a Vietnamese scholar [who] went as representative to China in olden times.

Nầy *tôi nói vầy...* (S) In these circumstances I say as follows...

Kìa *thì bụt, nọ thì tăng.* (Describing a monastery:) In one place a Buddha, in another a monk.—*Phan Trần*

Nào *hãy đi hỏi thăm.* Whatever [may be involved] we'd better go and inquire.

Ấy *là tiền của tôi.* That's my money.

Kia *ông ấy làm gì?* [Look] over there, what's he doing?

This category has certain troublesome features. First of all, the words in the class are far more common as descriptive complements. In fact, with the exception of *sao* and *vậy* these words are so limited in the kinds of circumstances in which they occur that they serve as markers of the class of substantives (8.5). From this point of view it would seem a more meaningful description of the facts to treat these words as occurring unusually in focal complement position. However, there seems to be no formal basis

for classifying them other than as focuses. The class meaning also involves some difficulties. The notion of manner should not be taken too
strictly. However, it is important to emphasize that the focuses appearing
in this position do not have the clear sort of locational or temporal notions
which can be established for other focuses (10.46-7) or the specific kind of
topic function of pronouns and proper names (10.41-4). The class meaning
may perhaps best be understood as a relational one: the speaker establishes
the way in which events or conditions are related to him.

10.46. Locational Focuses occur between outermost and innermost
position in normal order (10.31) of focal complexes; they also appear as
descriptive complements of verbs (9.62). The members of this class are
the place demonstratives (7.22).

đâu wherever
đây here
đấy (S **đó**) there

Đây *là nhà của tôi,* **đâu** *là nhà của ông?* Here's my house,
    where's yours?

Đây *đã đến nơi rồi.* Here [we] are, we've got [where we're
    going] already.

Đấy *ông thấy một người hiền lành.* There you see a good person.

Đấy *chỉ là một người thường.* He [that one] was just an ordinary
    person.

Đó *có ai phiền ông.* (S) Who's there to bother you? (i.e., there's
    no one)

Kìa **đấy** *là kẻ trộm!* Over there, that's the robber!

Đấy *hai ông xem quan-nha chúng tôi như thế* **đấy.** So there you
    (two) see our mandarin's office [i.e., the bureaucratic system]
    is like that [as just described].

Ông *đi* **đâu?** Where are you going?

Mời *ông ngồi* **đây.** Won't you sit here? ["invite gentleman sit
    here"]

Cô *ấy thích làng nhiều, nhưng không muốn ở* **đấy** *luôn.* She likes
    the village very much, but [she] doesn't want to live there all
    the time.

Chừng *nào ông nghĩ sẽ đến* **đó?** (S) When do you think you'll get
    there?

Locational focuses also occur as descriptive complements with substantival heads. Especially noteworthy is the usage in the southern dialect
area, where **đó** is the most common form meaning 'that' corresponding to
nầy 'this' (cf. 7.22 and 8.5). (In those dialects it largely supplants ấy, as
well as đấy.)

10.47. Temporal Focuses occur between outermost and innermost position in normal order of focal complexes, as locational focuses do; however, they are distinguished from the latter by the fact that they do not appear as descriptive complements to verbs. On the other hand, they are frequently descriptive complements to substantives. It is a small class, although its limits are not clear. The forms exemplified below are common.

xưa formerly, in former times, long ago
nay present time, now, today, nowadays
mai tomorrow
mốt (S) day after tomorrow

> **Xưa** *có người học trò rất thông-minh.* Long ago there was a very intelligent student.
>
> *Sách* **xưa** *chép một truyện thật lý-thú về hai cái phải.* Old time books record a really interesting story about the two truths.
>
> **Nay** *hai chúng tôi cùng sang Việt-nam du-lịch.* Now the two of us [exclusive] are taking a trip to Viet Nam together.
>
> *Tết năm* **nay** *nhằm ngày mồng hai tháng hai dương-lịch.* The [New Year] holiday this year falls on the second day of the second month of the solar calendar [i.e., February 2d].
>
> *Sao* **mai** *anh không đi?* Why won't you go tomorrow?
>
> **Mai** *chúng ta làm xong được.* Tomorrow we'll be able to finish.
>
> *Ngày* **mai** *ông đi đâu?* Where are you going tomorrow?
>
> **Mốt** *ai cũng có lễ.* (S) Day after tomorrow everybody has a holiday ["ceremony" (to perform)].
>
> *Bữa tiệc* **mốt** *là do ông bà Nam sửa soạn.* Day after tomorrow's banquet was prepared by Mr. and Mrs. Nam.

10.5. Logical Subjects. By far the most common focal complements are those in topic position (10.31). In a large number of cases these resemble the subjects of sentences in English and other western European languages. However, although a simple subject-predicate (actor-action) kind of translation is appropriate for many such sentences, it is important to remember that the relationship between the focal complement and its predicate head is fundamentally different from the relationship between subjects and their predicates in English. Topic focal complements appear in boldface type in the following examples.

> *Nay* **hai ông** *muốn biết* **người nhà quê** *nghĩ gì,* **tôi** *kể truyện sau đây,* **hai ông** *sẽ rõ.* Now you two want to know what the country people think, I'll tell the following story, you will [see] clearly. (The meaning of *hai ông sẽ rõ* is something like 'it will be clear for the two of you;' the relationship of

hai ông and *rõ* is unlike that of an English subject and predicate. The relationships of the other topic focal complements with their predicates in this sentence are similar, although on the surface they look more like English subjects.)

Hai thằng trộm *vội ra bờ ruộng và khiêng chum vàng về nhà định mở ra chia nhau. Nhưng* **vàng** *chả thấy đâu chỉ thấy toàn là rắn độc.* The two thieves hastened out to the edge of the [rice] field and together carried the pot of gold back home, determined to open [it] up and divide [the gold] between them. But gold [they] saw nowhere—[they] only saw that [it] was entirely [full of] poisonous snakes.

Sau này **nhiều nhà** *không có cành đào thì* **họ** *vẽ cành đào vào tờ giấy bùa và vẽ cả mặt hai thần Trà và Uất Lũy.* **Những bức vẽ này** *thường dán ở cửa ra vào.* After this many families [if they] didn't have peach branches, (they) drew peach branches on amulets and drew also the faces of the two [benevolent] spirits Trà and Uất Lũy. These drawings were often pasted on doors [where people] (were going out and coming in).

Ai đấy, **tiếng ai** *nghe như tiếng cô Hồng, phải không?* Who's there? Someone's voice sounds ["listen"] like cô Hồng's, [am I] right?

In many cases the categorization of a focal complement as topic (as opposed to one of the other types) would be artificial: the context justifies no such clear division. It is only the need arising in English translation which forces a decision to treat an element as similar to an English subject or an English preposed adverbial modifier of some sort. Focal complements of this sort appear in boldface in the following examples.

Đồng-hồ ông *mấy giờ rồi?* What time is it by your watch? ["time-piece gentleman indefinite-number hour already"]

Vùng này *lắm voi.* This area has plenty of elephants.

Ngoài cửa *là dãy nhà đồ-sộ, một bên thì bày những ảnh các tài-tử và những ảnh chụp các đoạn phim đã quay.* Outside (the door) was a row of imposing buildings, on one side [there were] displayed some portraits of the actors and some shots from completed films.

Thì giờ thấm-thoát mới ngày nào **dân-chúng Hà-thành đang rộn-rịp sửa-soạn đón xuân** *thì hai ông Dong và Vỹ đến, nay mùa xuân đã qua, mùa hạ đã đến và cũng đã sắp hết.* Time had flown [so] fast [it seemed] only a few days [before] that, with the populace of the city of Hanoi busy getting ready to greet spring, the two fellows Dong and Vỹ had arrived; now

spring had already passed, summer had come and very soon
would be over.

Chàng y phục nai nịt gọn gàng, **đầu** *đội nón lông đen,* **chân** *đi hia*
chẽn **cổ** *quấn một cái khăn lụa trắng thắt lỏng, mối bỏ rủ sau*
lưng. His clothes were neat battle dress—[his] head (wearing)
a black fur hat, feet (walking in) tight mandarin boots, [around
his] neck [there was] rolled a scarf of white silk, knotted
loosely, the end allowed to hang behind [his] back.—Khái Hưng

For the implicit lack of a regular distinction between active and passive
verbs, see 9.55. This is consistent with the character of topic focal complements as described here. That Vietnamese grammar groups focal complements into one large class (with little to distinguish subject-like entities
from temporal, locational and manner complements) is emphasized by the
fact that the focal head particle **thì** (11.51) appears as often setting off a
topic focal complement as it does with other types.

Rừng *thì rậm,* **đường lối đi lại** *thì khó-khăn.* **Chim rừng, thú dữ**
thì nhiều còn **bóng người** *thì thật là hiếm.* The forest was
dense, the routes of communication difficult. Forest birds
[and] wild animals were abundant, while the shadows of human
beings were truly rare.

CHAPTER 11

Particles

11.1. General. Words which do not belong to any of the classes described thus far (substantives, predicatives or focuses) are **particles**. In some cases the border line between particles and members of other word classes is not too clear. In general, particles are less restricted than the words of other classes which they resemble. On the other hand, some particles (especially those already identified as markers, 5.63) are in at least some respects quite limited in distribution. The majority of particles are dependent words, but there are important exceptions. The most meaningful classification of these forms is to be made in terms of their positions with respect to the other sentence elements—on the basis of the types of immediate constituent partners with which they appear.

The least restricted of particles (in fact, the least restricted of Vietnamese words) are **interjections** (11.2), which form their own pause groups, and appear with nothing at all or any type of phrase as sentence immediate constituent partner. Other particles are restricted in various ways as to partner, and this provides a basis on which to define several subtypes (11.3-8). These make up the balance of the grammatical machinery of the language, signaling the interrelationships of sentences and their parts.

11.2. Interjections are particles which occur consistently as the whole of a pause group; they are regularly in coordinate construction with the rest of a sentence or utterance of which they form one immediate constituent. They are so independent that they are in a sense at the margin of the linguistic material of the language: they resemble more the non-linguistic gestures used in the culture. They seem to have been little studied, but their general expressive function is quite clear. Far more difficult is the task of defining the precise province of individual forms. Only suggestive examples can be given here (interjections in boldface type).

258

Ái! *Đau quá!* Ow! [That] really hurts!
Chà, *cô ấy đẹp quá.* Gee, that girl is pretty!
Chà, *mất rồi.* Gee, [it] got lost already.
Ủa! *Thật thế phải không?* Oh [surprised], is that really the case?
Ôi. *Trễ rồi.* Alas, it's too late.

Many forms which are often called interjections in particular uses are simply words (or phrases composed of words) of other classes isolated as pause groups with increasing intonation and exclamative meaning. Informal vocatives (11.63) are especially common in this use.

Tội-nghiệp! *Chết non thế!* What a pity! To die so young! (*tội-nghiệp* 'something or someone pitiable', mass noun)
Này! *Anh hỏi ai?* Hey! Who is it you're asking for? (*này* 'this', manner focus [demonstrative marker])
Giời đất ơi! *Chúng ta mau lên, kẻo bị chết!* Heaven [help us]! We'd [better] hurry up, or else [we'll] be dead! (additive phrase with vocative particle)

Occasionally exclamatory pause groups occur which contain in coordinate construction a series of interjections, sometimes mixed with a word (or phrase composed of words) of some other class—the same elements which frequently appear alone in exclamative usage.

Trời ôi! *Nó định giết tôi!* Heaven [help me], alas! He's determined to kill me! (*trời* 'heaven', general categorical)
Ối giời ơi! *Nhà cháy rồi!* Good Lord! The house has caught fire! (*giời* 'heaven' [N], general categorical; *giời ơi*, informal vocative)

11.3. Initial Particles appear as the first element in utterances or utterance portions. They sometimes have as immediate constituent partner the entire remainder of their utterance; more often it is the balance of the first sentence of the utterance. They differ from interjections, however, in two respects: they frequently appear as part of pause groups comprising regular sentence elements, and they are always complements (interjections are always heads). They are important in that they signal the overall function of utterances. Four forms have been identified, all belonging primarily to the spoken language. There may be others.

à [general introductory particle, announcing beginning of speech on new or revived topic]
À *ông để xây gì đó?* (S) What have you put on [the tape recorder] there? (opening conversation) ["introductory-particle gentleman put turn whatever there?"]

dạ [polite responsive particle, signalling a courteous reaction to the speech of another speaker]

> *Người ấy là ai?–Dạ tôi không biết.* Who is that person?–I don't know. (deferent answer) ["person just-referred-to identificational-marker whoever?–polite-responsive-particle I not know"]

ừ [familiar particle, signalling a speech addressed to someone with whom the speaker is on familiar terms, or one whom he considers inferior; occurs both in introductory and responsive situations]

> *Ừ, mày làm gì đấy?* Hey, what are you doing there? (rude)
> *Đi không?–Ừ, đến giờ rồi.* [Shall we] go?–Yeah, it's already time.

nào [exhortative particle] come on!...

> **Nào** *làm đi xem!* Come on, do it [and] see [what happens]!

Of these, the particle dạ is extremely common, especially in the more southerly dialects. In the Saigonese materials it was recorded on several occasions in the middle of a sentence where it served as partner to an immediately following clause rather than to the entire sentence. (This use would place it as a clause particle, 11.5).

> *Nếu ông muốn,* **dạ** *tôi đi.* If you wish, I'll go.
> *Ông kêu,* **dạ** *tôi không nghe.* You called, [but] I didn't hear.

11.4. Final Particles

11.4. Final Particles appear at the ends of sentences. A final particle is one of the two immediate constituents of its sentence or of the remainder of a sentence serving as partner to an initial particle (11.3). They are dependent words and often are accompanied by weak stress (5.21). They cover a variety of meanings, usually conveying primarily some attitude or mood of the speaker.

ạ [deferent speech]

> *Ông ở đây mấy năm rồi ạ?* How many years have you lived here? (deferent)

à [mild surprise]

> *Không đi à?* Oh, you're not going?

chứ (S chớ) [mild contradiction] contrary to what is suggested or stated or might be expected; of course, as you ought to know (see also Appendix A)

> *Ông chủ không có nhà à?–Dạ có* **chứ.** Oh, the boss isn't home, eh?–Oh yes, he is.
> *Đi đâu đó?–Đi làm* **chớ.** (S) Where are [you] going?–To work, of course. [How come you didn't guess?]

mà [strong contradiction] (see also Appendix A)

> *Làm không được.–Được* **mà!** [It's] not possible to do.–Oh, yes it is!

nhé [expecting agreement] all right? O.K.?
> *Chúng ta đi bây giờ* nhé? Shall we go now?

11.5. Clause Particles serve as one of the immediate constituents of clauses (9.8, 12.2). They differ from initial and final particles in that they often appear in phrases which constitute only a part of a sentence, while initial and final particles operate regularly at sentence level. They are of two types: **principalizing particles**, signalling that their clause is a head; and **subordinating particles**, signalling that their clause is a complement. They appear regularly at the beginning of their clauses.

11.51. Principalizing Particles are clause particles which identify their clauses as heads. They are further of two types: **coordinating**, marking clauses whose partners are also heads; and **isolating**, marking clauses whose partners are not necessarily heads. Two **isolating particles** have been identified:

thì 'then, in that case' (the partner of its clause is marked as a focal complement; cf. 10.24)
> *Khi* thì *ba người đàm-luận trong phòng ngồi chơi của tầu.* At times the three people had discussions in the lounge of the ship.
> *Sau khi cụ Đàm ăn sáng xong đi ra boong tầu* thì *gặp hai ông Vỹ và Dong.* After cụ Đàm ate breakfast and went out on the deck of the ship, [he] ran into the two fellows Vỹ and Dong.
> *Rừng* thì *rậm, đường lối đi lại* thì *khó-khăn.* The forest was dense, the routes of communication difficult.
> *Một giờ sau tôi vào trong phòng chè,* thì *ông ấy đã bỏ đi rồi.* An hour later [when] I went into the drawing room, he had already left.

nên 'therefore, so, as a result' (see also Appendix A)
> *Tôi bị nhà tôi cháy,* nên *mất của hết.* My house burned, so I lost all my belongings.
> *Xưa nay không có cái gì là thật thường định. Vậy* nên *ta cứ phải tìm cách theo thời mà sửa-đổi sự sinh-hoạt của ta.* Since time immemorial ["in-former-times (and) now"] nothing has [ever] been really fixed [i.e., unchanging]. [Since this is] so, therefore we must in spite of this find a means of keeping up with ["following"] the times by modifying our way of living.
> *Trời còn sớm,* nên *tôi để anh ngủ.* It was still early—that was why I let you sleep.

Nên clearly often occurs with clauses whose partners are themselves heads, and is thus more like coordinating particles (see below) than thì. However, this distinction in the uses of the two particles is difficult to justify on formal grounds.

Coordinating Particles frequently occur with clauses which themselves constitute full sentences, although they are also common in clauses with a preceding head clause in coordinate construction.

nhưng but, however

> *Tôi muốn đi xem hát,* **nhưng** *không có tiền.* I'd like to go to see a play, but [I] don't have the money.
>
> *Tôi bằng lòng đi,* **nhưng** *cha tôi không cho phép.* I'd be happy to go, but my father won't give [me] permission.
>
> *Vua cha thấy thế liền cho tìm anh thuyền chài vào và bảo nàng công-chúa nếu muốn kết-hôn, vua sẽ cho phép.* **Nhưng** *một sự bất-ngờ đã xẩy ra. Lúc trông thấy mặt anh Trương-Tri, nàng công-chúa đã thất-vọng vì anh xấu quá.* The king [her] father, seeing [that things were] that way, immediately sent for the fisherman to come in and told the princess if she wished to marry [him] he (the king) would give permission. But an unexpected thing took place. When [she] saw Trương-Tri's face, the princess despaired, for he was very ugly.

song however (also **song le**, with the bound morpheme **le**, which seems not to occur elsewhere) (primarily written)

> *Tuy cuộc đời có thay đổi,* **song** *cái lòng ái-quốc vẫn còn.* In spite of the fact that life does change, still patriotism remains [the same].
>
> *Tôi chờ nó,* **song le** *nó không đến.* I waited for him; however, he didn't come.

mà but (often accompanied by weak stress) (Note that this is different from *mà* [descriptive complement particle], 11.52; see also Appendix A.)

> *Tôi muốn được gặp ông ấy,* **mà** *ông đi rồi.* I wanted to get to meet him, but he's left already.

chứ (S **chớ**) and [not], [but] to the contrary, still, as a matter of fact (see also Appendix A)

> *Cái này của tôi,* **chứ** *không phải là của anh.* This belongs to me and not to you.
>
> *Lúc ấy cả quan và nha chỉ giương mắt ra mà nhìn sự thật* **chứ** *còn hống-hách gì được nữa.* Then both the mandarin and [his] office staff will just be wide-eyed and stare at the truth, and no more intimidation of any sort will be possible.

11.52. Subordinating Particles are clause particles which identify their clauses as complements. They are **focal** (introducing focal complements) and **relative** (introducing descriptive complements).

A single **relative particle** has been identified: it is regularly accompanied by weak stress (5.21) and marks its clause as a descriptive complement (12.22).

mà [descriptive complement particle] (Note that this is different from the coordinating particle *mà* 'but', 11.51; see also Appendix A.)

>*Nó sợ* mà *chạy trốn.* He was [so] frightened that [he] ran away.
>
>*Anh* mà *không giúp nó, thì việc ấy hỏng.* If you don't help him, it'll be a failure. ["elder-brother descriptive-complement not help him, then affair just-referred-to fail": focal phrase with *anh* and its descriptive complement clause (introduced by *mà*) as focal modifier]
>
>*Tôi đã tìm thấy quyển sách* mà *anh nói hôm nọ.* I found the book you were talking [about] the other day.

Focal Particles identify clauses serving as focal complements.

nếu if
>**Nếu** *không trông thấy tre và cau thì là cánh đồng lúa mông-mênh.* If [they] weren't seeing bamboo and areca palms, then it was endless rice-fields.

vì because
>**Vì** *tàu sẽ đỗ ở Nhật-bản và Hồng-kông nên hai ông cũng xin cả chữ chiếu-khán của sứ-quán Nhật và Anh nữa.* Because the boat would dock in Japan and Hong Kong, the two fellows also requested visas from the Japanese and British embassies as well.

dù (or dầu, dẫu) although; whether, whatever, however, even ...
>**Dù** *ông hết sức muốn đi, người ta không cho phép.* Although you want very much to go, they won't give [you] permission.
>
>**Dù** *ai buôn đâu, bán đâu. /Mồng mười tháng tám chọi trâu thì về.* Wherever it is that someone may be doing business, on the tenth of the eighth month he returns home for the buffalo contest.—Folk saying

tuy although (somewhat more literary than *dù* in flavor)
>**Tuy** *không có trận-chiến ở đây, nhưng chúng tôi vẫn còn trong tình-trạng chiến-tranh.* Although there is no battle [going on right] here, still we remain in war [time] circumstances.

263

Focal complement clauses thus marked often appear following the head clause. There is an obvious difference in emphasis in such sentences, but it is difficult to say whether the subordinate clause has rather more of a descriptive than a restrictive function.

> *Không nguy-hiểm lắm* vì *suốt dọc đường đều có đồn binh đóng.*
> [It's] not very dangerous because all along the road at regular intervals military posts have been set up.

11.6. Substantival Particles are used only or primarily with immediate constituent partners which are substantives or substantival phrases. They include the **plural markers**, which occur only before substantives and substantival phrases (8.1); **descriptive particles**, which occur only as descriptive complements following nominals (8.6); and **vocative particles**, which form elements appearing only as initial or final complements in sentences, or as separate sentences by themselves (cf. 12.41).

11.61. Plural Markers help define the class of substantives (8.1). They include the forms *những* 'plural', *các* 'plural [implying all of a given set]', *mỗi* 'each', *mọi* 'every', and *từng* 'each [in turn]'. For examples, see 8.2.

11.62. Descriptive Particles are substantival particles which occur only as descriptive complements following nominals (8.6), or rarely following verbals (9.5) or certain other particles. They form a small class of forms with specialized meanings, each fairly restricted by virtue of this specialization. However, most forms serve on at least some occasions as complements to classifiers, as well as to general categoricals and nouns. In the material studied forms belonging to some minor semantic sets have been identified. There may well be others.

A set of **sex gender** forms is conveniently further categorized in terms of their usage with humans, animals in general, or birds in particular.

	HUMANS	ANIMALS	BIRDS
Male	nam	đực	trống
Female	nữ	cái	mái

phái nam the male sex, *phái* nữ the female sex [referring to humans], *bò* đực steer, *bò* cái cow, *con* đực [the] male [of an animal], *gà* trống rooster, *gà* mái hen, *chim* mái female bird

The forms *trai* (N *giai*) 'boy, male', *gái* 'girl, female' are general categoricals: cf. *một trai* 'a boy', *một gái* 'a girl'. In the spoken language they are far more common than the forms of Chinese origin (*nam, nữ*) which belong to this class. The recurrence of the element *-ái* in the words denoting females is interesting.

A set which may be termed **directional** includes the names of the points of the compass and the designations for right and left. They occur occasionally as descriptive complements to verbals (9.5) and with certain other particles, notably the postpositive noncontained particle *từ* 'departing from' (11.82).

bắc north	*đông* east	*phải* right [side]
nam south	*tây* west	*trái* left [side]

phương **bắc** north [as a region or direction]
phía **nam** south [as a cardinal point or direction]
người **tây** westerners, esp. Frenchmen
bên **đông** the east side, the East [as a region]
tay **phải** the right hand
bên **trái** the left side, to the left
từ **bắc** *đến* **nam** from north to south

It should be noted that the compound compass designations involve an order of elements different from that of English: *đông bắc* northeast, *đông nam* southeast, *tây bắc* northwest, *tây nam* southwest.

The remaining forms include a set distinguishing relative size or age and a temporal element denoting present time.

cả immense, large; eldest	*rày* now, present time, today (cf. the
út smallest, youngest	temporal focus *nay* 'present time')
anh **cả** eldest brother	
con **út** youngest child	

Rày has an extremely limited distribution, occurring apparently only with *ngày* 'day', *độ* 'approximate time', and *từ* 'departing from.'

Ngày **rày** *nó đã chịu học.* He's managing to study these days.
Độ **rày** *thóc gạo cao lắm.* Right about this time rice is very high [i.e., expensive].
từ **rày** *(trở đi)* from now on

In the last case (following *từ*) it appears to fill a head position with the prepositive particle (11.81), but since its occurrence is otherwise limited to complement positions, this case is probably best considered a compound (cf. 11.92).

11.63. Vocative Particles

accompany a small class of substantives forming phrases which appear as complements with heads varying from interjections (11.2) to all types of sentences; these phrases also occur on occasion as complete sentences by themselves (12.41). The order of elements distinguishes two types: **formal** vocative particles precede their heads and the phrases they form appear as preceding (restrictive) complements to their heads, which comprise the balance of the sentences involved.

Informal vocative particles follow their heads and the phrases they form appear as following (descriptive) complements to their heads, which again comprise the balance of the sentences involved.

Formal vocative particles also occur by themselves as the whole of vocative elements. The two forms exemplified below are the most common, but there are a few others, notably special honorifics. (In the examples the entire vocative elements are in boldface type.)

bẩm [subservient vocative particle, used in deference to social superiors]
   Bẩm công-tử *có mực Bắc Hải ngon lắm.* (In former times, waiter in a restaurant addressing mandarin's son): Sir, there's Bắc Hải squid [which is] very tasty.–Khái Hưng.
   Anh có xem quyển sách ấy không?–**Bẩm** *có.* Have you read that book?–[Yes, I] have, sir.
thưa [polite vocative particle, used with courtesy to social equals and superiors]
   Thưa cụ *chúng tôi ăn quà sáng rồi ạ. Còn cụ đã dùng chưa?*–
   Thưa *đã, bây giờ hai ông định làm gì?* (young man speaking to considerably older man:)(Sir,) we've had breakfast already. How about you, have you eaten yet?–[Yes, I] already [have]; what have the two of you decided to do now?

Informal Vocative Particles do not appear as the whole of vocative elements, although the form **ơi** does occur by itself as a responsive sentence. They are also used with proper names (10.41). They are regularly accompanied by heavy stress (5.21). Two forms have been identified in this category. (In the examples, vocative elements are in boldface type.)

à [casual vocative particle, implying a minimum of insistence]
   Đi chợ chưa, **bếp à?** Have you been to market yet, cook?
ơi [informal vocative particle, implying somewhat more insistence]
   Ông để tôi làm, **ông ơi.** Let me do it, sir.
These informal vocative elements are very common by themselves (especially those containing *ơi*) in situations where the function is to call the attention of a person at some distance.
   Ông ơi! Sir! Say, Mister! (somewhat less formal than these glosses imply, but more polite than 'Hey, there!')
   Hiền ơi. Say, Hiền ...
Informal vocative elements at the ends of sentences are also quite common without any identifying particle.
   Bây giờ mấy giờ, **ông?** What time is it now, sir?
   Mạnh giỏi, **ông?** (S) How are you, sir?

11.7. Predicative Particles are those particles which are always part of predicates. They are **predicative markers** (11.71), which have the balance of an entire predicate as immediate constituent partner and occur with substantival as well as verbal predicates; and **verbal particles,** which occur only in verbal predicates. Verbal particles are further **preverbs** (11.72), preceding their head; and **postverbs** (11.73), following their head.

11.71. Predicative Markers are the defining elements for predicates (9.1). They include the identificational marker *là* 'be, which is (are), that is, namely' (for examples, see 9.7); and the tense markers *đã* 'anterior' and *sẽ* 'subsequent' (for examples, see 9.3).

11.72. Preverbs are verbal particles which precede their head. The following are examples of this small class. (In the examples boldface type marks the particles with their heads.)

rất very

> *Anh này có một giọng hát* **rất hay,** *nhưng mặt thì* **rất xấu.** This fellow had a very beautiful singing voice, but [his] face was very ugly.
>
> *Cô ấy* **rất có tiếng.** She is very famous. ["unmarried-lady just-referred-to very exist fame"]

hơi slightly, somewhat, rather

> *Tôi* **hơi hiểu** *cái thuyết ấy.* I understand that theory slightly.
>
> *Cô ấy ốm nặng, hôm nay mới* **hơi cười cười.** She's gravely ill— only smiled a little bit today.

vừa only just, right now (then) (see also Appendix A)

> *Hôm qua nó* **vừa làm xong** *bài, thì tôi đến.* Yesterday he had just finished doing [his] lessons when I came.

cứ continuing without interruption, definitely, insistently, in spite of adverse circumstances (see also Appendix A)

> *Tôi đã cấm mà anh* **cứ làm.** I forbade [it], but you did [it] anyway.
>
> **Cứ làm lấy** *bài của mình, đừng nhờ ai giúp.* Go ahead and do your lessons by yourself, don't rely on anyone to help.

hay often, frequently, customarily (see also Appendix A)

> *Ông* **hay đi** *Đà-lạt không?* Do you go to Dalat often?
>
> *Chúng tôi sẽ không* **hay đi** *thăm ông Bính.* We shan't go to visit Mr. Bính often.
>
> *Người Việt-nam* **hay uống** *nước chè.* The Vietnamese [as a custom] drink tea.

mới [after something just mentioned is accomplished] only then, now, recently, just; [if something just mentioned is true] only then; [in contrast with preceding] really, truly (see also Appendix A)

>Ăn cơm rồi mới đi chơi. [Let's not] go out till after [we've] eaten.

>Ếch-Hoa thương Cóc lắm, nhưng vì không quen việc luật-pháp mới bảo Cóc đi tìm Nhái Bén giúp đỡ công việc. Leopard-Frog was very fond of Toad, but because [he] was not acquainted with legal matters—for that reason alone [he] told Toad to go look for Tree-Frog to help with the matter.

>Tôi còn truyện này mới thật mỉa-mai. I have this other story which is *really* ironic [if you thought the last one was].

sắp on the point of, about to

>Xe hỏa sắp chạy. The train is about to leave.

>Nó đang sắp vào thì anh ra. He was just coming in when you went out.

>Sắp mưa. It's going to rain [right away].

11.73. Postverbs are verbal particles which follow their head. Four forms have been identified; there may well be others. (Particles and their heads are in boldface type.)

lấy [by or for] oneself

>Cứ làm lấy bài của mình, đừng nhờ ai giúp. Go ahead and do your lessons by yourself, don't rely on anyone to help.

thay to a surprising or unusual extent (mildly exlamative)

>Lạ thay! How strange!

>Đau-đớn thay phận đàn bà. How painful is the lot of women!

>—Nguyễn Du

lại repeating, doing over [generally with notion of attempted improvement], continuing [uninterruptedly] (see also Appendix A)

>Anh nói lại, tôi không nghe rõ. Say [it] again, I didn't hear [it] clearly.

>Lúc bạn tôi ra Hà-nội tôi ở lại Sài-gòn làm việc. At the time my friend went to Hanoi I remained in Saigon working..

luôn directly, without break, all at once, in a single operation, without stopping, extending to another situation or person (see also Appendix A)

>Bạn tôi bị ốm đi luôn nhà thương, không được về nhà lấy đồ. My friend got sick and went directly to the hospital—[he] wasn't permitted to go home to get [his] things.

Thầy thuốc chữa bịnh truyền-nhiễm **bị đau luôn** *nữa.* (S) Doctors
treating contagious diseases [sometimes] take sick themselves.

11.8. Movable Particles are the particles which remain. They are less
limited than other particles in the positions in which they occur, although
they generally have as immediate constituent partner a single word or short
phrase. The important difference of these elements from more specialized
particles, especially preverbs and postverbs, is that their immediate constituent partners are not limited to particular word classes, and these
partners frequently are phrases containing other particles. They are subdivided according to position relative to their partners: **prepositive** (11.81),
preceding their partners; **postpositive** (11.82), following their partners;
and **versatile** (11.83), occurring either before or after partners, sometimes
with slight differences in meaning.

11.81. Prepositive Particles are movable particles occurring before
their immediate constituent partner. Several are exemplified in the quotation which follows. (Particles and their partners are in boldface type. In
one case a pertinent phrase includes a smaller one, which is shown by
underscoring. Sentences are numbered correspondingly in the text and
translation.)

   chỉ only (see also Appendix A)
   cũng likewise, still, nevertheless
   và and
   hay or (see also Appendix A)
   như like, similar to

(1) Bần **chỉ là một**
anh nghèo xác, *ngày*
ngày lang-thang khắp
xóm này qua xóm khác
xin ăn. (2) Quần áo
rách-mướp Bần **cũng**
chả coi sao, *chân*
không có giày **và**
đầu <u>**cũng chẳng có**</u>
<u>**mũ**</u>*. (3) Giời nắng* **hay**
giời mưa *Bần không*
bao giờ quan-tâm. (4)
Một người **như Bần** *thì*
ai **cũng** *tưởng là không*

(1) Bần was just a very poor fellow [who] day
after day wandered about from one place to
another ["all-over neighborhood this cross-over
neighborhood different"] begging food. (2) [His]
clothes were tattered and torn [but] Bần didn't
care, [on his] feet were no shoes and [on his]
head likewise there was no hat. (3) [Whether]
it was sunny or rainy Bần paid no attention. (4)
A person like Bần everyone believes has nothing
left that he values ["identificational-marker not
remain exist whatever identificational marker
precious-object any-more"]. (5) [That may be
the] way [it seems], but we're mistaken because Bần has [his] areca-palm fan [which]

269

còn có gì là quí-vật nữa.
(5) Thế nhưng ta nhằm
vì Bằn có cái quạt mo,
Bằn quí lắm. (6) Bằn
quí và **giữ luôn** *không*
rời bỏ bao giờ. (7) Giời
nắng thì Bằn che đầu,
giời mưa Bằn **cũng nhờ**
nó mà đỡ ướt. (8) Muốn
ngồi Bằn dùng làm chiếu
và đêm đến các chú
muỗi vo-ve thì Bằn
dùng để đánh đuổi
các chú ấy.

Bằn values a great deal. (6) Bằn values [it] and keeps [it] always, never abandoning [it]. (7) [When] it's sunny Bằn shields [his] head, [when] it rains Bằn likewise depends on it to get less wet. (8) [If he] wants to sit down Bằn uses [it] as a mat, and [when] night comes [with] mosquitoes ["plural-total father's-younger-brother mosquito"] buzzing [around], then Bằn uses [it] to chase them away.

Some other important prepositive particles are exemplified below. They include the proportion demonstratives (7.24).

bao to whatever extent, **bây** to this extent, **bấy** to that [such] extent.
> *Có* bao nhiêu, *xài* **bấy nhiêu.** Whatever [you] have [you] spend.
> **Bây giờ** *mấy giờ?* What time is it now?

dương (N đang) in the act of, during, while
> *Nó* **đang sắp vào** *thì anh ra.* He was just coming in when you went out.
> *Xuân* **đương tới,** *nghĩa là xuân đương qua.* Spring is coming, [actually that] means that spring is passing.—Xuân-Diệu
> **Đang lúc giời mưa** *các cô ở nhà đọc sách.* During the time it was raining the girls stayed at home reading.

từ starting from, since (cf. Appendix A: *tự 2.*)
> **Từ đây** *lên Đà-lạt độ chừng hai trăm cây số.* From here up to Dalat [is] about two hundred kilometers.
> **Từ ngày hai ông Vỹ và Dong gặp cụ Đàm,** *ba người thường-thường nói chuyện với nhau luôn.* From the day the two fellows Vỹ and Dong met cụ Đàm, the three of them were continually talking together.

The particle **như** 'like, similar to' is special in two ways: it sometimes introduces a clause, and it occasionally appears with the postpositive contained particle *nhau* (11.82) following it. In the latter respect it appears much like the postpositive noncontained particle *với* 'with', but seems not to occur as a descriptive complement by itself. The sequence *như nhau* 'like each other' is here treated as a compound particle (11.92).
> *Tiệm nầy nhỏ lắm* **như ông thấy.** (S) This ship is very small, as you see.

Tập giấy nầy với tập giấy kia cũng **như nhau.** (S) This notebook
and that one are alike ["like one-another"].

11.82. Postpositive Particles are movable particles occurring as complement after their immediate constituent partner. There are two types:
non-contained postpositive particles sometimes have their own following
complements, while **contained** postpositive particles do not.

Contained Postpositive Particles include some very common and
important forms. (Particles and their partners are in boldface type in the
following examples.)

nhau reciprocally, one another
> *Hai đứa con* **đánh nhau.** The two children are fighting ["hit one-
> another"].
>
> *Mấy cái nhà kia cất* **gần nhau.** Those houses are built close to-
> gether ["near one-another"].

nữa any more, in addition, further
> *Ông* **dùng cơm nữa** *thôi?* Are you going to eat any more rice?
>
> *Ít lâu nay anh ta* **không được bán khế nữa** *vì hễ có quả nào chín
> thì chim đến ăn hết.* Not long after this he could not manage
> to sell any more carambola because whenever there was any
> fruit ripe the birds came [and] ate it all up.
>
> *Hôm qua tôi hụt tàu, bữa nay tôi* **còn gần hụt máy bay nữa.** (S)
> Yesterday I missed the boat; today I nearly missed the plane,
> too.

hoài continually, incessantly, without stopping
> *Nói phải có người nói đi nói lại chớ bắt người ta* **nói một mình
> hoài!** (S) For a conversation [you] ought to have people talk-
> ing back and forth, not make somebody talk alone all the time.
>
> *Đừng* **khóc-lóc khóc-liếc hoài** *như thế!* (S) Don't be such a cry-
> baby all the time!

ngay directly, right away, straightaway
> *Tôi nghe ông bị ốm, nên tôi* **đến ngay.** I heard that you were
> sick, so I came right over.
>
> *Đích-thân tôi* **vô ngay** *trong rừng tìm-kiếm, nhưng không thấy tăm
> dạng con chó nào hết.* (S) I myself went right into the forest
> to search, but found neither hide nor hair ["trace (or) form"]
> of any dog at all.
>
> *Anh ấy vay tiền rồi* **trả lại ngay.** He borrowed [some] money,
> [and] returned [it] right away.

lắm to a great extent, very much

> *Con chó* **la lắm.** The dog barks a lot.
>
> *Cô ấy* **đẹp lắm.** She's very beautiful.
>
> *Ông ấy đem đồ đi Sài-gòn* **nhiều lần lắm** *rồi.* He has already
> taken things to Saigon very many times.

The particle **lắm** also appears as a numerator (8.31) on a few occasions:

> **Lắm người** *có hằng-tâm mà không có hằng-sản.* Many people have
> generous hearts but no property.

Noncontained Postpositive Particles differ from most other particles
in that special capacity of introducing descriptive complements in which
they themselves serve as head. Some of them introduce clauses as descriptive complements in these positions; others do not. (In the example particles and their partners are in boldface type. In cases where particles have
following complements, they appear in roman type.)

với along with, in company of

> *Anh đi chơi, tôi cùng* **đi với.** [If] you're going [off to] have a
> good time I'm going along. ["elder-brother go do-something-
> for-pleasure, I accompany go with"]
>
> *Thưa cụ, tên Việt tôi là Lê Vỹ* **cùng học tiếng Việt-nam với**
> ông bạn tôi là Trần Dong. Sir, my Vietnamese name is Lê Vỹ,
> [I] studied Vietnamese together with my friend Trần Dong.
> ["polite-vocative venerable-old-person, name Viet (Nam) is
> Lê Vỹ accompany study language Viet Nam with gentleman
> friend I is Trần Dong"]

luôn always, continually, anyway (less common with following complements) (independent) (see also Appendix A)

> *Tôi ở* **Đà-lạt luôn**-khi. (S) I stay at Dalat all the time.
>
> *Hãy ăn cơm* **luôn** *đi cho rồi.* Go on, keep eating so as to finish.
>
> *Ông* **làm công việc nầy rồi luôn** *không?*–**Luôn.** (S) Will you
> finish this work anyhow?–Just the same.

cả all of, also, including, as a whole, at all (see also Appendix A)

> **Không ai đến cả.** No one at all arrived.
>
> *Tôi* **uống cả** *một cốc rượu rồi.* I've drunk a whole glass of wine.

The noncontained particle **rằng** 'to the effect that, as follows, saying' is
used in modern formal prose to introduce direct or indirect quotations and
other similar elements. Earlier literary usage suggests that it was originally a verb meaning something like 'to say [that], speak as follows.'

> *Anh ta* **bảo rằng:** Cứ yên-tâm. He said: 'Don't worry.'
>
> *Khổng-tử* **nói rằng** những người xảo ngôn lệnh sắc là ít có nhân.
> Confucius said that people of clever words and great beauty
> are not very kind-hearted.

These noncontained particles, together with their following complements are occasionally found as focal complements.

> *Nàng* **luôn miệng** *ca-tụng những buổi chiều yêu-đương ấy.* She had constantly in her mouth a song of praise for those much loved afternoons. ["young-woman constantly mouth sing-praise..."]

> *Nếu tiểu-thư thuận-tình thì chúng ta sẽ kết làm vợ chồng, bằng không thì* **với lưỡi kiếm này** *hai ta cùng chết.* If you (young lady of good family) consent, then you and I will unite as man and wife; if not, then with this sword the two of us will die together.

> **Cả nhà nầy** *làm bằng cây.* (S) This whole house is made of wood.

> **Cả mười người nầy** *đi Sài-gòn.* (S) All these ten people are going to Saigon.

Note also that contained particles sometimes occur as complements to noncontained (and perhaps other) particles.

> *Chúng ta cùng đi chợ* **với nhau.** You and I will go to market together [...with one-another]

11.83. Versatile Particles are movable particles occurring either before or after their immediate constituent partners, sometimes with slight differences in meaning. In the following examples particles and their partners are in boldface. Only a few have been isolated, but it likely there are others.

hẳn [preceding head] definitely, certainly; [following head] completely, thoroughly

> *Ông ấy* **hẳn thích** *ở Đà-lạt.* He certainly likes living in Dalat.

> *Cảnh náo-nhiệt ngày thường đêm nay* **mất hẳn** *đi.* The usual daily bustle this evening is entirely missing.

> *Sao anh biết chúng tôi là Mỹ?–Có khó gì mà không biết, quần-áo các ông mặc giống trong màn ảnh lắm, cả mầu lẫn kiểu* **khác hẳn** *người Âu-châu.* How did you know we're Americans?– Nothing hard [about it] (so that [I] wouldn't know): the clothes you're wearing are very much like [those we see] in the movies, then, [your] color and manners are completely different from [those of] Europeans.

luôn-luôn always, continuously (see also Appendix A)

> *Tôi ở* **Đà-lạt luôn-luôn.** ⎱ I'm always in Dalat.
> *Tôi* **luôn-luôn** *ở Đà-lạt.* ⎰

bộ [preceding head] apparently, manifestly, seemingly; [following head] making a pretense, leading one to believe

> *Anh ấy* **bộ làm lính.** He seems to be a soldier.
> *Anh ấy* **làm bộ** *lính.* He pretends to be a soldier.

11.9. Special Features. Particles are the most difficult forms in the language to describe, partly because their meanings are not easy to define precisely, partly because positional frames in the language are so elusive. The picture is further complicated by the utilization of words of other classes in positions where they greatly resemble particles (11.91), and by some apparent cases of compounding of particles and similar elements (11.92). It is also important to note that a few particles appear in correlative uses (11.93).

11.91. Other Words in Uses Resembling Particles. A variety of substantives and predicatives appear as complements in stylized circumstances in which they very much resemble certain particles. In some cases, it may be that they would be better treated as separate words, but where the meanings are clearly related there is usually an advantage in considering special uses as extensions of the basic form.

Words resembling interjections are discussed in 11.2. Note also that auxiliaries (9.54) in some ways resemble preverbs (11.72). However, preverbs are dependent words, while auxiliaries are independent.

A few examples of other forms follow.

> **Khi** *tôi đi chợ, thì giời mưa.* When I went to market, it rained. (*khi* 'time when' is a general categorical: cf. *mấy khi* 'a few times', *khi nào* 'when, whenever.' Here it resembles focal particles like *nếu* 'if.')
> *Ông ấy đi về* **rồi.** He's gone home already. (The definitive *rồi* 'be over and done with', 9.51, resembles postverbs like *lấy* '[by or for] oneself.')
> *Ông ấy không khỏi lại nhà tôi* **đâu.** He mustn't fail to come to my house at any cost. (The locational focus *đâu* 'where, wherever,' 7.22, 10.46, resembles contained postpositive particles like *lắm* 'very much.')

11.92. Compound Particles are quite common with a few basic forms. Sequences of interjections of this sort are discussed in 11.2. Focal particles (11.52) frequently are followed by the relative particle **mà** (11.52), which adds a note of specialization: 'only in the case at hand, just in this way', etc. In some cases it seems merely to lend a kind of emphatic or special stylistic touch. (This usage may very well reflect the stylistic preference for dissyllabic elements; cf. 13.5.)

Nếu mà *kiếm được cuốn sách đó, thì tôi sung-sướng lắm.* (S) If only I can find that book, I'll be happy.

Certain focal and coordinating (11.51) particles occur compounded together. It may be significant that these double forms appear to be more common when the clauses they introduce are transposed to the position following the head clause.

Tôi không biết chỗ ở người nầy, **bởi vì** *người nầy dời chỗ ở luôn-luôn.* (S) I don't know where this person lives because he's always moving.

Hôm qua tôi có ý mua quyển sách ấy, **nhưng mà** *có bạn đến nhà thăm, tôi quên.* Yesterday I intended to buy that book, but a friend dropped by [and] I forgot.

Movable particles (11.8) frequently seem to be compounded.

Nó ăn **tất-cả.** He ate the entire thing.

Tập giấy nầy với tập giấy kia cũng **như nhau.** (S) This notebook and that one are alike. [...like one-another]

Some cases which must be treated as compound particles suggest that one or other of the entities involved may originally have had a less restricted distribution and may have belonged to one of the major word classes (i.e., substantives, predicatives or focuses).

từ rày (*trở đi*) from now on (**rày** otherwise has been observed only as a descriptive particle, 11.62, but may earlier have been a focus like *nay* 'present time')

Still other cases show particles of various sorts apparently compounded with words of other classes in uses resembling particles.

Hãy còn *sớm.* It's still early.

Chúng ta ít có thì giờ, để cùng nhau nói chuyện ở phòng giấy, **cho nên** *tôi muốn gặp hai anh ở nhà tôi.* We rarely have time to converse with one another at the office; that's why I wanted to have ["meet"] the two of you over at my house.

11.93. Correlative Particles.

A few particles appear only or predominantly in correlative uses.

vừa...vừa both...and (prepositive, 11.81) (see also Appendix A)

Ngày xưa có người hiếu-lợi, một hôm ra chợ, gặp ngày chợ phiên **vừa** *đông người đến buôn bán* **vừa** *lắm đồ hàng.* Once upon a time there was a greedy person, [who] one day went out into

275

the market-place on the day of a fair [when there were] both a great many people who had come to do business and a great deal of merchandise.

nào...nào...(nào...) not only...but also..., ...all these (prepositive, 11.81) (see also Appendix A)

Nào *tiền,* nào *tình,* nào *hạnh-phúc...* Money, love, happiness—all these...

CHAPTER 12

Sentence Structure

12.1. **Sentences** in spoken Vietnamese are separated from one another by terminal intonations (5.3). A sequence of one or more pause groups ending with a terminal intonation and preceded by silence or by another such sequence is a **sentence** (5.41). The autonomy of such elements is symbolized in writing by the use of a capital letter at the beginning and a sentence end sign (period, question mark or exclamation point) at the end (3.54).

The structure of sentences is varied, but one type is overwhelmingly predominant—the sort of sentence which consists of a clause (9.8, 12.2) or series of clauses, at least one of which is a head. Such sentences are **major** (12.3); others are **minor** (12.4). This structural classification is intersected by one based on relative autonomy—**dependent sentences** occur only as second or later sentences in utterances or as opening sentences in responsive utterances, while **independent sentences** appear as opening sentences in independent utterances (5.41).

By the patterning of stresses (5.2) speakers signal elements of greater or lesser informational importance in their sentences; the general principles of this system are discussed in 12.5. Positionally emphatic elements are discussed in 12.6.

12.2. **Clauses.** A **clause** is a predicate (together with any complement it may have) viewed as a sentence constituent (9.8). In other words, each time a predicate occurs, from the point of view of the sentence in which it stands, it is a clause (or, if it has complements, the head of a clause). Some clauses contain restrictive or descriptive complements which are themselves smaller clauses. Like other sentence elements, clauses are sometimes heads, sometimes complements.

Ông Vỹ đang hút thuốc lá, mắt nhìn mấy con hải-âu bay theo tầu thì có một cụ già độ ngoài 60 tuổi tay cầm một cuốn sách đến xin ông một que diêm để hút thuốc lá. Vỹ was smoking a cigarette, (eyes) watching some seagulls flying after the ship, when an old man over sixty years old, holding a book in his hand, came and asked him for a match to light a cigarette.

Each clause in this example[1] is listed below with a notation in brackets of of its function (see 5.4ff for type of analysis used):

Ông Vỹ đang hút thuốc lá Vỹ was smoking a cigarette (head)

mắt nhìn mấy con hải-âu bay theo tầu [with his] eyes watching some seagulls flying after the ship (descriptive complement to preceding clause)

   bay theo tầu fly after [the] ship (descriptive complement to *mấy con hải-âu*)

     bay fly (head)

     theo tầu follow ship (head)

thì có một cụ già độ ngoài 60 tuổi tay cầm một cuốn sách (then) there was an old man (approximately) more than sixty years old holding a book in his hand (head)

   tay cầm một cuốn sách [with his] hand holding a book (descriptive complement to *có một cụ già độ ngoài 60 tuổi*)

đến xin ông một que diêm để hút thuốc lá [who] came and asked him for a match to light a cigarette (descriptive complement to *thì có một cụ già...sách*)

   đến xin ông một que diêm arrived [and] asked him for a match (head)

     đến arrive (head)

     xin ông một que diêm ask him for a match (head)

   để hút thuốc lá permit to smoke a cigarette (descriptive complement to *đến xin ông một que diêm*)

Clauses are of two principal types: **main clauses** (12.21) appear as heads or as the whole of certain sentences; other clauses are **subordinate**, appearing as complements to other sentence elements. Subordinate clauses are further **descriptive,** following their heads (12.22); and **restrictive,** preceding their heads (12.23).

12.21. Main clauses occur both marked and unmarked. Marked clauses are introduced by principalizing particles (11.51); they appear as second

---

[1] This same sentence is discussed in 9.8 from the point of view of the uses of its predicates.

or later elements in independent sentences, but sometimes constitute the whole of a dependent sentence (5.41, 12.1). Main clauses appear in bold-face type in the following examples.

UNMARKED MAIN CLAUSES

Người nhà giàu xin chuộc, người kia đòi nhiều tiền. The person from the rich family asked to buy back [something he had lost], the other person [who had found it] demanded a great deal of money. (two main clauses separated by comma)

Tuy thế **ảnh-hưởng xưa vẫn còn ăn sâu trong đầu óc các bạn thanh-niên nam nữ.** Although this is the case, the influence of former times still penetrates ["eats"] deeply in the minds of young friends of the two sexes. (*Tuy thế* is a marked restrictive clause [focal complement] containing the unmarked predicate *thế.*]

MAIN CLAUSES MARKED BY COORDINATING PARTICLES

Tôi bằng lòng đi, **nhưng cha tôi không cho phép.** I'd be happy to go, but my father won't give [me] permission.

Vua cha thấy thế liền cho tìm anh thuyền chài vào và bảo nàng công-chúa nếu muốn kết-hôn, vua sẽ cho phép. **Nhưng một sự bất-ngờ đã xảy ra.** *Lúc trông thấy mặt anh Trương-Tri, nàng công-chúa đã thất-vọng vì anh xấu quá.* The king [her] father, seeing [that things were] that way, immediately sent for the fisherman to come in and told the princess if she wished to marry [him] he (the king) would give permission. But an unexpected thing took place. When [she] saw Trương-Tri's face, the princess despaired, for he was very ugly.

MAIN CLAUSES MARKED BY ISOLATING PARTICLES

Nay **thì các bậc phụ-huynh đã cho phép con gái được tiếp bạn giai ở nhà.** Nowadays the elders [of the family] have given persission to girls to receive their boy-friends at home.

Anh muốn đi bây giờ, **thì đi đi.** You want to go now, so go ahead.

Tôi bị nhà tôi cháy, **nên mất của hết.** My house burned, so I lost all my belongings.

Tại nó ăn bậy **nên đau.** (S) He's sick because he's eaten haphazardly [off unclean dishes, etc.].

Nếu tiểu-thư thuận-tình **thì chúng ta sẽ kết làm vợ chồng,** *bằng không* **thì với lưỡi kiếm này hai ta cùng chết.** If you [young lady of good family] consent, then you and I will unite as man and wife; if not, then with this sword the two of us will die together.

Ba giờ tôi phải đi làm.—**Thì nên mau lên!** I am supposed to go
to work at three.—Then [you'd] better hurry up!
Thì nếu ông muốn đi bây giờ tôi cùng đi được. [So] then, if
you want to go now I can go along [with you].

A few unmarked main clauses are not found as the opening clause of an
independent sentence: they appear only in dependent sentences or as noninitial clauses in independent sentences. They are **secondary main
clauses.**

Ông đi chợ, **còn tôi không.** You're going to market, but I'm not.
Tôi đi chợ.—**Còn tôi không.** I'm going to market.—*I'm* not.

12.22. Descriptive Clauses are common as complements both of other
clauses and of shorter sentence elements. Especially when they complement single words or (non-clause) phrases they are very frequently marked
by the relative particle **mà** (11.52). Clauses consisting of identificational
predicates with **là** are also common in this use. Descriptive clauses are
in boldface type in the following examples.

Xưa có người học trò **đi dạm vợ.** Long ago there was a student
[who] went to bargain for a wife. (complement to main head
clause)
Ngày xưa có người hiếu-lợi, **một hôm ra chợ, gặp ngày chợ
phiên vừa đông người đến buôn bán vừa lắm đồ hàng.**
Once upon a time there was a greedy person, [who] one day
went out into the market-place on the day of a fair [when there
were] both a great many people who had come to do business
and a great deal of merchandise. (The long element in boldface
type is a clause sequence serving as descriptive complement
to the main head clause of the sentence; it contains two coordinate clauses. Within the second a shorter clause *đến buôn bán*
complements *đông người.* For a detailed analysis of this sentence see 5.4ff.)
Nó sợ **mà chạy trốn.** It [an animal] was so afraid it ran away.
(complement to the main clause)
Anh **mà không giúp nó,** *thì việc ấy hỏng.* Unless you help him
out it'll be a failure. [elder-brother relative-particle not help
him, then affair just-referred-to spoil] (complement to *anh*)
Tôi đã tìm thấy quyển sách **mà anh nói hôm nọ.** I found the book
you were talking about the other day. (complement to *quyển
sách*)
Điều **mà các ông chú-trọng đến nhất** *là đem theo máy ảnh và
máy quay phim đi.* The thing they attached the most importance

to was bringing along a [still] camera and a movie camera.
["detail relative-particle plural gentleman consider-important
arrive-at first..."] (complement to *điều*)

Hai ông là bạn thân và cùng có chung một ý-tưởng **là đi sang
Việt-nam du-lịch.** The two fellows were close friends and
had the same idea—to go over to Viet Nam on a trip. (complement to preceding clause *và...ý-tưởng*)

12.23. Restrictive Clauses are focal complements containing a predicate as head, or consisting of a predicate alone. Lone (unmarked) predicates are rare in this use (see 10.24). More often restrictive clauses are
marked by focal particles (11.52).

Tuy thế *ảnh-hưởng xưa vẫn còn ăn sâu trong đầu óc các bạn
thanh-niên nam nữ.* Although this is the case, the influence
of former times still penetrates ["eats"] deeply in the minds
of young friends of the two sexes. (*thế* is an unmarked substantival predicate; cf. 9.1.)

Nếu tiểu-thư thuận-tình *thì chúng ta sẽ kết làm vợ chồng, bằng
không thì với lưỡi kiếm này hai ta cùng chết.* If you (young
lady of good family) consent, then you and I will unite as man
and wife; if not, then with this sword the two of us will die
together. (For the construction of *bằng không*, see next paragraph in this section.)

Vì tầu sẽ đỗ ở Nhật-bản và Hồng-kông *nên hai ông cũng xin
cả chữ chiếu-khán của sứ-quán Nhật và Anh nữa.* Because the
boat would dock in Japan and Hong Kong, the two fellows also
requested visas from the Japanese and British embassies as
well.

Many focal complements containing predicates appear at first to have
this same structure. Actually they are different: in each case the head of
the focal complement element is a substantive with a predicate as complement.

Sau khi cụ Đàm ăn sáng xong đi ra boong tầu *thì gặp hai ông
Vỹ và Dong.* After cụ Đàm ate breakfast and went out on the
deck of the ship, [he] ran into the two fellows Vỹ and Dong.
(The focal complement in boldface type has as head the relator noun *sau* 'time after', complemented in turn by another
substantival phrase with the general categorical *khi* 'time
when' as head; the clause, consisting of two predicates in
sequential construction, complements *khi*.)

281

Nếu tiểu-thư thuận-tình thì chúng ta sẽ kết làm vợ chồng, **bằng không** *thì với lưỡi kiếm này hai ta cùng chết.* If you (young lady of good family) consent, then you and I will unite as man and wife; if not, then with this sword the two of us will die together. (Relator noun *bằng* 'demonstrated proportion' is complemented by the negative *không* 'not'.)

Khi mặt trời đang bắt đầu khuất *thì cả một vùng chân trời và bể chỗ đó đỏ ối như một đám cháy khổng-lồ.* When the sun was beginning to disappear, a whole area of the sky and sea at that point of the horizon was completely red, like a colossal fire. ["time face sky in-act-of seize beginning disappear then including one section foot sky and sea place there be-red great similar-to one compact-item burn giant"]

Marked restrictive clauses are not infrequent in descriptive complement position, with little apparent difference in meaning: the reversed order seems simply to achieve a difference in emphasis (see also 11.52, 12.62). Clauses marked by **vì** are most common.

Cậu Thanh đến nhà vợ chưa cưới để giúp việc **vì ngày mai là ngày ăn mừng nhà mới.** Cậu Thanh went to the house of [his] bride-to-be to help out because tomorrow was the day [they were to] celebrate the new household.

12.24. Clause Composition.
Beyond the fact that they all contain a predicate, clauses are infinitely varied as to their internal structure. The simplest clause consists of a one-word predicate:

Đi. Go [ahead]. (e.g., said to a child who has asked permission to go somewhere)

Ăn *thì no, không ăn thì đói.* [If you] eat [you're] full, [if you] don't eat [you're] hungry.—Folk saying

However, most clauses consist of somewhat more complex predicates and often have focal complements. (Predicates appear in boldface type.)

Ông ấy **đã lấy tiền rồi.** He already took the money.

Con chó **bị chết.** The dog died.

Ngày **đi chơi,** *đêm* **ngủ ngon.** In the daytime [they] went out and had a good time, at night [they] slept well.

Clauses often contain several parts which are themselves clauses.

Trời mưa tôi thích ở nhà đọc sách. When it rains I prefer to stay at home and read.

trời mưa (restrictive clause: focal complement)

tôi thích ở nhà đọc sách (main clause)

tôi (focal complement)
thích ở nhà đọc sách (predicate: head)
  thích (head)
  ở nhà đọc sách (descriptive complement containing two smaller clauses:)
    ở nhà ⎫
    đọc sách ⎬ (sequential construction)

12.3. Major Sentences are those sentences consisting of a sequence of one or more clauses, at least one of which is a head (i.e., a main clause). They are as varied as the clauses they contain (cf. 12.24). The examples analyzed below furnish a notion of this variety.

Thưa thầy, ở làng bên có người muốn bán một ngôi nhà, thầy có mua không? Sir, in the next village there's a fellow [who] wants to sell a house, do you [want to] buy it?

ở làng bên có người muốn bán một ngôi nhà (head: main clause)
  ở làng bên (restrictive clause: focal complement)
  có người muốn bán một ngôi nhà (head)
    có người (head)
    muốn bán một ngôi nhà (descriptive clause)
thầy có mua không? (head: main clause)

Ngày xưa có người hiếu-lợi, một hôm ra chợ, gặp ngày chợ phiên vừa đông người đến buôn bán vừa lắm đồ hàng. Once upon a time there was a greedy person, [who] one day went out [into] the market-place on the day of a fair [when there were] both a great many people who had come to do business and a great deal of merchandise.

Ngày xưa có người hiếu-lợi (head: main clause)
  ngày xưa (focal complement)
  có người hiếu-lợi (head)
    có (head)
    người hiếu-lợi (descriptive complement)
      người (head)
      hiếu-lợi (descriptive complement)
một hôm ra chợ, gặp ngày chợ phiên vừa đông người đến buôn bán vừa lắm đồ hàng (descriptive complement)
  một hôm ra chợ (head)
  gặp ngày chợ phiên vừa đông người đến buôn bán vừa lắm đồ hàng (head)
    gặp ngày chợ phiên (head)
    vừa đông người đến buôn bán vừa lắm đồ hàng (descriptive complement)

>   *vừa...vừa* (correlative prepositive particle)
>   *đông người đến buôn bán* (descriptive complement)
>   *đông người* (head)
>   *đến buôn bán* (descriptive clause)
>   *lắm đồ hàng* (descriptive complement)

Sau khi cụ Đàm ăn sáng xong đi ra boong tầu thì gặp hai ông Vỹ và Dong. After cụ Đàm ate breakfast and went out on the deck of the ship, [he] ran into the two fellows Vỹ and Dong.

>   *sau khi cụ Đàm ăn sáng xong đi ra boong tầu* (focal complement)
>   *sau* time after (head)
>   *khi cụ Đàm ăn sáng xong đi ra boong tầu* the time [when] cụ Đàm finished eating breakfast [and] went out onto the deck of the ship (descriptive complement)
>   *khi* (head)
>   *cụ Đàm ăn sáng xong đi ra boong tầu* (descriptive clause)
>   *cụ Đàm* (focal complement)
>   *ăn sáng xong đi ra boong tầu* (head)
>   *ăn sáng xong* (head)
>   *ăn sáng* (head)
>   *xong* (descriptive complement)
>   *đi ra boong tầu* (head)
>   *đi ra* (head)
>   *boong tầu* (descriptive complement)
>   *thì gặp hai ông Vỹ và Dong* (head: main clause)
>   *thì* (isolating particle)
>   *gặp hai ông Vỹ và Dong* (head)

Từ thượng-cổ dân Việt-nam bao giờ cũng tin có Giời. Since earliest times the Vietnamese people have always believed there is a God.

>   *từ thượng-cổ* (focal complement)
>   *dân Việt-nam bao giờ cũng tin có Giời* (head)
>   *dân Việt-nam* (focal complement)
>   *bao giờ cũng tin có Giời* (head)
>   *bao giờ* (focal complement)
>   *cũng tin có Giời* (head)
>   *cũng tin* (head)
>   *có Giời* (descriptive clause)

It should be especially noted that substantival predicates form regular clauses and major sentences just as verbal predicates do (9.1).

Bây giờ hai giờ rưỡi. It's two-thirty now.

Em nhỏ đó mấy tuổi? (S) How old is that child?

284

12.4. Minor Sentences are those sentences which do not contain a clause as head. They are of two principal types: **independent** (that is, independent sentences [5.41] containing no clause as head), and **dependent**. Independent minor sentences are relatively few; they are discussed in 12.41. Dependent minor sentences are **fragments** (that is, words and phrases generally found as parts of sentences) of various sorts: predicative (12.42), substantival (12.43), focal (12.44), particular (12.45), and clausal (12.46).

12.41. Independent Minor Sentences are independent sentences (5.41) containing no clause as head. They are relatively rare, serving as exclamations or attention getting devices. In keeping with their frequent exclamatory function they are often accompanied by increasing intonation (5.32). Sentences of this sort consist of interjections (11.2), vocative elements (11.63), initial particles (11.3), or demonstrative markers (8.5, 10.45).

> Chà! Gee! (interjection)
> Chị ơi! Say, there... (speaking to female equal or inferior)
> (vocative element)
> À. Uh...(calling attention) (initial particle)
> Này. There now... (calling attention) (demonstrative marker)

12.42 Predicative Fragments are minor sentences containing a predicative element (9.2) which does not generally appear as predicate head. They are most frequent as responsive utterance opening sentences (5.41), but also appear in other dependent positions. Most frequent are negatives (9.4), auxiliaries (9.54), and the definitive (9.51), but it is also quite usual to find a predicate repeated from a preceding sentence or the utterance of another speaker, where it served as complement. Such minor sentences are often accompanied by final particles, just as major sentences are (11.4).

> Ông mua cái này không?-Không. Do you [want to] buy this?-No. (negative)
> Ăn cơm chưa?-Chưa. Have [you] eaten yet?-No. (negative)
> Ông đi nhà thương thăm bạn Hiền không?-Có chứ. Are you going to the hospital to see [your] friend Hiền?-Of course. (auxiliary, with final particle)
> Anh còn ở Đà-lạt không?-Còn. Do you still live in Dalat?-Yes. (auxiliary)
> Làm rồi à?-Rồi. [You've] already done it, eh?-Yes [I have]. (definitive)
> Đi được không?-Được. Can [one] go?-Yes. (descriptive complement)

Predicative fragments frequently repeat elements from a previous sentence with the addition of a descriptive complement.

 Ăn được không?–**Được lắm.** Can [you] eat [it]? (e.g., said by
  polite host to guest)–[It's] very good! (with postpositive
  particle)

 Tôi nghe nói là người ấy có tiền nhiều.–**Nhiều quá!** I've heard
  that that fellow has a lot of money.–An awful lot! (with
  comparative)

12.43. Substantival Fragments are minor sentences containing a substantival element (8.1) which does not constitute a clause (12.2). Like
predicative fragments (12.42) they are most frequent as responsive utterance opening sentences (5.41), but also appear in other dependent positions. These fragments are substantives or substantival phrases repeated
from the immediately preceding context, sometimes with certain additions
or logically replacing some element in a preceding sentence or utterance.

 Anh ấy làm ở đây bốn mươi hai năm rồi.–*Chà!* **Bốn mươi hai năm!**
  He's worked here for forty-two years.–Gee! Forty-two years!

 Cái này bao nhiêu tiền?–**Sáu mươi lăm đồng.** How much does this
  this cost?–Sixty-five piastres.

 Ông mua vé một lượt hay vé khú-hồi?–**Một lượt thôi.** Do you
  [want to] buy a one-way ticket or a round trip (ticket)?–Just
  one-way.

Dependent predicates which are substantival phrases (9.11) belong in this
category.

 Em đó mấy tuổi?–**Ba tuổi.** (S) How old is that child?–Three
  (years old).

Occasionally a substantival fragment occurs as an independent sentence
with exclamative or vocative force (cf. 12.41).   ᐟ

 Giời! Heavens!

 Ông Lâm! Say, Mr. Lâm! (calling him)

12.44. Focal Fragments are minor sentences consisting of a focus as
head. They occur primarily as opening sentences in responsive utterances,
but some also occasionally appear as independent sentences, serving as
exclamations or vocative elements.

 Ai nói bây giờ?–**Tôi.** Who's going to talk now?–I [am].

 Khi nào ông định đi Hà-nội?–**Mai.** When did you decide to go to
  Hanoi?–Tomorrow.

 Anh ở đâu?–**Đây.** Where are you?–Here.

 Này! Say, now!

 Bần. Bần. (calling him)

12.45. Particular Fragments are minor sentences containing a particle as head. Independent particles are not infrequent as dependent sentences; noncontained postpositive particles (11.82) often appear with their complements in similar uses.

> *Ông còn ở đây luôn à?*–**Luôn.** You're still here right along, eh?– Right along.
> *Chị ấy nói với ai?*–**Với bạn.** Who's she talking with?–With a friend.

12.46. Clausal Fragments are minor sentences consisting of restrictive clauses (12.23). They appear regularly as dependent sentences..

> *Mai anh đi xem hát không?*–**Nếu có thì giờ.** Are you going to the play tomorrow?–If there's time.
> *Tại sao ông Nam không đến?*–**Vì ông bị ốm.** Why didn't Mr. Nam come?–Because he got sick.

12.5. Emphatic Patterning is the system by which stresses are distributed in pause groups and sentences. Until now there has been too little investigation of these phenomena to furnish more than the general outlines of the system. However, the principles involved seem helpful in understanding the way the relative importance of forms is signalled. By far the great majority of syllables are accompanied by medium stress; it is deviation from this in either direction which marks a particular form as conveying an especially heavy or light load in conveying information. In general weak stress signals information already known or obvious in the context; heavy stress signals new or contrastive information.

12.51. Weak Stress accompanies many monosyllabic words whose meanings have more to do with the grammatical structure than with the designation of entities in the natural universe. It also accompanies the next to last syllable of many polysyllabic words. Along with a few special cases, these instances may be regarded as basic, since they are found in even rather careful speech and in some varieties of reading pronunciation. In more rapid conversational speech many other syllables are accompanied by weak stress; they seem always to be relatively low in the informational load they carry in the context.

The following examples show weak stress with monosyllabic words of primarily grammatical meanings.

> *Ông ấy* °là 'bạn tôi. He's a friend of mine.
> *Điều* °mà °các ông chú-trọng đến 'nhất °là *đem theo máy* 'ảnh °và *máy quay phim* 'đi. The thing they attached the most importance to was bringing along a [still] camera and a movie

camera. ["detail relative-particle plural-total gentleman
consider-important arrive-at first identificational-marker carry
follow machine photograph and machine turn film go"]

Common polysyllabic words often have weak stress accompanying their
penultimate syllable (see also emphatic patterning in compounds, 5.56,
6.2). However, there are frequent exceptions and a good deal of variation
from speaker to speaker and from slow to rapid speech.

ᵒHà-nội, ˢSài-gòn, ᵒĐà-lạt, Thủ-ᵒdầu-một, ᵒViệt-nam (place names)
Nguyễn ˢthị Lan, Phạm ᵒduy Khiêm, Trần ˢvăn Ngọc (personal names)
ˢngười ta one, someone, [an indefinite] person, ᵒdây thép telegram (compounds)
ᵒgia-đình family (pseudo-compound)
ˢva-li suitcase (dissyllabic single-morpheme word)

In many exceptions it can be seen that the penultimate syllable carries a
heavy informational load; for example:

sạch-sẽ be clean (emphatic) (sạch is base of an emphatic
derivative; cf. 7.5)
Mỹ-quốc America, Trung-quốc China (in which Mỹ and Trung
carry the primary informational load, while quốc is nearly
predictable)

In complex numerals (8.45) the word mười (mươi when itself numerated)
'ten' is regularly accompanied by weak stress wherever it is followed by
another number in an additive phrase (8.33).

ˢmười hai twelve, hai ˢmươi lăm twenty-five, bốn ˢmươi mốt forty-
one, năm ˢmươi lăm ngàn fifty-five thousand

Note that this has led to contractions for such numbers in rapid speech—
contractions which are even sometimes written (8.45).

Classifiers with descriptive complements (8.61) which are not clauses
are regularly accompanied by weak stress.

hai ᵒquyển sách two books
ᵒcái gì which(ever) [one]
một ᵒcái 'to, hai ᵒcái 'nhỏ one large, two small

12.52. Heavy Stress appears at least once in each pause group, signal-
ling the most important form in the context. It also sometimes accompanies
other syllables in the pause group, pointing up contrasts, singling out
forms which convey new or unexpected information.

A single heavy stress generally occurs close to the end of the pause
group. With substantival phrases it often accompanies the final syllable
of the descriptive complement, except that demonstrative markers are so
accompanied only in special cases, to signal contrast.

hai ᵒcái nhà 'nhỏ này these two small houses
hai 'cái này these two

hai ⁰cái 'nhà (the) two houses

Không phải ⁰cái 'này, ⁰cái 'kia. It's not this one [I'm talking about], [it's] that one.

Where a pause group ends with a complex predicate, the predicate center normally is accompanied by heavy stress if a following descriptive complement does not add more specific information: in the latter case, however, the final syllable of the descriptive complement has heavy stress.

⁰Cái này ᵗôi 'ăn được, ⁰cái này ᵗôi 'mặc được, ⁰cái này ᵗôi 'dùng được, ⁰cái này tôi 'thích lắm. This I can eat, this I can wear, this I can use, this I like. (pause groups here are set off by commas)

Chúng ta ⁰đi 'chợ. Let's go to market.

Khi nào ăn 'cơm rồi, ... After [you] have eaten, ...

In alternative phrases (9.67) generally a syllable of the first element (which is set up for contrast) is accompanied by heavy stress. The second element usually has medium stress and the result is a relatively neutral question. With heavy stress accompanying the second element instead or as well, the importance of the alternative is emphasized.

Ông đi ⁰bây 'giờ chưa? Are you leaving now?

Ông đi ⁰bây 'giờ 'chưa? Are you leaving now, or not yet?

Ăn 'cơm không? Shall [we] eat?

Các ông uống nước nữa 'thôi? [Will] you drink any more tea ["water"] or [are you] stopping?

Other cases of heavy stress single out the forms with which they occur for special attention.

Con 'chó đó dữ lắm, ⁰con 'chó này thật cũng 'dữ ⁰như vậy. (S) That dog [emphasized as new topic] is very vicious; this dog [emphasized for comparison] is really just as vicious [emphasized for comparison].

Trời 'ít mưa lắm. Còn khi nào 'có mưa, thì mưa 'ít. It rains very rarely. And when it does rain, it rains just a few drops.

Ông ấy lại 'còn ⁰đương ăn, khi tôi đến hồi ⁰sáu 'giờ. What's more, he was *still* eating when I arrived around six o'clock.

Occasionally heavy stress appears every few syllables; the result is a colorful, rather lively sentence.

'Nói phải 'có người nói đi nói 'lại chớ 'bắt ⁰người ᵗa 'nói ⁰một mình 'hoài! (S) For a conversation you ought to have people talking back and forth, not make somebody talk alone all the time! ["speak ought exist person speak go speak come prohibit constrain someone (*người ta*) speak alone (*một mình*) continually"]

12.6. Emphatic Positions in the Sentence. Over and above the general framework of word order as described in Chapters 8-11, certain positions in the sentence are also more emphatic than others. Initial position commands first attention of the hearer or reader; final position has the advantages of leaving its content as the most recent impression of the audience, of reserving a conclusion until after a case is stated, or of conserving an element of surprise while the circumstances are built up. Although every sentence thus has two more or less emphatic elements—those which come first and last—it is most significantly in unusual sentences that this appears as a special emphatic device: with the limitations imposed by the general syntactic system, elements are sometimes found transposed from their usual place in the sentence to beginning or end position and thus command special attention.

12.61. Sentence Initial Position is very commonly occupied by a regular focal complement (10.2). Transposed elements appearing in this position are special focal complements, called emphatic topics (10.33).

> **Ngày xưa** *có ông Trạng đi sứ Tàu.* Once upon a time there was a scholar [who] went as representative to China. (regular focal complement)
>
> **Cái nầy** *tiếng Việt gọi chi?* (S) What is this called in Vietnamese? (emphatic topic)
>
> **Đi Sài-gòn,** *tôi đi mỗi tuần ba lần.* As for going to Saigon, I go three times a ["each"] week. (emphatic topic)

12.62. Sentence Final Position usually is occupied by a predicate (9.1) or a descriptive complement to a predicate (9.62).

> *Nàng vì cảm-động, không giữ được nỗi thổn-thức,* **oà lên khóc.** The girl, because she was deeply moved, was unable to withstand the disturbing emotion [and] burst into tears. (predicate)
>
> *Khi mặt trời đang bắt đầu khuất thì cả một vùng chân trời và bể chỗ đó đỏ ối* **như một đám cháy khổng-lồ.** When the sun was beginning to disappear, a whole area of the sky and sea at that point of the horizon was completely red, like a colossal fire. (descriptive complement to predicate *đỏ ối*)

Identificational predicates with *là* (9.7) quite often serve the function of placing an element in emphatic final position.

> *Chỉ còn một tuần-lễ nữa* **là tầu đi.** It's just one more week until the boat leaves.

Những người được chọn lựa là những người có địa-vị trong xã-hội,
giàu có, lắm con, nhất là có học-thức và làm ăn may-mắn.
People are chosen [who] are persons of [high] position in
the society, wealthy, [blessed with] many children, especially
[those with] knowledge and good jobs.

Marked restrictive clauses often appear simply transposed to final position
(cf. 12.23); those marked by *vì* 'because' are most common.

Cậu Thanh đến nhà vợ chưa cưới để giúp việc vì ngày mai là
ngày ăn mừng nhà mới. Cậu Thanh went to the house of
[his] bride-to-be to help out because tomorrow was the day
[they were to] celebrate the new household.

Lúc trông thấy mặt anh Trương-Tri, nàng công-chúa đã thất-vọng
vì anh xấu quá. When [she] saw Trương-Tri's face, the
princess despaired because he was very ugly.

CHAPTER 13

Style

13.1. Levels of Discourse. Three major factors affect the grossest
stylistic choices of the Vietnamese speaker or writer: the relative
formality of the situation in which he is speaking or writing; his **status**
in direct relation to his audience and to other persons mentioned; and his
attitude toward the persons addressed and discussed.

Situations may be roughly divided into three classes. **Formal** situations
are those in which an individual is dealing with persons with whom he has
only a limited (or perhaps no prior) acquaintance. They include also public
ceremonies and large ritualistic gatherings. **Familiar** situations, on the
other end of the scale, are those in which the speaker is intimately related
to the other persons involved. Between these two extremes lies the realm
of **informal** situations, involving persons who are fairly well acquainted,
but not intimate. Since most general writing is directed to audiences consisting of unknown or little known people, published materials reflect a
preponderantly formal approach. However, in narratives and especially in
popular novels a more informal tone prevails. Letters between personal
friends or intimates evoke informal or familiar situations. It is important
to note that in sharp contrast to the general aspect of American social
relationships, Vietnamese formal situations are far more common, and extend well down into circumstances to which the average American would
react less formally. Familiar situations are nearly limited to relationships
involving the extended family and a very few specially close friends.

Status in Viet Nam is reckoned in terms of age, sex and social position.
Elders are venerated over younger persons; males enjoy more prestige than
females. To some extent overriding these two other factors is the matter of
the individual's standing in the community: there is a class hierarchy in
which prestige is accorded persons of sociopolitical rank, intellectual
achievement and wealth. Actually the majority of the status distinctions

are recognized within the family structure, and certain of the basic kin terms (13.21) are extended to cover the majority of relationships outside the family. Of all the factors, certainly the most important is relative age.

The attitude of the speaker or writer is generally polite, but on occasion it is honorific or abrupt. With **polite** attitude appropriate forms are chosen on the basis of formality and status (13.22). **Honorific** attitude, however, is appropriate only for a highly formal situation; it involves mainly the use of special status terms and particles (13.23). At the other extreme, **abrupt** attitude indicates that the speaker specifically identifies himself as superior; he makes use of pronominal forms which do not appear in polite speech (13.24).

There is, of course, a good deal of difference between the levels of discourse involved in ordinary conversation (13.3) and the usual relatively formal documents of the written language (13.4).

It is beyond the purpose of this volume to treat finer points of style. However, there is one general tendency which needs discussion: there seems to be an underlying favoring of dissyllabic sequences, in both spoken and written texts (13.5).

13.2. Address and Reference.
It is especially in the forms of address and reference of the basic spoken language that the levels of discourse play an important role. In striking contrast to English and other European languages, the category of person is nearly an optional one in Vietnamese: little in the structure of the language itself forces the speaker to indicate specifically whether he refers to himself, to his listener or to another person. On the other hand, the status of the various persons involved must nearly always be clearly stated. There is a good deal of talking in the third person, making use of nouns and general categoricals denoting family relationships, professions and the like, when actually the speaker may refer to himself or to his hearer. This is not unlike the practice in many American families of using third person forms (rather than *I* and *you*) with small children—"Johnny can do it if he tries," "Daddy has to go to work now," etc. But while this is "baby talk" in English, it is an integral part of the normal system in Vietnamese. For example, consider the following passage in which a young lady around twenty talks with her mother:

–*Thưa má, truyện giầu-cau* con *nói có đúng và hay không, má?*

"Mother, is the story of betel [chewing] I've told correct and well [told]?

–Con *nói đúng và hay lắm, nhưng tại sao* con *không nói các ích-lợi của giầu-cau?*

"You've told [it] correctly and well, but why didn't you talk [about] the useful aspects of betel [chewing]?"

—*Vâng,* con *quên mất vì* con *không*	"Yes, I forgot all about [that] be-
ăn giầu. Con *xin* má *nói về ích lợi*	cause I don't chew betel. (I ask you
của giầu-cau cho hai ông nghe.	to) tell about the useful aspects of
	betel for the two gentlemen to hear."

The fact of the matter is that in polite conversation the distinction between speaker, hearer and referent is unemphasized, but the social relationships involved are vital categories. Since the words which are used
for address and reference to specific persons are kin terms within the
family, and these terms are to a large extent extended to function with
situations outside the family, it is essential to describe the kinship system
in some detail (13.21). It will then be possible to describe the utilization of
these terms outside the family, and discuss as additions or substitutions the
other terms used for polite (13.22), honorific (13.23), and abrupt (13.24)
reference. It is impossible, however, to cover fully here the more specialized usages of older literary texts.

13.21. The Kinship System reflects the patrilineal organization of the
Vietnamese family.[1] The **extended family** includes, beyond the persons
immediately related to ego (father, mother, brothers, sisters, children),
those persons who are related to him through males (father's immediate
relatives, father's father's immediate relatives, father's brothers' offspring,
brothers' offspring, grandsons' offspring, sons' offspring, etc). These
persons are termed **nội** 'inside.' All other relatives are designated **ngoại**
'outside'; they include all relatives through females—foremost, of course,
are the members of the mother's extended family, but the term refers as
well to father's sisters' children, sisters' children, and daughters' and
granddaughters' offspring, and so on.

The system provides the most extensive set of differentiating terms for
the members of the extended family. Besides the clear designation of the
male lineal relatives the important distinctions represented are generation,
relative age within generation, and sex for individuals regarded as older
than ego.[2] Specifically different from American kinship is the application
of the same kin terms as those used for immediate relatives to collateral
relatives of the same generation: for example, the father's elder brother's

---

[1]For discussions of various aspects of the kinship system, see Spencer 1945 and
Benedict 1947. I am also grateful to H. Merrill Jackson for making available to me his unpublished study (Jackson 1960). As is the practice in discussions of kinship, the term
"ego" is here used to refer to the person viewed as center of the system—the individual to
whom various others are related in the ways described.

[2]This includes some persons who may actually be younger than ego, but are related in
such a way that the system treats them as older—e.g., father's elder brother's children.

children (ego's first cousins) are called **anh** 'elder brother' and **chị** 'elder sister' just as ego's own elder siblings are. Similarly, his father's younger brother's children are called **em** 'younger sibling' (even though some of them may actually be chronologically older), just as his own younger brothers and sisters are. In a similar way, children of the grandparents' siblings are called by the same terms as the parents' siblings, and so on. In the descending generation, ego's nieces and nephews are called **cháu**, basically the term for his grandchildren.

In the third ascending generation the nuclear term **cụ** 'great-grandparent' does not in itself distinguish sex. In the same way the nuclear terms for all relatives reckoned as younger than ego are single terms for both sexes: **em** 'younger sibling', **con** 'child', **cháu** 'grandchild', **chắt** 'great-grandchild', **chít** 'great-great-grandchild', **chút** 'great-great-great-grandchild'.

In keeping with the patrilineal descent pattern, nuclear terms distinguish father's elder brother (**bác**) from his younger brother (**chú**), while the same term is used for father's elder and younger sisters (**cô**), for mother's elder and younger brothers (**cậu**) and for mother's elder and younger sisters (**dì**).

The most important terms in average family relationships are presented in tabular form below. Boldface items are nuclear terms and (in parentheses) descriptive complements used with them, where precision is desired (not, however, used in direct address). Where there are special terms for the spouses of the related persons, these are listed parenthetically in italics next to the basic nuclear term. Thus *chị dâu* means the wife of **anh**, *anh rể* means the husband of **chị** , etc.

MALE	FEMALE
SIBLINGS Included are parents' siblings' children and grandparents' siblings' grandchildren, etc.	
Elder **anh** *(chị dâu)*	**chị** *(anh rể)*
Younger **em (trai)** *(em dâu)*	**em (gái)** *(em rể)*
PARENTS	
cha, thầy, bố, ba	**mẹ, me, má**
PARENTS' SIBLINGS Included are grandparents' siblings' children, and great-grandparents' siblings' grandchildren, etc.	
Father's side	
Elder **bác** *(bác gái)*	**cô** *(dượng)*
Younger **chú** *(thím)*	**cô** *(dượng)*
Mother's side	
cậu *(mợ)*	**dì** *(dượng)*

GRANDPARENTS Included are grandparents' siblings, great-grandparents' siblings' children, etc.

Father's side	ông (nội)	bà (nội)
Mother's side	ông (ngoại)	bà (ngoại)

GREAT-GRANDPARENTS

    cụ (ông), cố   cụ (bà)

CHILDREN

    con (trai) *(dâu)*   con (gái) *(rể)*

GRANDCHILDREN Included are siblings' children, parents' siblings' grandchildren, etc.

    cháu (trai)*(cháu dâu)* cháu (gái)*(cháu rể)*

Some items need further comment. Of the terms for parents, cha and mẹ are the most widespread for reference; for direct address the other four terms are common (ba and má seem most frequently encountered). The word thầy (basically 'master') is used for 'father' in many dialect areas, especially in the north. At the great-grandparent level the term cố refers specifically to the paternal grandfather's father—in other words, the great-grandfather in the direct male line; it is little used in ordinary conversation and in some dialects refers to an older ancestor. At the child level, although both dâu 'daughter-in-law' and rể 'son-in-law' are used by themselves, they also commonly appear in referential use as complements to *con* 'child': *con dâu, con rể* (same meanings as simple terms).

There are sets of opposing secondary terms which serve to clarify certain aspects left vague by the nuclear words. For the most part they occur only in referential use, not in direct use.

Trai—gái. *Trai* (N *giai*) 'male' and *gái* 'female' serve to distinguish the sex of relatives where the nuclear term leaves this unspecified. However, they are not used at the level of the grandparents' generation or above— there they are replaced by ông for males and bà for females (cf. *cụ ông* great-grandfather, *cụ bà* great-grandmother). Although basically the term *bác* designates the father's elder brother, in modern Vietnamese his wife is addressed by the same term, and the distinctive reference for her is commonly *bác gái*. On a few occasions where it is desirable to make clear that it is the uncle himself who is referred to, the expression *bác trai* (or *giai*) is utilized.

Nội—ngoại. The 'inside' family (*nội*)—immediate relatives and persons related to ego through males—is distinguished from all other relatives (*ngoại* 'outside'). The words appear most commonly to separate paternal grandparents (*ông bà nội*) from maternal grandparents (*ông bà ngoại*), and to separate ego's son's children (*cháu nội*) from his daughter's children (*cháu ngoại*).

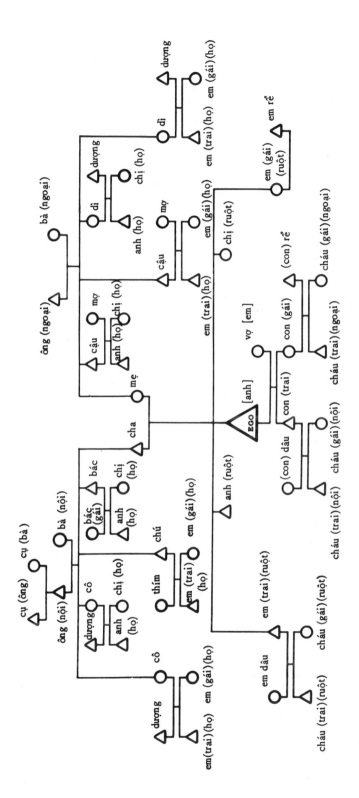

Fig. 1. Some Important Relationships and their Terms

Ruột–họ. A different opposition separated the members of ego's line of descent ancestors and descendants (*ruột* entrails; blood line)—from other blood relatives who are not in the direct line—collateral relatives (*họ* collaterally extended family, clan). Thus *anh ruột* is one's own elder brother, while *anh họ* refers to cousins—the male children of the parents' elder siblings. *Cháu ruột,* however, refers to ego's nieces and nephews, while *cháu họ* specifies cousins' children. Grandchildren are specifically *cháu nội* or *cháu ngoại* (see above).

Rể–dâu. These terms are extended from their basic meanings to serve as complements covering the spouses of blood relatives. *Rể* 'son-in-law' then means 'connected by marriage to female relative' and *dâu* 'daughter-in-law' means 'connected by marriage to male relative.' They are even added on occasion to terms like *thím, mợ, dượng,* which already refer specifically to affinal relatives: *thím dâu* father's younger brother's wife, *mợ dâu* mother's brother's wife, *dượng rể* husband of parent's sister. In some areas the wife of father's elder brother (*bác*) is referred to precisely as *bác dâu,* although *bác gái* is more widespread. Relatives through one's own spouse, however, are handled in a different way. For the most part ego adopts the terms used by his or her spouse to designate various members of the family (see 13.22 below). There are the terms **nhạc** and **gia** which mean 'related through one's spouse', but they are used with terms which imply greater formality. So, for example, the father-in-law may be designated *ông nhạc* or *ông gia,* the mother-in-law *bà nhạc* or *bà gia.* Fig. 1 shows the most common relationships to a male ego in a family tree kind of diagram.

There are a number of differences of usage in the southern dialect area. Here the term **cố** replaces the northern **cụ** for 'great-grandparent' in general, and the specific terms are *ông cố* 'great-grandfather', *bà cố* 'great-grandmother' (cf. N *cụ ông, cụ bà*). Occasionally the next ascending generation is referred to: the general term is **sơ** 'great-great-grandparent', and again specific reference is accomplished by *ông sơ, bà sơ.* A different affectionate word for father is common: **tía,** generally coupled with **má** for mother. In the descending generations, the term *chút* (N great-great-great-grandchild) is lacking. (As a matter of fact, as is often the case with the more remote relationships, there is some confusion about the application of this term in the north: some sources cite it for 'great-great-grandchild', the final descending generation then cited as rather *chít.*) For collateral relations, the term **bà con** is in use in the south: cousins, then, are distinguished from brothers and sisters by the expressions *anh bà con, chị bà con, em bà con.*

13.22. Polite Address and Reference. Within the extended family persons are called by nuclear kin terms (13.21) and are referred to by these same nuclear terms, sometimes with secondary complements. Certain basic items from this reservoir are extended to cover situations involving persons outside the family. For the latter purpose there are also a few additional (non-kin) terms.

Children and young people under twenty address their relatives by the appropriate nuclear term and call themselves by whatever kin term would be appropriate for the relative in question to use with them. Thus a child addressing his father calls himself *con* and his father *cha* (or one of the affectionate substitutes); speaking to his father's elder brother he calls himself *cháu* and his uncle *bác*. Reciprocally, adult members of the family return these appellations in kind: the father calls his son *con*, himself *cha* (or a substitute); the elder brother of the father calls the boy *cháu*, himself *bác*. However, young people on more or less even footing use the appropriate kin term for the hearer or referent, but use the pronoun *tôi* 'I' to refer to themselves. Adults over twenty extend this use of *tôi* for designating themselves to most situations, but use kin terms for addressing others or referring to them. In the case of adults, the use of the appropriate kin term to designate oneself when talking with other adults connotes special humility or obsequiousness (if it is a younger person addressing an elder), or rather great formality, severity or arrogance (if it is an older person addressing a younger one).

A husband fits himself into the family pattern of his wife, adopting roughly the position of her elder brother. He then calls people in her family by the same terms that her elder brother uses. It is a special feature that she not only calls him *anh* but refers to herself as *em* when talking with him. (The pronoun *mình* is also used reciprocally by husband and wife in direct address.) He calls her elder brother *anh*, and is called *em* by that person, regardless of their relative ages.

In some families *cậu* and *dì* are used only for the younger brothers and sisters of the mother, and the term *bác* is extended to her elder siblings as a special courtesy.

Outside the extended family polite usage maintains *tôi* for the first person, but makes use of certain kin terms for addressing or referring to others. These terms almost invariably involve an exaggeration of the relative age and status of the hearer or referent. The degree of exaggeration depends upon how well the persons talking know one another. The system is most economically described from the point of view of rather formal acquaintances—that is, persons who either have just met one another or have known each other only in formal circumstances (although perhaps

over a long period of time). In such cases the following uses are standard
(from the point of view of a speaker over twenty):

cụ for persons of advanced age, roughly the age of one's own
grandparents or older

ông for all men twenty and older unless they merit *cụ*

bà for all married women and for women the same age as the
speaker or older, unless they merit *cụ*

cô for unmarried girls and women from about ten years old, unless
they merit *bà* or *cụ*

anh for boys roughly over twelve and under twenty

em for younger children

In situations where social class is clearly defined, persons of lower
social class are generally called *anh* (for males) and *chị* (for females). In
modern Viet Nam this cleavage is most obvious between the aristocracy,
professional families, landowners and business executives on the one hand,
and laborers and servants on the other. Even here age plays a great part:
an elderly person of laborer class is most often politely addressed as *ông*
or *bà*.

As a person comes to know people better reductions take place, but for
the most part some exaggeration remains. Age persists as the most telling
point. Persons older than the speaker often come to be called *ông* or *bà*,
rather than *cụ*. But the movement from *ông, bà* and *cô* to *anh* and *chị* implies
a great deal closer acquaintance, often a certain amount of intimacy. Only
in one case is there a reduction to *em*: a man paying court to a young lady
may likely begin with *cô* when they are first introduced, change to *chị* as
they grow to know one another better, and then finally call her *em* when
they become sweethearts. (Note that this is what he will call her as his
wife if they are subsequently married. In arranged betrothals the engaged
couple generally call one another *anh* and *em*, just as they will when they
are married.)

A few other kin terms are used for special relationships. Cậu is very
common in northern Viet Nam for designating the male youngster of a
person of higher social standing (rather than *em* or *anh* and more or less
parallel to *cô* for girls). (In the south *cậu* in this sense is generally replaced by the word thầy 'master', which in other dialect areas is used for
the father; see 13.21 above.) In a very different situation, cậu is used to
designate a male friend of the family, much in the way that 'uncles' are
often appointed in American culture. For somewhat more formal special
relations, bác is sometimes used (for both males and females), connoting
a responsible influence just outside the family with a good deal of concern
for its welfare; and chú (for males) connoting a less responsible, but perhaps more friendly outsider.

For the most part older adults with educated backgrounds retain the humility of their earlier years. They tend to address younger adults using *ông*, *bà* and *cô*, just as they did when they were twenty or thirty.

A number of terms denoting professional status are used in address, as well as in reference. **Bác-sĩ** 'doctor' and **giáo-sư** 'teacher, professor' (both general categoricals) are quite common, for example. (In some parts of the country, the colloquial equivalents of these rather learned terms are in use among the general populace: **thầy thuốc** 'medicine master' for doctors; **thầy giáo** 'teaching master' for teachers.) However, the extended use of titles for persons other than doctors and teachers smacks rather of honorific usage (13.23), and in ordinary circumstances may give a notion of pomposity.[3]

The general categorical **bạn** 'friend' is extremely common, especially to refer to a male acquaintance or colleague with whom one is not on intimate terms. (More intimate friends are called **anh, chị.**)

The general categoricals **chàng** 'young man' and **nàng** 'young woman' (designating persons roughly between the ages of eighteen and thirty) belong primarily to the written language or somewhat old-fashioned usage. They are extremely common as forms of address and reference in written texts.

The only personal pronouns (10.43) appearing in polite usage are **tôi** 'I', **ta** (perhaps somewhat superior, now seldom used except in the meaning 'you and I'), and **mình**. This last form has a rather wide variety of disparate uses (see also 10.43 end): it appears as descriptive complement referring reflexively to whatever actor is clear in the context (myself, yourself, himself, herself, ourselves, yourselves, themselves, oneself). As already noted above, it is also used by married couples to address one another ('you'). Further, it is used by women who are on intimate terms with one another to mean 'you and I' or, on occasion, 'you.' The plural forms of the pronouns involved are formed with **chúng** 'group of animate beings' (10.42). This same form is used with kin terms which are used to designate the speaker: *chúng con* we children, *chúng cháu* we grandchildren (*or* we nephews and nieces). When, however, the kin term refers to another person—either the person addressed or the person talked about—the plural form has its regular plural marker **các**: *các con* (you) children, *các ông* (you) gentlemen, *các bà* (you) ladies, etc.

The absolute pronoun **người ta** 'one, we, they, someone, people in general' belongs to the realm of polite usage in reference to a vague sort of third-person entity. There are also the familiar third person pronouns y

[3] Material is lacking to provide a description of the usage with persons of religious orders.

and **hắn**, of which the latter is on the verge of being abrupt. For examples, see 10.44. The collective *chúng* is also used by itself for reference to groups of people (10.42).

Beyond this, reference to persons and things is handled by means of the appropriate specific substantives (cf. 8.6).

The use of kin terms and titles with given names (3.52) is quite common, although more frequent in reference than in address. When used in direct address, this lends at the same time a note of increased formality and a touch of more personal concern.

Names are also used alone in address and reference. However, the use of the given name by itself implies great intimacy. In practice it occurs only among very close friends and family members. In some families given names are used reciprocally by members of the same generation to address one another; they are also often used by elders to address younger members of the family.

Children of some families are called by a number which designates their position in the order of births for that generation. (Details of the practice differ in different dialect areas. In the north the eldest child is called **Cả** 'eldest', the second **Hai** 'two', the third **Ba**, 'three', etc. In the south, however, the first child is called **Hai**, the second **Ba**, the third **Tư**, etc. It has been variously suggested that this reflects some superstition about designating the eldest as such, or that the designation *cả* always belongs to the father, never to any of the children.) In some families these are the only given names the children have; in others they provide familiar alternates. In some parts of the country it is common practice to call servants by such number-names, together with *anh* or *chị*. Otherwise, however, the use seems more or less limited to children, and the connotation is as familiar and intimate as that of personal names. (Of course, where these numbers actually serve their owners as names, adults are addressed *ông Hai, cô Ba,* etc., just as with other personal given names.)

Polite speech makes use of a number of other elements to convey respect for the hearer or referent. There are polite particles like **dạ** (11.3) and **ạ** (11.4), as well as the vocative particles (11.63). There are also occasions where it is more polite to refer to the (potential or actual) action of a hearer by a euphemism. For example, the verb **xơi** replaces *ăn* 'eat' and *uống* 'drink' in such situations:

> *Mời ông* **xơi** *cơm.–Cám ơn ông. Tôi* **ăn** *cơm rồi.* Have something to eat.–Thank you, I've already eaten.

In many circumstances persons who normally address and refer to one another in a familiar way use much more formal terms in order to create an atmosphere of courtesy for other persons present who are not as well acquainted. It is similar to an American woman's referring to or addressing her husband as *Dr. Jones* and his calling her *Mrs. Jones*—speaking from the point of view of the outsider. However, this principle is much more common in Vietnamese. Specifically, for example, a parent will call his own children **cháu** in the presence of adult visitors, on the basis that his children should address the visitors with appropriate terms chosen from those designating uncles and aunts, and would be called *cháu* (i.e., 'niece' or 'nephew') by the visitors. If, on the other hand, the outsider is of his children's own age group, he then designates his children as **em** (younger sibling), suggesting that the visitor has the status of an elder brother or sister. At the same time, the American parallel cited above is somewhat unfortunate: it would generally seem haughty in a Vietnamese situation for a host to refer to his wife by the term the guests would probably use for her (i.e., usually **bà**). In such cases a Vietnamese often refers to his or her spouse as **nhà tôi**, even as he (or she) does in less formal circumstances.

13.23. Honorific Address and Reference is structurally similar to polite usage (13.22), but the kin terms are replaced by special words which connote still greater respect. The most common of these are **Ngài, Người,** used to address high ranking officials (for example, ministers of cabinet rank). As mentioned in the preceding section, the use of **bác-sĩ** 'doctor' and **giáo-sư** 'teacher' is similar, and perhaps belongs here rather than under polite usage. The term **cố**, which as a kin term designates the paternal grandfather's father, is used as an honorific term for Catholic missionaries, especially those of high rank or an earlier historical period (e.g., *Cố Alexandre de Rhodes*).

In replying to a person who has addressed him as *Ngài*, an official today generally uses the polite *ông, bà* or *cô* commensurate with the person's status. However, there is a form **người** which such persons sometimes use in addressing their inferiors.

The vocative particle **bẩm** is suggestive of honorific usage, although it is often used with **ông** or **bà**.

In the days of the Vietnamese kingdoms and empires there were a number of special terms used only in conversation with the king or emperor. For example, the monarch used **Trẫm** to designate himself, and was addressed or referred to as **Hoàng-thượng** 'Sire, His Majesty', **Điện-hạ, Bệ-hạ** 'Sire', **Hoàng-đế, Thánh-hoàng, Thánh-thượng** (various forms meaning 'emperor'), etc., while a person of lower rank was designated **thần** 'subject [of a king]' (cf. *tôi*, which also seems originally to have meant 'subject of the king'). There were also special verbs (similar to the polite verbs mentioned in

13.22) in use to refer to actions of royalty—for example, **ngự** 'be on the throne' used to cover meanings such as 'sit, go, stay.' Lesser personalities also merited special forms: such words as **chúa** 'lord, prince' and **quan** 'mandarin, official' were used with appropriate modifiers (e.g., *Ông Chúa, Bà Chúa, Ông Quan, Quan lớn*) in direct address. The noun **đức** 'virtue' served as a kind of honorific prefix (*Đức Ông, Đức Bà*, etc.).

The honorific forms in general seem to be going out of use in the modern language. There is a clear tendency in the direction of formal polite address. (Note that the same leveling is also eliminating abrupt forms; see 13.24).

13.24. Abrupt Address and Reference are important to understand, although the system is breaking down in the modern language and these forms are little used. In the main abrupt address forms today are limited to situations in which a person is talking to animals or small children; in any other contexts it constitutes extremely arrogant behavior or suggests limited education and rude upbringing. The reference forms are less offensive and continue to be used, especially for persons who are rather removed in one way or another—they are not known personally to the speaker or hearer, or they are not present and the speaker feels no particular constraint to demonstrate respect in their absence. The tone is impersonal or slightly superior. The address forms are primarily conversational and, as might be guessed from their force, appear in written passages only where the author reports the speech of a person of this category.

It is only in abrupt usage that the distinction between the second person—the individual(s) addressed—and the third person—the individual(s) spoken about—is clearly designated in formal terms. These forms are personal pronouns (10.43), like *tôi* and *ta* (which belong to polite usage), and they distinguish all three persons. Since there is a difference in force between the address forms (first and second persons) and reference forms (third person), it is convenient to discuss them separately.

Address forms include the first person **tao** 'I', and the second person forms **mày** (or **mầy**) 'you [singular]' and **bay** (or **bây**) 'you [plural].' All forms occur with a preceding **chúng** 'group of animate beings': *chúng tao* 'we [exclusive]', *chúng mày, chúng bay* 'you [plural]'. The lack of an inclusive first person plural form (you and I) is not surprising since elevation of the self and scorn for the hearer are not easily linked as an inclusive concept (see also 10.43, *ta*). Evidence from written texts indicates that these abrupt forms were formerly less arrogant, presumably reflecting less self-consciousness about the disparity in social relationships. Note that logically enough the use of one of the ordinary polite general categoricals to refer to oneself in most instances produces an arrogant speech. While it is perfectly polite for a grandfather to call himself *ông* in addressing his five-year-old grandson, the same person would seldom if ever use *ông* for himself while speaking to any adult, including his grown grandson. It is an interesting grammatical feature, however, that when such forms are used for designating the speaker himself, the corresponding plural form has **chúng** (10.42, 13.22).

Reference forms include the personal pronoun **nó** 'he, she, it, him, her' (10.43), which is scarcely more abrupt than *hắn* (10.44, 13.22); the general categorical **họ** 'they, them'; and certain classifiers, like **đứa** (for children or persons of low social status) and **thằng** (for boys and for older males meriting some contempt).

The distinction between abrupt and polite speech is obviously not a clear one; it is especially vague in reference forms. It appears that in the modern language, at the same time there is a tendency to use fewer abrupt forms in direct address, there is perhaps identifiable the contrary drift in the case of third person reference. In general however, it seems that the category of abrupt speech, with what earlier was a fairly extensive formal system, is becoming a less and less significant part of the language structure, just as honorific speech is on the opposing side of the social ledger (13.23).

13.25. Distinctions between Address and Reference are seldom

formal; which is involved is usually clear in the context. It can be generalized, however, that the demonstrative marker **ấy** quite often serves primarily to make clear that third person reference (and not second person address) is intended. Still clearer is the use of anaphorics (7.3) in southern and south central dialects. Nevertheless there are many cases where the forms described in the foregoing sections appear without any formal signal that they refer to a person other than the hearer or reader.

Nguyễn Công-trứ *vốn thích chơi-bời nên không để trí gì đến sách-đèn. Trước còn học-hành ít chút, sau mê cờ-bạc thì bỏ hẳn việc học.* **Ông** *ham-mê quá đánh thua hết cả tiền,* **ông** **Trứ** *liền bán cả cửa hàng. Một hôm* **ông** *không còn gì bán nữa,* **ông** *làm văn-tự bán vợ cho người Tàu chủ sòng-bạc. Nguyễn Công-Trứ* was at heart a lover of the carefree life, so did not concentrate on [his] studies. At first [he] still studied a little, [but] later [he] became empassioned of gambling and renounced studies completely. *He* was so addicted that [he] gambled away all his money; *Mr. Trứ* then promptly sold [his] shop as well. One day *he* had nothing left to sell, [so] *he* made a contract to sell [his] wife to a Chinese [who was] proprietor of the gambling house.

In this passage the variety of usage can be seen. At times where a pronoun is required in the corresponding English rendition there is no referent whatever (e.g., second sentence). The most specific reference appears at the very beginning, where the full name is cited. In the third sentence *ông* appears in the first part, and this same form is used twice in the final sentence. The use of the given name *Trứ* with *ông* in the second part of the third sentence lends a subtle kind of emphasis—only Mr. Trứ would behave in this way.

The form **ta** (in a use similar to that of *ấy*) is common in narrative passages. It is presumably the pronoun meaning 'you and I' and it lends a connotation of pleasant relationship between story-teller and audience not unlike that found in the earlier English use of *our* in forms like *our hero, our man*, etc.

Ngày hôm sau đàn chim lại đến ăn, người chồng đưa cái túi ra thì đàn chim bảo nhắm mắt lại rồi hóa-phép cõng anh ta *bay đi nhanh lắm. Đến một quả núi giữa bể, chim hạ cánh xuống và* anh ta *mở mắt ra thì thấy toàn là vàng bạc, châu-báu.* Anh ta *lấy đầy túi rồi lại cưỡi lên mình chim mà về.* The next day the flock of birds returned to eat; the husband brought the pouch out and the flock of birds told [him] to close [his] eyes, then performed a miracle [and] carried *him* on [their] backs, flying away very fast. Arriving at a mountain in the midst of the sea, the birds alighted and *he* opened [his] eyes and saw [that] everywhere was gold and silver, [and] precious pearls. *He* filled the pouch, then again mounted astride the body [of one of the] birds to return home.

13.3. Conversational Style

is characterized by relatively short sentences, a predominance of clauses consisting of predicates alone, frequent repetition of elements from the immediately preceding context as emphatic tie-ins with what follows, and a liberal sprinkling of particles which maintain the formal or informal tone of the situation. Generally it is also rich with particles which convey hints about the speakers' attitudes and emotional responses. The sequential construction (9.66) is especially common, filling many of the uses which in a corresponding English equivalent would involve some sort of subordinate clause. Focal complements are common enough in ordinary conversation, but those here termed topics (10.31), which often resemble the subjects of corresponding English clauses, are certainly far less frequent than in English. While the sentences are characteristically short, it is important to note that absolute minimal sentences (consisting, for example, of a single verb alone) are unusual. This stems partly from a speaker's usual desire to convey some kind of attitude he has about things, partly from the notion that a somewhat longer utterance is more polite. The tendency to avoid monosyllabic entities (13.5) also plays a part here.

This is properly the style of ordinary everyday conversation. It is also used in most informal correspondence—personal letters, diaries, etc.—and even in some very chatty types of prose.

13.31. Opening Utterances in conversations are very apt to begin with the initial particle à (11.3). In fact this is on occasion the entire utterance, followed by an utterance on the part of the person thus addressed. On other occasions it is the whole of the first sentence, then followed by one or more longer sentences. More usually it forms the first immediate constituent of a longer sentence. This is, of course, the defining frame for independent sentences (5.41), and such sentences regularly contain a predication (9.1). Opening utterances not beginning with à are very apt to start with a polite vocative or to be some kind of polite formula.

Xin lỗi ông. I beg your pardon. (said to a man)

Thưa cụ, *cụ là người Việt, phải không?* Sir, you're a Vietnamese, aren't you? (said to an old man)

13.32. Questions are posed by means of sustaining intonation (5.34), sometimes by itself, but more often in combination with indefinite words (14.2), certain final particles with questioning content (11.4), or alternative phrases (9.67). Sometimes questions are accompanied by fading (5.33) or increasing intonation (5.32), and in these cases are discerned as such largely by context.

Those involving the alternative construction have been called **choice questions** (9.67). They often (but not always) correspond to what are sometimes called yes-or-no answer questions in English. The most common of these have a negative as the second alternative, so that the effect of the choice is '...or not?' or '...or not yet?' etc. However, there are a few other words which appear in this position, and there are also choice questions making use of the particle hay 'or.'

Mai anh đi xem hát **không?** Are you going to the play tomorrow?

Ăn cơm **chưa?** Have [you] eaten yet?

Ông uống nước nữa **thôi?** Are you going to drink any more tea? (servant preparing to take away the teapot) ["gentleman drink liquid in-addition stop?"]

Ông ở đây lâu **mau?** (S) will you be here long?

Quyển sách mà anh tìm xanh **hay nâu?** Is the book you're looking for green or brown?

There are three special purpose formulas used in connection with choice questions. The **có...không?** formula, in which the predicate is preceded by the auxiliary *có*, is much the most common way of asking a simple

307

choice question with the negative *không*. (Such questions also occur with **chưa**, but they are hardly the rule.) Without this device (that is, without *có* preceding the predicate) a question seems to have some connotation of expecting an affirmative reply, while with the formula the speaker signals no suspicion of the answer. The **có phải...không?** formula, in which the predicate (or the whole predication) is preceded by *có phải*, is used to ask this type of question with a substantival or identificational predicate. The **...phải không?** formula simply asks for confirmation (equivalent of the French *n'est-ce pas?* or the English *...isn't it? ...don't you?* and the like).

Ông **có** *biết nói tiếng tây* **không?** Do you (know how to) speak French?

Thưa cụ, người thông-thạo pháp-luật cụ vừa nói **có phải** *là trạng-sư* **không?** [Sir] is the person experienced with [matters of] law you just mentioned a lawyer?

Có phải *bây giờ là mùa cưới* **không?** Is now the season for marriages?

Cụ là người Việt, **phải không?** You're a Vietnamese, aren't you?

Ai đấy, tiếng ai nghe như tiếng cô Hồng **phải không?** Who's there? Someone's voice sounds like cô Hồng's—am I right?

Final questioning particles for the most part ask for confirmation or agreement. Sentences containing them are actually marginal as questions.

Không đi **à?** Oh, you're not going?

Chúng ta đi bây giờ **nhé?** Shall we go now?

Questions signalled by sustaining intonation alone are rare. For the most part they indicate uncertainty on the part of the speaker that he understands something correctly.

Ông hỏi tôi? Are you asking me?

Anh muốn đi bây giờ? You want to go now?

All other questions involve the use of some indefinite word (14.2) at its appropriate position in the sentence. They may conveniently be labeled **information questions.** (Indefinite words appear in boldface in the following examples.)

Bây giờ **mấy** *giờ?* What time is it?

Anh đi **đâu** *về?* Where have you been?

Ai *nói bây giờ?* Who's going to talk now?

Ông muốn hỏi về chuyện **gì?** What do you want to ask about?

Khi **nào** *ông định lên Đà-lạt?* When have you decided to go up to Dalat?

Tại **sao** *ông Nam không đến?* Why didn't Mr. Nam come?

13.33. Responsive Utterances are far more varied than opening utterances, and they frequently involve fragments (12.4). In formal situations there occur short answers to questions about which certain generalizations can be made. Negative answers to choice questions (9.67, 13.32) frequently consist merely of the appropriate negative (9.4)–the one used or implied in the stimulus. Most common are **không** 'not' and **chưa** 'not yet.' Prohibitives do not appear in this use.

> *Ông mua cái này không?*–**Không.** Do you [want to] buy this?–No.
> *Ăn cơm chưa?*– **Chưa.** Have [you] eaten yet?–No.

Affirmative answers to choice questions frequently make use of the auxiliary **có** (9.54) alone to stand for the main verb. This usage is nearly obligatory in response to a question which uses the formula *Có...không?* (13.32). However, in answer to questions making use of the special formula *Có phải...không?* the appropriate affirmative short answer is **phải** rather than *có.* Questions having with the main verb a complement which is also a verbal (9.5) prompt short answers consisting of this modifying word (except for questions where the *có...không?* formula is used, to which the short reply **có** is more usual).

> *Ông mua cái này không*–**Có.** Do you [want to] buy this?–Yes.
> *Ăn cơm chưa?*–**Có.** (or **Có rồi.**) Have [you] eaten yet?–Yes.
> *Ông có hiểu câu này không?*–**Có.** Do you understand this sentence?–Yes.
> *Có phải ông ấy là người Việt-nam không?*–**Phải.** Is that man a Vietnamese?–Yes.
> *Anh còn ở Đà-lạt không?*–**Còn.** Do you still live in Dalat?–Yes.
> *Làm rồi à?*–**Rồi.** [You've] already done it, eh?–Yes.
> *Đi được không?*–**Được.** Can [one] go?–Yes.
> *Ông ấy có đi được không?*–**Có.** (or **Được.**) Can he go?–Yes.

Questions involving a sequential phrase with two main verbs invite the simple affirmative answer **có.**

> *Anh đi chợ mua rau không?*–**Có.** Are you going to market to buy vegetables?–Yes.
> *Anh muốn lấy quyển sách này không?*–**Có.** Do you want to take this book?–Yes.

Other complements are frequently added to short responses, either to make them more polite (13.31) or to add some special flavor or emphatic notion.

> *Ăn được không?*–**Được lắm.** Can [you] eat it? (e.g., said by polite host to guest)– [It's] very good! (postpositive particle added)

309

Tôi nghe nói là người ấy có tiền nhiều.—**Nhiều quá!** I've heard that that fellow has a lot of money.—An awful lot. (comparative added)
Làm được không?—**Được chớ.** (S) Can [it] be done?—Of course! (final particle added)

Short answers to information questions (13.32) are generally of types other than predicative fragments. They supply the information requested without restating the predication.

Cái này bao nhiêu tiền?—**Sáu mươi lăm đồng.** How much does this cost?—Sixty-five piastres. (substantival fragment)
Ai nói bây giờ?—**Tôi.** Who's going to talk now?—I [am]. (focal fragment)
Chị ấy nói với ai?—**Với bạn.** Who's she talking with?—With a friend. (particular fragment)

Some questions, however, invite a clausal fragment.

Tại sao ông Nam không đến?—**Vì ốm.** Why didn't Mr. Nam come?—Because [he's] sick.

13.4. Learnèd Style differs from conversational style (13.3) primarily in greater complexity of sentence structure and especially in the use of a special vocabulary, nearly wholly of Chinese origin (to a large extent pseudo-compounds, 6.3). At the same time, compounds (6.2) and specializing and emphatic derivatives (7.4, 7.5) are more common than in conversational usage. Several constructions are more frequent: focal complements of the topic type (10.31) (similar to clause subjects in English), logical passive expressions (9.64), descriptive clauses (12.22). restrictive clauses (12.23). By the same token, the characteristic sequential construction of the ordinary spoken language is less in evidence.

Learnèd style appears mainly in written texts of a formal nature—this includes most newspaper writing, as well as formal letters and both popular and more scholarly books. It is also evident in formal speeches and scholarly addresses which are delivered orally. As in other literatures there are gradations of formality, showing mainly in the percentage of (learnèd) Chinese loan words in the text. However, some modern writers make extensive use of everyday conversational style.

13.5. Tendency toward Dissyllabic Forms. In many circumstances where it would seem to a foreigner that a monosyllabic form would convey the desired meaning, the Vietnamese speaker insists on a two-syllable expression of some sort—a phrase, compound, pseudo-compound or derivative. This is especially noticeable in the kind of short responses reported in 13.33. Actually single-syllable responses are relatively rare; dissyllabic phrases are extremely common. For example, in response to the question *Đi được không?* 'Is it possible to go? (Can one go?)' the monosyllabic affirmative answer *Được* is perfectly possible. However, one is much more apt to hear any one of the following disyllabic answers.

Dạ được. Yes.

Được chớ. (S) Of course.

Được lắm. Very much so.

Được rồi. Already possible.

In other cases embedded in longer sentences, examples of the tendency are harder to detect. It seems particularly compelling at the ends of clauses, especially those in sentence final position. For example one informant rejected as unnatural *Chị ấy rửa cái nhà sạch.* She washed the house clean. He offered the following substitutes for it:

Chị ấy rửa sạch nhà. She washed the house clean.

Chị ấy rửa cái nhà sạch-sẽ. She washed the house clean.

Chị ấy rửa cái nhà sạch lắm. She washed the house very clean.

Chị ấy rửa cái nhà rất sạch. She washed the house very clean.

Chị ấy rửa cái nhà sạch-nhách. She washed the house very clean.

Chị ấy rửa cái nhà sạch trơn. She made the house slickly clean.

The tendency is probably more active in learnèd style than in conversational usage. In any case, it appears to merit some careful consideration and study to determine in what kinds of circumstances it operates.

CHAPTER 14

Lexical Complexities

14.1. Introductory. Although not strictly matters of grammar as it is usually construed, a number of problems involving the use of words in particular semantic categories are of special concern to students learning Vietnamese. The language's structuring of human experience is understandably different from that of other languages, especially those of western Europe. In this chapter are covered a number of cases in which the representation of the universe seems of quite different organization from that implied by the corresponding English expressions.

14.2. Indefinite Words constitute a small semantic class characterized by their denial of specific reference to any particular entities or concepts. They are of extremely high frequency and are clear essentials for most questions (13.32) and many negative statements (14.3). They belong to several different word classes, providing one or more generalizing indefinite forms for each.

Four indefinites are morphologically related: they are demonstratives (7.2), with the element *-ao/-âu* 'unspecified.' They include the demonstrative marker **nào** 'whichever' (8.5), the locational focus **đâu** 'wherever' (10.46), the manner focus **sao** 'however' (10.45), and the noncontained postpositive particle **bao** 'to whatever extent' (11.82). Three others are indefinite nouns (8.65): **ai** 'whoever', **chi** 'whatever' (polite), **gì** 'whatever' (informal). Finally, there is the indefinite number **mấy** 'however many (generally fewer than ten)' (8.42). The poetic word **nao** 'which(ever)' and the local form in Huế popular speech **mô** 'which(ever), where(ver)' also belong to this class; examples of these are to be found in 7.23.

The following examples are provided primarily to highlight the elusive force which indefinites sometimes have.

Có nói **sao,** *phải làm vậy.* However [you] say [you do], [you] should act that way. (I.e., Practice what you preach.)

Dù **ai** *buôn đâu bán đâu,/Mồng 10 tháng 8 chọi trâu thì về.* Wherever anyone may be doing business, he always returns for the buffalo fight on August 10th.

Phải của trời cho thì đứa **nào** *lấy được.* [If it's] really given by heaven, then whoever could take it [away]! (negative implication without a negative in the sentence)

Ông đi Sài-gòn làm **chi.** (S) There's no point in your going to Saigon. (with fading intonation)

Ở Đà-lạt những **ai** *trồng rau đều trúng lắm.* (S) At Dalat those who plant [i.e., grow] vegetables are all prosperous.

Gì *có cánh đều bay được.* (S) Whatever has wings can fly.

Ở gần chợ có **mấy** *người đứng nói chuyện.* Near the market there were a few people standing talking.

Certain of these words (notably **ai, gì,** and **đâu**) are common with negative emphatic force. They often accompany ironic emphatics (7.62) in the southern dialects.

Tôi mắc công việc nhiều quá, rồi-riệc **gì** *mà đi chơi.* (S) I'm terribly busy with many things, never have time to go out for a good time.

Biết **gì đâu!** [Doesn't] know a thing!

Đừng nói lăng-nhăng nữa, **ai** *mà tin được!* Don't tell any more fantasies, [there's] no one that can believe [them].

With the prepositive particle **cũng** 'likewise' and the auxiliary **đều** 'be equal; equally, as well' indefinite words convey the notion of totality, or of general inclusiveness.

Ai cũng *biết truyện ấy.* Everyone knows that story.

Tôi ăn **gì cũng** *được.* I can eat anything.

Mấy *người trong nhà này* **đều** *điên-dại.* Everyone in this house is crazy.

Làm **sao cũng** *được hết.* Any way at all is fine.

Truyện **nào** *của tác-giả ấy* **đều** *hay lắm.* All of that author's stories are very good.

Đi **đâu cũng** *vậy.* Wherever [you] go it's the same.

In some sentences both *cũng* and *đều* occur, with the former a preceding complement.

Chiều ấy người nào **cũng đều** *vui-vẻ.* That afternoon everyone was having an (equally) good time.

Most typically, however, indefinites appear in interrogative (13.32) and negative (14.3) sentences, in which they take on the force of question or denial words. Extensive examples of these uses are to be found in the sections referred to.

There seem to be a number of gaps in the semantic range covered by indefinites. Actually they are filled by phrases containing one or another of these forms. A list of the most common follows.

bao giờ whenever
bao lâu however long [in time]
bao nhiêu however much, many
chừng nào whenever; however much
hồi nào whenever, at whatever moment [generally in the past]
khi nào whenever, on whatever occasion
lúc nào whenever, during whatever period
cách nào however, by whatever means
thế nào however, in whatever fashion
tại sao for whatever reason, why
vì sao for whatever cause, why

14.3. Negation is accomplished primarily by means of the negatives (9.4), although indefinite words sometimes have negative force (14.2). The negation of verbal predicates (14.31) may be taken as standard. Negatives are also used with non-predicates on occasion (14.32). Certain complications arise in the negation of non-verbal predicates (14.33).

14.31. Negation of Verbal Predicates. Overwhelmingly the most common negative sentences involve **không** 'not' or **chưa** 'not yet' placed directly before the verbal serving as predicate center. Less frequent is **chẳng** 'definitely not', which is stronger than *không* and has something of a literary flavor. The usual prohibitive is **đừng** 'don't', less common than the others by virtue of the fact that prohibitions are less often called for than factual negations. (For examples see 9.4.)

The fact that the negative goes with the predicate center sometimes reveals that what appears to be a single affirmative sentence actually has two analyses with different predicate centers. Compare the following sentences:

Tôi đi được. I can go.
Tôi đi không được. I can't go (I'm ill, have no transportation, am physically unable, etc.)
Tôi không đi được. I can't go. (I have other things to do, another engagement, too much work, etc.)

314

The simple affirmative sentence incorporates the opposing ideas of both negative sentences. In the first negative sentence, however, the center is *được*, the extended state verb meaning 'become a reality, be physically possible', in the second *đi* 'go' is the center, and *được* is a postpositive particle meaning 'successfully, with a good result' (cf. *được* 2 and 3, Appendix A). The affirmative sentence corresponding to the first negative sentence should then be analyzed as containing the center *được*: that corresponding to the second as containing the center *đi*.

14.32. Negation of Non-Predicates. Negatives also appear as restrictive complements to heads which are not predicatives; the result in these cases is a denial of the concept denoted by the head. (The heads are generally substantives or substantival phrases, but some focuses also occur.)

Không ai *thấy con phèn ở đâu.* No one [had] seen where the brown [dog] was.

Tôi không bao giờ *quên.* I'll never forget.

Anh Bính là một người không tiền. Bính is a fellow without money.

Không sao. It doesn't matter.

Chẳng chè chẳng chén *sao say,/Chẳng thương, chẳng nhớ sao hay đi tìm?* No drink, no cup, how [can one] be drunk?/[If you] don't love, don't recall nostalgically, why so often [do you] go looking [for someone]?—Folk saying

In the folk verse which serves as last example, the negative *chẳng* appears with verbs *thương* 'like, love' and *nhớ* 'remember, recall nostalgically' in the second line; but in the first line it negates *chè* ('tea', euphemistic for alcohol) and *chén* 'cup [in which tea and alcohol are served]'. *Chè-chén* 'drinking' is generalizing compound (6.22), appearing here in interlocking order (6.4) with *chẳng*.

These phrases do not constitute regular predicates, although they sometimes appear (like the fourth example above) as minor sentences.

14.33. Negation of Non-Verbal Predicates. Substantival and identificational predicates (9.1) are not generally negated directly. Instead the verb phải 'be true, be the case [that]' is supplied, and the negative appears as restrictive complement to it.

Cái này của tôi. This belongs to me. (*Của* 'possession, belonging' is a general categorical, 8.62.)

Cái này không phải *của tôi.* This doesn't belong to me.

Ông ấy là lính. He's a soldier. (identificational marker *là*)

315

Ông ấy **không phải** *là lính.* He's not a soldier.

Tiếng pháo bây giờ **không phải** *là để tế Trời, Phật hay lễ tổ-tiên mà là tiếng pháo mừng tuổi các người còn sống.* The sound of fire-crackers now is not for the purpose of performing a sacrifice to Heaven or Buddha or to honor the ancestors but is (a sound of firecrackers) to wish Happy New Year to the people still living.

On rare occasions a substantival predicate appears negated by a negative directly (the circumstances of its occurrence require recognition of a major sentence [12.3] rather than a substantival fragment [12.43]). It is perhaps significant that the only examples found involve *chưa* rather than *không*.

Chưa ba giờ. [It's] not three o'clock yet.

14.4. Spatial Elements involve certain complications which seem unexpected from the point of view of the English speaker. They concern the ways of stating position (14.41), direction to and from which an entity is moving (14.42), and changes of position or direction (14.43).

14.41. Positional Expressions most commonly make use of the general positional verb *ở* 'be located'. Its descriptive complement specifies the location.

Anh ở đâu? Where are you?

Ông chủ ở nhà. The boss is at home.

Ngày xưa ở Việt-nam việc hôn-nhân là do ở bố mẹ kén chọn cho con cái. In the olden days in Viet Nam for a marriage the responsibility rested with the father and mother to choose for [their] daughter. (Note that the second *ở* has a meaning of figurative position—relating to responsibility.)

To clarify relative position, the complement of *ở* is often one of the relator nouns (8.63), the most common of which are listed here:

dưới the under or lower part, bottom, foot, base

giữa the middle, part between

ngoài the outside, exterior

sau the back part, rear

trên the top or higher part

trong the inside, interior

trước the front

These words are very often followed by another substantive as descriptive complement, clarifying with relation to what the position is described as under, middle, outside, etc. In translation to western languages the normal colloquial result is a prepositional phrase; for this reason these words (with or without *ở*) have been called prepositions.

Khi ngoảnh lại thì con phèn của tôi đã biến mất **trong** *đám cỏ*
dưới *triền núi.* When I looked back my brown [dog] had vanished in a clump of grass at the bottom of the mountain slope.
Cái bút ở **trên** *bàn.* The pen is on the table.
Nhiều khi tôi thích ăn ở **ngoài.** Often I prefer to eat out.
Gần nhà có hai cây to, một cây ở **trước,** *một cây ở* **sau.** There were
two big trees near the house, one in front, one in back.

These relator nouns also occur as complements to other verbs, sometimes
to those denoting motion or change of position, but the reference of the
relator noun remains that of relative position.

Chốc nữa một đôi người qua đi chợ, chồng **đi trước,** *vợ* **đi sau.**
In a short while a couple came by on their way to market the
husband going first, the wife behind.

There are also some extended state verbs (9.55) which appear as complements to *ở* denoting position. The two most common are exemplified
here.

gần be near: *Nhà tôi ở* **gần** *đây.* My house is near here.
xa be far: *Khi ở* **xa** *nhà thì nhớ nhà lắm.* When [one] is far
from home, [one] misses home a lot.

There are a few common verbs which denote static position of a very
specific nature:

đứng stand: *Mời ông* **đứng** *đây xem.* (Invite) you stand here [and]
look.
ngồi sit: *Cả ngày người ấy* **ngồi** *nghĩ-ngợi.* The whole day the
fellow sat thinking.
nằm lie: *Bạn tôi* **nằm** *nhà thương.* A friend of mine is (lying) in
the hospital.

14.42. Directional Expressions make use of verbs which indicate mo-
tion and their descriptive complements specify the goals involved. The
most common verb of all is **đi** 'go', but there are also many specifically
directional words such as **xuống** 'go down', **ra** 'go out', **vào** (S **vô**) 'go in',
lên 'go up', **sang** 'traverse', **về** 'return to point of origin'. (Southern
speakers often replace *sang* by **qua**.)

Đi *đâu đó?—* **Đi** *chợ.* (S) Where [you] going?—To market.
Ngày mai chúng ta **đi** *Hà-nội.* Let's go to Hanoi tomorrow.
Tuần tới tôi **lên** *Đà-lạt chơi.* Next week I'm going up to Dalat on
a pleasure trip. (Dalat is located on a high plateau.)
Ba bốn ngày ở Đà-lạt thì tôi **xuống** *Nha-trang nghỉ-ngơi.* [After]
three or four days in Dalat I'll go down to Nha Trang for a rest.

(Nha Trang is located on a lovely beach on the ocean, down off the plateau from Dalat.)

Sáng nay ông ấy **ra** *nhà sớm.* This morning he left the house early.

Mời ông **vào** *phòng trà.* Please come into the living room.

Khi nào ông định **sang** *bên Mỹ?* (S *Chừng nào ông định* **qua** *bên Mỹ?*) When have you decided to go to America? (Crossing the ocean is involved.)

Năm tới tôi hy-vọng **về** *Hà-nội.* Next year I hope to return to Hanoi.

Certain of these commonly have as complement a relator noun (or a phrase with relator noun as head), expressing the logical terminal position the direction verb implies:

> *lên* **trên** go up (on top)
>
> *xuống* **dưới** go down (under, *or* to the bottom)
>
> *ra* **ngoài** go out (outside)
>
> *vào* **trong** go in (inside)

There are specializations of directional verbs, some similar to those of English, others different. As in English the picture of a map on the wall is often pertinent: direction north then is signalled by **lên**, south by **xuống**, and travel east or west is described by **sang** (somewhat like English *go over to*). These are in effect, however, only if there is not some quite obvious difference in altitude (in which case the primary meanings of *lên* and *xuống* apply) or another kind of difference is not involved—the distinction between the urban center and the rural provinces, and sometimes that between the interior and the coast. In northern Viet Nam in particular, the capital Hanoi is regarded as 'out' (perhaps 'out in the open, in civilization'), and travel to and from the city is described accordingly with **ra** when coming from the provinces to Hanoi: and **vào** when going from Hanoi into the rural areas. This includes even major cities like Saigon and Huế: *ở Hà-nội* **vào** *Sài-gòn, Huế;* *ở Sài-gòn, Huế* **ra** *Hà-nội.* The rest of the country in general fits into this pattern, and for the south any major destination in the more northerly parts of Viet Nam is 'out': *ở Sài-gòn* **ra** *Hải-phòng, Huế.* In the provinces in general, too, any destination on the coast is 'out', as we might expect.

Finally, for the multitudes in the cities who come originally from some rural area, travel to their original home province is termed **về**, even though their permanent home may now be in the city. It is thus not uncommon to hear a person say

> *Tuần tới tôi* **về** *Nam-định. Ở đấy sáu ngày thì* **về** *Hà-nội làm.*
>
> Next week I'm going home to Nam-định. After six days I'll be back to Hanoi for work.

14.43. Change of Position or Direction is generally covered by a sequential phrase which states first the initial position or direction, then the fact of departure or the new direction. This contrasts vividly with English usage, where there are special verbs like *leave, depart*.

> *Ba giờ tôi ở Hà-nội* **đi.** I left Hanoi at three o'clock.
> **Đi** *Hải-phòng* **về** *rồi.* [I]'ve gotten back from [my trip to] Haiphong.
> *Anh* **đi** *đâu* **về** *?* Where have you been?

With the exact timing clear only from the context, identical sentences can cover a rather wide range of meanings in corresponding English translation.

> **Đi** *Hải-phòng thứ hai mới* **về** . [I]'m going to Haiphong and won't be back till Monday *or* Just returned from Haiphong Monday *or* Went to Haiphong and returned only on Monday.

This same type of construction is used to specify points of origin.

> *Ông ấy ở Sài-gòn* **lên** *đây.* He came up here from Saigon.

Where point of origin is to be stated very precisely, especially where distance is being measured from it, use is often made of the prepositive particle **từ** (occasionally **tự**) 'starting from.'

> **Từ Sài-gòn** *đến Đà-lạt độ chừng ba trăm cây số.* From Saigon to Dalat it's about 300 km.

Again the construction is used with an appropriate change in focal complement to indicate that an outside agency changes the position or direction of an entity (which then appears as descriptive complement).

> *Chị* **đổ** *nước* **vô** *bình trà.* (S) She poured water into the teapot.
> *Tôi* **lấy** *quần-áo trong tủ* **ra.** I took some clothes out of the wardrobe.
> *Tôi* **lấy** *quyển sách trên tủ* **xuống.** I took the book down from the bookcase.

14.5. Temporal Elements involve several important differences from English usage. Some of these have to do with the designation of time periods in serial order: in older usage two special sets of words borrowed from Chinese tradition served this purpose (14.51). Clock time and various periods of the day are discussed in 14.52; longer periods (days, weeks, months, years) are treated in 14.53. For a discussion of relative time or tense, see 9.3, 9.55.

14.51. Cyclical Terms. Two series of words borrowed from Chinese are used in some traditional time expressions (and a few other situations) to designate serial order.

Địa-chi 'earth's branches' (often referred to simply as *chi*) is a cycle of twelve elements which in more traditional usage is applied to months and years (14.53), as well as to the twelve two-hour periods of the day (14.52). The meanings of the elements beyond their serial values are un-known, but at some point in the history of the system in China they came to be associated with a system of twelve animals similar to the western zodiac. (With certain differences in the identity of the animals involved and their order, such systems are in use in most of the civilizations of central and eastern Asia, and comparable usages are described in the Near East as far west as Egypt.) In everyday Vietnamese speech the formal terms are often replaced by the native words for the associated animals (listed below together with their serial values).

ĐỊA-CHI	ASSOCIATED ANIMAL	SERIAL VALUE
tý (or tí)	*chuột* rat	first
sửu	*trâu* buffalo (or *bò* ox)	second
dần	*hùm* tiger	third
mão	*mèo* cat (or *thỏ* hare)	fourth
thìn	*rồng* dragon	fifth
tỵ (or tị)	*rắn* serpent	sixth
ngọ	*ngựa* horse	seventh
mùi	*dê* goat	eighth
thân	*khỉ* monkey	ninth
dậu	*gà* cock	tenth
tuất	*chó* dog	eleventh
hợi	*lợn* (or *heo*) pig	twelfth

The substitution of 'buffalo' for 'ox' of the Chinese system is shared by some other peoples of the area, but only the Vietnamese seem to have replaced 'hare' by 'cat.' It is possible that this reflects a misinterpreta-tion of the formal term *mão*, which is very similar to the word for 'cat.'

Thiên-can 'heaven's stems' (also *Thập-can* 'the ten stems' or simply *can*) is a cycle of ten elements. They have been used to designate the order of kings or emperors and occasionally the sequence of volumes in a series. They also appear in some reckoning of years. The meanings of the forms beyond their serial values are obscure.

giáp	first	kỷ	sixth
ất	second	canh	seventh
bính	third	tân	eighth
đinh	fourth	nhâm	ninth
mậu	fifth	quí	tenth

Some representative references on these cyclical elements are Chavannes 1906, Halévy 1906, Li Fang-Kuei 1945, Pelliot 1913, Porée-Maspero 1962, and von Staël-Holstein 1935-36.

14.52. The Times of Day. In broad terms the day is divided into several vaguely delimited parts. First of all daylight time (**ban ngày**) is separated from night time (**ban đêm**). The two major parts of the daylight hours are called **buổi sáng** 'morning' (also **buổi sớm**) and **buổi chiều** 'afternoon', and the term **cả hai buổi** means 'all day, morning and afternoon.' The twenty-four hour period is also divided into five rough parts as follows:

4 a.m. to 10 a.m.	**sáng**	morning
10 a.m. to 3 p.m.	**trưa**	noon
3 p.m. to 6 p.m.	**chiều**	afternoon
6 p.m. to 11 p.m.	**tối**	evening
11 p.m. to 4 a.m.	**khuya**	late at night

These times are very approximate. Each of the Vietnamese words appears as descriptive complement to the word **buổi** 'division of the day' (cf. above) except *khuya*. There is also the term **buổi bình-minh** 'dawn.'

More specifically, the western clock is now in standard use in the country; the word **giờ** 'hour' is used with the numbers one through twelve for the large divisions of clock time: *một giờ* 'one o'clock', *hai giờ* 'two o'clock', *bốn giờ* 'four o'clock', *mấy giờ?* 'what time?' etc. Minutes are designated **phút** and seconds **giây**, where such precision is called for. A very common way of telling time is similar to the English pattern *ten-fifteen, ten-forty-three*: *mười giờ mười lăm, mười giờ bốn mươi ba*. However, for the half-hour generally the term **rưỡi** 'and one half' is used: *ba giờ rưỡi* 'half-past three, three-thirty.' For the time after the half-hour and before the next hour, there is another usage, stating the next hour less a certain number of minutes: *ba giờ thiếu mười lăm* 'fifteen minutes to three', *mười một giờ thiếu hai mươi hai* 'twenty-two minutes before eleven.' When the numbers in these expressions are simple, there is a strong tendency to add the word *phút* 'minute', which is otherwise rare in colloquial time-telling: *hai giờ ba phút* 'three minutes past two', *bảy giờ thiếu mười phút* 'ten minutes to seven.' This is perhaps another example of the tendency toward dissyllabic elements (cf. 13.5). Some speakers use *kém* 'be less' in place of *thiếu* in such expressions. Some add *phút* regularly to the number of minutes, unless it is a multiple of five, where they do not use it at all. (These special usages are probably primarily southern, although their geographical distribution is not clear.)

There are survivals of older time systems. In the countryside one still meets with the usage of identifying the night hours by watches and references are of course common in written texts. This system used the word **canh** 'watch' followed by a number as descriptive complement, with *bốn* replaced by **tư** 'four.' The five watches, then, were designated:

canh một from about 7 to 9 p.m.
canh hai from about 9 to 11 p.m.
canh ba from about 11 p.m. to 1 a.m.
canh tư from about 1 a.m. to 3 a.m.
canh năm from about 3 a.m. to 5 a.m.

Another earlier system divided the entire twenty-four hour day into periods of two hours each (the original use of the word **giờ**); these were designated by the elements of the *địa-chi* (14.51), beginning at 11 p.m.:

giờ tý (tí)	11 p.m. to 1 a.m.	*giờ ngọ*	11 a.m. to 1 p.m.
giờ sửu	1 a.m. to 3 a.m.	*giờ mùi*	1 p.m. to 3 p.m.
giờ dần	3 a.m. to 5 a.m.	*giờ thân*	3 p.m. to 5 p.m.
giờ mão	5 a.m. to 7 a.m.	*giờ dậu*	5 p.m. to 7 p.m.
giờ thìn	7 a.m. to 9 a.m.	*giờ tuất*	7 p.m. to 9 p.m.
giờ ty (tị)	9 a.m. to 11 a.m.	*giờ hợi*	9 p.m. to 11 p.m.

14.53. Larger Time Divisions. In former times reckoning of time beyond the limit of days depended on the lunar calendar (**âm-lịch**); with the coming of western influence the solar calendar (**dương-lịch**) was adopted. Modern usage reflects a mixture of the two systems: for most everyday things, the solar calendar serves, but in certain details of ordinary usage and in most special connections the lunar calendar continues in force. In the following discussion these elements of the lunar calendar are specially indicated.

There are several words corresponding to the English word *day*. It is extremely difficult to separate them from one another, and the picture is complicated by a good deal of dialectal variation. Presented here are the most common expressions in use in Hanoi and Saigon.

hôm day (as time when, primarily in present or past)
bữa (S) day (as one of a series, or time when, primarily in present or future)
ngày day (as one of a series, or time when, in future)

	HANOI	SAIGON
today	*hôm nay*	*bữa nay*
yesterday	*hôm qua*	*hôm qua, bữa qua*
day before yesterday	*hôm kia*	*hôm kia*
two days before yesterday	*hôm kìa*	*hôm kìa*
tomorrow	*(ngày) mai*	*(ngày) mai*
day after tomorrow	*ngày kia*	*(ngày) mốt, bữa mốt*
two days after tomorrow	*ngày kìa*	*ngày kia, bữa kia*
three days after tomorrow		*ngày kìa, bữa kìa*
three days	*ba ngày*	*ba ngày, ba bữa*

	HANOI	SAIGON
what day?	*hôm nào?*	*bữa nào? hôm nào?*
the preceding day	*hôm trước*	*bữa trước*
the following day	*hôm sau*	*bữa sau*

Especially in written material one finds combinations of these terms, such as *ngày hôm nay* today, *ngày hôm qua* yesterday, etc.; in the south *bữa hôm nay* today, *bữa hôm qua* yesterday. There are also a few common special expressions: *ngày hôm ấy* (S *bữa hôm*) the other day (also, as expected, 'that day [just referred to])', *ngày nay* nowadays.

The days of the week (western calendar) are for the most part descriptive phrases with the general categorical **thứ** as head and the numbers two through seven as complements (with **tư** replacing *bốn*). The exception is Sunday, which is a pseudo-compound.

chủ-nhật ["master's day"] or *chúa-nhật* ["lord's day"] Sunday
thứ hai Monday
thứ ba Tuesday
thứ tư Wednesday
thứ năm Thursday
thứ sáu Friday
thứ bẩy (or *bảy*) Saturday
thứ mấy? what day of the week?

The western week is specifically **tuần-lễ**, often shortened to **tuần**, although this designates also the ten-day periods of the lunar month (see below).

The days of the month are designated with the word **ngày** followed by the appropriate number, except that for the first ten the word **mồng** (or **mùng**) appears between *ngày* and the number; in the latter case *ngày* is often omitted. This is a survival of the older lunar calendar usage.

(ngày) mồng một the first [day of a particular month]
(ngày) mồng hai the second
(ngày) mồng bốn the fourth
(ngày) mồng mười the tenth
ngày mười một the eleventh
ngày mười lăm the fifteenth (also called *ngày mười rằm*; see below)
ngày hai mươi ba the twenty-third
ngày ba mươi the thirtieth

For reference to days in the past *ngày* is often replaced by **hôm** (cf. above).

The month is designated **tháng**, and the names of the months, except for the first and last, are simply numbers in serial order (with **tư** replacing *bốn*): November, however, is usually simply *tháng một*.

tháng giêng	January		*tháng bảy* (or *bẩy*)	July
tháng hai	February		*tháng tám*	August
tháng ba	March		*tháng chín*	September
tháng tư	April		*tháng mười*	October
tháng năm	May		*tháng (mười) một*	November
tháng sáu	June		*tháng chạp*	December

tháng mấy? what month?

In contrast to these expressions designating specific time periods according to the basic organization of time, ordinal numbers appear as descriptive complements to **ngày, hôm** and **tháng**, marking particular periods in reference to some other arbitrary serial order.

Ngày thứ hai *tôi ở đây là* **thứ năm**. The second day I'm here is Thursday.

Tháng thứ nhất *tôi ở Việt-nam là* **tháng tám**. The first month I was in Viet Nam was August.

According to the lunar calendar the months were generally named in the same way, but on occasion they were designated by the elements of the *địa-chi* (14.51). However, the year started with **dần**: *tháng dần* first month [of lunar year], *tháng mão* second month, *tháng thìn* third month, *tháng tý* eleventh month, *tháng sửu* twelfth month. These months had either twenty-nine (**tháng thiếu** 'incomplete month') or thirty (**tháng đủ** 'full month') days. Every third year there was an intercalary month (**tháng nhuận**), to make up the discrepancy in timing. The lunar months were divided into three decades, called **tuần**: **thượng tuần** waxing decade (first ten days of month, designated **mồng** [or **mùng**]), **trung-tuần** middle decade (11th through 20th), and **hạ-tuần** waning decade (last nine or ten days). The fifteenth day was called **ngày rằm** day of the full moon. The first day was optionally designated **ngày sóc**, the last **ngày hối**. There are also special terms for the first quarter (**thượng-huyền** waxing quarter) and the last quarter (**hạ-huyền** waning quarter) of the moon.

The seasons of the year are traditionally four: **mùa xuân** spring, **mùa hè** (or **hạ**) summer (*hạ* is more formal), **mùa thu** autumn, **mùa đông** winter. Each season is thought of as having three parts: **mạnh** beginning, **trọng** middle, and **quý** end. Thus we find *mạnh xuân* early spring (or first month of spring), *trọng hạ* mid-summer, *quý đông* end of winter. In the southern part of the country there are actually two seasons, **mùa mưa** rainy season, and **mùa nóng** hot [dry] season. However, even there, the four-way division is often recognized. Winter is the coolest season with short days at the end of the lunar year; the new year is heralded as the arrival of spring (**tân xuân** new spring).

324

Years (năm) are designated according to the western calendar for the most part; the word *năm* is simply followed by the number of the year as descriptive complement. This number is often shortened to the last two digits for dates in the present century, just as is the practice in English.

> *năm một nghìn chín trăm năm mươi ba* 1953 (short form: *năm năm mươi ba*)
>
> *năm một nghìn tám trăm tám mươi chín* 1889

In giving dates, the day is generally mentioned first, then the month, finally the year. The word *năm* 'year' is often omitted from such citations. In writing, figures are nearly always used.

> *(ngày) mồng tám tháng chín (năm) sáu mươi mốt* September 8th, (19)61 (generally written *(ngày) mồng 8 tháng 9, 1961*)

In older usage years were indicated by the word *năm* and the appropriate element of the *địa-chi* (14.51). The specific reference was to be deduced from the context—for example, if a person was speaking of his own birth date a rough estimate of his age would lead to the correct series of years involved. In annals and the like the reference was clarified by reference to the reigning monarch.

Note also the expressions **năm nay** this year, **năm ngoái** or **năm rồi** last year, **sang năm** next year.

14.6. Measures.

In addition to the divisions of time (treated in 14.5) there are special expressions for measuring size, distance, weight, quantity and value. A general statement can be made about one typical construction of such measuring expressions: the dimension involved is stated by an extended state verb (9.55) and the specification of measurement is added as a following complement:

> *Cái nhà này* **dài bao nhiêu?** How long is this house?
>
> *Cái nhà này* **dài tám thước.** This house is eight metres long.
>
> *Hà-nội* **cách** *đây* **mấy cây số?** How many kilometres is Hanoi from here?
>
> *Hà-nội* **cách** *đây* **hai chục cây số.** Hanoi is around twenty kilometres from here.
>
> *Thùng ấy* **nặng bao nhiêu?** How heavy is that crate?
>
> *Thùng ấy* **nặng** *độ chừng* **mười cân.** That crate weighs about ten pounds.
>
> *Đồi ấy* **cao bao nhiêu?** How high is that hill?
>
> *Đồi ấy* **cao ba mươi thước.** That hill is thirty metres high.

In the case of price the general categorical **giá** 'price' serves in place of a verb in a question (and is generally omitted in the answer). The predicates are of course substantival.

Cái áo này **giá bao nhiêu?** What's the price of this tunic?
Cái áo này **một trăm đồng.** This tunic [costs] one hundred
piastres.

However, questions about quantity simply make use of the indefinite forms
bao nhiêu 'however much, many' and **mấy** 'however much, many (often
presuming a quantity less than ten)' with appropriate substantives. This
includes the use of **bao nhiêu tiền?** 'how much money', a very common
colloquial way of asking price.

Ở trong phòng có **bao nhiêu người?** How many people are there
in the room?
Ở trong phòng có **sáu mươi mấy người.** There are sixty-odd
people in the room.
Ông mua **mấy quyển sách?** How many books are you buying?
Tôi mua **ba quyển.** I'm buying three.
Quyển này **bao nhiêu tiền?** How much is this one [book]?
Quyển này **tám mươi hai đồng.** This one [book] is eighty-two
piastres.

In the following sections the exact values of the more common units of
measure are given.

14.61. Size and Distance

are measured primarily in terms of linear and
square units. In this case some of the units from the traditional system of
measurement have been readapted to fit the European system brought by
the French. The actual measurements involved are different, but the context generally makes clear which system is involved. In cases where it
does not, the term **tây** 'west' is added as a descriptive complement to a
measurement to signal that the European system is referred to; in some
other cases the word **ta** (presumably here 'you and I', i.e., 'our') signals
that the native system is involved.

UNIT	CONSISTING OF	ORIGINAL VALUE (IN METRIC TERMS)		TRANSFERRED VALUE (IN METRIC SYSTEM)
ly		0 m 0004,	0 m²04	millimeter
phân	10 *ly* (6 sq *ly*)	0 m 004,	0 m²24	centimeter
tấc [thốn]	10 *phân*	0 m 04,	2 m²40	decimeter [inch]
thước [xích]	10 *tấc*	0 m 40,	24 m²	meter [yard]
bộ [ngũ]	5 *thước*	2 m		
trượng	10 *thước*	4 m		
lý	360 *bộ*	720 m		[mile]
sào [cao]	15 sq *thước*	360 m²		
mẫu	10 *sào*	3600 m²		

326

Note among the values for square measurement that **phân** referred in the traditional system to 6 square *ly*. The Vietnamese forms in brackets are pseudo-bases appearing in forms borrowed from Chinese. The English values in brackets refer to Anglo-American (rough) equivalents. Longer distances are measured in kilometers (**cây số**).

14.62. Weight was traditionally measured by a system in which the smaller units were designated by the same words as those in the linear-square system (14.61). Here, however, the words were for the most part not transferred to the metric system. Only the word **cân** (generally with complement **tây**) is occasionally used for kilogram, and the direct borrowing **ki-lô** is more common.

UNIT	CONSISTING OF	VALUE (IN METRIC TERMS)
hào		0 gr 0037
ly	10 *hào*	0 gr 037
phân	10 *ly*	0 gr 37
đồng or tiền	10 *phân*	3 gr 778
lạng	10 *đồng*	37 gr 783
cân	16 *lạng*	604 gr 50
yến	10 *cân*	6 kg 045
tạ	10 *yến*	60 kg 450

Some of these terms are used as rough equivalents of Anglo-American weights: **lạng** ounce, **cân** pound.

14.63. Money is based on a unit called the **đồng (bạc)**, probably originally 3.778 grams of silver (see 14.62), the French equivalent of which is *piastre* (English *piaster*). This system, of course, dates from the French colonial period. No earlier monetary system is discussed here. In the earlier economy the *đồng* was valuable enough so that a hundredth part of it was coined, as well as pieces of one- and two-tenths (still in use until quite recently). At the time of this writing international exchange recognizes approximately seventy-two *đồng* as the equivalent of the US dollar.

UNIT	CONSISTING OF
xu	
cắc [hào, giác]	10 *xu*
đồng	10 *cắc*

In citing monetary values the additive construction is used (8.33); they are written with the dollar sign or a lower case *đ* (especially in more recent usage) following the number of *đồng*:

5$, 5đ	*năm đồng (bạc)*	five piasters
5$20, 5đ20	*năm đồng hai (cắc)*	five piasters and twenty cents

0$52, 0đ52	*không đồng năm cắc hai*	(no piasters and) fifty-two cents
5$10, 5đ10	*năm đồng mốt* or	five piasters and ten cents
	năm đồng một cắc	
5$40, 5đ40	*năm đồng tư* or	five piasters and forty cents
	năm đồng bốn cắc	
5$02, 5đ02	*năm đồng hai xu* or	five piasters and two cents
	năm đồng lẻ hai (xu)	
120$, 120đ	*một trăm hai mươi đồng*	one hundred and twenty piasters
2$35, 2đ35	*hai đồng ba cắc năm (xu)*	two piasters and thirty-five cents
	or	
	hai đồng ba mươi lăm (xu)	

The terms **hào** and **giác** for units of ten *xu* are more formal; they appear in written texts and in some more careful speech.

14.7. Patterns of Modification

14.7. Patterns of Modification involve a number of differences from those characteristic in English. Several devices serve to maintain the social context of a conversation—the relationship between the speaker and his surroundings (14.71). In both speech and writing the descriptive complement is exceedingly popular, primarily as a means of specifying something more clearly or in more detail (14.72). Expressions covering accompaniment and transport (14.73) involve a pattern which seems inverse to that of English. There are special uses of the sequential construction (9.66) which may be called **causative-resultive** (14.72) and **purposive** (14.75). The designation of colors involves some special features (14.76).

14.71. Social Context Signals

14.71. Social Context Signals. Especially in conversation there appear numerous expressions which serve to maintain a clear picture of the social context. This includes not only the use of appropriate status words referring to the people involved and various particles and special vocabulary for certain levels of speech (13.2), but the addition of complements (especially descriptive complements) referring to certain obvious elements of the situation at hand which, strictly speaking, might seem quite unnecessary to mention. For example, in the southern dialect area speakers make a great deal of use of the demonstrative **đó** 'there [near you]'; it serves roughly the purpose of a final particle (11.4) in many sentences, simply relating the question or comment involved to the hearer. (In this use it regularly has weak stress [5.21].)

> *Chà! Đường 'xấu lắm °đó.* Gee! It's a terrible road [as you know].
> *°Cái 'để °cho một °cái 'để °đó!* The topic—give [us] a topic [so we can discuss it]—it's your responsibility!
> *Đi 'đâu °đó?—Đi 'chợ °đó.* Where you going?—To market—you know.

The same tendency may be seen in complements which occur with greetings. For example, a servant at the house often greets the returning employer:

Chào ông **mới về**. [I] greet you [who have] just returned.

Some other examples of this sort of usage follow:

Chào anh Lâm **đã đến**. Hello, Mr. Lâm. ["greet elder-brother Lâm anterior arrive"]

Chào anh **về**. Goodbye. (You're going home.)

14.72. Specification makes extensive use of the descriptive complement. Since the pattern involves adding these complements after their respective heads, sequences are often found where more and more specifiers are added, bit by bit, sometimes accompanied by repetition of the head, sometimes not. The following conversation, reported in a story, shows several examples:

—*Thưa thầy, ở làng bên có người muốn bán một ngôi nhà, thầy có mua không?*

'Sir [young man speaking to future father-in-law], in a neighboring village there's a fellow [who] wants to sell a villa, do you [want to] buy it?'

—*Nhà* **to hay nhỏ**, có tốt không *cậu?*

'A big or small house? Is it a good one?'

—*Thưa thầy* **tốt lắm** *ạ, nhà* **ngói năm gian**, cột bằng lim, cửa bằng gụ *và* cột cũng khá to.

'Yes, sir, it's a very good one—a house with a tiled roof, five rooms, pillars of iron-wood, doors of *gụ* [a fine hard wood] and the pillars are quite big.'

—*Thế* cột bằng nào?

'So, the pillars are how big?'

—*Thưa thầy,* cột to bằng này.

'Sir, this big [demonstrating by gesture].'

A descriptive passage from a novel (Khái Hưng, *Tiêu Sơn Tráng Sĩ* [The Hero of Tiêu-sơn], Hanoi, 1951, p.7) shows similar features.

Chàng y phục nai nịt gàng, đầu đội nón lông đen, chân đi hia chẽn, cổ quấn một cái khăn lụa trắng thắt lỏng, mối bỏ rủ sau lưng. His clothes were neat battle dress—[his] head (wearing) a black fur hat, feet (walking in) tight mandarin boots, [around his] neck [there was] rolled a scarf of white silk, knotted loosely, the end allowed to hang behind [his] back.

14.73. Accompaniment and Transport. While in English a verb denoting directional movement or some other action is generally modified by an expression specifying accompaniment or transport of persons or things (*go carrying one's belongings, come bearing gifts, eat together,* etc.), the typical pattern is in reverse in Vietnamese: the main verb signals accompaniment or transport (often with a descriptive complement denoting the persons or objects involved), and it is followed by a verb (often with its own complement) stating the direction or more specific action involved; the construction is sequential (9.66).

> *Cách mấy hôm sau hai cha con cậu nhỏ* **đưa nhau đến đền vua.**
> A few days later the father and his young son went together to the king's palace.

> *Hai thằng trộm vội ra bờ ruộng và* **khiêng chum vàng về nhà**
> *định mở ra chia nhau.* The two thieves hurried out to the edge of the rice field and brought home the pot of gold, carrying it between the two of them, intending to open it up and divide [the contents] between them.

> *Ba ông bạn đồng-hành Mỹ-Việt lại* **cùng nhau đàm-đạo** *như*
> *thường-lệ.* The three friends—American and Vietnamese fellow travelers—again were conversing together as usual.

On the other hand, these expressions often correspond to English sequences of verb with a following adverbial modifier—*take away, bring up, fall down,* etc.

> *Xin anh* **đem cái va-li này đi.** Please take this suitcase away.

> *Ngày hôm sau đàn chim lại đến ăn, người chồng* **đưa cái túi ra**
> *thì đàn chim bảo nhắm mắt lại rồi hóa-phép* **cõng anh ta bay**
> **đi** *nhanh lắm.* The next day the flock of birds returned to eat; the husband brought the pouch out and the flock of birds told [him] to close [his] eyes, then performed a miracle [and] carried him on [their] backs, flying away very fast.

Sometimes the second verb follows the first immediately, and the expression denoting the person or thing conveyed or accompanied appears as complement to this verb phrase. This seems especially frequent where the expression denoting the person or thing conveyed or accompanied is a long one, and the second verb has no complement of its own.

> *Điều mà các ông chú-trọng đến nhất là* **đem theo** *mấy ảnh và máy*
> *quay phim đi.* The thing they were most particular about was bringing along a [still] camera and a movie camera. (Note that the expression **máy quay phim đi** 'movie camera' involves this same type of expression: 'a machine [for] turning film [and] going.')

14.74. Causative-Resultive Expressions make use of the sequential
construction (9.66) with a momentary action verb (9.55) in first position stating the causal action or condition, and another verb in second position

(often an extended state verb) stating the result or effect, generally with a following complement specifying the person or thing affected. The most common verb in first position is **làm** 'do, make', but a variety of others also occur.

> *Tôi* **làm đau** *con mèo.* I hurt the cat. (Cf. *Con mèo đau.* The cat is in pain.)
>
> *Loài chuột* **phá hại** *chúng ta lắm.* Rats make a lot of trouble for us. (Cf. *Loài chuột hại lắm.* Rats are very destructive.)
>
> *Ngày hôm sau đàn chim lại đến ăn, người chồng đưa cái túi ra thì đàn chim* **bảo nhắm** *mắt lại rồi hóa-phép cõng anh ta bay đi nhanh lắm.* The next day the flock of birds returned to eat; the husband brought the pouch out and the flock of birds told [him] to close [his] eyes, then performed a miracle [and] carried him on [their] backs, flying away very fast.
>
> *Anh ta* **lấy đầy** *túi rồi lại cười lên mình chim mà về.* He filled ["take be-full"] the pouch, then climbed back on the bird's back to return home.

Note that this type of expression does not in itself connote intention; this is conveyed rather by purposive expressions (14.75). Compare the following:

> *Tôi làm đau con mèo.* I hurt the cat [as a result of something I did, but it was not necessarily intentional].
>
> *Tôi làm cho con mèo đau.* I hurt the cat [intentionally, e.g., as a punishment].

14.75. Purposive Expressions make use of the sequential construction

(9.66) with the verb **cho** 'give' in second position, usually followed by a complement specifying the person, thing or situation served. It not only states the responsibility for the action but also implies intention (cf. 14.74). The complement is sometimes a substantival phrase or focus, sometimes a clause. The verb *cho* is nearly always accompanied by weak stress unless the following complement is lacking.

> *Nó không 'biết làm, anh đi* **làm 'cho.** He [a child] doesn't know how to do [it], you go do [it] for [him].
>
> *Đêm ngày tôi thường °cầu-nguyện để xin Thượng-đế cho cha tôi sinh mấy đứa em 'nữa để chúng °nó chơi °với tôi °cho 'vui.* Night and day I (customarily) pray (to ask) God to permit my father to give birth to some more younger brothers and sisters so that they [can] play with me to make things pleasant.
>
> *Hai họ thường ngồi chung để* **nói chuyện cho** *dễ.* The two families usually sit together to make it easy to converse.
>
> *Anh làm ơn* **mở cửa cho** *tôi.* Please open the door for me.

331

Xin ông **viết thơ cho** *tôi biết.* Please write and let me know.
Ông ấy **mua thóc cho** *một người tàu.* He's buying [unhusked]
rice for [the account of] a Chinese.
In some cases there is ambiguity (usually cleared up by the context) as to
whether the action is accomplished for someone to relieve him of the burden or to supply him with something.

Chị ấy **viết thơ cho** *tôi.* She wrote me a letter (i.e., wrote a
letter addressed to me) *or* She wrote a letter for me.
Anh **bán quyển sách này cho** *tôi không?* Will you sell this book
to (*or* for) me?

14.76. Color Designations.
The basic words denoting colors are ex-
tended state verbs (9.55). One important difference in segmentation of the
spectrum is that the shades generally called *blue* and *green* in English are
included under one general word in Vietnamese: **xanh** (formal **thanh**, a
pseudo-base). Descriptive complements are of course often added to specify
which of various shades is referred to: *xanh biếc* sky blue, *xanh lá* leaf
green, etc.

Many words specifying colors, however, are not verbs, but substantives.
In sentences where such words serve as predicates, they appear as complements to the general categorical **màu** (or **mầu**) 'color', and the predicate
is of the substantival type (9.11). (Verb color words appear in this use as
well of course.)

Cái này **màu vàng.** This (thing) is yellow. (*vàng* gold)
Thứ này không phải **màu da cam.** This kind is not orange-colored.
["color skin orange"]

In older usage, and still surviving in idiomatic speech today, descriptive complements denoting colors of certain inanimate objects and animals
are not the usual color words. There is rather an extensive usage similar
to the limited pattern exhibited by English *bay mare*, etc. For example,
the general word for 'black' is the extended state verb **đen** 'be black' but
note the following expressions:

chó **mực** black dog (*mực* ink)
mèo **mun** black cat (*mun* ebony)
đũa **mun** black chopsticks
ngựa **ô** black horse, (*ô* crow, raven, pseudo-base)
bò **hóng** black steer, cow (*hóng* soot, pseudo-base)
khăn **thâm** black turban (*thâm* be deep; blue-black)

14.8. Taboo Replacement Forms. In former times, and still today in families which have been little affected by western culture, ordinary words which are homonymous or very similar to proper names of special significance in the locality are avoided. These are the names of persons and places commanding special respect or dread—revered ancestors, recent dead, powerful nobility, persons touched by insanity or crime, places haunted by some crime or disaster. For example, in one family, the father's given name was *Đậu*, which is nearly homonymous with *đậu* 'bean.' Other members of the family avoided this form, saying instead [dịw].

The homonymous (or nearly homonymous) words are replaced either by synonyms which bear little or no phonemic resemblance to the original, or by variants of the words themselves in which the vowel nucleus is altered. Some of the latter types are well known as dialectal variants, others seem to occur only in this specialized usage. Only a careful study of a full body of data will reveal whether there is an underlying derivative pattern. The hundred-odd forms collected are insufficient for this purpose, but some of them are listed below (in Hanoi pronunciation) to give a notion of the character of the phenomenon. (No attempt is made here to separate dialectal variants from apparent taboo derivatives.)

ORIGINAL FORM		TABOO REPLACEMENT FORM
kim	actual, present	[kâm]
minh	clear, bright	[mênh]
nghĩa	idea	[ngãj]
nếp	glutinous [rice]	[niếp]
đều	be equal	[dìw]
tết	New Year festival	[tiết]
thu	autumn	[thâw]
mò	to grope [for]	[mùw]
khom	be bent, curved	[khum]
nước	liquid	[nák]
đường	road	[dàng]
khá	be rather good	[khóγ]
mai	tomorrow	[moj]
cao	be high, tall	[kiw]
màu	color	[mìw]
tâm	heart	[tim]
tầng	story [of building]	[từng]
sanh	be born	[sinh]
ăn	eat	[en]

14.9. Problems of Semantic Range. One startling way that languages
represent special facets of the cultures they serve is in the relative number
of distinctions in unitary vocabulary items made as compared with the
items of the real universe for which they stand. While in English there are
many discrete forms denoting various kinds of garments worn over the
shoulders and extending down the trunk of the body (*shirt, blouse, sweater,
coat, jacket, slip, shawl, cape, smock, tunic,* etc.) Vietnamese makes do
with a single basic item **áo**, which covers all these meanings in general.
It can be modified by descriptive complements to express more exactly
what is meant if this is desired, but the speaker is not forced to do so as
he is by the selection of different words in English: *áo sơ-mi* [western
style] shirt, *áo len* sweater ["tunic wool"], *áo mưa* raincoat ["tunic rain"],
etc. This reflects something about the basic simplicity of traditional Vietnamese dress. On the other hand, the English word *rice* has no general
consistent equivalent in Vietnamese, simply because the Vietnamese
speaker is forced to distinguish the various forms of this basic staple of
his diet:

> *mạ* rice seedling [at time of transplanting]
> *lúa* rice growing in field
> *thóc* harvested but unhusked rice
> *gạo* husked rice
> *cơm* cooked rice

It is not the purpose of this section to provide any full accounting of
these varying systems of vocabulary reference, but rather to alert the
student to the kind of problem involved. Another example, however, is
interesting: corresponding to the English verb 'carry' (and some special
directional substitutes like *bring, take,* which have no precise equivalents
in Vietnamese; cf. 14.73) there are several words which specify different
manners of carrying, including two rather general forms.

> *đem* carry [in general]
> *đưa* carry or convey [with notion of delivery]
> *mang* carry or wear on body [especially strapped over shoulder],
>   take with oneself
> *vác* carry [generally something reasonably heavy] on shoulder;
>   on back of animal
> *xách* carry suspended from hand [usually by a handle]
> *đội* carry or wear on head
> *cõng* carry on one's back
> *cầm* carry grasped in hand [usually something relatively light]
> *ôm* carry in both arms and hugged against body
> *bồng* carry [a child] in one's arms

ẵm carry [a baby] in one's arms
khiêng [two people] carry, sharing the weight
gánh carry two things balanced, one suspended at each end of a
   shoulder bar
quẩy carry suspended at one end of a shoulder bar
đeo wear [as jewelry, glasses, etc.]
đèo carry on one's vehicle
bưng carry in both hands and held relatively high before one
bê carry in both hands and held relatively low

Glossary of Difficult Forms

A few forms involve special difficulties, either because there are two or more homonymous forms with disparate meanings and uses,[1] or because there is a single word with a wide range of meanings in conjunction with other words (idioms) so that it is nearly impossible to supply a gloss which will suggest this range, or because the use of a word in a construction different from its usual one involves semantic shifts not predictable from the English gloss. These problems relate to a number of grammatical topics, but it would not be feasible to treat them under any one of these. It has therefore seemed wise to include an alphabetical list of such difficult forms, together with illustrative examples. Note that certain other individual forms are conveniently treated in connection with specific items of structure; reference to them may be found in the index.

ăn [momentary action verb, 9.55]
Several quite different English translations correspond to this Vietnamese form; it is difficult to say whether some four different words are involved, or whether some or all of them are related. They are presented here as separate entities.

    ăn 1. eat; bite, chew
        ăn cơm eat, have a meal
        ăn đói not have enough to eat
        ăn đường eat enroute, on the road
        ăn giầu chew betel
        ăn ngon be delicious, make fine eating
        ăn uống eat and drink; live, get along
        làm ăn make a living, earn one's livelihood

---

[1] It is sometimes difficult or impossible to determine precisely whether these are single words with a wide range of meaning, or several homonymous forms. Unless the relationships of meanings are quite clear, they are treated here as separate homonymous forms.

ăn 2. celebrate; do something seriously, wholeheartedly
> ăn *chơi* have a good time
> ăn *hỏi* celebrate a betrothal
> ăn *mừng* celebrate, rejoice
> ăn *nói* talk, be a talker
> ăn *tiêu* spend [a good deal of money]

ăn 3. conform to, harmonize with
> ăn *mặc* to dress [in a particular way]
> ăn *ở* behave [in a particular way]
> ăn *chịu* withstand, endure, undergo
> ăn *giá* be of appropriate price

ăn 4. absorb, attack, penetrate, seize, overwhelm, win, procure illegally (generally pejorative)
> ăn *cắp* steal, pilfer
> ăn *cướp* seize, take by force
> ăn *hại* live at the expense of [someone]
> ăn *hiếp* to bully, oppress
> ăn *béo* to practice the "squeeze," misappropriate employer's funds
> ăn *tiền* take a bribe
> ăn *gian* to cheat
> ăn *giải* win a prize
> ăn *đêm* ply one's trade at night [speaking of thieves, prostitutes, etc.]

cả
> cả 1. descriptive particle, 11.62] large, immense; eldest, first born
>> *Ao sâu nước* cả, *khôn tìm cá.* [In a] deep pond [with] a large amount of water, [one must be] clever to catch fish.—Ngơ Khuyến
>> *Người ấy là con* cả *của ông Lâm.* That fellow is Mr. Lâm's eldest child.

> cả 2. [postpositive noncontained particle, 11.82] all of, also, including, as a whole, at all (emphasizes entirety; cf. *cùng* 3., *hết*)
>> *Không ai đến* cả. No one at all arrived.
>> *Tôi uống* cả *một cốc rượu rồi.* I've drunk a whole glass of wine.
>> *Bán* cả *nhà cũng không đủ trả nợ.* Even selling the house, [we] still won't have enough to pay off the debt.
>> *Mất* cả *vợ* cả *con.* [He] lost both his wife and his children.

Note that phrases consisting of this postpositive particle with its own following complement sometimes appear as focal complements:
> Cả nhà nầy *làm bằng cây.* (S) This whole house is made of wood.

cách

cách 1. [general categorical, 8.62] fashion, manner, way
Các người ấy luôn-luôn làm việc một **cách** *khí-lực.* Those people
always work energetically.
Ông định đi bằng **cách** *nào?* How [by what means of transporta-
tion] did you decide to go?

cách 2. [extended state verb, 9.55] be separated by [a certain]
distance from
Làng ấy **cách** *đây hai cây số.* That village is two kilometers
from here.
Note there is also a pseudo-base **cách** 'to change, disrupt', as in *cách-
mạng* 'to revolt.'

càng [prepositive particle, 11.81] increasingly; often used correlatively:
càng...càng the more ..., the more ...
Anh khôn tôi đã mừng, anh biết tôi lại **càng** *mừng.* [If] you're
clever I'm delighted (already), [if] you [really] know [some-
thing] I'm still more delighted.
*Tiếng âm-nhạc du-dương ở góc phòng do một máy phóng-thanh tung
ra* **càng** *làm cho câu truyện ba người thêm vui-vẻ.* The sound of
harmonious music coming from a loudspeaker in the corner of
the room added to the stories of the three people so that they
were still more pleasant.
Con tầu **càng** *ra xa bờ* **càng** *chạy nhanh hơn.* The farther the boat
got from the shore, the faster it went.
Mùa nầy trời **càng** *ngày* **càng** *nóng.* (S) This season it gets
hotter by the day.

chỉ

chỉ 1. [item noun, 8.66] thread, string
*Người ta tin là khi hai người lấy nhau thì có một vị-thần ở trên
Giời lấy hai sợi* **chỉ** *hồng xe lại với nhau thành một sợi.*
People believe that when two people get married ["take one-
another"] there is a benevolent spirit up in heaven [who]
takes the two pink strands [representing their individual
destinies] [and] spins [them] together (with each other),
making a single strand.

chỉ 2. [momentary action verb, 9.55] point out, direct, indicate, show,
demonstrate
Ông làm ơn **chỉ** *đường cho tôi.* Please show me the way.

Đang nói thì cụ Đàm lại **chỉ** *cho hai ông xem một đoàn thuyền
khác.* While talking cụ Đàm pointed out (for the two fellows
to look at) another group of different boats.

chỉ 3. [prepositive particle, 11.81] just, only, nothing but

Vợ ông **chỉ** *biết khóc mà thương cho duyên-kiếp mình không ra
gì, không hề oán-trách chồng.* His wife was of such a personality [that she] only wept, regretting that her predestination
turned out to be so disappointing ["came to nothing"]; she
never reproached [her] husband.

Tôi **chỉ** *có bốn đồng thôi.* I have only four piasters.

Chỉ *tôi và anh biết việc ấy thôi.* Only you and I know about that
affair.

chỉ 4. [pseudo-base] command, order

*Khi dân làng nhận được chiếu-***chỉ** *của vua và cả số trâu, gạo thì
mọi người lấy làm kỳ-dị quá sức.* When the people of the village received the order of the king and the [specified] quantity
of buffalo [and] rice, everyone took it to be enormously strange.

chớ

chớ 1. [negative, prohibitive 9.4] better not, avoid, keep from, don't

Chớ *nên hút thuốc.* One shouldn't smoke.

Chớ *uống rượu.* Don't drink alcoholic beverages.

Phải chi ông **chớ** *cờ bạc, thì không đến đỗi nghèo.* (S) If he had
kept from gambling he wouldn't have turned into a poor man.

Note that this form appears as second head in choice questions (9.67).
However, this usage is infrequent in the north.

Ông ấy đương ăn cơm **chớ***?* (S) Is he having his meal [right now]?

Ông đi Sài-gòn **chớ***?* Are you going to Saigon?

chớ 2. (N **chứ**, which see) [coordinating particle, 11.51] and [not],
[but] to the contrary, still, as a matter of fact (introducing contradictory
clause)

Dầu cha tôi khó ở, **chớ** *chẳng phải là đau nặng.* (S) Although my
father's not too well, still [he's] not seriously ill.

Tờ giấy nầy là chánh, **chớ** *không phải giả.* (S) This document is
authentic, not false.

chớ 3. (N **chứ**, which see) [final particle, 11.4] contrary to what is
suggested or stated or might be expected; of course, as you ought to
know.

Đi đâu đó?–Đi làm **chớ***!* (S) Where [you] going?–To work, of
course!

Tôi ở Việt-nam hai năm, rồi mới đi **chớ***!* (S) I'll be in Viet Nam for two years before I leave. (contradicting the suggestion of only a short stay)

chứ (S **chớ**, which see)
  chứ 1. [coordinating particle, 11.51] and [not], [but] to the contrary, still, as a matter of fact

Mày muốn có em thì cha mày phải lấy vợ nữa **chứ** *một mình cha mày thì để làm sao được!* [If] you want to have younger brothers and sisters, then your father will have to marry again, otherwise how can your father alone have children?

Cái này của tôi, **chứ** *không phải là của anh.* This belongs to me and not to you.

Lúc ấy cả quan và nha chỉ giương mắt ra mà nhìn sự thật **chứ** *còn hống-hách gì được nữa.* Then both the mandarin and [his] office staff will just be wide-eyed and stare at the truth, and no more intimidation of any sort will be possible.

  chứ 2. [final particle, 11.4] contrary to what is suggested or stated or might be expected; of course, as you ought to know

Vậy khi chúng tôi sang Việt-nam có được hân-hạnh gặp các cô, các bà không?—Có lắm **chứ.** So when we get to Viet Nam will we have the pleasure of meeting girls and married ladies?—Of course.

Anh chưa làm à?—Làm rồi **chứ***!* You haven't done it yet, eh?—Oh, yes I have!

của [general categorical, 8.62]
This word is often translated 'belong(ing) to' and thought of as some kind of verbal, but it is clearly a general categorical which is very common as the center of a substantival predicate (9.11). (Note the negated predicate in the second example below.)

Tôi bị nhà tôi cháy, nên mất **của** *hết.* My house burned, so I lost all my belongings.

Cái này **của** *tôi, chứ không phải là* **của** *anh.* This belongs to me, not to you.

It is also common as head of a substantival descriptive phrase which itself serves as descriptive complement to a longer head, specifying the possessor of an object or quality or the agent responsible for some action or idea.

mấy lời tỏ ý khen ngợi **của** *thày giáo* a few words of congratulation from the teacher

340

Trong cuộc tiến-hóa của *nhân-loại, cứ đến mỗi thời-kỳ nhất định lại xảy ra những cuộc cách-mạng. Hiện-tượng ấy như là một định-luật tự-nhiên* của *con người khi sự sống của con người gặp phải những trở-lực ngăn-cản và muốn vượt qua, phải đánh ngã trở-lực ấy.* In the evolution of the human species, as each [new] era arrives revolutions are again sure to come about. This phenomenon is like a natural law of mankind [to the effect that] when [in] human life [one] has the misfortune to meet with impeding obstacles and wishes to overcome [them], [one] must strike down those obstacles.

cùng [verb, 9.55]
This may be a single word with the basic meaning 'coincide, be coterminous' and successively more abstract special developments connected with the terminal portion of the concept involved: 'accompany, coincide [with]; be coterminous with the whole of something, all the way to the end; be arrived at the end of something, be at the end of one's resources.' It seems most helpful to separate the uses into four categories:

cùng 1. accompany; coincide, be simultaneous [with]; act in the same way
> *Hai đứa con nầy* **cùng** *một cha mẹ.* (S) These two children are of the same parents.
> *Hai cái nhà kia cất gần nhau* **cùng** *trên một miếng đất.* Those two houses are built close together on the same lot.
> *Chúng ta* **cùng** *nhau đi thăm ông Bính nằm nhà thương.* Let's go together to visit Mr. Bính (lying) [in] the hospital.

cùng 2. be everywhere, all inclusive, along the whole extent of
> *Nước* **cùng** *hết.* There's water everywhere.
> *Tôi quét* **cùng** *nhà.* I've swept the entire house.
> *Hồi ở Việt-nam tôi đã đi* **cùng**. When [I] was in Viet Nam I went everywhere.

cùng 3. be at the end [of something] [with the notion of complete coverage], terminate, be at an end, be final, definitive (emphasizes final portion; cf. *hết, cả* 2.)
> *Ở gần Cam-ly đường* **cùng** *rồi.* Near Cam-Ly the road ends.
> *Tôi muốn cố gắng làm việc này tới* **cùng**. I want to see this work through to the end.

cùng 4. be poor, destitute
> **Cùng** *quá hóa liều.* [If one] is excessively poor [one is apt to] be transformed [and] take foolhardy risks. (i.e., Poverty makes men desperate.)—Folk saying

cứ

The verb with the meaning 'be based on, dependent on, persistent' is rare. The preverb with the meaning 'continuing without interruption, definitely, insistently' could be considered an extended use of the verb (and it would be reclassified as an auxiliary, 9.54); the prepositive particle meaning 'coinciding with every...' is perhaps a further specialization. It seems most helpful with the present analysis to consider them separate forms.

cứ 1. [extended state verb, 9.55] be based on, dependent on, essential, continual, perpetual, persistent

Anh **cứ** *việc ăn.* You're always eating. ["elder-brother be-perpetual business-of eat"]

Chẳng **cứ.** That's not necessarily [the case].

Mật nghe hát không thèm để trí, **cứ** *việc làm thinh như không nghe biết gì.* Mật heard [him] sing [but] felt no urge to pay attention, continued ignoring [him] as if [she] was unaware of hearing anything.

cứ 2. [preverb, 11.72] continuing without interruption, definitely, insistently, in spite of adverse circumstances

Anh ấy **cứ** *làm việc.* He continued to work.

Tôi muốn cho em tôi **cứ** *đi học, nên tôi phải đi làm.* I want to [arrange it so that] my younger brother [can] continue going to school [without interruption], so I must work.

Tôi gọi anh ấy hai ba lần, mà anh ấy vẫn **cứ** *ngủ.* I called him two or three times, but he went right on sleeping.

Cứ *đọc sách đi.* Keep on reading [i.e., don't stop].

cứ 3. [prepositive particle, 11.81] coinciding with every ..., on each [occasion], whenever

Cứ *hai mươi phút một, anh ấy lại đi mở cửa.* Every twenty minutes he goes and opens the door (again).

Trong cuộc tiến-hóa của nhân-loại, **cứ** *đến mỗi thời-kỳ nhất định lại xảy ra những cuộc cách-mạng.* In the evolution of the human species, as each [new] era arrives revolutions are again sure to come about.

đã [tense marker, 9.3] anterior

Khi ông ấy đương đau, tôi **đã** *có ở đó lâu.* (S) When he was sick, I had already been there for a long time.

Tôi **đã** *không chịu đi Sài-gòn mà họ biểu tôi đi hoài.* (S) I wasn't willing to go to Saigon, but they made me go anyway.

Hai tháng rồi tôi **đã** *nói Việt-minh sẽ vô Lèo.* (S) I said two months
ago that the Viet Minh would go into Laos.

This word is fairly common as a descriptive complement, signalling that
its head denotes a circumstance viewed as completed prior to some other
circumstance (often, but not always, previously mentioned).

Ông uống nước **đã** *không?* Have you had enough (water) to drink?

Tôi đi chợ coi coi **đã**, *rồi sẽ mua.* Let me go to market and have
a look, then [if there are any things you want] I'll buy [them].

Thôi, nghỉ **đã**. [That's] enough, [let's] rest [before we do anything else].

Đừng nói lớn tiếng. Để cho những người lính Nhật ấy đi qua **đã**.
Don't raise [your] voice. Let those Japanese soldiers go past
first.

đánh [momentary action verb, 9.55]
This verb covers a much wider variety of meanings than any comparable
English word. The basic meaning is generally given as 'beat, hit, strike',
and many of the more specialized meanings can easily be seen to be related. In other uses the connections are less obvious. The following examples give a notion of the range.

đánh bạc gamble
đánh bài play cards
đánh bạn befriend
đánh bóng to polish
đánh cá to fish
đánh chén to eat and drink
đánh cờ to play chess
đánh cuộc to bet, wager
đánh dấu to mark; esp. to
place a diacritic by a
letter
đánh dây thép send a telegram

đánh ghen make a scene because
one is jealous
đánh giá appraise
đánh giày shine shoes
đánh lưới catch [birds, fish] with
a net
đánh máy (*chữ*) to type, use a type-
writer
đánh răng brush one's teeth
đánh thuế impose, levy a tax
đánh thuốc (*độc*) to poison
đánh vảy to scale [a fish]
đánh vần to spell [a word]

đi

đi 1. [momentary action verb as center 9.55] go; away (see also 9.64)
Tôi **đi** *chợ.* I'm going to market.
Chúng ta **đi** *bây giờ.* Let's go [i.e., leave a particular scene] now.
Đi *đâu đó?* Where [you] going?
Xin anh đem cái va-li này **đi**. Please take this suitcase away.

đi 2. [momentary action verb as complement, 9.62] go ahead ...
(exhortation often connotes impatience)

> *Đi đâu đi điếc gì, thì đi* **đi!** (S) Wherever you want to go, go
> ahead!
> *Anh nói* **đi!** Go ahead and talk!

đi 3. [final particle, 11.4] say! well! do you get it? you know what I
mean (adds exclamative note to sentence; together with notion of some
collusion or secret understanding with hearer) (conversational; generally
accompanied by weak stress)

> *Cô ấy đẹp quá* **đi!** That girl certainly is pretty [both you and I
> appreciate that kind of beauty]!
> *Không có xu nào* **đi!** I don't have a red cent [you know how it is
> to be low on funds]!

đi 4. [postpositive contained particle, 11.82] [emphasizes preceding
form] more intensely, definitely, extremely

> *Cảnh náo-nhiệt ngày thường đêm nay mất hẳn* **đi.** The usual daily
> bustle this evening is entirely missing. ["circumstance bustle
> day ordinary night now lose completely emphatic-particle"]

được

được 1. [momentary action verb, 9.55] receive, get, obtain; be benefited by, get to be, reach (see also 9.64)

> *Sáng nay chị tôi* **được** *thơ.* My [elder] sister got a letter this
> morning.
> *Em* **được** *mấy tuổi rồi?* How old are you? (speaking to a child)
> *Hôm nay tôi* **được** *bớt đau.* (S) I'm less ill today.
> *Vậy khi chúng tôi sang Việt-nam có* **được** *hân-hạnh gặp các cô,
> các bà không?* So when we get to Viet Nam will we have the
> pleasure of meeting girls and ladies?
> *Tôi* **được** *ông thương-yêu vì tôi siêng-năng.* I am esteemed by you
> because I am diligent.
> *Tôi* **được** *giàu có như ngày nay nhờ tôi cần-kiệm.* I'm as rich as I am
> today thanks to [the fact that] I've been thrifty.
> *Chỗ nầy làm cho người ta* **được** *mạnh-khỏe.* (S) This place makes
> one healthy.
> *Tôi* **được** *ăn.* I am permitted to eat.
> *Ông qua Việt-nam* **được** *bao lâu rồi?* (S) How long have you been
> in Viet Nam?

được 2. [extended state verb, 9.55] become a reality, result in something good; be (physically) possible, able

> *Trọn ngày đó và qua hôm sau tôi kiếm mãi, kiếm luôn, không*
> được. (S) All that day and the next I kept searching and search-
> ing, [but] it was no use.
> *Anh đi không* được. You can't go [because of ill health].
> *Món này ăn* được *không?*—Được *lắm!* (Host to guest:) Is this dish
> edible?—(Guest replying:) Very much so [i.e., delicious]!
> *Người đó làm việc hay lính hay quýnh quá, nên không* được *gì hết.*
> (S) That fellow works with such a fearful attitude so much of
> the time that he can't accomplish anything.

được 3. [postpositive contained particle, 11.82] fortunately, successfully, with a good result (cf. *phải* 3)

> *Ông ấy mua* được *một ngôi nhà to.* He purchased a large villa.
> *Chúng tôi sinh* được *một đứa con giai.* We've had a son born to us.
> *Anh không đi* được. You can't go [because of circumstances].

Structurally, *được* 1. 'receive' is set off fairly clearly from the other two
forms. It is frequently followed directly by a substantival complement;
when another predicate is involved, it follows *được*. The other two forms,
however, are less clearly separated from one another, and presumably they
are divergent uses of what was originally the same word. Wherever *được*
is predicate center (and *được* 1. is not involved) it is clearly *được* 2.
'become a reality; be physically possible', the extended state verb. In
some situations where *được* follows another verb or predicate phrase the
particle (*được* 3. 'successfully') is not distinguishable from the extended
state verb. In the following two cases the distinction is clear: (1) if *được*
is negated directly (e.g., *không được, chưa được*) the verb is involved; (2)
if *được* intervenes between the main verb and its substantival complement,
(e.g., *mua được nhà, bắt được hai con cá*) the particle is involved. Compare the following examples:

> *Tôi không* được *đi.* I am not permitted to go. (*được* 1.)
> *Tôi đi không* được. I am physically unable to go [e.g., because
> of poor health]. (*được* 2.)
> *Tôi không đi* được. I can't go [because of circumstance which
> makes it impossible]. (*được* 3.)
> *Tôi* được *bắt hai con cá.* I'm permitted to catch two fish. (*được* 1.)
> *Tôi bắt hai con cá* được. I'm able to catch two fish (presumably
> *được* 2.)
> *Tôi bắt* được *hai con cá.* I caught two fish. (*được* 3.)

hay

hay 1. [momentary action verb, 9.55] find out, learn, come to know [about something]

Ông hay *tin chưa?* Did you hear the news?

Khi nào ông nhất định đi, ông làm ơn cho tôi hay. Whenever you decide to go, please let me know.

hay 2. [extended state verb, 9.55] be good, interesting

Phim này hay *quá!* This film is very interesting!

Người ấy nói hay, *hát* hay, *cũng* hay *cờ.* That fellow speaks well, sings well, and is good at chess.

hay 3. [preverb, 11.72] often, frequently, customarily

Ông hay *đi Đà-lạt không?*—Hay *chớ.* (S) Do you go to Dalat often?— Sure!

Người đỏ làm việc hay *lính* hay *quýnh quá, nên không được gì hết.* That fellow works with such a fearful attitude so much of the time that he can't accomplish anything. (in interlocking order with *lính-quýnh,* cf. 7.8)

Chúng tôi sẽ không hay *đi thăm ông Bính.* We shan't go to visit Mr. Bính often.

Người Việt-nam hay *uống nước chè.* The Vietnamese [as a custom] drink tea.

This form differs from most preverbs in that it appears as a short answer (as in the first example above) and is negated as an auxiliary (9.54), but no environments supporting it as a predicative have been found.

hay 4. [prepositive particle, 11.81] 'or' (often with weak stress)

Ông ấy đi ra hay *đi về.* He went out [somewhere] or went home.

Tôi hay *ông sẽ đi chợ.* You or I will go to market.

Anh hay *em đứa nào mười lăm tuổi.* Which one is fifteen, the elder or younger brother?

Frequently the head which accompanies this particle is an identificational predicate introduced by là; in this case somewhat greater emphasis is given to the second alternative—it is more likely or more desirable.

Chiều nay chúng ta ở nhà, hay là *đi nhà anh Ba chơi?* This evening shall we stay home, or rather go to Mr. Ba's house to call?

Hay 4 is common in choice questions (9.67), as exemplified immediately above; in statements the somewhat more literary particle hoặc 'or' appears in similar environments, with the connotation that the alternatives are not mutually exclusive, while *hay* gives more the idea that if one alternative is in force the other cannot be.

Anh thích ăn cam hay *măng cụt?—Cam* hoặc *măng cụt cũng được.*
Do you like [to eat] oranges or mangosteens?—Oranges or
mangosteens—they're both all right. (*Hay* might well occur in
this sentence with little or no difference in force.)
Mặc dầu chậm tiến-hóa, hoặc *vì nghèo,* hoặc *vì nhiều lẽ khác,*
nhưng sự cạnh tranh cũng đã đưa người ta đến mỹ-thuật. Although progress is slow, either because of poverty, or for
many other reasons, still competition has led people to achieve
[something] artistic.

hãy

hãy 1. [preverb, 11.72] (let's) be sure to ...
Hãy *theo gương những kẻ nhân-đức.* [One should] follow the ex-
ample of virtuous people.
Ta hãy *chịu khó làm việc.* Let us work with patience.

hãy 2. [versatile particle, 11.83] still [before head]; ...first, before
[following head]
Hãy *còn sớm.* It's still early.
Chúng ta làm cái này hãy. Let's do this first.

hết [auxiliary, 9.54] be completely finished, all used up, all gone; no
longer; completely, to the very end (emphasizes aftermath of completion;
cf. *cả* 2., *cúng* 3.)
Đường hết *rồi.* The sugar is all used up.
Công việc ấy gần hết. That job is nearly complete.
Ăn cơm hết *thì ăn cháo.* [When you] finish eating rice then [you]
eat [rice] gruel.
Anh ấy tiêu hết *cả tiền rồi.* He's spent all the money already.
Lúc này tôi hết *đi Sài-gòn.* (S) I no longer go to Saigon now.
This verbal appears in a use much like that of postpositive particles
(11.82) emphasizing negative notions.
Chẳng thấy gì hết! Can't see a blessed thing!
Ông ấy không đi đâu hết. He's not going anywhere at all.
With certain descriptive complements of its own, it appears meaning 'with
all one's might, as ... as one can', etc.
Anh ấy ở đấy làm hết lòng. He's over there working as hard as
he can.
Bạn tôi nằm nhà thương, tôi hết sức *buồn cho bạn.* My friend is
(lying) in the hospital; I'm terribly sorry for him.

347

Following the comparative **hơn** (9.52) it adds the notion of a superlative.
Cô ấy đẹp **hơn hết**. She's the prettiest (of all).
Trong mấy người đó ông Hai nói tiếng Anh giỏi **hơn hết**. (S) Among
those people, Mr. Hai speaks English best.

lại

lại 1. [momentary action verb, 9.55] come [to], arrive [at]
Mời ông **lại** *thăm chúng tôi.* Please come and visit us.
Anh làm ơn mang **lại** *đây hai cái ghế.* Please bring two chairs
here. (cf. 14.73)
Ông muốn gặp tôi, tôi sẽ **lại** *nhà ông.* [If] you want to see
["meet"] me I'll come to your house.

lại 2. [preverb, 11.72] resuming, continuing, extending [activity which
has been interrupted, or is threatened with interruption], accomplishing
[another act of the same sort]
Anh muốn thi đỗ thì anh **lại** *học một năm nữa.* [If] you want to
pass your exams you [should] continue studying another year.
Nó định hại anh, nhưng anh **lại** *tránh khỏi.* He determined to kill
you, but you escaped once more.
Nó đã thôi rồi, sau nó **lại** *làm.* He had stopped [but] later he went
to doing [it] again.
Đang nói thì cụ Đàm **lại** *chỉ cho hai ông xem một đoàn thuyền
khác.* While talking cụ Đàm pointed out (for the two fellows to
look at) another group of different boats.

lại 3. [postverb, 11.73] repeating, doing over [generally with notion
of attempted improvement], continuing [uninterruptedly]
Anh nói **lại**, *tôi không nghe rõ.* Say [it] again, I didn't hear [it]
clearly.
Dẹp **lại** *một chỗ.* Put [them] away [neatly] again in the same
place.
Anh ấy vay tiền rồi trả **lại** *ngay.* He borrowed [some] money,
[and] returned [it] right away.
Lúc bạn tôi ra Hà-nội tôi ở **lại** *Sài-gòn làm việc.* At the same
time my friend went to Hanoi I remained in Saigon working.
Cuốn sách nầy cũ, người ta mới in **lại**. (S) This book is old [i.e.,
was first published long ago], they've just reprinted [it].

lại 4. [prepositive particle, 11.81] on the other hand, changing
decision, in contrast, contrary to expectation; moreover, besides
Sao anh **lại** *không đánh dây thép trước?* Why didn't you send a
telegram first?

Tôi định đi Sài-gòn, nhưng **lại** *hơi không muốn đi, vì gặp trời mưa—tôi không thích ướt-át.* (S) I had decided to go to Saigon, but (on the contrary) I was rather unenthusiastic about going because I ran into rain—I don't like wet weather.

Nó đã không cho tôi làm, nó **lại** *dọa đánh tôi.* He didn't allow me to do [it]; moreover he threatened to hit me.

Xưa có người học trò rất thông-minh. Học một biết hai, tính **lại** *chăm học.* Long ago there was a very intelligent student. He learned very quickly; moreover he was by nature studious.

lại 5. [postpositive contained particle, 11.82] back, behind, reduced to original condition or position, to closed position, tight together.

Người ta làm mới cuốn sách nầy **lại.** (S) They have rebound this book [making it seem like new again].

Tôi vặn trễ đồng-hồ tôi **lại** *hai phút.* I've set my watch back two minutes. ["I twist late timepiece I back two minutes"]

Chị ấy đóng cửa **lại.** She closed the door.

Bài nầy dài thướt, nên thâu ngắn **lại.** (S) This lesson is very ["dragging"] long, [we] must shorten it.

Tôi dừng bước bạn tôi **lại** *để nói chuyện.* (S) I stopped my friend ["his walking"] to talk [with him].

Khi nào tôi xuống Sài-gòn **lại,** *tôi hy-vọng gặp ông.* (S) Whenever I get back down to Saigon, I'll hope to see you.

Người ta tin là khi hai người lấy nhau thì có một vị-thần ở trên Giời lấy hai sợi chỉ hồng xe **lại** *với nhau thành một sợi.* People believe that when two people get married ["take one-another"] there is a benevolent spirit up in heaven [who] takes the two pink strands [representing their individual destinies] [and] spins [them] together (with each other) making a single strand.

Note that in certain sentences, these contrasting uses of *lại* make for some rather subtle differences.

Người ta làm mới **lại** *cuốn sách nầy.* (S) They've repaired this [damaged] book again. (postverb, *lại* 3.)

Người ta làm mới cuốn sách nầy **lại.** (S) They've rebound this book [making it like new again]. (postpositive contained particle, *lại* 5.)

Ông **lại** *viết thơ nữa.* Write another letter. (preverb, *lại* 2.)

Ông viết **lại** *cái thơ này.* Rewrite [i.e., revise] this letter. (postverb, *lại* 3.)

Ông viết cái thơ này **lại**. Rewrite this letter [in its proper or original form]. (postpositive contained particle, *lại* 5.)

Cha tôi không thích đi chợ, **lại** *ổng khó ở.* (S) My father doesn't like to go to market; what's more he's indisposed. (prepositive particle *lại* 4.)

Cha tôi không thích đi chợ, ổng **lại** *khó ở.* (S) My father doesn't like to go to market—he's gotten indisposed again (preverb *lại* 2.)

Cha tôi không thích đi chợ, ổng khó ở **lại**. (S) My father doesn't like to go to market—he's back to being indisposed again. (postpositive contained particle *lại* 5.)

There are some other forms with the shape *lại*, but the material is insufficient to provide good examples of their use. They are less common than those exemplified above, and it will be sufficient for the present purposes to list the more important with glosses and suggest their grammatical functions.

lại public servant, official [probably a pseudo-base, appearing in such pseudo-compounds as *quan-lại* 'mandarins, officials', *nha-lại* 'public servants, personnel, staff' if a free form, then presumably some kind of substantive]

lại rely on [probably a pseudo-base, appearing in such pseudo-compounds as *ỷ-lại* 'rely (on)', *vô-lại* 'good-for-nothing, dishonest person'; if a free form, apparently some kind of verbal]

lại resist, stand, withstand, overcome, be a match for [verb]
    Tôi nói không **lại** *nó.* He out-talked me. ["I talk not be-a-match-for him"]

luôn

luôn 1. [postverb 11.73] directly, without break, all at once, in a single operation, without stopping, extending to another situation or person

Bạn tôi bị ốm đi **luôn** *nhà thương, không được về nhà lấy đồ.* My friend got sick and went directly to the hospital—[he] wasn't permitted to go home to get [his] things.

Thầy thuốc chữa bịnh truyền-nhiễm bị đau **luôn** *nữa.* (S) Doctors treating contagious deseases [sometimes] take sick themselves.

Hãy ăn cơm **luôn** *đi cho rồi.* Go ahead and keep eating so as to finish.

luôn 2. [prepositive particle, 11.81] profiting from this fact, going on from this [just referred to]

Anh tôi chị tôi ở đây, **luôn** *tôi cũng ở đây nữa.* My [elder] brother and sister are here; profiting from [their presence] I'll stay here, too.

luôn 3. [postpositive noncontained particle, 11.82] often, frequently; always, continually; just the same, anyhow

Tôi ở Đà-lạt **luôn** *khi.* (S) I stay in Dalat all the time.

Ông đi về, tôi ở lại đây mãi, hằng nhớ ông **luôn.** [When] you return home [and] I remain here (permanently), [I'll] (habitually) remember you often.

Tôi làm công việc nầy rồi **luôn.** (S) I'll finish this work just the same.

Nàng **luôn** *miệng ca-tụng những buổi chiều yêu-đương ấy.* She had constantly in her mouth a song of praise for those much-loved afternoons. (used as focal complement, cf. 11.82)

The derivative **luôn-luôn** 'always, continuously' seems to be a versatile particle (11.83) with little or no gross difference of meaning for different positions.

Tôi ở Đà-lạt **luôn-luôn.** I'm always in Dalat.

Tôi **luôn-luôn** *ở Đà-lạt.* I'm always in Dalat.

Luôn-luôn *tôi ở Đà-lạt, không đi đâu hết.* I'm always in Dalat, don't go anywhere at all.

mà

mà 1. [coordinating particle, 11.51] but

Tiếng pháo bây giờ không phải là để tế Trời, Phật hay lễ tổ-tiên **mà** *là tiếng pháo mừng tuổi các người còn sống.* The sound of firecrackers now is not for the purpose of performing a sacrifice to Heaven or Buddha or to honor the ancestors but is (a sound of firecrackers) to wish Happy New Year to the people still living.

In some instances this particle serves in exclamative expressions where the meaning is something like 'why...!'

Nóng, **mà** *nó nóng bức!* (S) Hot? Why it's stifling!

mà 2. [relative particle, 11.52] [descriptive complement marker]

Trạng Việt-nam đưa lên trước nên được vua hỏi trước là trạng vẽ cái gì **mà** *nhanh thế?* The Vietnamese scholar brought [his drawing] up first, so [he] was asked first by the king what he had drawn so quickly.

Vợ ông chỉ biết khóc **mà** *thương cho duyên-kiếp mình không ra gì, không hề oán-trách chồng.* His wife was of such a personality [that she] only wept, regretting that her predestination turned out to be so disappointing ["came to nothing"]; she never reproached [her] husband.

351

Anh ta lấy đầy túi rồi lại cưỡi lên mình chim **mà** *về.* He filled the
pouch, then again mounted astride the body of the bird to
return.

Giời **mà** *cho thì nó bò về nhà.* [If it's really] Heaven that gave
it, then it'll crawl back to the house [on its own].

Đừng nói lăng-nhăng nữa, ai **mà** *tin được.* Don't tell any more fantasies, [there's] no one that can believe [them].

Cô ở đó rồi **mà** *ông thấy.* (S) She's over there already, as you
[can] see.

This relative particle often conveys the notion that the descriptive complement it marks is the only appropriate one in the situation.

Mấy câu tôi hiểu không hay. Some of the sentences I understand
are not interesting.

Mấy câu **mà** *tôi hiểu không hay.* The [only] sentences I understand are not interesting.

Nếu tôi kiếm được cuốn sách đó, thì sung-sướng lắm. (S) If I can
find that book I'll be very happy.

Nếu **mà** *tôi kiếm được cuốn sách đó, thì sung-sướng lắm.* (S) If
only I can find that book I'll be very happy.

mà 3. [final particle, 11.4] [strong contradiction]

Làm không được.—Được **mà!** [It's] not possible to do.—Oh, yes
it is!

Ông ấy đã cưới vợ lâu rồi **mà!** Why, he's been married for a long
time [contrary to what you suggest]!

Thế **mà!** That *is* the way it is! (occasionally also used as a
mocking comment: 'Oh, is that so? [I don't believe it.]')

The probable relationship of these three words is seen in the very similar
flavor which the first and third often lend to sentences, and especially in
the numerous examples where it is impossible to decide whether the first
or second particle is involved.

Hoa vờ là thứ hoa ông đã biết rồi **mà** *còn vờ như không biết.* The
"pretense" flower is a kind of flower which a man already
knows [what it is] but still pretends not to know [so as to be
able to talk about it and avoid talking about something un-
pleasant].'

Còn gì bằng là hai ông đang đi sang Việt-nam du-lịch **mà** *được
nghe một cụ già lịch-duyệt kể chuyện về Việt-nam.* Nothing
[could be] better than that two fellows going over to Viet Nam
on a trip should get to hear an experienced old man tell about
Viet Nam.

Rắn **mà** *nó trông ra vàng.* Snakes that he sees as gold! (*or* [They're] snakes, but he sees [them] as gold!)

mình

mình 1. [general categorical, 8.62] body

Anh ta lấy đầy túi rồi lại cười lên **mình** *chim mà về.* He filled the pouch, then again mounted astride the body of the bird to return.

mình 2. [personal pronoun, 10.43] self, oneself, myself, yourself, himself, herself, ourselves, yourselves, themselves; you, I [speaking to spouse or very intimate friend] (in latter case either speaker or hearer is female [or both are])

Anh đánh nó, nó phải giữ **mình.** You hit him, he has to defend himself.

Vợ ông chỉ biết khóc mà thương cho duyên-kiếp **mình** *không ra gì, không hề oán-trách chồng.* His wife was of such a personality [that she] only wept, regretting that her predestination turned out to be so disappointing ["came to nothing"]; she never reproached [her] husband.

Này **mình** *ơi!* Say, there! (farmer calling wife)

Mình *nói đùa mà ai cũng tưởng thật.* I said [it] in jest but everyone took it seriously. ["self speak tease but whoever likewise think true"]

Chúng **mình** *đi xem hát đi.* Let's go see a play.

mới

mới 1. [extended state verb, 9.55] be new

Quyển sách này **mới.** This book is new.

Tết Nguyên-đán là lễ ăn mừng năm **mới.** The Nguyên-đán festival is the holiday celebrating the new year.

mới 2. [preverb, 11.72] [after something just mentioned is accomplished] only then, now, recently, just; [if something just mentioned is true] only then; [in contrast with preceding] really, truly

Còn hai ngày nữa chúng ta **mới** *đến Sài-gòn.* Only after another two days will we get to Saigon.

Ăn cơm rồi **mới** *đi chơi.* [Let's not] go out till after [we've] eaten.

Tôi **mới** *làm xong công việc ấy.* I just finished that work.

Ếch-Hoa thương Cóc lắm, nhưng vì không quen việc luật-pháp **mới** *bảo Cóc đi tìm Nhái-bén giúp đỡ công việc.* Leopard-Frog was very fond of Toad, but because [he] was not acquainted with legal matters—for that reason alone [he] told Toad to go look for Tree-Frog to help with the matter.

Tôi còn truyện này **mới** *thật mỉa-mai.* I have this other story which is *really* ironic [if you thought the last one was].

Thế **mới** *lạ!* It's really astonishing [if that's the way it is]!

nào

nào 1. [negative, 9.4] on the contrary, not

Tôi **nào** *đi.* I'm definitely not going [although someone said I was].

Tôi đã **nào** *ngủ.* I certainly didn't sleep.

Nào *ai còn dám nói-năng một lời.* Not a single person dared say a word more.—*Kim-Vân-Kiều*

nào 2. [reference demonstrative, 10.45] whichever (see also 14.2)

Anh muốn lấy quyển **nào** *thì lấy đi.* Whichever [book] you want to take, go ahead.

Nhà **nào** *của ông?* Which house is yours?

Bài **nào** *cũng khó.* Every lesson is difficult.

Không có việc **nào** *làm.* There isn't anything to do.

nào 3. [initial particle, 11.3] come on! ...

Nào, *làm đi xem!* Come on, do it [and] see [what happens]!

nào 4. [final particle, 11.4] [mild exhortation] won't you?

Hai ông đi tầu xem thấy những gì lạ kể cho tôi nghe **nào?** [If] the two of you saw anything new on your trip on the train tell me about it, won't you? ["two gentleman go conveyance look perceive plural-marker whatever strange narrate give I listen won't-you?"]

nào 5. [prepositive particle, 11.81] [in series] both ... and ...; not only ... but also ...; ...—all these

Nào *tiền,* **nào** *tình,* **nào** *hạnh-phúc* ... Money, love, happiness—all these ...

Nào *cây to bóng mát,* **nào** *hoa thơm bốn mùa.* Not only [were there] great trees [with their] cool shade, but also fragrant flowers [during all] four seasons.

nên

nên 1. [auxiliary, 9.54] be appropriate, necessary, have an obligation to

Nên *chăng?* It is appropriate?

Không **nên** *đi.* [One] shouldn't go.

Chúng ta **nên** *tập thể-thao.* We should have physical exercise.
["animate-group you-and-I ought practice sports"]
Bài nầy dài thượt, **nên** *thâu ngắn lại.* (S) This lesson is very
["dragging"] long, [we] must shorten it.

nên 2. [momentary action verb, 9.55] develop into, become, result in
Anh ấy đã **nên** *người rồi.* He has already become a personage.
Cười **nên** *tiếng khóc, hát* **nên** *giọng sầu.* Laughter leads to
(sound of) weeping, singing leads to (accent of) sadness.
–Nguyễn-Gia-Thiều

nên 3. [isolating particle, 11.51] therefore, so, as a result
Tôi bị nhà tôi cháy, **nên** *mất của hết.* My house burned, so I lost
all my belongings.

Tại nó ăn bậy **nên** *đau.* (S) He's sick because he's eaten
haphazardly [off unclean dishes, etc.]
Vì sức yếu **nên** *nhờ cây gậy chống đi.* (S) Because [he] is weak
[he] has to walk leaning on [his] stick. ["because strength
weak therefore depend-on stick cane lean-on go"]
Trời còn sớm, **nên** *tôi để anh ngủ.* It was still early–that was why
I let you sleep.
The second and third forms may well be different uses of the same word,
but it has seemed best to separate them here; in the material collected
there were no examples which would mark instances of *nên* 3. as centers
of predicates (see also 11.91).

những
những 1. [plural marker, 8.2, 11.61] some, several [of same category]
[indefinite plural]
Như vậy các ông đến nơi thì gặp **những** *ngày cuối năm âm-lịch.*
In this way they [would] arrive (there) [and] run into some of
the final days of the year [according to] the moon calendar.
Những *làn sóng lớn bị tầu cắt đôi, đập vào hai bên mạn tầu, tung
lên* **những** *bọt trắng-xóa.* Large waves were cut in two by the
ship, [they] struck against the two sides of the ship, [and]
threw up bubbles of glistening white spray.
Anh ấy ăn **những** *tám bát cơm.* He ate all of [i.e., as many as]
eight bowls of rice.

những 2. [prepositive particle, 11.81] only, exclusively
Cái va-li ấy đầy **những** *quần-áo.* That suitcase is full of nothing
but clothes.

Không **những** *anh ấy bỏ tôi đi, mà anh ấy còn lấy hết tiền của tôi.* Not only did he abandon me, but he also took all my money.

Tôi chẳng **những** *chỉ biết tiếng Việt mà thôi, tôi còn biết tiếng Pháp nữa.* It's not only Vietnamese that I know, but also French.

In older usage *những* 2. was common with a predicate as head, but this is now considered old fashioned unless the whole expression is negated as in the last two examples above; in other cases it is replaced by **chỉ** 3. or the compound **những chỉ** (as in the last example above), or **chỉ những** is used.

Tôi **những** *lo đến việc ấy.* I am worried only about that matter.

More commonly: *Tôi* **chỉ** *lo đến việc ấy.*

Anh ấy nghe tôi nói thế, **chỉ** *(***những***) cười.* [When] he heard me say that, he only laughed.

phải

phải 1. [extended state verb, 9.55] be correct; right [hand, side]

Nó **phải**, *tôi trái.* He's right, I'm wrong.

Lời của ông nói **phải** *lắm.* Your remarks are quite true.

Hai với hai là bốn, **phải** *không?*—**Phải.** Two and two are four, isn't that right?—Yes.

Đi đến nhà hát lớn thì rẽ tay **phải.** [You] go as far as the municipal theatre, then turn right. (giving directions)

It serves to mark emphatic affirmatives and is presumably the verb involved in the negation of non-verbal predicates (14.33) and in the question formula *có phải ... không?* (13.22)

Ấy **phải** *cái nhà mà chúng ta đã đến thăm hôm qua.* It *is* the house where we came visiting yesterday.

Không **phải** *việc tôi.* It's not my affair.

Ông ấy không **phải** *là lính.* He's not a soldier.

Có **phải** *bây giờ là mùa cưới không?* Is now the season for marriages?

phải 2. [extended state verb, 9.55] ought to, must

Xin lỗi ông, tôi **phải** *đi.* [I] beg your pardon, I have to leave.

Tôi nghĩ lỗi tại tôi, tôi **phải** *ngừa lúc bất-trắc ấy.* I thought it was my fault, I should have taken precautions against that [sort of] unexpected occasion.

Ta **phải** *giúp kẻ nghèo-khó.* We should help the poor and unfortunate.

phải 3. [momentary action verb, 9.55] suffer, sustain, be adversely affected by, contract [a disease]

Nó **phải** *bắt, bị phạt.* He was caught and punished.

Bạn tôi **phải** *bệnh nên nằm nhà thương.* My friend contracted a disease, so [he's] (lying) in the hospital.

As a complement to a main verb it adds the notion 'to one's misfortune, chagrin.'

Anh ta ngồi **phải** *cọc.* He had the misfortune to sit on a fence picket.

Tôi mua **phải** *gạo hạng ba.* I made the unfortunate mistake of buying third-quality rice.

Hiện-tượng ấy như là một định-luật tự-nhiên của con người khi sự sống của con người gặp **phải** *những trở-lực ngăn-cản và muốn vượt qua, phải đánh ngã trở-lực ấy.* This phenomenon is like a natural law of mankind [to the effect that] when [in] human life [one] has the misfortune to meet with impeding obstacles and wishes to overcome [them], [one] must strike down those obstacles.

tự

tự 1. [preverb, 11.72] acting for or upon oneself, of one's own accord

Nó **tự** *nói.* He [a child] is talking to himself.

Tôi không **tự** *đi.* I'm not going of my own accord.

Anh ấy định **tự**- *tử.* He decided to commit suicide. (The form is hyphenated since it is recognized as a Chinese loan form.)

Khi nào mà anh ấy hát, thì tôi **tự** *thấy khó chịu.* As soon as he sings I feel I can't endure it. ["... perceive myself ..."]

Tôi **tự** *làm lấy được.* I can do it myself.

tự 2. [prepositive particle, 11.81] starting from; because of, according to

Anh ấy đi làm việc **tự** *tháng trước.* He went to work (starting from) the preceding month.

Tự *ông ấy sinh sự ra.* Because of him [the thing] became a reality.

Tôi đi hay không đi **tự** *tôi.* I go or don't go, as I please.

Tôi đi không **tự** *tôi.* I was forced to go against my will.

In the meaning 'starting from' *tự* 2. appears to be a variant of the prepositive particle **từ** (cf. 14.43); however, there are many contexts in which the two forms are not interchangeable.

tự 3. [pseudo-base] written word, [Chinese] character, letter, symbol; courtesy name (see also 5.57)

Hán-tự Chinese character
tự-vi, tự-điển dictionary
biểu-tự fancy name, nickname
văn-tự writing, spelling, orthography, written language

There are a number of other less common forms with the shape tự; they are not thoroughly analyzable with the material at hand, but they seem for the most part to be pseudo-bases. We may note here the following:

tự [Buddhist] temple: Phật-tự Buddhist temple
tự order, series: thứ tự order, series
tự preceding: tiểu-tự, tự-luận foreword, preface
tự resembling: tương-tự similar, identical
tự offspring, heir: thừa-tự to succeed, carry on [a family line], tuyệt-tự heirless

từng
từng 1. [general categorical, 8.62] layer, stratum; floor, storey [of building] [dialectal variant of tầng]

Nhà này có mấy **từng**? How many storeys does this building have?
Lúc này người ta đang dò-xét về thượng-**từng** không-khí. These days they're investigating the upper atmosphere.

từng 2. [plural marker, 8.2, 11.61] each in turn, so many by so many

Công-an đi đến **từng** nhà mà điều-tra. The police went from house to house investigating.
Chia thành phố ra **từng** khu mà kiểm-soát. Divide the city up by districts for [purposes of] control.
Chúng ta vào **từng** người, hay vào cả một lần? Shall we go in one by one ["person by person"], or all at once?

A peculiarity of this word is that when it appears in phrases serving as focal complements the substantival phrase ends with the word một 'one' as final complement. (Một is also often found as final complement when the whole phrase serves as descriptive complement.)

Từng gia-đình một đi bỏ phiếu. Family by family they went to cast [their] votes.
Anh giắt những con trâu này **từng** con một đi tắm. Lead these buffalo to bathe one by one.

Note that this một serves to signal that unified groups are involved, not to limit the series to individual items.

Từng ba người một chạy thi. Three by three they ran races.

vừa

vừa 1. [extended state verb, 9.55] fit, suit, be just the right quantity or quality, be pleasing, satisfying; be moderate, reasonable

Nếm hộ xem dã **vừa** *chưa hay mặn quá.* Please taste it to see whether it's about right or too salty.

Đôi giầy này anh đi **vừa** *không?* Does this pair of shoes fit you?

Vừa rồi! [That's] enough! Just the right amount!

Cô ấy có **vừa** *mắt anh không?* Did that girl please your eye?

Nó không **vừa** *đâu.* He has a terrible temper. ["he not moderate at-all"]

Học **vừa** *chứ!* Don't study too hard! ["study moderate contrary-to-what-you-might-do"]

vừa 2. [preverb, 11.72] just this moment, recently

Chuối này **vừa** *chín.* These bananas are just ripe.

Ông ấy **vừa** *đi xong.* He just this moment left.

vừa 3. [prepositive particle, 11.81, usually correlative] both ...and ...; ... and at the same time ...

Nó **vừa** *khóc* **vừa** *cười.* He [a child] was crying and laughing at the same time.

Chị ấy phải **vừa** *đi học* **vừa** *đi làm.* She had to work while going to school.

Nhà tôi có tới một trăm con, **vừa** *trâu,* **vừa** *bò.* My family has up to a hundred animals, both buffalo and cattle.

Word Classes

In the following list numbers refer to treatments in the text. Indentations clarify class and subclass membership.

SUBSTANTIVES (8)

NUMERALS (8.4)
 Unit Numbers (8.41)
  Indefinite Number (8.42)
 Multiple Numbers (8.43)
NOMINALS (8.6)
 Categoricals (8.6)
  Classifiers (8.61)
   General Classifier (8.61)
  General Categoricals (8.62)
 Nouns (8.6)
  Relator Nouns (8.63)
  Mass Nouns (8.64)
  Indefinite Nouns (8.65)
  Item Nouns (8.66)

PREDICATIVES (9)

NEGATIVES (9.4)
VERBALS (9.5)
 Definitive (9.51)
 Comparatives (9.52)
 Quantifiers (9.53)
 Auxiliaries (9.54)
 Verbs (9.55)
  Momentary Action Verbs (9.55)
  Extended State Verbs (9.55)

FOCUSES (10)

Proper Names (10.41)
Pronouns (10.4)
 Collective (10.42)
 Personal Pronouns (10.43)
 Absolute Pronouns (10.44)
Manner Focuses (10.45)
Locational Focuses (10.46)
Temporal Focuses (10.47)

PARTICLES (11)

INTERJECTIONS (11.2)
SENTENCE PARTICLES (11.1)
 Initial Particles (11.3)
 Final Particles (11.4)
CLAUSE PARTICLES (11.5)
 Principalizing Particles (11.51)
  Isolating Particles (11.51)
  Coordinating Particles (11.51)
 Subordinating Particles (11.52)
  Relative Particle (11.52)
  Focal Particles (11.52)
 Substantival Particles (11.6)
  Plural Markers (11.61, 8.2)
  Descriptive Particles (11.62)
  Vocative Particles (11.63)
   Formal Vocative Particles (11.63)
   Informal Vocative Particles (11.63)
PREDICATIVE PARTICLES (11.7)
 Predicative Markers (11.71, 9.3, 9.7)
 Verbal Particles (11.7)
  Preverbs (11.72)
  Postverbs (11.73)
MOVABLE PARTICLES (11.8)
 Prepositive Particles (11.81)
 Postpositive Particles (11.82)
  Contained Particles (11.82)
  Non-Contained Particles (11.82)
 Versatile Particles (11.83)

Selected Bibliography

Listed here are references cited in the text and selected other works on the language. Journals and series publications are cited with abbreviations. These abbreviations appear alphabetized in the same list with full titles supplied. A period separates volume or part number from page numbers; where it is necessary to include the number of a separately paginated part or fascicle, it appears following the volume number, separated from it by a colon. Series numbers appear in roman numerals preceding volume numbers. For additional references see Embree and Dotson 1950 (under Vietnam: Language and Writing) and the forthcoming chapter on linguistics in Vietnam (Thompson and Thomas, in press).

Alešina, I.E., 1961. O formirovanii v'etnamskogo nacional'nogo literaturnogo jazyka. *NAA* 3.139-46.

An-đò-rế-ép (= N.D. Andreev), 1956. Vấn đê bình thường hóa cách phắt âm tiếng Việt-nam. *VSĐ 1956.* No. 18.

Andreev, N.D., 1956. *V'etnamskaja transkripcija russkix slov.* Leningrad.

——, 1958a. K voprosu o proisxoždenii v'etnamskogo jazyka. *SovV 1958* 2.101-11.

——, 1958b. Struktura v'etnamskogo sloga. *UZLU (Istorija i filologija stran vostoka)* 256.152-7.

——, D.A. Batova, V.S. Panfilov, and V.M. Petrova, 1958. Elementy nezavisimogo analiza vo v'etnamsko-russkom algoritme mašinnogo perevoda. *Materialy po mašinnomu perevodu,* Sbornik 1.199-208. Leningrad.

——, and M.V. Gordina, 1957. Sistema tonov v'etnamskogo jazyka (po èksperimental'nym dannym). *VLU 1957* 8.132-48.

Anh-Đao et al (Thanh-Nguyễn, ed.), 1957. *Tự-điển Nga-Việt thực-dung.* Hanoi.

Barker, Milton E., 1963. Proto-Vietnamuong initial labial consonants. *VHNS* 12.491-500.

BEFEO = *Bulletin de l'École Française d'Extrême-Orient.* Hanoi, Paris.

Benedict, Paul K., 1947. An analysis of Annamese kinship terms. *SJA* 3.371-92.

——, 1948. Tonal systems in Southeast Asia. *JAOS* 68.184-91.

BSEI = *Bulletin de la Société des études Indochinoises* [n.s. = new series]. Saigon.

BSL = *Bulletin de la Société de Linguistique de Paris.*

BSOAS = *Bulletin of the School of Oriental and African Studies.* London.

Bùi đức Tịnh, 1948. *Những nhận xét về văn-phạm Việt-nam.* Saigon.

——, 1952. *Văn-phạm Việt-nam.* Saigon.

Bulteau, R., 1950. *Cours d'annamite,* 3rd ed. Paris. (4th ed., 1953)

Bystrov, I.S., 1961. K voprosu o klassifikacii častej reči vo v'etnamskom jazyke: slova so smešannymi priznakami imeni i predikativa. *UZLU (Jazyki narodov vostoka)* 305.3-14.

——, and N.V. Stankevič, 1961. Sposoby vyraženija vremeni vo v'etnamskom jazyke. *UZLU (Vostokov 12)* 294. 84-91.

——, (see also Gordina, M.V., and I.S. Bystrov, 1961).

Cadière, Léopold, 1902. *Phonétique Annamite* (dialecte du Haut-Annam). PEFEO 3. Paris.

——, 1904. La question du quốc-ngữ, ap. Textes et documents relatifs à la réforme du quốc-ngữ. *RI* May: 585-600, 700-5, 784-8, 872-6; Jul: 58-63.

——, 1908-9. Monographie de la semivoyelle labiale en sino-annamite et en annamite. *BEFEO* 8.93-148, 381-477; 9.51-90, 315-46, 681-706.

——, 1911. Le dialecte du Bas-Annam. *BEFEO* 11.67-100.

——, 1958. *Syntaxe de la langue viêtnamienne.* PEFEO 42. Paris.

Carte ethnolinguistique de l'Indochine. 1949. PEFEO. Hanoi.

Chao Yuen Ren, 1948. *Mandarin Primer.* Cambridge, Mass.

Chavannes, Edouard, 1906. Le cycle turc des douze animaux. *TP* II 7.51-122.

Cordier, G., 1932. *Cours de langue annamite. Année préparatoire: Grammaire et exercices.* Hanoi.

Cuisinier, Jeanne, 1951. *Prières accompagnant les rites agraires chez les Mường de Mãn đức.* PEFEO 33. Hanoi.

Day, Arthur Colin, 1962. Final consonants in northern Vietnamese. *Transactions of the Historical Research Institute* 3.89-109. Saigon.

de Rhodes, Alexandre, 1651a. *Dictionarium annamiticum, latinum et lusitanum.* Rome.

——, 1651b. *Linguae annamiticae seu tunchinensis brevis declaratio.* Rome.

——, 1651c. *Catechismus in octo dies (Phép giảng tám ngày)*. Rome.
[Republished on the occasion of the tricentenary of the death of the
author, 1961, Saigon.]

Doàn Quan Tân, 1954. Le français et le viêtnamien dans l'enseignement
au Viêt-Nam. *BSEI* n.s. 29.59-97.

Donaldson, Jean, 1963. A study of the "nặng" tone in the northern dialect
of Vietnamese. *VHNS* 12. 1151-4.

Durand, Maurice, 1953. L'avenir des études viêtnamiennes. *BSEI* n.s.
28.69-71.

——, 1957. Alexandre de Rhodes. *BSEI* n.s. 32.5-30.

——, 1961a. Conclusions sémantiques et syntaxiques tirées de l'étude
des impressifs en viêtnamien. *BSL* 56.xii-xiv (résumé).

——, 1961b. Les impressifs en viêtnamien. Étude préliminaire. *BSEI* n.s.
36.5-50.

Dương quảng Hàm, 1951. *Việt-nam văn-học sử-yếu*. Hanoi.

DVN = *Dân Việt-nam* (published by the École Française d'Extrême-Orient).
Hanoi.

Đào duy Anh, 1950. Pháp-Việt Từ-điển. 2nd ed. Paris.

——, 1951. *Giản-yếu Hán-Việt tự-điển*. 3rd ed., revised and enlarged by
Hãn Mạn Tử. Paris.

Đào văn Tập, 1949. *Tự-điển Pháp-Việt phổ-thông*. Saigon.

——, 1951. *Tự-điển Việt-Pháp phổ-thông*. Saigon.

Efimova, O.E., et al (Nguyễn văn Thành, ed.), 1960. *Russko-V'etnamskij
slovar'*. Moscow.

Embree, John F., and Lillian Ota Dotson, 1950. *Bibliography of the
peoples and cultures of mainland Southeast Asia*. New Haven.

Emeneau, Murray B., 1947. Homonyms and puns in Annamese. *Lg* 23.239-44.

——, 1950. Language and non-linguistic patterns. *Lg* 26.199-209.

——, 1951. *Studies in Vietnamese (Annamese) grammar*. UCPL 8.
Berkeley and Los Angeles.

——, and Diether von den Steinen, 1944. *A course in Annamese: Lessons
in the pronunciation and grammar of the Annamese language*.
Berkeley. (dittoed)

——, and Diether von den Steinen, 1945. *Annamese-English dictionary*.
Berkeley. (dittoed)

Ferkinghoff, Klaus, 1962. *Deutsch-vietnamesisches Wörterbuch: Từ-điển
Đức-Việt*. Wiesbaden.

Gage, William W., and H. Merrill Jackson, 1953. *Verb constructions in
Vietnamese*. SEAP Cornell, Data Paper No. 9. Ithaca. (mimeo)

Glebova, I.I., 1961. Grammatičeskie osobennosti v'etnamskix prilagatel'nyx.
UZ IMO (Ser. filolog.) 5.190-213.

363

——, et al (I.M. Ošanina and Vũ Đăng Ất, eds.), 1961. *V'etnamsko-russkij slovar'*. Moscow.

Gordina, M.V., 1959. K voprosu o foneme vo v'etnamskom jazyke. *VJa* 8:6.103-9.

——, 1960a. *Osnovnye voprosy foneticeskogo stroja v'etnamskogo jazyka. Avtoreferat kandidatskoj dissertacii*. Leningrad.

——, 1960b. O nekotoryx spornyx voprosax foneticeskogo stroja v'etnamskogo jazyka. *UZLU (Ser. filolog.)* 237.170-87.

——, 1961. O fonologiceskoj traktovke v'etnamskix diftongov. *UZLU (Ser. filolog.)* 301.29-36.

——, and I.S. Bystrov, 1961. Priznaki sintagmaticeskogo členenija i frazovaja intonacija vo v'etnamskom jazyke. *UZLU (Jazyki narodov vostoka)* 305.15-29.

Gouin, Eugène, 1957. *Dictionnaire viêtnamien-chinois-français*. Saigon.

Grammont, Maurice, 1909-10. Recherches expérimentales sur la prononciation du cochinchinois. *MSL* 16.69-86.

——, and Lê quang Trinh, 1912. Études sur la langue annamite. *MSL* 17.201-41, 295-310.

Gregerson, Kenneth J., 1963. *The phonemes of Middle Vietnamese*. (Unpublished MA thesis, University of Washington)

Halévy, Joseph, 1906. Nouvelles considérations sur le cycle turc des animaux. *TP* II 7.270-95.

Haudricourt, André-G., 1949. Origine des particularités de l'alphabet viêtnamien. *DVN* 3.61-8.

——, 1951. Statistique phonologique du viêtnamien. *BSL* 47.xvi (résumé).

——, 1952. Les voyelles brèves du viêtnamien. *BSL* 48.90-3.

——, 1953. La place du viêtnamien dans les langues austroasiatiques. *BSL* 49.122-8.

——, 1954. De l'origine des tons en viêtnamien. *JA* 242.69-82.

Henderson, Eugénie J.A., 1951. The phonology of loan words in some Southeast Asian languages. *TPS 1951*. 131-58.

——, 1961. Tonal exponents of pronominal concord in southern Vietnamese. *IL* 22.86-97.

HJAS = *Harvard Journal of Asiatic Studies*.

Ho Ch'eng, Cheng Wo-lung, Chu Fu-tan, and Wang Te-lun, 1960. *Yüeh-Han tz'u-tien*. Peking.

Hockett, Charles F., 1958. *A course in modern linguistics*. New York.

Honey, Patrick J., 1956. Word classes in Vietnamese. *BSOAS* 18.534-44..

——, and E.H.S. Simmonds, 1963. Thai and Vietnamese: some elements of nominal structure compared. *Linguistic comparison in South East Asia and the Pacific*, pp. 71-8. London.

Huỳnh Tịnh (Paulus) Của, 1895-6. *Đại-Nam quấc-âm tự-vị*. Saigon.
IL = *Indian Linguistics*, Journal of the Linguistic Society of India.
JA = *Journal Asiatique*. Paris.
Jackson, H. Merrill, 1960. *Dimensions of social relationships indicated in Vietnamese forms of address*. Preprint No. 32, Mental Health Research Institute, University of Michigan. (unpublished)
JAOS = *Journal of the American Oriental Society*.
Jones, Robert B., Jr., and Huỳnh Sanh Thông, 1960. *Introduction to spoken Vietnamese*. Revised ed. Washington, D.C.
JPRS = U.S. Joint Publication Research Society.
KSIV = *Kratkie Soobščenija Akademii Nauk SSSR, Institut Vostokovedenija*.
Lekomcev, Ju. K., 1958. Stroenie v'etnamskoj glagol'noj sintagmy. *Voprosy statistiki reči*, pp. 131-48. Leningrad. [English translation in: Foreign developments in machine translation and information processing 13 (*JPRS* 6543) 12 Jan 1961.]
———, 1960. K principu klassifikacii prostyx predloženij vo v'etnamskom jazyke. *VJa* 9:1.52-9.
Lê bá Khanh and Lê bá Kông, 1955. *Standard pronouncing Vietnamese-English and English-Vietnamese dictionary*. New York.
Lê văn Hùng (Dr. and Mrs.), 1955. *Vietnamese-English dictionary*. Paris.
Lê văn Lý, 1948. *Le parler viêtnamien*. Paris. (2nd ed., 1960, Saigon.)
Lg = *Language*, Journal of the Linguistic Society of America.
Li Fang-Kuei, 1945. Some old Chinese loan words in the Tai languages. *HJAS* 8.333-42.
Lý Đức Lâm, M.B. Emeneau, and Diether von den Steinen, 1944. *An Annamese reader*. Berkeley. (dittoed)
Martini, François, 1950. L'opposition nom et verbe en viêtnamien et en siamois. *BSL* 46.183-96
———, 1952. De la morphématisation du verbe en viêtnamien. *BSL* 48.94-110.
———, 1958. Notices bibliographiques: langue viêtnamienne (review article treating Emeneau 1951 and Lê văn Lý 1948). *BEFEO* 49.337-48.
———, 1959. Tournures impersonnelles en cambodgien et en viêtnamien. *BSL* 54.136-48.
Maspero, Henri, 1912. Études sur la phonétique historique de la langue annamite: les initiales. *BEFEO* 12:1.1-127.
Meillon, G., 1953. L'expression du genre en viêtnamien. *BSL* 49.xix (résumé).
Miller, John D., 1961. Word tone recognition in Vietnamese whispered speech. *Word* 17.11-15.
MSL = *Mémoires de la Société de linguistique de Paris*.
Mxitarjan, T.T., 1959a. Opyt èksperimental'nogo issledovanija glasnyx fonem sovremennogo v'etnamskogo literaturnogo yazyka. *KSIV* 29.3-15.

———, 1959b. *Fonetika v'etnamskogo jazyka.* Moscow.

NAA = *Narody Azii i Afriki. Istorija, èkonomika, kul'tura.* Moscow.

Nguyễn Bạt-Tuỵ, 1954. *Tên Người Việt-nam.* Saigon.

———, 1959. *Ngôn-ngữ-học Việt-nam.* Saigon. (Includes revised edition of author's *Chữ và vần Việt khoa-học,* 1949, with separate pagination.)

Nguyễn dình Hòa, 1955. *Quốc-ngữ: The modern writing system in Vietnam.* Washington, D.C.

———, 1957a. Classifiers in Vietnamese. *Word* 13.124-52.

———, 1957b. *Speak Vietnamese.* Saigon. (Revised ed., 1963)

———, 1959a. Chữ nôm, the demotic system of writing in Vietnam. *JAOS* 79.270-4.

———, 1959b. *Hòa's Vietnamese-English dictionary.* Saigon. (Revised ed. in press)

———, 1962. Reading list on Vietnamese language and writing. *VHNS* 11.685-97.

Nguyễn Khắc Xuyên, 1963. Thử tìm hiểu nguồn gốc ba chữ *d, đ* và *s* trong Việt-ngữ. *VHNS* 12.681-8.

———, and Phạm Đình Khiêm, 1961. *Giáo-sĩ Đắc-lộ và Tác phẩm Quốc-ngữ đầu tiên.* Saigon. (published with an annotated and modernized edition of the full text of Alexandre de Rhodes' *Catechismus in octo dies,* prepared by André Marillier, Saigon.)

Nguyễn Năng An (P.I. Alešin and Hồng-Hà, eds.), 1959. *Russko-V'etnamskij slovar'.* Moscow.

Nguyễn Tài Cẩn, 1960. Gruppa suščestvitel'nogo vo v'etnamskom jazyke. *VLU 1960* 14.99-112.

Nguyễn văn Liễn, 1934. La langue annamite dans ses tendances actuelles. *BSEI* n.s. 9.63-73.

PEFEO = Publications de l'École Française d'Extrême-Orient.

Pelliot, Paul, 1913. Le cycle sexagénaire dans la chronologie tibétaine. *JA* XI 1.633-67.

Pho-can Tham (Fu Ken-shen), 1955. *Việt-Hán tự-diển.* Cholon.

Porée-Maspero, Eveline, 1962. Le cycle des douze animaux dans la vie des cambodgiens. *BEFEO* 50.311-65.

Przyluski, Jean, 1912. Les formes pronominales de l'annamite. *BEFEO* 12.5-9.

RI = *Revue Indochinoise.* Hanoi.

SEAP Cornell = Southeast Asia Program, Department of Far Eastern Studies, Cornell University.

Ser. filolog. = *Serija filologiceskix nauk* (see *UZ*).

SJA = *Southwestern Journal of Anthropology.* Albuquerque, N.M.

Smalley, William A. and Nguyễn văn Vạn, 1954. *Tiếng Việt cho các Giáo-sĩ* [Vietnamese for Missionaries, a course in the spoken and written language of Central Vietnam]. Books I, II and III. Dalat. (2nd ed., 1957, Saigon.)

Solncev, V.M., Ju. K. Lekomcev, T.T. Mxitarjan, and I.I. Glebova, 1960. V'etnamskij jazyk. *Jazyki zarubežnogo Vostoka i Afriki.* Moscow.

SovV = *Sovetskoe Vostokovedanie.* Moscow.

Spencer, Robert F.,1945. The Annamese kinship system. *SJA* 1.284-310.

Stankevič, N.V., 1961a. O granicax kategorii prilagatel'nogo vo v'etnamskom jazyke. *UZLU (Jazyki narodov vostoka)* 305.43-50.

——, 1961b. Opredelenie k suščestvitel'nomu vo v'etnamskom jazyke. *UZLU (Jazyki narodov vostoka)* 305.30-42.

——, 1961c. Sintaksičeskoe upotreblenie izobražitel'nyx slov v klassičeskom v'etnamskom jazyke. *VLU 1961* 14.106-17.

Thanh-Nghị, 1952. *Việt-nam tân tự-diển.* Saigon.

Thomas, David D., 1962. On defining the "word" in Vietnamese. *VHNS* 11.519-23.

Thompson, Laurence C., 1959. Saigon phonemics. *Lg* 35.454-76.

——, 1963. The problem of the word in Vietnamese. *Word* 19.39-52.

——, and Nguyễn đức Hiệp, 1961. *A Vietnamese reader.* Seattle.

——, and David D. Thomas (in press). Vietnam, in Thomas A. Sebeok, ed., *Current trends in linguistics,* Vol. 2.

TP = *T'oung Pao.*

TPS = *Transactions of the Philological Society.* London.

Trần trọng Kim et al, 1950. *Việt-nam văn-phạm.* 6th ed. Saigon.

Trương vĩnh Ký, 1883. *Grammaire de la langue annamite.* Saigon.

UCPL = University of California Publications in Linguistics.

U.S. Army Language School, 1954-56. *Vietnamese basic course.* Monterey.

——, 1962. *Vietnamese (Saigon dialect): special course (12 weeks).* Monterey.

UZ IMO = *Institut meždunarodnyx otnošenij: učenye zapiski.* Moscow.

UZLU = *Učenye zapiski Leningradskogo ordena Lenina gosudarstvennogo Universiteta im. A.A. Ždanova.* Leningrad.

VHNS = *Văn-hóa Nguyệt-san: cơ-quan nghiên-cứu và phổ-thông.* Saigon.

VJa = *Voprosy jazykoznanija.* Moscow.

VLU = *Vestnik Leningradskogo gosudarstvennogo Universiteta.*

von Staël-Holstein, A., 1935-36. On the sexagenary cycle of the Tibetans. *Monumenta Serica* 1.277-314.

VSĐ = *Tập San Nghiên cứu Văn Sử Địa.* Hanoi.

Wells, Rulon S., 1947. Immediate constituents. *Lg* 23.81-117.

Index

family (see kinship terms)
family names (see names)
figurative reference 6.24, 6.32
final particles 11.4 (see particles)
focal elements 8.32, 9.62, 10, 11.92,
12.44, 14.32, 14.75 (see demonstratives); manner focuses 7.23,
8.5, 10.4, 10.45, 14.2; complements
10.2 (see complements); complexes
10.3; topic focuses 10.3, 10.4,
13.3; proper names 10.4 (see
names); pronouns (collective,
personal, absolute) 10.4 (see
pronouns); locational focuses 10.4,
10.46, 14.2, 14.41; temporal
focuses 10.2-10.4, 10.47; focal
particles 11.52 (see particles);
focal sentence fragments 12.44
(see sentences)
formal and literary language 13.1 (see
levels of discourse); reinforcing
compounds 6.24; attributive
pseudo-compounds 6.24; interlocking order of compounds and
pseudo-compounds 6.4; derivatives
7.7; plural markers (substantives)
8.2, 11.61; numbers 8.41, 8.45,
14.62; honorifics 11.63, 13.1;
narratives 13.1; novels 13.1; older
texts 13.2; forms of address 13.22;
letters 13.3, 13.4; diaries 13.3;
prose 13.3; learnèd style 13.4,
13.5; newspapers 13.4; speeches
13.4; negative 9.4, 14.31
fortis consonants: Hanoi 2.11, 2.15,
2.2; Saigon 4.21
fortis tones 2.15
fractions 8.44 (see numbers)
fragmentary sentences 12.4 (see
sentences)
free forms: basic free forms 5.51,

5.53; free morphemes 5.52, 5.53;
Chinese borrowings 6.25
French borrowings 2.81 (see
borrowings)
future (time) (see tense); in
extended state verbs 9.55; basic
future reference 10.22

G

gender 11.2 (see particles, substantive)
generalizing compounds 6.22 (see
compounds)
generalizing pseudo-compounds 6.31
(see pseudo-compounds)
glottal stop: standard pronunciation
1.2; Hanoi (as a phoneme) 2.15;
Hanoi tones 2.71; Hanoi syllable-
initial 2.81; in earlier language
3.21, 3.22; Vĩnh dialect 4.12;
Huế dialect 4.13; Saigon dialect
4.16, 4.25; Saigon (as a phoneme)
4.27; in alliterative chameleon
affixes 7.11
glottal stricture 2.71 (see tones)
goals and objects (Vietnamese
equivalents of English verbal
goals and objects) 9.55, 9.63
grammatical classes (see word
classes)
greetings (with complements) 14.71

H

(H) = recorded only for Huế
speech
Hanoi dialect 2 (see dialects)
Haut-Annam dialect 4.1 (see
dialects)
heads 5.43, 7.23, 8.34, 8.41, 9.1,
9.5, 12.2 (see constituent
analysis)
historical present (time) 9.3 (see
tense; time)

purposive construction 14.75 (see construction types)

Q

quantity, units of 8.62, 14.6 (see categoricals; measure, units of)
questions 9.54, 13.32, 14.2; negative 9.4; choice 9.4, 13.32, 13.33; information 13.32, 13.33
intonation of 1.5, 2.73, 5.32, 5.4, 7.21, 13.32; interrogative words in 7.21, 14.2; auxiliaries in 9.54; alternative phrases 9.67, 12.52, 13.32
quotation (quote marks) 3.55

R

ranks (and status) 13.1 (see names)
reading pronunciation 3.6
reduplicatives 5.54, 7.11, 7.75 (see derivatives); perfect 5.54, 7.11; partial 5.54, 7.11
reference:
figurative reference 6.24, 6.32; demonstratives 7.23 (see demonstratives); anaphorics 7.3
address and reference 13.2
reinforcing:
compounds 6.24 (see compounds)
pseudo-compounds 6.32 (see pseudo-compounds)
relationship terms (see kinship terms)
relative particles 11.52 (see particles)
relative time 9.55 (see time)
relator nouns 8.63 (see nouns)
repetitives (iterative derivatives) 7.42
responsibility 14.75
responsive utterances 5.41, 11.63, 12.1, 12.42-12.44, 13.33

restricted words (see morphemes, bound)
restrictive elements:
clauses 12.23 (see clauses); complements 5.64, 8.35 (see complements); phrases 9.61 (see phrases); subordinating construction 5.61 (see construction types)
resultative (causative-resultative) 14.74
rhetorical usage (see formal and literary language)
Rhodes, Alexandre de 3.1, 13.23
riming reduplicatives 5.54; chameleon affixes 7.11 (see derivatives)
roman alphabet (see writing system)

S

(S) = recorded only for southern speech; or occurring in certain southern (Cochinchinese) dialects
Saigon dialect 4.2 (see dialects)
school pronunciation 1.1
seasons 14.53 (see time)
semantic range, problems of 14.9
semivowels (see vocalics)
sentences 5.41, 12; independent 5.41, 9.1, 9.54, 12.1, 12.4; dependent 5.41, 12.1, 12.4, 13.31; negative 9.53, 9.54; affirmative 9.54; interrogative 9.54
fragments 12.4, 13.33; predicative 12.42; substantival 12.43; focal 12.44; particular 12.45; clausal 12.46
punctuation of 3.54; immediate constituent analysis of 5.4; morphology of 5.5; structure of 5.65, 12
sequential phrases 9.66 (see phrases)

Index of Vietnamese Forms

chục 8.43

chúng 10.42, 10.43, 10.44, 13.22, 13.24

chứ 11.4, 11.51, App. A

chữ 3.1, 3.51, 5.57; chữ hán 3.1; chữ nho 3.1; chữ nôm 3.1; chữ hoa 3.51; chữ cái 3.51

chưa 9.4, 9.67, 13.32, 13.33, 14.31

D

dạ 11.3, 13.22

dấu ngoặc đơn 3.54

dấu ngoặc kép 3.55

dầu (see dù)

dẫu (see dù)

do 9.64

dù 11.52

Đ

đã 9.1, 9.3, 11.71, App. A

đam 8.61

đang (N) 11.81

đánh App. A

đâu 7.2, 7.22, 7.23, 10.46, 11.91, 13.32, 14.2

đây 7.2, 7.22, 10.46

đấy (S đó) 7.2, 7.22, 10.46

đầy 9.53

đến 9.66

đều 8.2, 14.2

đi 9.55, 9.62, 9.64, 9.66, App. A

địa-chi 14.5

đó (S) 7.22, 7.23, 7.3, 10.46, 14.71 (see also đấy)

đôi 8.45, 8.61

đông 9.53

đừng 9.4, 9.55, 14.31

được 9.64, 13.33, 14.31, App. A

dưới 8.63, 14.41, 14.42

đương (N đang) 11.81

G

gạch: gạch giữa 3.53; gạch nối 3.53; gạch dài 3.55

gần 9.54, 14.41

góa 2.81, 4.17, 4.25

góc (S) 8.44 (see phần)

GI

gì 8.65, 13.32, 14.2

giữa 8.63, 14.41

H

hai chấm 3.54

hay 9.67, 11.72, 11.81, 13.32, App. A

hãy 9.55, App. A

hẳn 11.83

hết 9.54, App. A; hơn hết 9.52

hoài 11.82

hoặc, App. A (see hay 4)

hỏi 1.4, 2.15, 2.71, 2.73, 3.42, 4.12-4.14, 4.16. 4.23, 4.3, 7.12, 7.51, 7.61, 7.71, 8.43

hòn 8.61

hơi 7.43, 11.72, 11.81

hơn 9.52; hơn hết 9.52

huyền 1.4, 2.15, 2.71, 2.73, 4.12-4.14, 4.16, 4.23, 4.3, 7.12, 7.61

I

ít 9.53, 9.54

K

kia 10.45

kìa 10.45

KH

không 9.4, 9.67, 13.32, 13.33, 14.31; phải không 9.67